ADVANCE PRAISE FOR COSMIC NAVIGATOR

"Gahl Sasson is well described by the words of the Old Testament: 'Behold now, there is in this city a man of God, and he is an honorable man; all that he says is sure to come about: now let us go there; perhaps he can show us our way that we should go.' (Samuel 1, 9:6)

"Gahl's radiance as teacher and oracle shines through the words of this book. The insight and wisdom that have improved the lives of his many clients and students are translated here into an approachable program for self-empowerment and realization. Personally and collectively, we now have clear directions for a divine life experience."

> —Rabbi Karen Deitsch

"Gahl is blessed with a unique gift. He is a spiritual sherpa: one who lights the path, who leads the way, and who holds the hand of all of us—spiritual trekkers—who seek the pathway to happiness and peace in our hearts."

> —Terri New, founder, Capital Strategies, National Political and Non-profit Fundraising Consultants

"[Sasson's] brand of astrology draws from Kabbalah and the tarot. A favorite of the film crowd."

> —W magazine

"Gahl blends myths and philosophy from many different traditions into an exciting spiritual system that makes room for people of every background and belief. His workshops on Kabbalah and astrology [are] both practical and profound. Gahl is a humorous, wise, and highly spirited storyteller, and his message of unity among all religious traditions—past, present, and future—is one that we need to hear as often as possible."

> —Gurmukh Kaur Khalsa, cofounder and director of Golden Bridge Yoga, Los Angeles

"Gahl Sasson is one of the most extraordinarily talented spiritual healers on the planet. I count him among the top few original thinkers in the world today."

> —Dr. Julian Neil, psychoanalyst, yoga master, and head of the nutritional department of the National Association of Child Development

"Gahl gleans patterns and cycles from mythology, blends them with astrology, looks at them metaphorically, brings to life the archetypes, personifies the characteristics, and unfolds a drama that is not only compelling but informative and educational. His messages and stories are unique and need to be heard. It is not often that one comes across such a well-informed, humorous, and enticing writer so ready and able to shed a fresh light on the ever-changing world and our position in it."

> —Michael Leifer, president and CEO, guerillaPR, Inc.

"Gahl's advice is always accurate, meaningful, and precise. He is a master storyteller and a true light warrior. I recommend this book and his teachings to everyone who wants to better themselves."

> —Noa Tishby, Coproducer of HBO's *In Treatment*

"I thank my lucky stars for Gahl Sasson—adviser, mentor, and inspiration! I'm charmed by his elegant telling of the astrological story. And his accurate predictions astound."

> —Holiday Mathis, syndicated astrology columnist

"Gahl leads his students towards transformation through an understanding and awareness of myths and stories gathered from all religions, folktales, world mythology, and more."

> —*Yogi Times*

COSMIC NAVIGATOR

Design Your Destiny with Astrology and Kabbalah

GAHL EDEN SASSON

WEISERBOOKS
San Francisco, CA / Newburyport, MA

In tribute to all who dedicated their lives to the propagation of the understanding that everything is One. Without their sensitivity and sacrifice, the information found in this book would never have been available to any of us.

First published in 2008 by
Red Wheel/Weiser, LLC
With offices at:
665 Third Street, Suite 400
San Francisco, CA 94107
www.redwheelweiser.com

Library of Congress Cataloging-in-Publication Data

Sasson, Gahl.
  Cosmic navigator : design your destiny with astrology and Kabbalah/Gahl Eden Sasson.
    p. cm.
  Includes bibliographical references.
  ISBN 978-1-57863-420-0 (alk. paper)
  1. Astrology. 2. Cabala. I. Title.
  BF1711.S155 2008
  135'.47—dc22
                    2008003488

Cover and interior design by Maija Tollefson
Typeset in Electra
Cover photograph © Nicholas Monu/iStockphoto.com

Printed in the United States of America

10 9 8 7 6 5 4 3 2

Contents

Part III: The Twelve Kingdoms of Light

Acknowledgments

Giving thanks to the people who were involved, supported and inspired this manuscript is a very hard job since I should really start with whoever was the person who introduced my parents to each other and end with you the reader who took the time to read the book. That being said, I would like to first thank my partner, friend, and inspiration Igor Orlovsky, who was by my side the whole time, editing and directing the flow of information. I would also like to thank Helen Zimmermann for believing in the book when it was nothing more than a proposal. I also thank Brenda Knight, Caroline Pincus, and the wonderful people at Red Wheel/Weiser for seeing the big picture and helping give birth to this book. Without their heartfelt enthusiasm this book would have never been completed and published. Many thanks to Lisa Buccieri, Amy Clark, and Steve Weinstein for editing the book. Uri Auerbuch, my very good friend and artist, and Lisa Jannone for the illustrations, and all my clients who provided me with a wealth of stories and live examples of how the wisdom of the stars manifest in life on Earth.

I thank my family for raising me to be who I am, to my friends who push me when I am slow and elevate me when I am low.

Many thanks and much love to you, the anonymous reader whom I might never meet but surely have in a past lifetime.

May the Presence be with you all . . .

Preface: How I Became a Cosmic Navigator

It was for this purpose that the stars and their planets were created. Through their cycles, all phenomena rooted in the spiritual realm are transmitted and reflected to their physical counterparts.
—RABBI CHAYIM MOSHE LUZZATTO, *THE WAY OF GOD*

I was twenty-three when I returned from a journey to India and the Far East. It was time, I thought, to settle down and choose a career path. Reared in an ultra-academic family in Haifa, Israel, I felt pressure to further my education. But what should I study? I could not avoid answering the question, "Who am I?"

I remember the day I finally made my decision. I took a swim in the Mediterranean Sea and stopped by my parents' house on my way home. I looked at the sign on the building where I had lived most of my life. It read "Freud Street 26." I said to myself, "Could it be so obvious?" The next day, I enrolled in the psychology department at Haifa University. Years later, as I deepened my studies in Kabbalah and numerology, I discovered that twenty-six represents the numerological value of the unpronounceable name of God, associated with the archetypal energy called Wisdom. I realized then that the sign on my parents' house had not only directed me to learn about Freud, but it had also launched me on a path to explore the wisdom of Kabbalah.

I completed my B.A. and planned to pursue my master's and Ph.D. in clinical psychology. However, in Israel, there are more individuals who yearn to heal than people who require healing. Most years, the university accepts only one in every four hundred or so applicants. The crucial requirement is a recommendation from a senior professor. I thought I had that sewn up. I had excelled in my studies. My grades were first rate. And I believed that the head of my program believed in me as well. I had been one of eight students specially selected by that professor to participate in an exclusive psychoanalysis workshop. I was certain that my stellar performance in his class had insured his endorsement and a spot in graduate school.

I was wrong.

When I asked for the letter, the professor refused. He told me that my outlook on life and healing deviated markedly from those of mainstream psychologists. Since I had shared my interest in symbolism, synchronicity, and mysticism during the course of his workshop, he argued that my overactive imagination, in conjunction with my bizarre theories about life, death, and spirituality, would constitute "a threat to the system."

"You have too much creativity to be a good clinical psychologist," he told me in what I perceived to be a patronizing voice.

I was devastated. I was shocked and humiliated. Most of all, I was furious. Being an Aries, the warrior sign, blood rushed to my head. I saw him suddenly as my archenemy. My sudden feelings of anger signaled nothing less than a mental declaration of war. And if you had stopped me there and then, I would have told you that this denunciation was the worst thing that I had ever endured.

But then something else happened, as it always does. The universe is more creative than we are. My best friend called and asked

Becoming a cosmic navigator means accepting the notion that everything that happens in life—good or bad, harmonious or challenging—is designed by the Creator to help us to grow and reach our authentic destiny. Your worst enemy might be your soul mate in disguise; an aversive situation might be your breakthrough. Accepting what life offers allows you to receive Light. This book was written as a wake-up call, summoning you to surf the waves of life, beckoning you to embark on the journey you were always meant to take.

me to join him on a surfing trip to Mexico. I was still mourning my recently deceased career, and my initial reaction was, "Are you out of your mind? Can't you see how miserable I am?" But then I thought about it for a second. *Gahl*, my name in Hebrew, means "wave." I figured that the only way to truly understand waves, and therefore myself, was to learn how to surf. In hindsight, I recognize that I simply followed the course that was inscribed for me when I was born. I did not know it then, but my astrological rising sign is Pisces—the fish. The rising sign is the symbol that shows us our path, our road to self-awareness. I was not summoned to the waters of Mexico by my friend, but by my astrological constitution and my name. My friend—and indeed my nemesis, the professor—were just the messengers.

I traveled west to follow the message of my name. And I found myself in Mexico, chasing Gahl, chasing waves, and learning the art of flowing with life. The mantra I picked up from my surfer friends was, "No fear." It has served me just as well outside the waters as it did in the swelling sea.

After a month, my friend had to return to Israel via Guadalajara's international airport. Since I had a few more months to burn before I could reapply to the university, I decided to accompany him to Guadalajara for a couple of days and from there make plans to visit South America.

On my fifth day in Guadalajara, a muscular young man approached me as I wandered the streets looking for something to do on my last day in the city. He offered to show me the "real Mexico." My first instinct told me to politely refuse. I had all my money, my passport, and my expensive camera with me. Surely he was out to take it all, and perhaps he planned to take my organs for black-market transport while he was at it as well.

But a deeper voice inside me told me to surrender. No fear. Surf the waves. So I thrust my hand inside my pocket to protect my wallet and climbed on a bus with him.

We traveled for more than an hour to a rather impoverished—some would say sketchy—part of the city. We ended up working out at his gym and then meeting up with his tequila-drinking buddies, who sang boisterously about the Mexican revolution. On the way back, we heard live music blasting from a little house. We wandered inside and found two guys playing their instruments. I saw a wired-up microphone standing unused beside the musicians. I had always dreamed of being a rock singer. On an impulse, I grabbed the mike, and I sang and screamed until my throat ached from the strain. After hours of rocking improvisation, I went back to my hotel. It had been one of the most fantastic days of my life. And I still had my wallet.

The next morning, as I was packing to leave Mexico for good, the two musicians, accompanied by a team of three translators—each of them apparently understood a different third of the English language—showed up at my hotel and asked me to join their band. The previous day, they had set up the mic to hold auditions for a lead singer. And I had been the only one who'd showed up. I told them, thanks, but I was leaving that afternoon for Guatemala. They asked me, why?

"To learn Spanish," I said.

The five men looked bemusedly at each other.

"Well, we can teach you Spanish," one of them said.

Within three weeks, the band and I were performing in clubs all over Guadalajara. I also found myself adopted by a family that provided me with free lodging, meals, transportation, and love. I was humbled by the generosity and open heartedness of the people. It seemed everywhere I went, I bumped into another lucky synchronicity.

One day as I was taking a run in the park, I saw a group of people dressed all in white. They sat on the ground and chanted some words in a strange language. I inched closer, and I witnessed for the first time in this incarnation yogis practicing yoga. Without waiting for an invitation, I joined them. And from that day forward, I eagerly went to yoga class nearly every day.

After about a month, the yoga teacher asked me to join him on a visit to one of his students who had been laid up ill at home. While we sat with the ailing man, I offered to try out on him some Tibetan energetic healing that I had learned a few years back. It seemed to invigorate the man, and his grateful wife insisted on giving me a gift.

She ushered me into another room, and she asked me three questions that since that day I have never stopped asking anyone who comes to me for help. I call it the Trinity: What is your date of birth? Where were you born? And at what time? I gave her the information, and for the first time in my life I witnessed the casting of an astrological chart. She was new to interpreting charts. She constantly turned to her books and read from them. But her comments were stunningly accurate. By that point in my life I had gone to see five different psychologists, who, after innumerous sessions, could not understand me as well as this novice astrologer.

I closed my eyes and whispered to my higher self: "If I am supposed to study this art that feels so familiar, please show me the way."

Less than two weeks later, the guitar player in my band dragged me to some mysterious meeting. I was suspicious. "What do they do? Why do they meet?" He dismissed my queries and said, "There are great looking girls in the group." I stopped talking and followed. I walked into the meeting and sat in the back, close to the door to insure an easy escape. The teacher talked in Spanish, which, at that time, I did not understand, but every once in a while he slipped in a Hebrew word. And then to my amazement, thousands of miles away from Israel, surrounded by Mexicans, the teacher began to write Hebrew letters—my native alphabet—on the blackboard. I had stumbled upon a group that studied Kabbalah and astrology. The guitarist somehow figured I would like it. He was another messenger.

I joined the esoteric school *Circulo Dorado* and studied with them for two years. I suppose that program in Guadalajara served as a substitute for my master's in psychology back in Haifa.

Did I plan to dive into Kabbalah, astrology, and yoga? No. Did I think it was my destiny? No. I just followed the direction of my name as well as the other signs and synchronicities I encountered along the way. Now, looking back, I consider my old professor who refused me access to the academy to be the most influential person in my life. He is perhaps the most important Kabbalist or mystic that I have ever met, even if he would reject both of these titles. He was not the enemy I thought he was that day years before, when I left his office without a letter of recommendation, without my hopes for any sort of worthwhile future. He was my savior, my guide, and my healer.

Introduction: Why Astrology *and* Kabbalah?

Astrology: *Astron,* "star" + *Logos,* "word" (Greek)

Kabbalah: "to receive," "to accept" (Hebrew)

What is the meaning of life?

When will I find my soul mate?

What happens to me after I die?

Am I bound to my astrological fate, or can I change it?

How do I get along with my Virgo boss?

Even in a turbulent world rife with fears of terrorism and pandemic, environmental degradation, wars, tsunamis, and depleting energy supplies, philosophical and spiritual concerns like these preoccupy people from all walks of life, cultural backgrounds, ages, and genders. By combining the ageless personality insights of astrology with the deeper archetypal wisdom of Kabbalah, this book provides answers to these and many other questions. It affords you the opportunity to learn why you are the way you are and how you can use the potent tools supplied by these spiritual traditions to create purpose, serenity, and a life exactly as you'd like it.

With *Cosmic Navigator,* I have created an entirely new kind of astrology book. By marrying the famous constellations and planets to the mystical lore of Kabbalah, I aim to push astrology beyond the two-dimensional chart on the page, beyond the realm of mere fortune-telling and pick-up-line amusement. Kabbalistic interpretation of astrological charts adds a third dimension to the space-and-time structure of traditional astrology. It attaches an ancient and universal spiritual component that will enable you to tap into the collective energies of the astrological signs in order to carve out your own path or destiny. This new approach to astrology unveils the keys that will enable you to access the hidden powers of the twelve signs and to use those forces to build a better life. In workshops I have taught over the past decade, practitioners of the program outlined in this book have enjoyed growth in their leadership abilities, increased their financial and career prospects, enhanced their intimacy with their family and friends, found their true love, become pregnant when doctors had ruled it an impossibility, and drastically improved their health. You can expect all of this and more.

> Cosmic Navigator: One who surfs life's synchronicities in search of adventure, happiness, love and Light. A Cosmic Navigator recognizes that all sentient beings are fellow passengers on board the spacecraft called Earth. Therefore, he or she is committed to the service of these passengers as they navigate back home into Oneness...

THE WEDDING OF ASTROLOGY AND KABBALAH

While Kabbalah speaks in cosmic or universal terminology, astrology is local, focusing specifically on the energies of our solar system. Since we are part of the solar system (astrology) as well as the universe (Kabbalah), it is vital to learn about these two doctrines simultaneously. These two systems function like the zoom lens on a camera: Kabbalah allows us to zoom out and see the big, wide picture of the universe as a whole, while astrology lets us zoom in on our own place in that universe.

Astrology explains that the heavenly bodies reflect both our physical and spiritual environment. It posits that by looking at the sky we can understand events and situations that occur on earth, that whatever happens above will be reflected below and vice versa. Transcending mere fortune telling, astrology provides a system of psychological analysis that can help us decipher synchronicities, symbols, and tendencies, which we then can use to forge a more productive and joyous life.

Like all explorers, cosmic navigators start the journey at the point of origin. That home base is mapped by astrology—the natal astrological chart of planets, houses, and signs that is cast according to the moment of birth. Astrology is personal. It provides every person an easy entrance into the numinous realm of Kabbalah, which offers more gravity, more spirituality, and greater possibility than astrology alone.

Kabbalah and its mystical techniques, which include myths, metaphors, and meditations with Hebrew letters, then demarcate the path that all cosmic navigators follow to attain their goals. For thousands of years, mostly in secret sects and lodges, Jews, Christians, and Muslims have all taken advantage of Kabbalah's system of spiritual empowerment to shape their destinies. Today, thanks in part to publicity from celebrities like Madonna, the clandestine mysteries of Kabbalah have been thrust into the mainstream. Kabbalah's mystical rituals and lore are now available to everyone, helping all of us to cope with challenges and to craft better lives. Kabbalah's mystical heritage and ritual meditations light the way for any of us to rewrite our destiny, to surmount the constraints of the astrological fate we were born with.

For example, one woman who worked with the techniques described in this book found that her chart featured Saturn in the fifth house. She longed desperately to have a child, but Saturn in the fifth house traditionally binds that person to a fate with no children. A routine astrological interpretation would have counseled this woman to forget that dream and instead to relish her happy marriage or good fortune in the stock market. Disappointed and crushed at first, this woman nonetheless worked with the Kabbalistic meditations and exercises prescribed in this book, and she soon received a stunning insight. She would expand her idea of having children. She would transcend the dictates of her chart and adopt a child that she'd love as her own. That affirmative act transformed her life, as this adopted child brought many blessings to her home, her marriage, and her disposition. And it also seemed to transform her astrological lot. Five years later—to the amazement of her doctor and her astrologer—she got pregnant and had a child.

Kabbalah teaches us how to receive Light in order to give it back to the rest of creation. In doing so, we rectify a challenging imbalance in our soul—an ongoing process called *Tikkun*. Kabbalah helps us to accept life, pushing us to realize that everything that happens to us, positive or aversive, stands ultimately as a vital component of our spiritual evolution.

Wedded to Kabbalah's magical tradition of hands-on spiritual virility, astrology becomes far more rich. It moves from just a psychological game that tells Scorpios that they are obsessed with sex to a comprehensive spiritual system that resonates with the powerful idea that Scorpio is actually the name of a marvelously powerful archetype—a vessel of energy that animates such core human concerns as sexuality, intimacy, and life after death. Retrograde Mercury likewise transforms from the source of a devilish travel nuisances and computer snafus to a beloved messenger of the divine that brings us—when we pay attention—astonishing synchronicities and inspirations that literally can change our lives. After years of teaching both Kabbalah and astrology and interpreting dozens of astrological charts each week in private consultations, I have discovered indisputably that Kabbalah fused with astrology can empower our lives in a way that traditional astrology cannot. My hope is that you will find this hybrid as useful and liberating as I have.

The link between Kabbalah and astrology is not some New Age fad. The two systems have been inextricably linked since the earliest development of each doctrine. This relationship dates back 4,000 years to the *Sefer Yetzirah*, or the *Book of Creation*, one of the oldest and perhaps the most mystical text in the Kabbalistic canon. Kabbalists believe that the patriarch Abraham, who is said to have authored the *Book of Creation,* relied heavily on the stars and planets in the *Sefer Yetzirah* to describe the ongoing mysteries and mechanics of the universe. Kabbalah's Tree of Life and the letters of the Hebrew alphabet, the centerpieces of the Kabbalistic lore, are embedded with all the crucial astrological symbols. When combined, as the sage mystics of the past always intended, Kabbalah and astrology provide a comprehensive spiritual system that can be studied and then applied in a way that will bolster the purpose, fulfillment, and happiness of every human being.

THE ASTROLOGY OF BECOMING: HOW TO USE THIS BOOK

This book enables you to use the powerful archetypes of the zodiac as allies in a program of self-improvement. The cosmic navigator pursues this journey by focusing not just on his or her own sun and rising sign, but also by personifying and thus becoming every sign in the zodiac. Each of us—whether we identify ourselves as a Sagittarius, Cancer, or Capricorn—have all of the signs somewhere within our astrological chart. This book teaches you how to recognize the wondrous complexity of your astrological constitution, while at the same time providing the methodology for activating all the hidden powers of your potential.

Part I offers a panoramic view of the basics and mysteries of astrology and Kabbalah that will appeal to both the novice and the experienced astrologer. It presents a holistic view of the Zodiac that teaches how the energies of the various signs and the planets interact with one another. And it also contains a fascinating original myth that explains the genesis of twelve signs of the Zodiac and why they represent the various personality characteristics that astrology for thousands of years has ascribed to them.

Part I also delves into the evolutionary proof of the authenticity of astrology and its symbols, while introducing such Kabbalistic concepts as Tikkun (rectification) and compassion. The overlay of Kabbalah atop traditional astrological interpretations teaches readers to view their natal chart not as a happenstance of birth, but as a divine contract designed to help all of us to overcome challenges and better ourselves and the world. It also provides a detailed primer on how to read astrological charts. And finally, Book I instructs readers to view the planets and stars as potent spiritual and psychological symbols, whose colors and physical totems on Earth enable anyone to manifest their wishes and change their lives for the good.

Part II focuses on getting to know yourself. You will learn how to examine, read, and interpret the snapshot of your soul: your natal chart. Part II presents what might seem to be a dizzying amount of factual information as we explore the ins and outs, ups and downs, and significance of all the planets, the twelve signs, and the twelve houses that compose the zodiac. I recommend reading this part all the way through to glean an overview of the myriad elements that make up any complete interpretation of an astrological chart. You might also want to return repeatedly to specific bits for reference as you continue to practice astrology in the future. Just remember that the more you know about the details of all the astrological symbols, the more you will gain when you work with their energies.

Where Can I Get My Natal Chart?

To benefit most from part II's compendium of facts and details, you should refer to a printout of your own astrological constitution. You can acquire your natal chart easily at *www.CosmicNavigator.com*. Simply scroll down the home page and click on the tab "Get a Chart."

The best way to learn astrology is to read as many charts as possible. I recommend that you first work with your own chart, then with the charts of people you know, and finally, when you feel confident, you can move on to interpreting the chart of anyone willing to sit with you.

Part III presents an interactive self-improvement program built around the twelve signs, the major energetic archetypes of the astrological system. It devotes one chapter to each of these signs, detailing a mystical and deeply psychological analysis of that particular archetype through myths, real-world or historical examples, and traditional descriptions of that sign's positive and negative characteristics. Each chapter includes a list of traits and symbols associated with that particular sign, and you will use these characteristics to invoke and then magnify the power of that particular archetype everywhere you go. For twelve weeks, you will embark on a revitalizing spiritual-training regimen, tapping the latent potential of each archetype that lies within each one of us. The book asks you to incarnate as each sign for one week. Like a method actor who thoroughly immerses himself into the character of a Mafia boss or the queen of England, you will place yourself into an Aries state of mind—a person of action, decisiveness, and adventure—for example. The following week, you move forward to Taurus and become an unapologetic sensualist, fascinated by food, art, money, and your own particular talents. The chapter on Libra tones the spiritual muscle that attracts your best romantic partner. Scorpio will stimulate intimacy, sexuality, and transformation, while Capricorn will facilitate career success. In this way, over the course of twelve weeks, you will invigorate every facet of your life, opening doors to success in money, love, health and family. This journey will reveal talents and opportunities you never knew existed. And, perhaps most importantly, it will energize and rejuvenate all of the archetypes that compose each one of us, bringing them into harmony and eliciting a profound sense of purpose, serenity, and joy.

In addition, this book personalizes this twelve-week journey by first teaching you how to interpret your own astrological chart like a pro. All of our natal charts feature every single astrological sign in some form or another. If you discover that Aries presides over your house of career, for example, then during the week dedicated to Aries, you will not only learn about the archetype of Aries in general, but you also will be guided to direct the Aries traits and tendencies toward advancing your career. You will be instructed, for example, to look for leadership opportunities at the office and to jump like an impulsive Aries at the chance to grab them.

Each chapter of the self-improvement program also features a Kabbalistic talisman and techniques that will amplify the particular energy of the archetype you are studying. Specially designed meditations on the Hebrew letter associated with a particular zodiac sign, for example, will embed you more firmly in the territory of the sign as well as trigger insights on how and where to use the energy of that archetype within your daily existence.

You also will learn how to surf the currents of the astrological archetypes by paying attention to synchronicities. Each zodiac sign is represented by a bank of symbols that include particular animals, colors, planets, personality traits, Tarot cards, famous people born under the sign, parts of the body, health implications, and all sorts of physical objects, such as water or arrows or doors. Encounters with these symbols out in the world will serve as clues about what to do, where to go, and how to think in order to make the most of the week's particular archetype.

Points of Emphasis for Each Astrological Sign

- Aries: Invoke the warrior within to reclaim power, leadership, and assertiveness.

- Taurus: Tap into your self-worth and talents to generate inner and material wealth.

- Gemini: Empower your intellect and improve your communication skills.

- Cancer: Enhance family relationships and the physical space you call home.

- Leo: Stimulate your creativity, love, and playfulness.

- Virgo: Emphasize work, health, and a better diet and focus on serving humanity.

- Libra: Attract partnerships and romantic relationships into your life.

- Scorpio: Infuse your life with intimacy, sexuality, and transformation.

- Sagittarius: Tap the miracles of luck, travel, and optimism.

- Capricorn: Strive to attain your career goals.

- Aquarius: Develop friendships and enhanced ties to your community.

- Pisces: Invoke your inner mystic and locate your personal spirit guide.

Paying attention to these signs and symbols turns astrology—and life—into a magical game. Many of my students have reported that the chief benefit of this program is not necessarily the new career prospects that arose as a result of the twelve-week practice, but the opening of themselves to the wizardry of synchronicity. These seemingly magical signs transform even the chores and challenges of life into moments of continual fun and miracles. They point you away from trouble, and they confer the gift of knowing that the universe is watching out for all of us.

Another act of synchronicity is that without my editor or me trying to make it happen, this book is 360 pages long, precisely reflecting the number of degrees in a natal chart. This kind of magic, I assure you, will start happening to you as you enter the wonderland of astrology and Kabbalah.

Most gratifying to me, this sort of studying and becoming the signs of zodiac seems to foster compassion both toward yourself and to all other people. The effort to embody the characteristics of all the signs will prompt you to experience firsthand both the positive and negative traits of that sign. Playacting the ram, crab, goat, lion, centaur, and water bearer inevitably leads to a sympathetic understanding of why certain people are the way they are. For example, in the week of Aries, you will discover why Aries talk about themselves all the time in part because you will probably spend the week talking profusely about yourself. You'll learn why it is dangerous to ask a favor of a Taurus when he's hungry; why the Gemini tells little fibs; why Cancers make you feel guilty, Leos demand so much attention, and Virgos are so critical that they even criticize criticism; why Libras cannot make up their minds, the Scorpio keeps so many secrets, the Sagittarius are always busy doing something close to nothing, and the Capricorn will sell her mother for a discount; why the Aquarius behaves as if he just returned from an alien abduction, and why the Pisces is always late.

Stepping into the shoes of someone else—in this case someone else's zodiac sign—is a sacred technique of both Kabbalists and Buddhists. It engenders compassion for their plight. It breeds understanding and forgiveness. The simple act of becoming each of these twelve signs, and the compassion and forgiveness that will surely ensue, can't help but upgrade your relationship with everyone you know. And understanding the darker side of your own sign, coupled with the knowledge that you are actually more than the obsessive-compulsive Virgo you always thought you were doomed to be, inevitably will generate more acceptance of your own self too.

PART I

THE PRINCIPLES OF KABBALISTIC ASTROLOGY

CHAPTER 1

The Myth of God's Children (or How the Twelve Signs Got Their Groove On)

Astrology and Kabbalah can be fully understood when we shift our mind from its usual preoccupation with cause and effect, beginning and end, to the more authentic truth of cycles that continue round and round to eternity. The following myth of God's children demonstrates the cyclical and eternal essence of astrology. There is no beginning and no end to any true system of symbolism. We might pinpoint Aries as the first sign and therefore the beginning, but as the story suggests, you can just as accurately finger Pisces (the last sign) as the energy that birthed the zodiac. The *Sefer Yetzirah* asserts, "Their end is embedded in the beginning and their beginning in the end."

Go back in time, some five billion years. Imagine the earth as a great hall, a chamber of multiple treasures, both physical and spiritual. Outside of it is an astral lobby—a waiting room for angels, if you will. Separating the two is a door, but not just any door—it is a portal of raging fire, a vortex of swirling flames.

God invited his twelve angelic children . . . into the waiting room and said, "This is the earth, a glorious garden that I'd like you to protect and serve. As a token of my appreciation for your dedication to this task, each one of you, one after the other, may take from the chamber of gifts whatever you can carry. Then you must ascend to the skies and fortify yourself as a constellation that will help to guide all sentient beings who navigate in darkness."

The magnificent dozen looked at each other, anxious to plunge into the chamber and retrieve their loot. But they were all paralyzed by the fear of the unfamiliar, and afraid, too, of the portal of fire that stood between them and the treasure-laden chamber called earth. Well, to be precise, eleven of the twelve were afraid.

Before the debate over who should go first even began, Aries jumped through the vortex with a wild warrior's cry. The others rushed to the window to witness the result. They anxiously watched the agile, lean, and athletic body of their crazy brother hurtle into the unknown. He survived, thank the Lord. Somehow he landed on his feet, and the fire of the portal did not destroy him. After all, Aries is a fire sign; how could fire destroy fire? How could a flame burn itself? He was the first, the initiator, the pioneer, and he liberated all the others from the bondage of their fear. He cleared the path and secured the room.

Brother Aries, who sometimes is called the ram, tends to be the sacrificial lamb, continually undertaking unspeakably bold feats. From that day on, Aries ruled as the first. He was granted the privilege of being the initiator of the astrological year. (According to the Bible, Aries is the first month of the year.) He marks the beginning of spring, and with spring comes the emergence of life. In the chamber of treasures, Aries naturally decided to take the ability to be first at everything. And in order to do that, he could not carry too much stuff. If you want to be number one, you need to run fast; you cannot allow bulky possessions to weigh you down. Cleverly, brother Aries picked up a seed from the ground. What could he do with a seed? Well, within the seed lies the DNA, and the DNA can be cloned into anything new.

Do you think our Aries brother knew where he was going when he jumped through the vortex? No. Do you think he was brave? Maybe, but often the Aries seems far more stupid than brave. And that explains why the Aries often appears with so many scars on his face.

Back in the lobby, a great commotion ensued. Now that the trail had been blazed, who would be second to descend to earth? With an enormous grunt, Taurus bullied herself right through the gate, pushing and shoving everyone in her path. Sister Taurus is a very practical woman. She is the empress. The minute she landed in the room, she looked around and smiled. "Fool of an Aries, he left everything valuable untouched," she thought to herself. Since Taurus is a beast of burden, she could carry quite a lot on her back. She started loading it all up. She took the trunk overflowing with money and jewelry, and since that day Taurus has ruled finance and precious stones. She adores beautiful things, especially if they are expensive. She collected every piece of art. She grabbed everything with material value, and that is why Taurus rules art, values, talents, and money. But the teaching of Taurus is not limited to material goods. Taurus also teaches that self-worth or how much you esteem your own valuable talents will determine how much money you make. The Taurus equation: self-worth equals bank-account worth.

After Taurus departed the chamber of treasures, Brother Gemini appeared out of thin air. What was he doing here? How did he manage to outflank the more ferocious and powerful signs and sneak in before them? Well, the answer, like always, lies embedded in the question. Gemini is the trickster, the magician. He schmoozed his way from the rear with his glib tongue. You see it today wherever you encounter a prestigious "in" nightclub. You'll see a doorman, a rope, and a line of beautiful women and men clamoring to get inside. Then, from out of a small but fast car, emerges Brother Gemini. He slaps a "press" sign on his chest and cuts right through the line. Why? Was he more famous than the people in the line? More beautiful or wealthy? No. Gemini is the messenger, and as such he gets everything for free: free movies, free gift bags, free everything. Just write up the product in a magazine, and it's all yours.

Gemini collected everything necessary for communication, intelligence, and business. He grabbed the phones, the faxes, the computers, the mail system, cables, cars, and all means of transportation, books, billboards, radio, TV, advertising, and all sources of information. His logic was simple. He watched Taurus leave the room with all that art and merchandise. Obviously she was going to need someone to sell it for her, and he planned to be the one to do that. He would take his commission, his finder's fee, 10 percent here or 15 percent there, and without having to warehouse or carry all that junk, he would wind up making more money than she. Gemini seized the concept of language, commerce, trade, the stock market, and numbers. For the first time, the beauty of the zodiac took shape: first we had Aries the man, then Taurus the woman, and now Gemini the messenger connecting the two. The Tarot card representing Gemini is called the Lovers. He is the connector, and here he connects the first masculine sign with the first feminine sign.

Gemini also scooped up the concept of lies and theft. I know it sounds harsh. But hey, I did not make Mercury—Gemini's ruler—the god of liars and thieves.

Anyone who writes, including me, is a liar and a thief. Writers translate their thoughts into words, and seldom are their thoughts complete and unbiased. Lao-Tzu, the founder of Taoism, once said that the truth cannot be spoken, and whoever even opens his mouth to speak of the truth has already lied. Traders, merchants, and businesspeople do the same. They sell you a banana for one dollar when it cost them only ten cents. Where did the extra ninety cents come from? Brother Gemini coined the term *profit*, which is actually a clever way to disguise a little theft. Gemini had no choice, because language, his prime booty from the chamber of treasures, is innately a kind of lie. But it's a necessary falsehood. After all, I am using that cosmic lie right now to convey this information about lies to you.

Suddenly, water flooded the chamber, and her highness the Queen of the Ocean, Sister Cancer, surged inside. Many astrologers and mystics call her Mother Cancer. She represents water, and she dripped her way through the cracks of the lobby in the astral world. She dripped and poured in so effectively that her waters covered 71 percent of the earth. She bathed the chamber and took what intrinsically belonged to her: birth, motherhood, compassion, and nourishment—all the qualities and concepts that esoteric lore assigns to the element of water. Mother Cancer also claimed the chamber itself—the actual real estate—and Cancer became the sign of home and family. The home represents the shell of the family, your family the shell of your personality, and your personality the shell of your soul. Cancer is symbolized by the crab, which carries its home—the place of sustenance, protection, and tender-loving care—wherever it goes.

Cancer represents the ultimate mother, but this archetype is not restricted to women with active wombs, nor is it limited to women in general. Anyone who adopts a child, who gives birth to a business, an idea, even a poem, is a mother too. For example, when you create a business, you invest unconditional love, energy, and dedication alongside your money. You see nothing in return for months, maybe years, and yet you stay up all night working, nourishing the enterprise as if it were an infant. Cancer gave birth to the concept of giving birth. And from that day on, the motherly energies of Cancer have supported us in our times of doubt and tribulation, watering us with feeling and compassion. Cancer also carried off the concept of the subconscious. She took reign over lost memories hidden by the waves of time. And, in her infinite compassion, she also took old age, so that in the best of all worlds, human beings would enjoy care and nurturing in infancy and years later in their dotage too.

Just as the sun appeared after the great flood in the time of Noah, the chamber of treasures next was infused with golden light. The sound of trumpets echoed in the hall and with a roar, finally, at last, the lion arrived. What an entrance! But with all due respect to Leo—or the king, as he prefers to be called—the question remains unasked (for fear of reprisal): why did he wait so long? By now, the chamber had been emptied of most tangible treasures. Why did he delay when he commanded enough authority and strength to demand to be first?

The answer was simple. At a regal feast, when the king sits at the head of the table and the food is served, who eats first? Nope, not the king. If he's a smart king, he will demand that someone else taste the food before him, just in case. The king allowed Aries, who is a fire sign, to taste from the fiery spirits that were offered on the table. Then Taurus, the earth sign, was asked to taste the food. Leo then required Gemini, an air sign, to breathe in the air (one can never be too cautious when dealing with poisonous gasses, not to mention chemical warfare), and finally he directed Cancer, the water sign, to sample the beverages. Only when the king saw that they all survived did he then start to eat.

The party had begun. Leo is the sign of happiness and fun. With little left in the chamber, Leo usurped the concept of creativity for himself. He roared in contagious laughter and enthusiasm: "If there are no gifts left in the chamber, well, let's create them, let's pretend!" So Brother Leo started playing around like a child. "Let's pretend I am a king and that I have a scepter and a crown and a cape, and you will be my subject, and when you talk to me you will say, 'Your Highness,' OK?" And indeed, from that day forward, Leo ruled children, playfulness, and entertainment. Leos love to occupy the center of attention, and since they are so entertaining, we all just play along and let them have their fun. This explains why movie stars and royal families fill the tabloids. Everyone wants to know what is happening with the prince and his lover or if one certain celebrity will divorce another. Leo took drama from the chamber along with control over stages, movie sets, and all creative endeavors.

Leo also snatched perhaps the most dramatic concept of all: love. And for that bit of ingenuity we all ought to doff our hats. Leo grabbed not only the love one feels toward a romantic partner, but also what the Sufis call love to "the Beloved," or love toward God. Leo chose to rule over romance and spirituality. Since love is childlike, innocent, and suffused with happiness, these qualities—think of the innocent mirthful monk—embody the spirit of true spirituality, the spirit bound up in the dramatic and playful crown of Leo.

After the glamorous fanfare of Leo, holy Sister Virgo arrived in the chamber, engendering a certain anticlimax in the cycle of the zodiac. Unable to out-party the Leo, Virgo looked around and found her purpose. She grabbed a broom and humbly began to clean the chamber, picking up the beer bottles, the plastic plates, cigarette butts, and everything else left over from the farewell party to the king. Without any resentment or hard feelings, she did what she does best: cleaned up the mess. Holding a burning bundle of sage (Virgo is the lady of herbs), she purified the chamber while chanting an old secret spell to ward off negativity. She became the Queen of the Angels, the nanny of the zodiac, the Mary Poppins of order, work, and service. After all, someone actually has to do the king's bidding. Virgo offered herself as the one to follow Leo's will, like a faithful babysitter who reads for the tenth time the same bedtime story to a stubborn little boy. Virgo emerged from the chamber of treasures with the concepts of service, work, diet, purification, and order. She became the energy accountant of the astrological wheel. One of the more famous members of her clan is the greatest queen Europe has ever known—England's Queen Elizabeth I, "the Virgin Queen." While Leo rules partying and getting high, Virgo cleanses the body. She represents the hangover and the rehabilitation center. Without Virgo, life just might destroy itself with excess.

With the chamber of treasures now spotless, shining, and purified, Sir Libra, the most handsome knightly brother appeared. The chamber was empty, vacant of treasures, but Libra did not mind, for he is the sign of design and symmetry. And it is easier to design a space when you have a space to design. In Zen, they tell us that design can be viewed as the relationship between object and space. In Zen art, as well as in Japanese gardens, space is part of the design. Libra, being an air sign, relates easily to space and its significance. In Western art, if you want to paint a tree, you usually place that tree smack in the middle of the composition, but in the East, the tree would be positioned on the side, leaving the other side empty. This way, the painting is not only about the tree, but also about the tree's relationship to space. Libra, therefore, became the sign that rules relationships and partnerships.

Relationships also give birth to another concept that Libra took from the chamber: justice. Justice represents the relationship between action and reaction—crime and punishment, for example, or, as the old laws of Hammurabi state, "An eye for an eye, a tooth for a tooth." These ancient tablets (circa 1850 B.C.E.) created the lucrative Libran profession we call lawyers. Let's face it—Libra, an air sign, knows how to make money out of thin air.

Then there was silence, the quiet before the storm or, better still, before the hurricane. Sister Scorpio appeared, veiled by a mist that filled the entire hall. The second that she landed in the chamber of treasures, it was changed. With little to choose from, Scorpio stashed away the concept of transformation, including the ultimate transformation, death. While Cancer, another water sign, brought us life and birth, Scorpio, the second water sign, introduced death. Water can quench, but it also can drown.

Scorpio also grabbed other forms of transformation, including sexuality. Sex, of course, often leads to conception, which enables souls to reincarnate back into life. In other words, the death of death is life. With sexuality came intimacy and secrets (behind closed doors). How do you know if someone is a Scorpio? You just ask, what's your sign? If she doesn't want to answer, then she is surely a secretive Scorpio, closely guarding her identity, just like an undercover spy. And with secrets came a whole chain reaction of associations, including healing, crime, research, paranoia, private investigations, inheritance (after death), other people's money, and joint financial affairs.

After the mists of Scorpio dispersed, a gorgeous creature arrived in the chamber. The centaur—half-horse, half-man; half-god, half-human—stood in the center of the room, radiating Light and force. Why did Sagittarius wait so long to descend to earth? With his power, speed, and athleticism, he easily could have fought his way through earlier and grabbed what was rightfully his. But Sagittarius is a natural-born traveler, always fascinated with foreign traditions and foreign planets. He also probably suffered a spasm of attention deficit disorder (ADD), which compelled him to gallop off to some other galaxy and some other task before he remembered the chamber and decided to return. When he finally arrived, relaxed, and peered around the chamber to choose a treasure, he found one invisible concept that no other sign had bothered to notice. It was the most valuable gift in the hall. What was it?

Love? No, Leo took that.

Money? Taurus had it all.

What about Life? Already Cancer's.

Sagittarius claimed truth. The truth, the whole truth, and nothing but the truth. (Lies already belonged to Sagittarius's opposite sign, Gemini.)

It took nine signs before anyone bothered to claim reign over truth. Isn't that something? Truth is a short but weighty word that includes many other concepts, such as wisdom, philosophy (the love of wisdom), teaching, religion, and higher education—all of which fell under the sway of Sagittarius. Sagittarius recognized that his love of travel and experiencing different cultures was the only way to truly know truth.

With so much adventure and unknown in his future, Sagittarius also needed to fortify himself with a few other trinkets from the chamber of treasures. And so he scooped up luck and optimism. Let's face it—when surrounded by Scorpio on one side and Capricorn on the other, you need to be optimistic. And, if we view the astrological ring as property, then you might say that Sagittarius is located in the worst real estate of the zodiac. Sagittarius marks the time in the year when the days get shorter and shorter and the nights are the longest. The message is clear: if Sagittarius rules over the darkest time of the year and also rules truth, then we find our truth in the darkest, most difficult moments of our life. Out of the Dark comes Light. Truth represents the light at the end of the tunnel.

Capricorn finally entered next. A cautious sister, she walked slowly and deliberately, and it took her a while to traverse the portal to the chamber of treasures. At this point, the building was completely empty. But Capricorn was persistent, diligent, and ingenious. She took the walls, foundations, and the structure of the chamber. Capricorn knew she could use the material to build something else.

Then she looked down and realized that no one had claimed what lurked underneath. The underworld (in the Tarot, Capricorn is represented by the Devil) lay undisturbed. Using a shovel, she started digging a hole in the ground. Slowly, grain by grain, the little hole became a crater. Because the digging lasted for centuries, she unwittingly exercised a great deal of patience, discipline, and endurance, and so she adopted these qualities too.

What did she unearth? All the riches of the earth. Gold, minerals, uranium, petroleum, diamonds—you name it—she extracted it all. It was a heavy load, and all that serious weight explains why Capricorn moves so slowly. But she has time. She is a late bloomer, and she knows that the older she grows, the better life will be. Capricorn accepted and incorporated the concept of time—the time that measures our achievements (or failures), the time that makes us old, the time that provides structure to our lives.

Then Aquarius appeared, landing from out of nowhere in a supersonic space-craft, emerging like the rugged renegade character Han Solo from *Star Wars*. After Capricorn departed, there was nothing left of the once magnificent vault—no floor, no walls, no ceiling, nothing. But Aquarius was smart. It was the sign of the genius, and Brother Aquarius had a genius moment. He took the future. Capricorn took the past, the millions of years that had transformed coal into diamonds and dinosaur remains into petroleum, and Aquarius countered by grabbing the future.

Does all this sound strange? Well, Aquarius is, after all, the sign that took domin-ion over things weird, strange, and unique. After all, he is the mad professor whose mind works at the threshold between genius and craziness, who can always invent a new gadget because he is not afraid to think outside the box.

How does one take the future? Brother Aquarius invented the concept of copy-rights and patents. Aquarius solemnly declared that any invention from this day forth would be registered under his name. It's called the trademark. By now you've seen his signature ™ everywhere, but at that time, it was a novel idea to assume owner-ship over an idea, an invention. Every future computer, the G6s, G7s, the flying car, and so forth will be registered under Aquarius Corp. Ltd. You predict that in the future nanotechnology will create miniature supercomputers? Aquarius would reply simply, "Thank you very much, it's ours." If advances in technology permit human-ity to occupy new planets, all these planets will be subject to the trademark of Aquarius. All future chambers of treasures would necessitate a visit by Aquarius before anyone else.

Thank God that Aquarius is also the most altruistic and democratic sign, which means that he generally will share ownership and use of all the new inventions. Aquarius's futuristic and sweet attitude also allowed him to adopt the concepts of humanitarian work, fraternity, cooperation, altruism, and friends. Brother Aquarius expressed no hard feelings toward the rest of the signs for leaving him nothing, because he could always make something out of nothing.

Last and never least arrived Sister Pisces, sometimes known as the mermaid. She showed up last because she loved to imagine, and she had a million imaginary friends who kept her tied up in their imaginary affairs. They took her to other dimensions and transported her to visit the land of elves and pixies. Finally, when the silence of the empty chamber of treasures snapped her out of her delicious daydream, she glided into the empty place where the room once stood. She smiled and breathed in. She sat down in the center of nothingness. She did not feel as if she had been cheated out of her inheritance or her treasures. She herself was the treasure. She understood that the chamber was an illusion, and that all the treasures her siblings had grabbed were illusory as well. "Form is emptiness" she chanted silently, "Emptiness is form." Sister Pisces did what only she could. She extracted from the empty space the ability to dream, sleep, and meditate. One does not need any *thing* for that; one can do it everywhere and at any time.

She sat cross-legged and meditated. She used her powers of imagination to reconstruct around her a magical chamber of treasures filled with artwork, computers, and seeds. A chamber of treasures stuffed with love and safety, truth, and life and death. A chamber situated upon a rich deposit of natural resources, filled with gadgets and futuristic inventions.

Then she imagined that out of a vortex of fire appeared her beloved brother Aries, who with such serious urgency had snatched a seed from the chamber. Then she imagined her beautiful sister Taurus gracefully amassing the jewelry that she imagined to be locked in a safe hidden deep in the wall. Pisces envisioned the rest of her siblings appearing one by one, all believing that the chamber and its treasures were really there. She even imagined herself entering the chamber, and then she imagined herself imagining the chamber and all her siblings entering one by one.

When she grew tired of imagining, she simply went to sleep and continued the construction of the chamber of treasures in her vivid dreams. Pisces loves to sleep because in her dreams she encounters so much. Like Alice who dreamt of her Wonderland, Pisces dreams up the zodiac, the planets, the treasures, and the rest of us. Next time you feel aggravated because some Pisces overslept, don't be so quick to judge or patronize him for being lazy. He might be dreaming you into existence. If this sounds far-fetched, let me remind you about another sleepyhead called Lord Vishnu, the magnificent god who, according to the Hindu tradition, sleeps on a lotus that floats upon a sea. (Pisces is the sign of sleep and the sea. The sea is the Indian version of a waterbed!) He is not an idle or lazy god, for in his sleep, the Hindus say, he dreams of us. Our joys and love are his blissful dreams; our challenges and suffering are his nightmares.

CHAPTER 2

The Historic Fusion
of Astrology and Kabbalah

ASTROLOGY AS THE COSMIC CLOCK

Astrology was born not as a form of entertainment or as a scheme for fortune telling, but as a vital tool for survival. With the advent of agriculture, humans adapted their planting and harvesting routines to the dictates of the seasons. The measuring of time—the fluctuations in darkness and daylight, the arrivals of the winter and summer solstices, the great rivers' tides and flooding—became essential to a successful harvest. There is evidence that suggest that over 4,500 years ago the Egyptians kept a detailed calendar to help them predict the rise of the Nile. Guided by the sun and the moon, these early farmers also noticed the other planets moving about the fixed constellations of stars. Attuning their lives to the repetitive rhythm of the seasons and the orbits of the planets simplified and insured their survival.

This dependable, clocklike rhythm of the skies became so critical to human life that humans began to view the planets, moons, and stars as gods. The people of Mesopotamia, circa 2000 B.C.E., for example, worshiped gods called Sin (the moon), Shamash (the sun), Ishtar (Venus), Nergal (Mars), Marduk (Jupiter), and Ninurta (Saturn). The earliest written evidence of astrology to be unearthed so far comes from the Babylonian Tablet of Amisaduqa, written around 1646 B.C.E:

In month XI, 15th day, Venus disappeared in the west. Three days it stayed away, then on the 18th day it became visible in the east. Springs will open and Adad (god of weather and abundance) will bring his rain and Ea (the Babylonian water deity) his floods. Messages of reconciliation will be sent from King to King.

The early astrologers of Babylon and elsewhere were the first to apply the old alchemical formula of "as above so below." They took note of the correlation between events in the heavens and those on the earth. For example, let's imagine a day when the king was angry, ranting and raving at his advisors and his servants. On that same day, multiple fights erupted between merchants in the market, and several people were murdered. The king's star gazer might have observed all these events and then noticed that Mars, the fiery red planet, was on that day in the sign of Aries, the constellation associated today with aggression and war. This early astrologer probably would note this correlation in his diary and then await the next time that Mars orbited into Aries to see if a similar sort of strife appeared then too.

When the heavenly movements repeatedly corresponded with the reality on the ground, the associations crystallized. Astrology then unfurled her wings and traveled from Babylonia to Greece and Rome. It was picked up by the Indian scholars and then transported to China. It was assimilated into Judaism through Kabbalah and embraced by Christians and Muslims as well. As it spread over the centuries, it was tweaked into a coherent body of knowledge. Slowly, star-and-human-gazers clothed and reclothed the signs and planets in the names, tendencies, and colors that we use today.

The Kaaba in Mecca, the holiest shrine in the Muslim faith, functioned as a religious center long before the days of Muhammad. Back then, the cubical structure was said to have housed 365 pagan idols, corresponding to the number of days in the astrological year. In addition, anthropological evidence suggests that the tawaf, *the ritualistic seven circumambulations of the Kaaba practiced by Muslim pilgrims to this day, was devised to mimic the orbits of the heavenly bodies around the sun.*

Notches carved on animal bones that date back to 15,000 B.C.E. reveal evidence of human attention to the lunar phases. The ancient wise men and women who carved the notches thought it necessary to trace the changes in the shape of the moon, which means these people could very well be the first lunar astrologers.

Evolutionary Astrologers?

Humans are not the only inhabitants of the planet to recognize a correlation between the above and the below, between the stars and life on earth. Every dawn, the faithful olive baboons in Sudan gather to await the rising of the sun. They salute the appearance of the solar disk with shrieks and screams, almost as if they believe that their cacophonic rejoicing insures that the sun will return every morning. Just as boisterous applause for an actor on a stage might encourage that performer to do it all again, the baboons reinforce the Sun with their loyal adoration.

The ancient Egyptians, who inhabited lands adjacent to the home of these baboons, surely noticed this unique worship of the sun because they portrayed Thoth, one of their oldest gods, as a baboon that held the solar disk in his hand. In the Egyptian pantheon, Thoth served as the god of writing, knowledge, magic, and astrology. As you can see, much of who and what we are derives from our evolution from primates . . .

STARS AND SPHERES

The author of *Sefer Yetzirah*—tradition suggests it was Abraham, the first monotheist of the Old Testament—provides precise associations between the zodiac signs and the Hebrew letters, yoking astrology to the sacred letters of the Torah. This manuscript details how God deployed the archetypal energies of the ten-sphered Kabbalistic Tree of Life and the twenty-two Hebrew letters to create the universe (see chapter 5).

The Midrash, a collection of Jewish myths and legends, tells us that King Solomon wore a magical ring engraved with Hebrew letters that afforded him the power to speak with animals. Since the word *zodiac* in Greek means "the wheel of animals," one can say that King Solomon's capacity to converse with animals referred to his ability to speak the language of the signs—to converse with rams (Aries), bulls (Taurus), lions (Leo), scorpions (Scorpio), horses (Sagittarius), goats (Capricorn), dolphins (Pisces), and so forth. Maybe King Solomon really did communicate with animals, but perhaps the fable is simply a metaphoric testament to the wise king's remarkable ability to speak to, persuade, befriend, and make peace with every single person, no matter his or her sign. King Solomon was also famed as being the wisest men ever born, and I believe his wisdom derived from mastering the art of astrology and Kabbalah. His ring and his ability to master animal speech might hint at his astrological aptitude.

King Solomon's father, King David, according to tradition the author of the Old Testament book of Psalms and whose name is mentioned more than that of any other person in the Bible, embodies another example of the relationship between Kabbalah and astrology: the Star of David, a six-pointed star comprised of two inter-locking triangles, one facing upwards and the other pointing down. In Hebrew, the Star of David is called *Magen David*, or the shield of David. While most people assume that David carved this symbol into his battle shield just as the Indianapolis Colts paint a horseshoe onto their football helmets, Jewish mystics ascribe a deeper import to the six-pointed logo. These mystics tell us that at the moment of King David's birth, six planets were aligned in a rare astrological formation that created a perfect six-pointed star within his astrological chart. This auspicious alignment— which I have witnessed just once in all of the thousands of charts I have ever read— astrologically reflected the protection King David enjoyed throughout his long, pro-ductive life. Hence "the [planetary] shield of David." Today, this ancient link between the two disciplines is proudly displayed on the flag of the modern state of Israel.

The *Zohar*, or the *Book of Splendor*, another crucial work of Kabbalistic lore (writ-ten in thirteenth-century Spain), adds further details to the intricate relationship between the Hebrew letters and the astrological symbols. This book classifies the Hebrew letters as the DNA of the universe, the building blocks of existence. It asserts that the Creator first fashioned the twenty-two letters and then with them manufactured all of life. Kabbalah teaches us that just as God used the archetypal letters to create the cosmos, any of us can create whatever we need in our own universe.

The book of Genesis depicts an enchanting example of the power of this hybrid system. Abraham, the so-called patriarch of Jews, Christians, and Muslims, was not always called Abraham. His given name was Abram. His wife's name was Sarai. And no matter how often they tried, they could not have children. One day, God felt sorry for Abram and urged him to "walk the talk."

God said, "You wrote a book on the Hebrew letters and their connection to the astrological signs. Maybe it's time to put the Hebrew letters to work for you." Abram was skeptical. Though God had kept promising that he would father many nations, he had passed his 100th birthday, and still he and Sarai had no children. But he decided to give the letters a whirl. He sank into a deep meditation, summoning all the Hebrew letters one by one. When he arrived at the letter *'Hey'* ה, he stopped and said to himself, "Hey, wait a minute. This is the letter of Aries, the sign that rules the sowing of seeds and the season of spring. Aries is the thing I need to up my dwindling sperm count. I will add the letter *Hey* to my name and my wife's name too (after all, she's ninety years old), and the power of Aries will bring some spring to our seeds."

He inserted the *Hey* (H). *Abram* became *AbraHam*, and *Sarai* turned into *SaraH*. A few months later, Sarah began to crave pickles and ice cream. The conception of Isaac, the son of Abraham and Sarah, seems to be the first reference to an individual invoking the tools of Kabbalistic astrology to change his fate. And it marks the *Sefer Yetzirah* as the first self-help book ever published on planet earth.

In part III of this book, you will find the particular Hebrew letters that will connect you to the archetypal power of each of the zodiac's twelve signs. By using these potent symbols as keys to accessing the energy of skies, you too will be able to manifest your dreams and transcend the confines of your astrological fate. This magic will transform you into a mystic, a creator. And rather than leaving yourself to be buffeted by the fatalistic luck of the astrological lotto, you, like Abraham, can become the master of your own destiny.

GIVING AND RECEIVING LIGHT

Kabbalah in Hebrew means both "to receive" and "to accept." These mystical Judaic teachings avow that life is a dance between giving and receiving. They show us how to accept light, love, or any other form of energy. And, most importantly, they instruct us on how to share this energy with others. Kabbalah challenges us to create a balance in our lives—to receive as much as we give, to give as much as we receive. For example, someone who invites a hundred people to his birthday party, relishes all of the gifts he amasses, but then mysteriously leaves town whenever his friends' birthdays roll around, is not a good Kabbalist. On the other hand, a saintly woman who continually offers her tender loving care to others but denies them the chance to help her lives in a similar state of disequilibrium.

Kabbalah views life as circular, nonlinear, and everlasting. When a person receives a gift and enthusiastically appreciates it, for example, he offers the giver an even greater gift. This gratitude generates a feeling of satisfaction in the giver that might very well exceed the value of the original present. Put more simply, Kabbalah is the spiritual art of receiving in order to give.

THE YIN AND YANG OF KABBALAH AND ASTROLOGY

Astrology similarly teaches us how to receive—specifically, how to receive the light and the energy of the sun, the moon, and the planets in order to share them with the entire universe. The moon and the planets signify diverse and sometimes contradictory energies, yet for billions of years these celestial bodies have peacefully shared the love and warmth of the sun. Astrology urges us to mimic this example of harmonious existence.

It designates the sun as the primary giver. In your own chart, the location of the sun represents the place in your life where you exude energy and vitality. Your sun sign illuminates your style of self-expression, how you radiate outward. Since the moon, in actuality, receives and then reflects the energy emitted by the sun, your moon sign provides clues to how effectively you receive light and energy. Thus, the moon epitomizes the primary principle of Kabbalah: it receives the light of the sun solely to give it back to all of us here on earth when we need it the most. In the darkness of the night, it is the moon that lights our way.

Early humans first recognized the sun and the moon, the two most conspicuous astrological bodies in the sky, as polarities, and up until about 12,000 years ago humanity had divided itself of necessity into two corresponding groups: lunar and solar, yin and yang.

The solar energy, typified by the masculine side of humanity or existence, engaged in venturing out, like the rays of the sun, to protect the clan, hunt for food, explore new territory, achieve fame and glory, and play around. Masculine energy is found in the zodiac signs Aries, Leo, Sagittarius, Libra, Aquarius, and Gemini. An arrow that shoots through the sky, a spear thrown far into the distance, or a rocket that soars to the moon all embody the energy of these macho archetypes. Masculine energy might have manifested in early human times as a bunch of hunters chasing a mammoth and might manifest today as some public relations company launching a presidential campaign.

The feminine or lunar energy, represented by Capricorn, Taurus, Virgo, Cancer, Scorpio, and Pisces, manifested in those humans who adopted the tasks of collecting and gathering nuts, fruits, and medicinal herbs that grew naturally near their caves. The cave represented the womb and all it implies: home, nurturing, and security, both physical and emotional. The feminine side of humanity tended to the newborns and the injured hunters and developed innovative ways to heal. Kabbalah considers the feminine energy as receptive, a vessel that welcomes and contains the exploratory masculine force. It facilitates the magic of birth. The feminine egg receives the masculine sperm and the result is a new life. The sperm, which vigorously travels to a new world, is assimilated by the vessel called the ovum, which then becomes a whole new being.

The masculine signs—Aries, Leo, Sagittarius, Gemini, Libra, and Aquarius—are generally more active, expressive, outgoing, childlike, and playful than the feminine signs. Their purpose is to explore the world and deliver what they discover to the feminine signs. The feminine signs—Capricorn, Taurus, Virgo, Cancer, Scorpio, and Pisces—are more introverted, deep, practical, and intimate. They receive the gifts and experiences hunted by the masculine signs and find practical applications that improve life. Those with these signs are generally more mature, responsible, and reliable than the masculine signs.

In Kabbalah, the masculine force is associated with giving as well as the right side of the body. From now on, when you want to give someone a present, a check, or a bottle of catsup, try doing so with your right hand and notice what happens. You will see that whatever you gave was received more openly. Whenever you receive a gift from someone or change from a cashier, accept it with your left, feminine hand—the hand astrologically as well as Kabbalistically designed to receive. Receiving with your left hand you are sending a message to the universe that you accept the gift and are in gratitude. This reinforces the universe to give you even more.

Astrology Hidden in Everyday Words

"The situation in Iraq is a *disaster*," commented the political correspondent.

"*Mazal tov!*" a renowned scientist shouted to his friend during a birthday party.

Both of the individuals above called on astrological terminology to make their points. The first chose the word *disaster*, which in Greek means "against the stars." The ancient Greeks, who were instrumental in bringing Babylonian astrology to the West, believed that events that violate the harmonious orbit of the stars signified bad news. For them, the orbit of the planets was symbolic of perfection; they called this silent symphony "the music of the spheres." Anything that proved incongruous with such perfection was inevitably deemed disastrous. The scientist who toasted his friend with *mazal tov* unwittingly dipped into the realm of astrology as well. The skeptical man of science probably would be appalled to learn that the Hebrew phrase *mazal tov* translates to "may a benevolent astrological constellation shine upon you." These common expressions illustrate how deeply astrology has embedded itself into everyone's lives, even the lives of those who might judge astrology as nothing but hogwash.

Is Astrology Real?

We wish to caution the public against the unquestioning acceptance of the predictions and advice given privately and publicly by astrologers.
—A STATEMENT OF 186 SCIENTISTS SIGNED IN 1975

Let me be frank. There is no scientific proof of the efficacy of astrology. But that does not mean that astrology does not work or that it is not a great tool for analyzing cycles and understanding life. No one knows how love works, and yet we all believe in love. No one has definitely proven the existence of God, and yet the overwhelming majority of the population of earth strongly believes in God. My attitude towards the validity of astrology can be summed by the words of Alexander Graham Bell: "What this power is I cannot say. All I know is that it exists."

I believe in astrology because I also believe in evolution—not just the evolution of species and advantageous mutations, like a larger brain or opposable thumbs, but also the evolution of ideas. According to the laws of Charles Darwin, only the strong survive. And astrology has survived. Cultures all over the world have adopted and refined astrology for thousands of years because it has served them well. It has conferred lasting benefits not in just one corner of the globe, but to myriad cultures everywhere. (This same evolutionary proof lends validity to many other intellectual properties. The Torah, Zohar, New Testament, Yoga, Jujitsu, Runes, Tarot, Upanishads, I Ching, and the Koran have all endured for thousands of years because the beliefs, ideas, and rituals they champion have proven constructive. They have helped and continue to help vast numbers of people.)

The evolutionary proof postulates that since astrology has helped so many people from so many different cultures for so many thousands of years, surviving buoyantly until this very day, then it must contain many a valid and universal truth.

CHAPTER 3

The Natal Chart: Your Divine Contract with God

Astrology is not a fortune-telling tool. Our astrological chart is actually a spiritual contract that we signed with God and a constant reminder of our chosen path in life. That means that we cannot bellyache to God, our mothers, or anyone else that we don't like our chart. We can't loathe the fact that we have eight planets in the house of death or six planets in the house of suffering. We—and only we—created and agreed to it. Accepting our chart marks the first step in changing our lives.

THE CYCLE OF OUR MANY LIVES

We know from the accounts of people who have died clinically and then returned to life that when we die, our entire life flashes in front of our eyes. Reportedly, it feels like we relive our lives all over again. It sounds as if we download our lives from our body, which contains our memories in its cells, brain, and other organs, into the part of ourselves that is eternal. After completing this file transfer, we are welcomed into the Light by an entity that most mythologies call the psychopompus, or the guide of the souls. This guide helps us travel up and down the divine highway, which has two lanes: one that runs from life to the Light and one that leads from the Light to life. The first is known as the path of death; the other is called the path of birth.

According to many spiritual traditions, we have all made this journey from death to life and back again many times, and we will experience it again and again until we attain enlightenment. It goes something like this. After recovering from the shock of dying, we slowly begin to accept the fact that this round is done and we are about to begin anew. We meet a guide, who often appears in the guise of a relative. This benevolent *sherpa* of our soul leads us to a place where we can review the file that we downloaded from our body and contemplate all that occurred in our life. Then, with the aid of our mentor, who is actually an ambassador of God, we identify the uncompleted trials and lessons that we probably ought to deal with in our next lifetime. Together with our guide, we figure out how best to do that. Should we be reborn a woman or a man, a Christian or a Jew, black or white, rich or poor?

As an example of how this all works, let's imagine a soul who lives as a bartender in a Chicago nightclub. He is a good man who strives to help his endless stream of imbibers with a sympathetic ear and savvy advice. As he serves up his words of wisdom, however, he also pours liquor into their empty glasses. And he soon realizes that by the time his counsel finally registers with his customers, they are too drunk to remember it. The next night, they inevitably return to the bar, complaining still about the same problems and misfortunes, without any recollection of the insights he had imparted just twenty-four hours before.

The barman dies. His soul travels to the Light (or God, if you want) and plays a melody, the music of his life. Because he lived a rather rough and rugged life amongst drunks and melancholy and frequent fisticuffs, he pumps out too much bass in his song. He lacks treble, the tenderness of the melodic instruments. His guide listens to this lively but discordant tune and suggests that he reincarnate as a woman psychologist. He—now she—is born once again and matures into a therapist in China.

She becomes a great healer, and when she dies, she returns to the Light and plays her song. It sounds so much fuller now, but it still does not match the perfect symphony of God. This soul yet misses the midrange tones and a few other crucial notes. And so she reincarnates as an inner city football coach in Los Angeles. With monumental strength and compassion, he single-handedly transforms the community. He fights the drug dealers, the skeptics, and even the board of education. When the coach dies, the entire city mourns. More than five thousand people arrive to grieve at his funeral. When he returns to the Light this time, his music rings so beautifully that it harmonizes perfectly with the melody of God. This soul is then ready to wash seamlessly into the Light, like a river that finally joins the sea.

Each of us sits with the ambassador of God before the Light between our every incarnation to outline our next plan of action on earth. Each of us decides what we will experience on this planet. All the challenges, joys, our parents, our hometown, our profession are selected by our soul prior to your arrival in your mother's womb. God merely gives us a seal of approval and perhaps a few editorial notes. The rest is up to us.

"GOD, WHY DID YOU DO THIS TO ME?"

According to Kabbalah and many other spiritual traditions, our prime mission in life is to fix our soul or "burn" our karma. Kabbalah's name for karma is *Tikkun*, which in Hebrew means "rectification." Your astrological chart outlines exactly how you can rectify your soul. Next time you find yourself in trouble, and you cry, "God, why have you done this to me?" you should not be surprised if God, or God's lawyer, replies, "What are you talking about? Haven't you looked at your chart? Don't you know that you agreed to embrace this obstacle? I warned you that it'd be difficult, but you assured me that you could handle it. So come on, face the challenge, don't start blaming me now!" Even in the face of such difficult challenges as a fatal disease or the loss of a loved one, we should remember that we signed up for it all.

Our astrological chart is a spiritual contract that we signed with God and a constant reminder of our chosen path in life. We—and only we—created and agreed to it. Accepting our chart marks the first step in changing our lives.

You might say to yourself, "Why don't I remember signing this contract? Was I drunk or something?" Well, yes, in a sense you were intoxicated by God's presence. When we find ourselves up there in the proximity of God, engulfed by so much perfection and Light, we are likely willing to sign just about anything that will propel us toward a day when we can sit there with God permanently. But you signed because you understood that the sorrows and challenges that you'd face on earth, that you might face today, would not be rotten, horrible misfortunes, but blessings in disguise that would push you closer to that everlasting embrace of Light.

At the moment of birth, every baby, fresh from the lap of God, remembers the rationale of his or her chart and his or her accepted mission. Yet this information could interfere with the process of pure experience. For example, would you truly enjoy a basketball game if you knew the outcome before the game was played? When we are born, one beautiful Kabbalist tale recounts, an angel of God with a finger of fire seals the lips of the newborn and quietly whispers, "Shhh, don't tell anyone you know all that you do. Don't even tell yourself." At the angel's touch, the story explains, the baby forgets everything—the divine contract, past lifetimes, the image as well as name of God. And that is why we all sport the finger-width indentation—what's known as the Cupid's bow—in the strip of skin between our upper lip and our nose.

THE DIVINE CONTRACT: A CASE STUDY

A Nobel Prize winner dies at the age of fifty-eight in a skiing accident. The world of science mourns. Indeed, much of the entire world mourns. A prestigious scientist who moved humankind closer and closer to a cure for cancer, he earned medals and fame and applause around the globe. Suddenly, he is gone.

The ambassador of Light meets him in the land beyond the living and asks, "So, my friend, what do you want to be in the next round?"

The brilliant soul thinks for a few minutes and then answers, "I want to work on my emotional side. As you surely know, I was a protégé; people were feeding me chemical formulas before I even had a chance to learn about the nourishment of love."

The guide listens, nods and asks, "How can we rectify that?"

The soul hesitates and then says quietly, "I wish to avoid the temptations of the mind, to shut down my intellectual faculties."

The guide pretends to be concerned. "Do you have the spiritual *credit* for this? Remember, you will not recall making this choice. I don't want you going about later slandering God."

The soul says, "Please, let me be born under a silent star."

The guide shakes his head. "Hmm, I am not sure about this. Do you have anyone to cosign for you?"

The prizewinning soul calls forth two other souls with whom he had traveled in many past lifetimes. "Here, these two soul mates of mine share the problem of an over-exercised and over-cherished intellect. They are too clever for their own good, and they too yearn to nurture their emotional potentials. They are willing to be born before me, and I will be their son."

Cosmic navigators take responsibility for everything that occurs in our lives. All that we do, all that we experience, is designed solely to make us better, stronger, and more equipped for our ascension back to the divine.

The guide knows them well; in fact, they were his two previous appointments. He looks at their charts, specifically into their house of children, to determine how the scientist might fit as their child. He finally smiles. "OK. You will be born in a body that has three of the twenty-first chromosome; you will be born with Down's syndrome. Your IQ will be one-third of what it was in the life you just concluded, but you will be an emotional genius. You will feel intensely everything that other people go through, and yet you won't possess the capacity to communicate it intellectually. Do you accept?"

All three agree.

Twenty-nine years later, a young and successful couple buys a huge loft in Manhattan. She is CEO of a software company, and he is a litigation attorney who has never lost a case. Everyone, including their so-called friends, envies them. They are masters of their little universes. They meet up on occasion late at night to have sex—a high-performance ritual, but not a truly intimate one. Finally, she becomes pregnant. They don't bother to check on the progress of the fetus. There is no need—they are both winners. Their confidence clouds their judgment. They plan to call the newborn Leonardo, after Leonardo da Vinci.

Leonardo's birth goes smoothly. And then, to their horror, they discover that little Leonardo has Trisomy 21.

"What does that mean?" the father asks.

In her frustration, the mother screams at him, "He's retarded!" She wails to the God she never believed in, "What did I do to deserve this? What am I being punished for?"

The father is perplexed. Nothing in law school prepared him for this. He suddenly despises his wife. He hypothesizes some genetic anomaly in her family that she kept secret from him. Then he suspects that she must have been unfaithful to him, because surely this child is the product of an inferior gene pool. And then he begins to sob. How can he possibly present this . . . this . . . *thing* to his colleagues?

The baby grows, slower and differently than others. Strangers in the park could see that something was different about the boy, but they were too polite to inquire. And yet anyone who looked at the smiling child could not help but notice some deeper understanding, a wisdom not spoken in words but communicated silently through his innocent and pure joy. The boy knows nothing but love and kindness. No matter what his parents think of him, he expresses nothing but love for them. He does not love them for their success or status. He has no means of evaluating their intellectual brilliance or professional acclaim. His IQ checks in at sixty-two, but what test can measure spiritual intelligence?

Of necessity, his parents alter their lifestyle. Since Leo demands extra attention and care, they start to spend more time together. After just four years, little Leonardo has generated more tears and hugs and authentic bursts of emotion from his parents than they had experienced in their entire lives. At the beginning, feelings of rejection, blame, anger, and guilt triggered these emotional displays. But soon these awful feelings transformed into nothing but love and compassion.

The two young parents slowly fall in love with the little Leo, and they learn to treasure him. The mother decides to work from home on a new Web design business. The logistics involved in raising Leo also compel her to spend time with her own mother, a woman she once disliked and shunned. Moved by the perspective gained in caring for this child, adult daughter and mother begin to appreciate each other in ways no one thought possible. Such was the powerful magic of little Leonardo. What his mother's highly intelligent therapist failed to mend in hundreds of long hours, Leo fixed with a smile.

His father changes too. He quits his job at the big firm in Manhattan to head up a nonprofit organization that supports children with special needs. Best of all, he begins to relish his softening, loving wife, often holding her for hours after they put their son to sleep. And this newfound intimacy delivers two more children. They name their second miracle Kuan, for the goddess of compassion, and the other John, after the Baptist.

This story illustrates the core premise of Kabbalistic astrology: you are the maker of your own chart. It is not fate that ordained you to be sick, broke, wealthy, happy, or miserable. You made that solemn decision yourself. Your chart, merely one page long but signed with your first breah of air, symbolizes your divine contract with God.

Cosmic navigators take responsibility for everything that occurs in our lives, the good and the bad, the beautiful and the ugly. All that we do, all that we experience—whether we soar, fall in love, or tumble hard against the rocks—is designed solely to make us better, stronger, and more equipped for our ascension back to the divine.

CHAPTER 4

Nuts and Bolts of the Zodiac

THE FOUR ELEMENTS

Navigators on sea and land rely on the four directions of the compass for orientation. Cosmic navigators use the four elements:

Fire, representing action and creativity, fuels the signs of Aries, Leo, and Sagittarius.

Water, symbolizing emotions, underlies the signs of Cancer, Scorpio, and Pisces.

Air, corresponding to intellect, is the dominating force for Libra, Aquarius, and Gemini.

Earth, which stands for substance and practicality, is the hallmark of Capricorn, Taurus, and Virgo.

According to the ancient wisdom of alchemy, these four elements form the basis of all life. Right now, as you hold this book in your hands, you embody the four elements. The *physical* aspect of the book (cover, paper, ink) belongs to the element of earth, the words and information that appeal to your *intellect* evoke air, the *action* of holding and reading the book falls under the rule of fire, while the *emotions* triggered by the information in the book come from the element of water. When you kiss your lover, you also create alchemy. You generate the physical touch of the lips (earth), the emotional rush (water), the thoughts running through your brain (air), as well as the passion and attraction (fire).

Alchemists endeavor to balance the four elements in order to transmute imperfect, ordinary, and mundane situations, symbolized by the metal lead, into the perfection of love, symbolized by the heart and the metal gold. The alchemist's or astrologer's laboratory is his or her own body.

We can group the four elements into two folders: feminine (water and earth) and masculine (fire and air), which mirrors the two major human archetypes, feminine (nurturing and practical) and masculine (active and communicative). That division tells us that for balance, to create a golden life, we need to honor and augment both our traditionally female and male characteristics, regardless of our gender.

THE THREE MODALITIES

The four elements form the backbone of all Western mysteries, including Kabbalah. So why do we need twelve signs?

Each of the four elements can be expressed in three different styles. These varied modes of expression are called the three modalities. Astrology follows the four seasons, which correspond to the four elements, and each of these three-month-long seasons is comprised of a beginning, middle, and end. Every month manifests in nature in a slightly varied way. The beginning of winter, for example, is not as frigid as the middle. The middle of summer is usually quite a bit hotter than the end. The three modalities represent those three parts of the seasons:

The **cardinal** modality marks the beginning of the season and the power of initiation.

The **fixed** modality corresponds to the middle of the season and the power of sustaining.

The **mutable** modality represents the end of the season and the power of change.

Elements and Modalities

	Fire	Water	Air	Earth
Cardinal	Aries	Cancer	Libra	Capricorn
Fixed	Leo	Scorpio	Aquarius	Taurus
Mutable	Sagittarius	Pisces	Gemini	Virgo

Each of the four elements presents a cardinal expression, a fixed expression, and a mutable expression. Four elements times three modalities equals twelve distinct energy fields and therefore the twelve signs. Even though Aries, Leo, and Sagittarius, for example, are all fire signs, they each represent a different archetype. Aries personifies the warrior or soldier. Leo embodies the king, who is protected by the warrior. And Sagittarius connotes the prophet, wizard, or adviser, who insures the upholding of the ethics of both the warrior and the king. In the Bible, David, the redheaded Aries warrior, was anointed by Samuel, a prophetic sage emblematic of Sagittarius. David usurped the kingdom from the old king Saul, initiating a dynasty. Aries, the cardinal fire sign, begins the process. Sagittarius, the mutable sign, acted as the messenger, the connector, the agent of change from one season to the next—in this case from one dynasty (Saul) to another (David). Leo, the fixed fire sign, then receives the flame from Aries and strives to maintain it. In this case, King Solomon, who symbolizes the born-a-king sign of Leo, inherited the kingdom from his father and ruled peaceably with his harem of a thousand wives. After all, a Leo is a Leo . . . . The cardinal signs initiate the seasons: Aries kicks off spring, Cancer births summer, Libra brings autumn, and Capricorn delivers us into winter. These cardinal signs push us forward, urging the best from us. They act as personal trainers who cajole our finest, our healthiest muscles, out into view.

The fixed signs, embedded in the middle of the season, radiate the full force of the seasonal trend. Taurus occurs when spring blooms everywhere; Leo falls under the strongest sun. Scorpio, the sign of death, rules when the leaves fall from the trees, and Aquarius rules when ice and cold fiercely grip the ground.

Kabbalah calls these four fixed signs *Hayot,* or "the Creatures." They are yoked to "the chariot," a mystical Kabbalistic code for the vehicle (or meditation) used to ascend to a communion with the divine. These creatures first appear in Ezekiel's transcendent vision (Ezekiel 11:10): "As for the likeness of their faces, they four had the face of a man [Aquarius], and the face of a lion [Leo] . . . they four had the face of an ox [Taurus] . . . they four also had the face of an eagle [Scorpio]." Later, Christian mystics associated the four creatures with the four apostles Mark, Matthew, Luke, and John. What is the significance of all this? Well, the fixed signs tend to take themselves very seriously and demand that we take them seriously too. No wonder the accounts ascribed to these apostles were later compiled into the New Testament and came to be regarded by close to a billion people as the word of God. The fixed signs stand as the pillars that support the zodiac, just as the four creatures support many of the esoteric mysteries of Kabbalah and the four gospels form the basis of Christendom.

The mutable signs, meanwhile, foster the transition of one season to the next in the same way that film editors endeavor to avoid jarring jump cuts between scenes. Gemini bridges spring and summer, Virgo ushers summer into autumn, Sagittarius shoots arrows from autumn to winter, and Pisces thaws winter into spring. Just as diversity and mutations in evolution insure the survival of many different species and therefore a dynamic and functioning biosphere, the mutable signs provide the change and diversity that permit survival amid the earth's changing physical states. The mutables guarantee our ability to adjust.

In Hinduism, these three modalities, or principles, gave birth to the Divine Triad: Brahma, the god of creation and initiation; Vishnu, the sustainer; and Shiva, the destroyer. The Greco-Roman culture mirrored this essential trio in the three goddesses of Fate; the first offers the thread of life, the second measures the thread, and the third cuts it. The Kabbalistic Tree of Life similarly features three pillars: a pillar on the right that expands, a pillar on the left that constricts, and a central pillar that balances and sustains.

THE CORE POWER OF THE SIGNS

You can learn much about any astrological sign simply by combining the characteristics of its element with those of its modality. This easy formula will help you determine the root power of any particular archetype, which will deepen your understanding of the people around you and the events that seem to occur during particular times of the calendar year.

Root Power = Modality + Element

Aries: You are cardinal fire. Your root power stems from an ability to initiate (cardinal) action (fire). Your success requires initiation, the pushing and furthering of your goals. You need to liberate (fire) yourself from any oppression so that you will be able to lead (cardinal) yourself and others.

Taurus: You are fixed earth. Your root power comes from stability (earth), patience, and sustaining (fixed) an effort for long periods of time. You need to connect to your five senses and ground yourself (earth and fixed) in matters that concern your talents, values, and finances.

Gemini: You are mutable air. Your root power manifests in the ability to adjust (mutable) the style of communication (air) to any fluctuating circumstance. As long as you improvise (mutable) and wield your intelligence (air), you will achieve your aspirations.

Cancer: You are cardinal water. Your root power derives from initiating (cardinal) emotional processes (water). You are a giver (cardinal) of life. To tap your potential, you need to give birth (cardinal) to situations that will allow you to nurture (water) people or projects.

Leo: You are fixed fire. Your root power comes from perseverance (fixed) in action (fire). You can become famous and respected in your circles if you maintain a steady and focused (fixed) creative force (fire) with the ultimate goal of benevolence.

Virgo: You are mutable earth. Your root power emerges from your ability to edit, fix, and adjust (mutable) situations so that life around you becomes more efficient and effective (earth). This editorial work ultimately ought to be directed toward service to humankind.

Libra: You are cardinal air. Your power root lies in initiating (cardinal) communication (air). This ability grants you mastery over relationships and justice, provided that you initiate (cardinal) conversations and work on your diplomacy (air).

Scorpio: You are fixed water. Your power root springs from the ability to remain (fixed) intensely emotional and intimate (water) in relationships. You can be successful if you allow yourself to expose and be exposed, to heal and be healed, and to dive as deep as you can into the fundamental (fixed) essence of the emotional (water) motives of others.

Sagittarius: You are mutable fire. Your root power emerges from your capacity to spread (mutable) philosophies, moral codes, and belief systems (fire), especially when you engage your innate sense of optimism. Your duty to humankind relates to teaching, learning, and adjusting (mutable) the negative attitudes and actions (fire) of others.

Capricorn: You are cardinal earth. Your root power comes from initiating (cardinal) practical applications of talents, assets, and resources (earth). You embody the business plan of the zodiac wheel. Your success is assured when you set a definite goal (cardinal) and then practice patience and discipline (earth).

Aquarius: You are fixed air. Your root power stems from a stable and consistent (fixed) interplay with your community and friends (air). You are the pillar (fixed) of a large group of people (air). Your success lies in cultivating innovative, funny, and futuristic ideas (air).

Pisces: You are mutable water. Your root power derives from your capacity to improve life and generate change (mutable) via imagination, mysticism, and compassion (water). You can cultivate success with your sensitivity to the emotional (water) states of others. Dreams and fantasy (water) often serve as the tools by which you manifest your preferred life.

The Merry-go-round of Astrology

We've all heard the old postulate that humankind's greatest invention is the wheel. I have always questioned that assumption. I guess it really depends on what wheel you're talking about. If you mean the ox-cart, wheelbarrow wheel, I have to point out that the Maya, Inca, and many other cultures in the Americas prospered just fine without it. Master architects and astronomers, they built complex and sophisticated civilizations without that particular bit of human ingenuity. However, these cultures were cognizant of the importance of the philosophical or symbolic wheel. They used advanced astronomy and math to chart space and time (the Mayan and Aztec calendar is written on a circular stone tablet) and investigated deeply the intricacies of astronomy and math (the Mayans invented the numerical zero).

In spirituality, the wheel represents completion, perfection, and equality (as proven by King Arthur's Round Table, which even the king could not sit at the head of). It also suggests the eternally repeating concept of reincarnation—life followed by death followed by life. In Kabbalah, the Tree of Life is composed of ten wheels or spheres. The Sanskrit word *chakra*, the fundamental building block of the Hindu tradition, translates as "wheel." In Sufism, the mystical tradition of Islam, the whirling dervishes worship God by spinning round and round in imitation of the wheel of life. Astrology uses the wheel of the zodiac as the symbol of life on earth, and it emphasizes degrees rather than sharp cliffs of yes-no, good-bad, wrong-right.

While it is true that year after year we travel in circles around the astrological cycle, when we work with astrology and Kabbalah, we nonetheless end up not in the same spot, but in a higher, more conscious place. Just think how much a baby learns and grows before the age of one and then between the ages of one to two, even though she finishes up each year in the same place on the zodiac circle. When we work with the wheel, we liberate ourselves from the repetitive cycles of the seasons. We mutate (in a good way) and elevate via the lessons and *Tikkun* (rectification) that we encounter on a daily basis. This work transforms the wheel into a spiral, the sacred symbol of the Crown, the loftiest sphere in the Kabbalistic Tree of Life (see chapter 5). A spiral is basically a three-dimensional wheel. Every time we return to the place of origin, we find ourselves in a slightly elevated spot. With every lesson we master, with every astrological sign we assimilate, we soar higher and higher, turning the monotonous

The cardinal signs make things happen. They ignite the energy and give it direction. They therefore tend to be bossy. The fixed signs maintain the energy. They crystallize and focus it. Thus they can be rather stubborn. The mutable signs induce change, destroying the old to create space for the new. This responsibility sometimes makes them a little wishy-washy or flaky.

circle into an enchanted spiral reaching for the heavens. It's like the rings of a tree, the central totem of Kabbalah. As it matures each year, the tree adds another ring to its core. Each year these rings grow larger and larger, a symbolic confirmation for us of the escalating vitality of the experiences gained, the lessons learned, and the growth invested in our own karmic bank.

CHAPTER 5

The Tree of Life

While astrology maps the energies of our solar system and galaxy, Kabbalah explores the entire creation—physical, astral, and whatever lies hidden and beyond. The Tree of Life blooms in the center of the mystical garden of Kabbalah. It functions as the spiritual organizer for all cosmic navigators, who can use its ever-present power to improve their lives and climb their way closer to God. Kabbalah teaches us how to transform ourselves into cables that transmit the divine to the earthly and to bridge— via the energetic magic of the Tree of Life—the above and the below.

The Tree of Life is made of ten archetypal energy spheres, or *Sefirot* in Hebrew. Only one of the ten spheres of the Tree of Life represents the physical existence that we can see, touch, hear, smell, and taste. The other nine all designate some form of "dark matter," the ethereal mysteries of the creation that resonate beyond our material world.

The Tree of Life endures as an ancient symbol, still used by different races and cultures, as it has been throughout history. For thousands of years, people everywhere have revered trees as a source of spiritual sustenance. From the esoteric traditions of Siberia, which claim that their shamans gestate on treetops, to the Buddhists, who contend that the Lord Buddha attained enlightenment under the Bodhi tree, trees always have served as an anchor for spiritual work. A tree also links Kabbalah and astrology. This connection emerges in the ancient association between the Kabbalistic spheres of the Tree of Life and the astrological planets, as well as in the correlation between the zodiac signs and the paths that connect the spheres. For a deeper understanding of the ten spheres of the Tree of Life and how to use this timeless, radiant tool for practical self-improvement, please refer to my first book, *A Wish Can Change Your Life*.

Planting Your Own Tree of Life

I urge you to plant a few trees as part of your study of astrology and Kabbalah. I have created two forests in which you can plant new trees via donations to nonprofit organizations. The first, located in Northern California, is managed by American Forests at *www.TreeofLifeGrove.org*. The second grove is situated in Israel, near the holy city of Tzfat, the legendary home of many of the most prominent Kabbalists in history. KKL oversees this forest at *www.TreeofLifeGrove.org.il*. I thank you in the name of all the trees you will plant.

Figure 1 depicts the Kabbalistic Tree of Life and its astrological attributes. Each of the ten spheres of the Tree of Life represents a different archetype or energy field. The term *archetype* derives from the Greek words *arkhe* meaning "first" and *typos* meaning "model" or "pattern." With this etymology, *archetype* appropriately describes the spheres since, according to Kabbalah, God first created the ten spheres, and then from that blueprint God then crafted all the rest of the creation.

The ten spheres are arranged in three pillars, which correspond to the three modalities in astrology (cardinal, fixed, and mutable). The right pillar is called the Pillar of Mercy or the Pillar of Expansion. It corresponds to the cardinal signs and holds the spheres Wisdom, Mercy, and Eternity. The left pillar, also called the Pillar of Severity or the Pillar or Restriction, correlates to the mutable signs and contains the spheres Understanding, Severity, and Splendor. The middle Pillar, the Pillar of Harmony, relates to the fixed signs and holds the spheres Crown, Beauty, Foundation, and Kingdom.

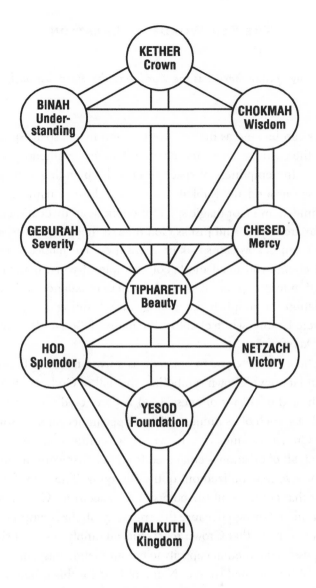

Figure 1: The Tree of Life

THE TEN WORDS OF CREATION

In the beginning of time there was the Word; and the Word was with God.
—JOHN 1:1

The ten spheres can be seen as the ten words or ten magic spells spoken by God at the creation of the cosmos. These ten divine utterances emitted ripples of energies that radiated into the emptiness of space, eventually blending and coalescing into everything we see around us. Kabbalah assigns a distinct name of God to each sphere. That name, mantra, or magic spell functions as an invocation of the energies of that particular archetype. And just as God uttered these ten words to manifest the energies of the cosmos, you can speak or chant these ten names to encase yourself in the ethereal energy you need most. For example, if you'd benefit from a more intense connection to the sphere Beauty, the sphere of balance and health, you can amplify that relationship simply by imagining yourself sitting in a golden sphere (the color of the sphere Beauty) while chanting the name of God for Beauty (*Yod Hey Vav Hey Eloha Va'Da'At*).

The first sphere or archetype to emanate as a word from God's mouth is called **Crown** (*Keter* in Hebrew). Crown symbolizes the will of God, and that will, according to Kabbalah, is the will for oneness. God is One. God's will is unity. Humans arrive as individuals, each of us unique in form, appearance, and personality. But the message of the Crown resounds clearly: we are all connected; we are all the same. All of us—in fact, all of creation—emanated from this first word uttered by God just as the entire universe materialized out of the Big Bang. The color for this sphere is white, the color that contains all the colors of the spectrum. Crown isn't associated with a particular planet or sign because this sphere symbolizes emptiness or nothingness. That does not mean that Crown represents an empty vessel. It simply suggests that we do not possess the mental capacity to comprehend, grasp, or contain the infinite magnitude of this original sphere. Name of God for this sphere is Eheye. Look at this name of God as a mantra, a key that can open before you the powers and potentials of the sphere. Just like you might need a web address to download a file, so does the name of God connect you to a certain aspect of the one God that can in turn help you access the content you need to connect with.

To learn more about how to connect to the ten spheres as well as the relevance of the names of God, please refer to my book *A Wish Can Change Your Life*. You can also find audio examples of each mantra at *www.CosmicNavigator.com*.

The next word uttered by God was **Wisdom** (*Hochma*). Wisdom represents reflection, meditation, intuition, and insights. Wisdom is the echo of the first archetype, Crown. It symbolizes the mirror in which God's Oneness reflects itself. Reflection—via meditation or other techniques of inner discovery—enables us to locate the divine part of ourselves. Kabbalists paint Wisdom in silver-gray to signify the wisdom we attain as we age. Gray also suggests that life is not black and white, all or nothing, good or bad. Wisdom correlates not to any particular planet, but to the zodiac wheel in its entirety. It is wise, then, to examine the entire, complicated, circular (endless) picture. As the source of the astrological wheel, Wisdom also generates and oversees the divine astrological contracts that guide our paths here on earth. Name of God: YOD HEY VAV HEY.

The word **Understanding** (*Binah*) follows next. No wonder few of us can understand Wisdom; Wisdom arrives in the creation before the sphere that gives birth to Understanding. This third sphere imparts the energies we need to comprehend ourselves, our identity, and our mission in life. It brings us logic, science, education, and discipline, as well as the concepts of time and space that provide a structure in which to practice all that science and discipline. This sphere is colored dark indigo. Understanding marks the first sphere to be assigned an astrological planet. It brings Saturn, the ruler of Aquarius and Capricorn and the planet associated in traditional astrology with malevolence, plagues, disasters, and other misfortunes. But Kabbalistic astrology places Saturn in the most lofty and vital domain, the closest of all the planets to Crown and the Will of God. In your chart, Understanding—represented by Saturn—highlights the area of life in which you must practice persistence and focus in order to succeed and grow. Saturn helps us in the Understanding of our *Tikkun* (fixing our soul), as well as with the construction of a structure (such as regular yoga, meditation, community and service) that will drive that rectification. Name of God: ELOHIM.

Next God spoke **Mercy** (*Hesed*). Mercy embodies the archetype of compassion, unconditional love, expansion, benevolence, and the grace of God. Whenever you feel good about yourself and those around you, you experience the energy of Mercy.

The sphere is associated with Jupiter, the ruler of Sagittarius and Pisces. Jupiter in our chart marks the area of our life in which we are likely to enjoy benevolence and boundless opportunities. Jupiter/Mercy also highlights the potential that you can transform into actuality. Mercy represents the most accepting and forgiving energy of the Tree of Life and creation as a whole. It works as a reinforcement of the prior sphere, Understanding. If you *gave* to the universe what Understanding asked of you, in Mercy you will *receive* or reap the rewards of that discipline and effort. The color of Mercy is blue, the color of the boundless seas and sky. Name of God: EL.

And fifth, God uttered **Severity** (*Gevurah*), which in Hebrew translates to "heroism," "bravery," or "valor." This sphere resonates with strength, power, pure energy, and force. It can also be severe. The biographies of heroes and heroines such as Moses or Superman often feature harsh childhoods or incidents that forged them into remarkable people. Kabbalah also calls this sphere *Din*, which means "judgment." This sphere is designed to balance the unconditionally expansive, loving, giving nature of Mercy. Severity is associated with Mars, the ruler of Aries and Scorpio. Since Mars is the red planet, it makes sense that Severity is also colored red. Red warns us of danger ("red alert"), protects (the Red Cross), and prevents us from crashing into each other (a red light). In astrological charts, this sphere underscores the area in your life in which you possess great courage, where you might need to be more of a hero, or where you fight for your rights as well as those of others. Severity/Mars asks us to put your foot down so that you might receive what is duly yours. Name of God: ELO-HIM GIBOR.

The sixth word in God's divine poem was **Beauty** (*Tiferet*). Located in the heart of the Tree of Life, Beauty balances constriction and expansion, feminine and masculine, and the above and the below. Some Kabbalists dub it the Throne of God, and Beauty is therefore associated with the higher self, as well as the sign Leo. The color of the sphere is bright yellow or gold; the latter is also the color and name of the most acclaimed of all metals and by far the most regal and royal. Beauty teaches that God's presence is felt most profoundly when you balance giving with receiving, masculine with feminine, judgment with forgiveness. Health, happiness, children, playfulness, and love all emanate from this beloved archetype. Just as all of the spheres revolve around this central sphere, all of the planets orbit the sun, the primary symbol of astrology and the celestial body associated with Beauty. The location of the sun in your chart describes the area in your life in which you can express most fervently your highest good and emit the greatest amount of light upon your fellow sentient beings. Name of God: YOD HEY VAV HEY ELOHA VA'DA'AT.

Then God whispered the word **Eternity** (*Netzach*). This marvelous archetype brings pleasure, art, talent, and all slices of life that provide us with sensuous joy. Because this sphere governs pleasure, it also generates the mechanism of repetition and reproduction. For example, when you dine at a delicious restaurant, you generally yearn to repeat that experience by going back there again and again. Mother Nature operates on this same principle. One tree seeds a second and then a third and fourth on into eternity until we find a gigantic forest. Green, the color of nature, is the color of the sphere. Eternity embodies the energy of Venus, the planet affiliated with both Taurus and Libra. This sphere oversees peace, diplomacy, negotiation, and relationships, as well as personal talents and money. Venus/Eternity in your chart underlines the area of your life in which your idiosyncratic talents can be deployed to generate financial security and abundance. Name of God: YOD HEY VAV HEY TZEVAOT.

The eighth word spoken by God was **Splendor**, or *Hod*, which is Hebrew for "reverberation." This sphere enables communication, that most human characteristic, which demands both speaking *and* listening. Splendor guides commerce, business, and trade. It enables us to absorb the messages, signs, and synchronicities that we encounter so that we can translate and transmit them to the rest of humankind. Splendor is associated with magic, spells, and the ability to manifest mind over matter. Orange—the color chosen to herald the new millennium, our information age—is the color of the sphere, and Mercury, the planet linked to Gemini and Virgo, is its ambassador. In your astrological chart, Splendor/Mercury signifies your antenna, highlighting your style of communication, as well as your strengths and perhaps your weaknesses when it comes to conveying and receiving messages and knowledge. Name of God: ELOHIM TZEVAOT.

Ninth came the word **Foundation** (*Yesod*). This sphere holds all the secrets and subconscious powers of the universe. The word *sod*, which is the root of the Hebrew name of this sphere, means "secret." Kabbalists have been stressing for millennia that at the foundation of the universe lies the secret of the law of attraction (the same law described in the bestselling book and DVD *The Secret*). That is one of the reasons why sexuality and passion are governed by this sphere. This intense and mysterious wheel of energy also governs transformation, healing, intimacy, and death. The law of attraction can transform your life and afford you what you always dreamt of. Foundation is linked to the moon, the ruler of the night, as well as the sign Scorpio. It is colored purple/violent, a rich tone that nonetheless emits the highest visible frequency in the spectrum. In your chart, Foundation/the moon exposes your inner reflexes—how you instinctively react to various situations in your life. It also might reveal hidden memories of early childhood or trauma, as well as the places in which you safeguard all your secrets. Name of God: SHADDAI EL CHAI.

And the last word to emerge from God's consciousness in the Kabbalistic story of creation is **Kingdom** (*Malchut*). In Kabbalistic astrology, Kingdom relates to your rising sign or ascendant, the path you chose to walk in this lifetime, the highway that leads to your destiny. This sphere encompasses the entire physical creation—from unseen viruses and your neighbor next door to alien starships and vast galaxies millions of light years away. Name of God: ADONI HA'ARETZ.

PART II

THE MAP OF YOUR SOUL

CHAPTER 6

The Horoscope: Mapping Space and Time

The wise man is the man who in any one thing can read another.
—PLUTONIUS, *THE ENNEADS*

Your astrological chart is called your horoscope. The word *horoscope* derives from the Greek words *horo*, "hour," and *scope*, "vision." Your horoscope represents the planetary vision at the hour of your birth. Up until the time of the ancient Greeks (the fifth century B.C.E.), horoscopes were cast only for countries, events, and kings. The ancient Greeks democratized astrology. They created the concept of the individual natal chart, which allowed commoners like you and me to benefit from the esoteric science of astrology.

The astrological chart maps both space and time. The chart in figure 2 is cast at the city of Los Angeles, California, on November 8, 2003, at 4:51 P.M., at the time of harmonious concordance, an auspicious moment that some astrologers and shamans consider to be a signpost that heralds the Age of Aquarius. Using this chart, you can familiarize yourself with the basic language and symbols of astrology, including:

1. The general structure of a chart;

2. The sun and its meaning (who are you?);

3. The ascendant, or rising sign (what is your path?);

4. The twelve houses of the chart (which aspects of your life are most influenced?);

5. Which house contains the sun (where do you shine the brightest?);

6. Which house contains the moon (how do you express your feelings?);

7. The locations of the visible planets (Mercury, Venus, Mars, Jupiter, and Saturn) and their meaning in the various signs and houses;

8. The global planets (Uranus, Neptune, and Pluto) and their meaning in the various signs and houses.

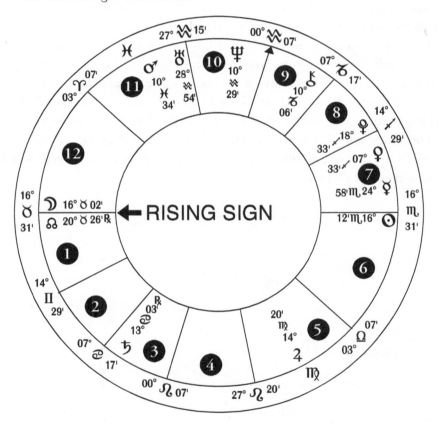

*Figure 2: Astrological chart cast at the city of Los Angeles,
California, November 8, 2003, at 4:51 P.M.*

I always recommend looking at the chart as a whole before plunging into any intricate analysis. Even if you know nothing about astrology, even if the chart looks like gibberish and haphazard squiggles, relax and continue to study it. Let the chart teach you. Here's a secret: the simple gesture of reading this book signifies that you possess an innate interest in the wisdom of the stars, which indicates that you already have delved into astrology in a past lifetime. (Perhaps in that past lifetime, it was me who read *your* book.)

Spend a few moments examining figure 2 as well as your own chart. What does the chart look like or remind you of? Can you see any shapes? It's like gazing at cloud formations in the sky and finding shapes or images, except here you are staring at star formations. Now do the same with your own chart.

The natal chart maps the position of the planets and constellations as viewed from the earth at the moment of your birth. It marks the place your soul landed in our material world, which is bound by the laws of space (place of birth) and time (the date and hour of birth). And it explains who you are, your purpose in this lifetime, what you have come to earth to fix (your *Tikkun*), and how you can do that.

The zodiac wheel of signs (or constellations of stars) can be viewed as a belt around the equator of the earth, approximately 15 degrees wide, through which all the planets except Pluto orbit.

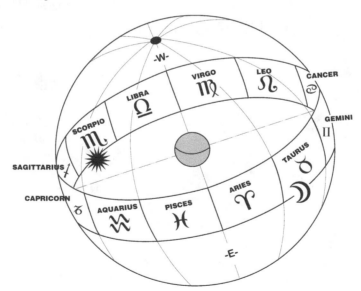

Figure 3: The zodiac belt

Imagine the earth as a circular room with a panoramic 360-degree window. The window is divided into twelve equal segments, each tinted a distinct color and each labeled with a distinct name. The first window is red and is called the Aries; the second is red-orange and is called Taurus. The next is orange and is called Gemini, and so forth. At night, you can sit in the center of the room and watch the planets and stars through the circular glass strip. You notice that the moon can be seen through the second window called Taurus; that means that the moon is in Taurus. If you draw a circle that represents the room's 360-degree view, divide it into twelve equal windows (30 degrees each) and then chart which planet you find in each window, you will have created the astrological chart of that night.

In figure 3, you can see that the sun shines through the part of the zodiac called Scorpio. That means that this image was taken when the sun, as viewed from the orbiting earth, was in Scorpio, roughly between October 23 and November 22.

Since every circle contains 360 degrees, each of the twelve signs occupies a 30-degree slice of the zodiac belt. These 30 degrees correspond to the roughly thirty days that the sun remains in each sign.

Aries (March 19–April 19)*

Taurus (April 20–May 20)

Gemini (May 21–June 20)

Cancer (June 21–July 22)

Leo (July 23–August 22)

Virgo (August 23–September 22)

Libra (September 23–October 22)

Scorpio (October 23–November 22)

Sagittarius (November 23–December 21)

Capricorn (December 22–January 19)

Aquarius (January 20–February 18)

Pisces (February 19–March 20)

*Note that the dates corresponding to the signs vary slightly from one year to another.

Symbols for the Planets and Signs

Here is a list of signs and symbols to assist you in identifying them within your own chart:

Aries ♈	Sun ☉
Taurus ♉	Moon ☽
Gemini ♊	Mercury ☿
Cancer ♋	Venus ♀
Leo ♌	Mars ♂
Virgo ♍	Jupiter ♃
Libra ♎	Saturn ♄
Scorpio ♏	Uranus ♅
Sagittarius ♐	Neptune ♆
Capricorn ♑	Pluto ♇
Aquarius ♒	
Pisces ♓	

THE COSMIC QUESTIONS: WHAT, HOW, AND WHERE?

Speaking the language of astrology requires us to master the three primary components of this intricate idiom: planets, signs, and houses.

The planets (including sun and moon) determine *what* type of energy is activated. The planets generate the energy of the archetypes. The sun, for example, serves as the engine for creativity and self-expression.

The twelve signs determine *how* the energy manifests in our lives. It might help to think of the signs as filters that alter the strength or color of the pure energy. For example, white light radiating from a lamp would appear blue if we placed a blue filter over the lamp and red if we used a red filter. With the sun in Pisces, for example, the energy of self-expression shows up through the filter of dance, poetry, dreaminess, and mysticism, while that same sun in Aries might reveal itself as vigorous athleticism, leadership, or militancy.

The twelve houses determine *where* all this filtered energy will appear in our lives. With the sun in Pisces in the tenth house, an individual might express herself (sun) in her career (tenth house) by becoming a professional dancer (Pisces).

Each one of the twelve houses governs a different slice of life. These arenas range from personality (first house), to money and talent (second house), siblings and communication (third house), home and family (fourth house), children and romance (fifth house), work and health (sixth house), relationships and marriage (seventh house), sexuality and death (eighth house), education and travel (ninth house), career and success (tenth house), community and friends (eleventh house), and finally, karma and challenges (twelfth house). Chapter 10 discusses the houses and their significance in more detail.

To help us with the big picture, let's ask the planets the *what* question. In other words, what type of energy does each planet symbolize?

What is my sun?

—It is my self-expression and creativity.

What is my moon?

—My emotional expression.

What is my Venus?

—It represents my relationships, my attitude toward money, and my artistic expression.

What is my Mars?

—It is my passion, my force, energy, and action.

What is my Mercury?

—It is my intellect and my communication skills.

What is my Saturn?

—It is my discipline, ambition, and endurance.

What is my Jupiter?

—It represents my best friend, signaling how I receive abundance, gifts, and expansion.

What is my Uranus?

—It is my individuality and uniqueness.

What is my Neptune?

—It is the mystic in me, my imagination.

What is my Pluto?

—It is my sexuality and power.

Of course, all of these energies can turn up or express themselves in myriad modes and fashions. That brings us to the *how*, which is represented and influenced by the signs. How does this particular energy (planet) come across here on earth? Each sign will deliver a different prism through which the planets reveal their presence in our lives. For example, Mars, the energy for pure force, filtered through Aries, will manifest in an aggressive style. If the same forceful Mars rushes through the filter called Capricorn, he will become a disciplined soldier, strictly obeying the orders and structure conferred by Capricorn.

The houses tell us *where* in life the energy of the planets and signs will appear most dramatically. If Mars in Capricorn is found in the second house, the house of money, it might induce the individual to be disciplined with his money. In the seventh house, the house of relationships, this same configuration might suggest that a person is likely to be attracted to disciplined people.

For practice, locate Venus in the sample chart (figure 2). You will find the symbol for Venus in the upper half of the seventh house in the sign of Sagittarius. It suggests that a good partner (seventh house) for the bearer of this chart might be a foreigner (Sagittarius rules foreign cultures) with a strong artistic sensibility (Venus).

Not all the houses in your chart will contain a planet. In the sample chart, the second and fourth houses are empty. Every house nonetheless is ruled by a sign, and that sign provides the energetic expression for that particular area of your life. For example, a man with Gemini in the sixth house, even if there are no planets in this house, is apt to work as a writer or similar processor of information, because the sixth house is the house of work and Gemini rules messages and writing.

I tend to look at the chart and the division of houses as a strategy map for war. (I concede that this metaphor is a little militant, but I am an Aries and therefore partial to such martial examples.) As you look at the chart, imagine it as a country called

USM (United States of Me). Each of the houses represents a state in your union with borders that need to be patrolled and protected. You have at your disposal ten legions (planets)—all possessed of different strengths, abilities, and weaknesses—to fight your wars, ward off invasions, and insure a thriving nation. Some of these forces are infantry (Saturn), airborne (Mercury), commando (Mars), magical warriors (the moon), spies (Pluto), intelligence (Uranus), artillery (Jupiter), and marine (Neptune). You also have your headquarters and capital (the sun), and since no army can march on an empty stomach, you enjoy a battalion in charge of food and supplies (Venus). Before you are born, your soul decides how to allocate your "armies" of energy to help you master as many areas of life as possible.

Since you might have been a bit stingy in your last incarnation, you might decide now to make piles of money for the purpose of philanthropy. You choose to put three battalions (planets), including your headquarters (sun), in the second house, the house of money, and you maneuver three other celestial forces into the eleventh house, the house that rules humanitarian causes. You realize that you will have to live as a charismatic leader to attract others to your cause, and so you put fiery Mars in your first house, the house of leadership. You then place several other legions in your house of career to provide ambition and success. With such a specific focus, your soul probably has left several houses naked. You have nothing in the house of family, the house of health, or the house of relationships. And so you might say to your secretary of defense (your guide in the afterlife), "Maybe I ought to transfer one legion from the house of money to the house of family? I really want to have kids, you know?" And so begins the tough negotiations with your higher self up there in the magical ether.

YOUR TWELVE APOSTLES: THE HOUSES OF YOUR CHART

The twelve houses serve as your apostles. They carry the energy of your life. Each house has a sign that governs it. You can view the sign as the doorman or as the key to the house. You must go through the doorman or use the key to access the energy stored inside. You can find the sign that rules each house in the outer wheel of your chart. The sign found at the beginning of the house governs that house.

The first house's doorkeeper is your rising sign (see chapter 8). The second house is ruled by the next sign you encounter moving down counterclockwise from the rising sign. You will find it adjacent to the line that demarcates the start of the second house. In our sample chart (figure 2), the second house is ruled by 14 degrees Gemini. Move down counterclockwise to find the sign for the third house; in this same chart, it is 7 degrees Cancer. This indicates that the access to the third house, the house of intellect, nests in the emotional energies of Cancer. If you want to gain entry to that house, you will have to make sure you communicate (third house) your emotions (Cancer).

The fact that we all have twelve houses ruled by the twelve signs reveals a vital premise of astrology: you contain all the signs inside you! Though you might view your sun sign as paramount, every other sign plays a role in your personality and development too. You might be an Aquarius with no planets in Sagittarius, but if Sagittarius rules your house of career, then you will have to nurture the Sagittarius archetype in order to succeed in that core area of your life. Some signs will exert a more significant influence on your particular life, but all of them serve some key purpose. A great cosmic navigator therefore speaks the language of every single sign.

The first house rules the body, physical appearance, leadership abilities, mannerisms, attitudes, and resistance to disease. Some astrologers describe it as your mask or how people see you. *Persona* in Greek means "mask," signifying your personality, or ego, if you want. It is your flagship, your rising sign/ascendant (see chapter 8).

The second house governs talents, money, finance, values, and self-worth. It reveals how you deal with money, assets, personal belongings, and budgets. Your self-worth will determine how much you believe in your talents and how well you can translate these talents into money.

The third house is the house of the mind, siblings, neighbors, and relatives (excluding your parents). It also rules lower education, communication, reading preferences, and the practical logical mind. This house also influences transportation, vehicles, cars, and airplanes, and one day soon, I hope, spaceships.

The fourth house represents the home and family, the place where you feel secure. It describes the home and family of your childhood as well as the family you build for yourself as an adult. It also relays information about your relationship with your mother, maternal figures, and old age.

The fifth house rules creativity, love, romance, fun, sports, speculations, entertainment, theater, and children. It's the house of happiness. This house also contains your inner child. You can connect (and help to heal) that inner child by working with the energies of the sign that governs your fifth house.

The sixth house is the house of physical health, disease, work, service, purification, hygiene, diets, and order. It also rules domestic animals and pets. This house reveals how you deal with employees and how well you delegate authority.

The seventh house governs beauty, marriage, partnerships, contracts, law, and justice. It also rules our known enemies as well as lawsuits. This house contains the key to your harmony and peace.

The eighth house is the house of death, sexuality, joint financial affairs, intimacy, the occult, other people's money, and inheritance. It rules taxes, insurance, your partner's earnings, alimony, as well as your business partner's finances. This house contains your secret chambers, the dungeons in which you hide the things you are afraid of.

The ninth house rules morality, traveling, prophecy, higher education, publishing, universities, churches, temples, philosophy, and religion. It is also the house of in-laws. This house describes how you experience truth and how you perceive the meaning of life.

The tenth house governs achievements, professional standing, success, status in the community, and career. It is the house of authority and society. It describes the mountain you need to climb in this lifetime, providing clues to your ambition and your capacity to bring the potential into the actual. In the Ancient Greek tradition it is called *Kleos*—our fame, glory, what we will be remembered for.

The eleventh house is the house of the future, freelance income, friendships, groups, cooperation, technology, hope, and philanthropy. This house reveals how well you function within group settings as well as the nature of your relationship to humanity.

The twelfth house rules karma, compassion, confinement, hospitals, mysticism, healing, imagination, faith, and past lifetimes. It is also associated with pain, personal limitations, and your hidden enemies. It shows what talents you possess from past lifetimes that are hard to access.

Interpreting the Planets in the Houses

The lists in chapters 7 through 10 provide a general interpretation of the sun, moon, and each planet as it appears in each of the signs and each of the houses. Understand that these are generalized and simplified interpretations and no one of them explains who you are. You must integrate together the various interpretations in this book that relate to you. Then you can catch a glimpse into your soul and destiny. Here are some general rules on how to use the lists to best interpret the planetary relationships you find in your own chart.

The houses and their energies correspond to the signs. The associations of the first house mirror those linked to Aries, the first sign. Both rule identity and personality; both represent the leader. The second house draws its attributes from Taurus, the second sign; the third house from Gemini, the third sign; and so forth. As you begin to interpret all the planets in your chart, first locate that particular planet and identify its sign. Then notice which house contains that planet. Then move to the list for that particular planet and read the paragraph for both the sign and the house. For example, in our sample chart (figure 2), you can see that the moon is in Taurus in the twelfth house. Read the paragraph in chapter 9 that describes the meaning of moon in the twelfth house. Also, read the description of moon in the second house since Taurus is the second sign and shares the associations ascribed to the second house.

Another example: In the sample chart we find the symbols 7° ♐ 37′ ♀ in the seventh house, which translates as Venus located at 7 degrees and 37 minutes of Sagittarius. To decipher the significance of this configuration, first refer to chapter 10's Venus list and read about Venus in Sagittarius. Then, to determine what area in your life this energy will exert the most dramatic effect upon, read about Venus in the seventh house, or Venus in Libra, since the qualities of Libra mimic those of the seventh house. These two paragraphs would then yield this kind of interpretation: a strong connection to foreigners (Venus in Sagittarius) that might lead to marriage (Venus in the seventh house—the house of marriage).

CHAPTER 7

Your Sun Sign: The Place Where You Shine the Brightest

"What sign are you?" Jane was asked.

"I'm a Virgo," she answered.

What Jane means is that her sun was in Virgo at the moment of her birth. But Virgo is only her sun sign. Besides her sun sign, Jane also has a moon sign, a rising sign, and signs pertaining to all the other planets. Perhaps her moon, Venus, and Mars are all in Leo. That configuration might cause her to act more like a Leo than a Virgo. With that caveat, the reason we all talk about our sun sign most often is because of its preeminence. You might not notice much if all the constellations and planets vanished for a day. You would notice if the sun disappeared. In fact, you wouldn't survive ten seconds.

The sun provides life, vitality, and strength. In your chart, it represents your mode of self-expression and individuality. The sun's energy is so powerful that when asked for our sign, we inevitably reply with the name of our sun sign.

The sun symbolizes your spiritual tribe, the energy that gives you life and an individual ego. In the chart, the sun's symbol is a circle with a dot inside. The symbol depicts the ancient Egyptian concept of the sun as the "all-seeing eye." In our sample chart (figure 2 in chapter 6), the sun (☉) is located on the right side at about three o'clock. Next to the symbol of the sun (going toward the center of the chart) the number 16 followed by a degrees sign, then the sign ♏, and finally the number 12. This astrological formula denotes the precise location of the sun. At the moment this chart was created, the sun was at the 16th degree of the sign Scorpio. The last number (12) represents the minutes of degree (each degree has sixty minutes). For our purposes, the minutes of any sign are not important, unless you are a Virgo and need to know the precise location down to the millimeter.

Since every sign occupies 30 degrees, and the sun in this case sits in the 16th degree of Scorpio, we can deduce that the chart was cast in the middle of the month ruled by Scorpio (October 23 to November 22). So let's count. Since Scorpio begins on October 23, all we have to do is count sixteen days from October 23. The result: November 8. If the chart had showed the sun at 2 degrees Scorpio, then the person would have been born two days after Scorpio began, which means she was born on October 25.

The degree of the planets' location is especially important when the planet is located at the beginning of the sign (0, 1, 2, 3 degrees) or at the tail end of the sign (27, 28, 29, and 30 degrees). These early or late degrees represent the cusp, or borderline position. If, for example, you were born on February 19, 1970, your sun is located at 0 degrees Pisces. Your personality would therefore sit on the cusp (border) between Pisces and Aquarius. Though your astrological passport would read "citizen of Pisces," you also would be heavily influenced and guided by the energies of Aquarius, the sign that precedes Pisces. You could say that you are a Pisces who speaks in a heavy Aquarius accent.

The sun provides life, vitality, and strength. In your chart, it represents your mode of self-expression and individuality. The sun's energy is so powerful that when asked for our sign, we inevitably reply with the name of our sun sign.

Similarly, a Swiss person born near the border with Germany would speak German, shop in Germany, and most likely be influenced by German culture, while a Swiss person born close to the Italian border likely would prefer linguine and speak Italian. They are both Swiss, and yet they each display a unique expression of "Swiss-ness." People born, for example, in the beginning of Gemini (2 degrees Gemini) will be more grounded (influenced by earthly Taurus) then a Gemini born in the middle of the sign (17 degrees Gemini).

The chart of Adolf Hitler demonstrates this principle. Hitler was born with his sun at 0 degrees Taurus, making him a Taurus under the waning influences of the energies of Aries, the sign that came just before. How was his personality shaped by this fact? We know that he was one the most influential leaders of the last century; he changed and destroyed the lives of millions of people. Aries is the sign of leadership and of war, and after all, Hitler tried to conquer the world. Taurus, the sign of art and material goods, explains his initial career as a painter as well as his obsession with stealing the art and possessions from those he murdered. If Hitler had been born deeper into Taurus, perhaps with the sun at 10 degrees Taurus, he probably would not have been so preoccupied with conquering the world. If, on the other hand, he had been born earlier, let's say at 25 degrees Aries, he might have lacked his stubborn fanaticism and racial prejudice, which probably would have given him victory in war. His obsession with killing Jews drove Jewish scientists such as Albert Einstein to flee to America, where they helped to build the atom bomb, and he also squandered soldiers, trains, and other resources on the Jewish genocide when they might have been marshaled to fight in the actual war. Aries is the sign of strategy, and no true Aries would accept such a waste of resources.

YOUR BEAUTY: FINDING THE PLACE WHERE YOU SHINE BRIGHTEST

Take a look at your own chart. Identify the house that contains your sun. This house indicates the area in your life in which you can shine and express yourself with gusto. It signifies your capital, your home field advantage, the place where you will find your destiny, the area of your life in which you can attract attention as well as grace.

The house of your sun also hosts the central sphere of Beauty in the Kabbalistic Tree of Life. This sublime archetype generates healing and balance, and you can therefore create much healing and harmony in this arena of your life.

The sun warms and invigorates. But it can also burn. If you abuse the powers of the sun, using them to advance and to feed your ego, then the house that holds your sun can become your prison.

The house that contains your sun highlights the area of your life touched by the sphere of Beauty in the Kabbalistic Tree of Life, the sphere of balance, health, radiance, spirituality, creativity, and love. It represents your throne—the kingdom in which your unique essence can be expressed with grace and vigor.

Sun in the First House or Sun in Aries: You shine when you are self-sufficient and independent and whenever you lead and initiate. In this lifetime, your job is to heal yourself, and in doing that, you help to heal the rest of the world. Strive to make your life an example. Be careful of self-obsession and egomania. You are great, but you are not God.

Sun in the Second House or Sun in Taurus: You shine when you generate money, art, or whenever you get paid handsomely for your talents. You can be successful with finance and money. You radiate gloriously in the proximity of beautiful objects. You also use sensuality, your five senses, to relate to the world. You will achieve your goals by developing your self-esteem. Be careful of exaggerated attention to materialism and of taking your talents or money for granted.

Sun in the Third House or Sun in Gemini: You shine as a writer, speaker, or communicator of any kind. You can thrive in business and trade. Your true allies are your siblings, relatives, and neighbors. You function chiefly as an antenna, and so you must learn how to listen and absorb information. You represent a junction of two roads, two ideas, two anythings. You are the connector. Be careful to avoid behaving in an overly rational way as opposed to emotional or spiritual way. Avoid creating conflicts with those that can help you.

Sun in the Fourth House or Sun in Cancer: You shine brightest when you live in a home that you love and when you enjoy the support of family. Work at beautifying your house and office on a regular basis. Feng shui could help you create a harmonious physical environment. You thrive and share your gifts most easily when you feel secure and nurtured. Be careful to avoid codependent attachments and guilt.

Sun in the Fifth House or Sun in Leo: You shine when you express your creativity, surround yourself with children or childlike people, and enter the center of attention. Romance, happiness, and love are crucial for your success. Others always enjoy your company because you are a natural performer. You are here to teach us about fun and happiness, which means you have to work on being happy yourself. Be careful of acting overly childish and of gambling too much with life.

Sun in the Sixth House or Sun in Virgo: You shine when surrounded with compatible employees and coworkers, as well as when you work in some service-oriented profession. You like to be busy and need to work all the time. Pay careful attention to your diet, because you excel when you feel purified both physically and emotionally. Watch your health closely and consider adopting a pet.

Sun in the Seventh House or Sun in Libra: You shine best when you have a partner in life as well as in business. Beauty and justice seem to be requirements for your fulfillment. You are a natural diplomat who seeks to avoid war at all costs. Be aware of your tendency to depend too heavily on others and your need for others to depend on you.

Sun in the Eighth House or Sun in Scorpio: You shine when you expose hidden things and when you heal or transform others. You excel when dealing with other people's money and talents. Intimacy and sexuality can help you to make the most of your potential. Be careful of clinginess, possessiveness, vindictiveness, and paranoia.

Sun in the Ninth House or Sun in Sagittarius: You shine when you teach, travel, study, and explore new places and ideas. Try living in a different culture for a while and make the most of mass-communication technologies. Be careful of allowing yourself too much freedom at the expense of others, and take care of your relationships with your in-laws.

Sun in the Tenth House or Sun in Capricorn: You shine when focused on your career. High status in your profession helps to bring out your potential. Career success is vital to feeling good about the rest of your life. Be careful to avoid abusing others as you climb the career ladder, and don't lose sight of the true meaning of life in the quest of your worldly aspirations.

The house that contains your sun highlights the area of your life touched by the sphere of Beauty in the Kabbalistic Tree of Life. It represents your throne—the kingdom in which your unique essence can be expressed with grace and vigor.

Sun in the Eleventh House or Sun in Aquarius: You shine when surrounded by your gang, your group of friends, or members of your community. You excel when you seek out change and the unexpected. Spontaneity, gadgets, and freedom are key to your success.

Be careful not to spread yourself too thin, and watch out for a tendency to be impersonal and inattentive to the feelings of individuals.

Sun in the Twelfth House or Sun in Pisces: You shine among mystical and imaginative people. You also require solitude to best manifest your talents. You likely will benefit from some strict limitations and boundaries. Success awaits you, but it probably will arrive after a sacrifice. Your father might be a source of karma or emotional blocks. Be careful of addictions.

Try now to create an equation made up of your sun sign and its corresponding house. This equation can inform your future behavior and allow you to shine most beautifully. For example, a woman with the sun in Capricorn in the seventh house might need to develop patience (Capricorn) with her partners (seventh house) in order to bring out her own sunlight. It also might mean that the older she gets, the more she appreciates the relationship.

CHAPTER 8

Your Rising Sign: The Path
You Chose This Lifetime

Many people find it difficult to differentiate between the rising sign and the sun sign. Here is an easy way to clarify the problem: consider the sun sign as your capital, your stronghold, the centerpiece of your kingdom. It is the sign that describes what you strive to master and rule—your destiny. You are like a princess or a prince who must advance spiritually to assume the post bequeathed to you by your sun sign. If you are an Aries, you must learn how to be a leader; if a Taurus, you need to master art, finance, and the art of manifestation; Gemini must master communication; Cancer must master emotional expression; Leo must learn to master his or her will; Virgo needs to master organization; Libra needs to master balance; Scorpio must master intimacy; a Sagittarius must perfect wisdom; Capricorn must learn structure; Aquarius must master knowledge; and Pisces needs to master mysticism. The sun sign presents our mission.

Your rising sign, on the other hand, represents the road you chose in order to reach that destiny. It marks the path you will take to become a leader (Aries) or a mystic (Pisces) or everything in between. If I am in Los Angeles and I wish to reach San Francisco, for example, I have many options. I might drive up the Pacific Coast Highway, which is beautiful but long and slow. I could take Interstate 5, which is fast, barren, and boring. I might fly on a plane (fast and expensive). I might also choose a boat, train, or hitchhiking. San Francisco can be viewed as my sun sign, my ultimate destiny. The route I follow to arrive there—indicative of all the experiences I might encounter on the way—is my rising sign. If, for example, I drive up the coast, it suggests that I am a Libra rising, because Libra is the sign of beauty. If I choose the fast and hot Interstate 5, I might be an Aries rising, because Aries is a fast and hot fire sign. If I opt to fly, then I am likely an airy Aquarius rising, and if I travel by ocean kayak, I'm probably a water-loving Pisces rising.

The rising sign, or ascendant, follows the sun sign in significance. It might even describe the nature of your personality and the course of your life far more accurately than your sun sign. It represents the path you walk towards the manifestation of your potential.

Muhammad Ali was born Cassius Marcellus Clay on January 17, 1942, at 6:35 P.M. in Louisville, Kentucky, which makes him a Capricorn with Leo rising. Leo rising supplied the three-time world-heavyweight champion with the path of a lion— unbeatable, confident, charismatic, and king of his sport and the world. The rising sign also rules the first house, which governs the appearance and the body. Ali performed inside the ring and out because Leo also rules entertainment, theater, and sports. His Capricorn sun provided his mission: an immense ambition and unprecedented success in his chosen career. Capricorn rules ambition and career. It is also the sign of tradition and social responsibility, and Ali, inevitably it would seem, became an inspiration to countless African Americans, fighting for civil rights, against injustice. Ali was even put in prison because he protested what he viewed as an immoral war in Vietnam.

On the other hand, Bill Clinton is a Leo with Libra rising. His sun in Leo represents his potential: he is destined to be king. As president of the United States in the late twentieth century, he was, practically speaking, the king of the solar system. His rising sign and path to his destiny is Libra, the sign of diplomacy and compromise. Libra also rules balance, marriage, and relationships, which might explain why his principle troubles (his affair with Monica Lewinsky) arose from this area of his life and nearly cost him his presidency (destiny).

The rising sign, or ascendant, follows the sun sign in significance. It might even describe the nature of your personality and the course of your life far more accurately than your sun sign. It represents the path you walk towards the manifestation of your potential.

Where Is My Rising Sign?

You will find the rising sign on the left center edge of any chart. If the chart is a clock, then the rising sign will be located at precisely nine o'clock. In our sample chart (figure 2), look at the outer ring at nine o'clock. Here you will find a little circle with two horns (♉), the symbol of Taurus. This chart indicates a Taurus rising.

The numbers above and below the symbol reveal the degrees and minutes of the rising sign. In this case, 16 degrees and 31 minutes Taurus. The rising sign time-stamps the exact moment of your birth, the portal through which all the energy of the cosmos enters your chart. It registers the sign that occupied the eastern horizon at the time you were born.

Spend a moment with your own chart and locate your rising sign. Notice too the degrees of your sign. If it falls near the cusp of two signs, then your path is likely to be influenced by your actual rising sign and the sign you just missed.

The rising sign is also called the first house, and it kicks off the division of the houses. In most charts, each of the twelve houses will be ruled by a different sign. In rare situations, you might encounter a chart (like the one provided in figure 2) where some signs fall in the middle of the house and not on its cusp. In figure 2, this is the case for both Pisces and Virgo. They are fully contained by the 11th and 5th house. This is called interception. In this case both the sign in the cusp and the sign in the middle of the house are said to co-rule that house. In the case of figure 2, the 11th house will be influenced by both Aquarius (on the cusp) and Pisces (intercepted in the house). It could be said that the individual's friends (11th house) seem to be very scientific (Aquarius) but also have a mystical bent (Pisces).

The zodiac wheel is divided into a pie with twelve slices. Each slice, numbered one through twelve, represents a specific house. We begin counting at your rising sign and continue around the circle counterclockwise. The first house occupies the slice just below (counterclockwise) your rising sign. The second house lies just beneath the first. Figure 2 indicates the numbers of houses, with the large numbers one to twelve. (The following chapter discusses each of the houses in detail.)

We calculate the rising sign with the time of birth. If you do not know your time of birth, you can still create your chart, but you will not be able to determine your rising sign. Since there are twenty-four hours in a day and twelve signs, the rising sign changes every two hours (24 ÷ 12 = 2). For example, a person who is born on September 8 at 9:30 A.M. in Cairo, Egypt, will most likely have a Libra rising. If he had been born at 11:30 A.M. that same day, his rising sign would have moved to the next sign, Scorpio, and if he'd been born at 9:30 P.M., he would be an Aries Rising.

Once you identify your rising sign, you can find the general characteristics of that energy in the following list. For the cosmic navigator, the rising sign represents the captain of your ship, the force that ushers you through life in pursuit of your destiny.

Aries Rising: Independent and outgoing, you follow the path of a leader and initiator. You are impatient and daring. Many see you as brave, a daredevil, even impetuous. You go and get what you need. You might be considered competitive, but you simply want to accomplish things as fast as possible and then move forward to the next task. Others like you: Louis Armstrong, Che Guevara, Henry Miller, Eva Peron, Ron Howard, and Richard Burton.

Taurus Rising: Your path is paved through Mother Nature. You are stable, determined, and focused, and you possess a love for art, beauty, and finance. You exhibit patience, but you might tend toward stubbornness. You have stamina and a bountiful intuition. Use your talents and hold fast to your values as you walk towards your destiny. Others like you: Carlos Santana, Liza Minnelli, Jean Cocteau, George Lucas, Queen Latifah, George Washington, Barbara Streisand, and Michael Jordan.

Gemini Rising: You travel the two-lane highway of communication and intelligence. You are a messenger. Always on the look out for people and places that need to be connected, you live to trade information. You are curious and jumpy, talkative and restless. You have the ability to mingle easily and get along, chameleon-like, with all kinds of people. Others like you: Johannes Kepler, George Bernard Shaw, Sir Laurence Olivier, Neil Armstrong, Miles Davis, Bruce Springsteen, and Orson Welles.

Cancer Rising: Your path runs along the ocean. You are nurturing and giving. You need to be needed, and you sometimes attract needy people. A sense of security is vital for you. You have a strong maternal instinct but can sometimes become overprotective or withdrawn. When you express your feelings and induce others to connect to theirs, then you know that you are on your path. Others like you: His Holiness the Fourteenth Dalai Lama, Steven Spielberg, Stephen King, Julia Roberts, John Travolta, Albert Einstein, and Bill Gates.

Leo Rising: You walk the royal road of creativity, constantly finding yourself in the center of attention. You need to be adored. You have a great deal of pride, strength, and love. You seek to protect those loyal to you as well as those in need, but you often seek to control life. It is hard for you to stay behind the scenes. Others like you: George W. Bush, Giorgio Armani, Johnny Depp, Donald Trump, Elton John, Marilyn Monroe, Al Pacino, and Saddam Hussein.

Virgo Rising: You walk the modest road of service and dedication. You possess powerful analytical capabilities and a perfectionist's outlook toward life. You tend to categorize and label experiences, and you can be overly preoccupied with your body image. As long as you purify, detoxify, and cleanse yourself on a regular basis, you will achieve your goals. Others like you: Igor Stravinsky, Tiger Woods, Cesar Chavez, Madonna, Howard Hughes, and Kurt Cobain.

Libra Rising: You travel the path of beauty, law, and justice. You tend to be good-looking and drawn to beauty in all its forms. Life is about creating harmony. You are a peacemaker and a diplomat, fair and likeable. Avoid war and conflict as you navigate your road, but don't forget to fight for your right to do so. Others like you: Mohandas K. Gandhi, Britney Spears, David Letterman, Anton Chekhov, Harrison Ford, John F. Kennedy, Bill Clinton, and Monica Lewinsky.

Scorpio Rising: Your path winds in the shadow of death. You are a healer and transformer. Some might call you an urban shaman. People change when they come in contact with you. You are fascinated with the occult, the forbidden, and the hidden. You are passionate and insightful, sexual, and sometimes paranoid. Others like you: Tom Cruise, Tori Amos, Prince, Vladimir Putin, Victor Hugo, D. H. Lawrence, and Dr. Phil (Phil McGraw).

Sagittarius Rising: You walk the path of the teacher and preacher—a route that transverses many foreign lands. You are lucky and optimistic, fun loving, popular, and enthusiastic. You live for adventure and expeditions. As long as you are guided by truth, you will be protected. Others like you: Nicholas Cage, Mother Teresa, Will Smith, Bob Dylan, Bruce Lee, Catherine Zeta-Jones, and Ted Turner.

Capricorn Rising: Your path is that of a mountain climber, who slowly but surely ascends to the top. Ambitious, focused, and resourceful, you move steadily toward worldly success. You are disciplined and persistent. You were old when you were young and will find your youth as you grow older. You tend to be a late bloomer. So rejoice—the future is bound to be better than the present and past. Others like you: George Burns, James Joyce, Niccolo Machiavelli, Malcolm X, and Yehudi Menuhin.

Aquarius Rising: You walk the path of freedom and equality. You are a democrat, always seeking to award power to the people. You are innovative, inventive, unique, and sometimes a bit strange. Often ahead of your time, you gravitate toward science fiction and futuristic ideas. Strive to think up new ways of doing things that can make the future happen now. Others like you: Larry King, Whoopi Goldberg, Jay Leno, Matt Damon, David Bowie, Billie Holiday, Jimmy Hoffa, Condoleezza Rice, and Immanuel Kant.

Pisces Rising: You traverse the path of the mystic, the dancer, and the poet, a road of ecstasy and union with the divine. You are sensitive, compassionate, and empathic. The road to your destiny at times might appear befogged and confused, but hold onto faith, and you will reach your goal. Be receptive, but be careful of succumbing to laziness. Others like you: Gwyneth Paltrow, Brad Pitt, Allen Ginsberg, and George Clooney.

CHAPTER 9

Your Moon Sign: The Foundation
of Your Psyche

The moon completes an orbital journey around the zodiac wheel roughly every twenty-eight days. Since there are twelve signs, the moon visits every sign for about two and a half days. As the closest and most visible heavenly body, the moon keeps a close watch on life on earth. Studies conducted on our biological clocks and sleep cycles have revealed that our body operates in tune with the phases of the moon. Women's menstrual cycles often sync up to the orbit of the moon too. The moon regulates the tides of the mighty ocean, raising and lowering the swells of the sea. Since we are all composed primarily of water, the moon likely exercises a strong influence on our swellings and ebbings as well.

Our moon sign is extremely important. It demonstrates how we express our emotions. The moon embodies our core animalistic nature that has never been tamed by reason and socialization. Your moon sign manifests when you are anxious or in danger (physical as well as emotional), whenever you shift to instinct mode, also known as the fight-or-flight mode. In legend, the werewolf, for example, transforms from a man (reason) to a wolf (instinct) at the time of the full moon, and Dracula transmutes from human (socially sensitive) to vampire (animal predator) in congruence with the cycles of the moon. The moon's powers have penetrated every language. Words such as *lunatic, moonstruck,* and *moony* constantly remind us of the authority Mother Moon wields on our emotions.

The moon is the ambassador of the sphere of Foundation in the Tree of Life. Therefore, the house that contains your moon is also the house that hosts the sphere Foundation. Foundation signifies the core of your psyche—the place in which you hide your demons and fears. It is also the seat of your subconscious, your dreams, your secret sexual desires, as well as your memories, both pleasant and traumatic.

Your moon represents how you react emotionally to the experiences you encounter. It serves as the sphere of Foundation in the Kabbalistic Tree of Life and indicates the area in your life that holds your subconscious power, instinct, and memories from past lifetimes.

YOUR MOON VS. YOUR SUN AND RISING SIGNS

How does your moon fit with your sun and rising signs? Imagine that four friends who share the same sun sign decide to travel from Barcelona to Rome. Remember that the sun sign equals destiny or destination, and the rising sign suggests the path these four will follow to reach their shared destiny. Two of the friends take a plane. They need to arrive early. And they probably share the same rising sign (path)—in this case probably Gemini, an air sign, since they chose to fly fast through the air. The other two friends jump on a yacht. They likely share a rising sign of water—let's say Scorpio.

The moon signs will reveal how these similar pals react emotionally to the situations they encounter on their path (rising sign) to their destiny (sun sign). One of the guys on the plane immediately falls asleep. His moon sign must be Pisces, the sign of sleep and dreams. His friend, meanwhile, spends the flight fighting over space in the overhead bin with the person across the aisle. Her moon sign is Aries, the sign of conflict, the sign that often views even a simple "good morning" as a declaration of war.

Meanwhile out at sea, the boater with a moon in Cancer, a water sign, rejoices at the up-and-down swells of the sea, while the other, who has a Capricorn moon (an earth sign), feels terribly seasick.

Sun sign = your destiny

Rising sign = the path you chose to reach your destiny

Moon sign = your emotional or instinctive reactions to the situations you encounter as you travel the path to your destiny

In the sample chart (figure 2), the moon (☽) is located in 16 degrees Taurus 02′—in other words, the 16th degree, two minutes of Taurus. It sits in the twelfth house, almost directly atop the rising sign. Whenever a planet falls in close proximity to the rising sign (within 0 to 5 degrees), it signifies that the individual lives a kind of exact personification of the energies of that planet. In this case, the person born at this moment would exhibit strong emotional and perhaps moody reactions to just about everything he encounters along his path. He might also exhibit an emotional (moon) attachment to material comfort (Taurus).

Your moon represents how you react emotionally to the experiences you encounter. It serves as the sphere of Foundation in the Kabbalistic Tree of Life and indicates the area in your life that holds your subconscious power, instinct, and memories from past lifetimes.

Moon in Aries or moon in the First House: You are a hotheaded, quick-tempered person. You shoot first and ask questions after. You tend toward sharp movements that can cause mishaps as well as physical injury. Your mother is viewed as exceedingly strong, perhaps the boss of the household. Family life can be competitive and aggressive.

Moon in Taurus or moon in the Second House: The moon thrives in Taurus, and so this position of the moon is considered one of success. You are highly creative and possess an instinct for moneymaking and art. Emotional stability can lead to financial stability. Your mother is stable and reliable.

Moon in Gemini or moon in the Third House: You have an instinct for gathering information and communicating it. You tend toward sharp, even jarring emotional swings. Intellect can stimulate emotions and vice versa. Your mother is viewed as intellectual, perhaps more like a sibling than a mother. She also might give off double or mixed messages.

Moon in Cancer or moon in the Fourth House: Your home and family are extremely important to you, and your relationships with family members can color your emotional moods. It helps to live near water or to place fountains around your home. You have a deep emotional concern for people and an instinct for nurturing others. Your mother is viewed as a homemaker.

Moon in Leo or moon in the Fifth House: Your instincts and talents lie in entertainment, or at least in entertaining your family and friends. You express emotions theatrically, dramatically, and sometimes ridiculously. You possess a great connection with children. Your home should be like a palace, grand and strategically located. Your mother is viewed as a strong and bossy queen.

Moon in Virgo or moon in the Sixth House: You have a gift for attending to the smallest details. This moon might restrain your expression of emotions in favor of logic and analysis. You possess a need for order and purity, especially in your home. Do you make your guests remove their shoes before entering your door? Your mother is very concerned with hygiene and cleanliness, and she might be overly critical.

Moon in Libra or moon in the Seventh House: You have an instinct for relationships and for sensing what other people need. However, you might end up overly concerned with what other people think and feel. You possess a need for peace and harmony, as well as an instinct for fashion, design, beauty, and human character. Be careful not to get trapped into thinking what your friends think you think they think. Your mother is viewed as overly concerned with society and has a gift for design.

Moon in Scorpio or moon in the Eighth House: You have an instinctive and deep understanding of the occult, magic, and healing. You can transform people, and you yourself shed your skin every so often. You express emotions intensely, and your emotions can sometimes border on possessiveness and vengeance. Your mother or family might be viewed as demanding or cold, but under that surface lie deep emotions.

Moon in Sagittarius or moon in the Ninth House: You have an indelible instinct for adventure and an emotional craving for freedom and movement. You probably ought to live in a different country or culture for a while. You are drawn to wisdom, religion, and philosophy. Your mother is viewed as a foreigner with different customs.

Moon in Capricorn or moon in the Tenth House: You have a deep need for planning and structure. You probably possess a bit of pessimism or skepticism downloaded to you from your mother or family. You tend to be late blooming in issues that relate to forming your own family or setting down roots. Your family and mother are traditional and set in their ways.

Moon in Aquarius or moon in the Eleventh House: You have an instinct for cultivating friends and joining groups as well as a deep need for freedom. You might tend toward emotional detachment and can treat people impersonally, spreading yourself thin among too many friends. You express your emotions in unusual or strange ways. Your mother or family setting is often eccentric or futuristic.

Moon in Pisces or moon in the Twelfth House: You have powerful psychic and imaginative abilities as well as an acute emotional sensitivity. You tend to absorb negative energies from people around you. Your home needs water (it can be located on a lakeside or seaside or filled with fountains) as well as a design that evokes a temple or sacred space. Your mother can be viewed as lacking boundaries and as very imaginative.

CHAPTER 10

The Significance of the Personal Planets

Just as you did with the sun and moon, identify the planets in your chart. Pay attention to the sign and house assigned to each of them. Then read the description of the planet in the sign as well as the house. This information will provide clarity about how each planet expresses its energy within the map of your soul.

YOUR SPLENDOR: MERCURY, THE MESSENGER OF THE GODS

Mercury, the ruler of Gemini and Virgo, represents your intellect. In the analogy of the journey to our destiny (sun sign) along our path (rising sign) that includes our emotional reactions (moon sign), Mercury highlights the way we express our intellect. Do you talk to other travelers along the way, and if so, how do you form these connections? Do you absorb information as you move forward? What type of information stimulates and attracts you? How and when do you share what you discover? Mercury also marks the area in your life where you can convey the most information and share your intelligence. Be aware that it also highlights the area in which you might encounter tricksters, thieves, and liars.

In the sample chart (figure 2), Mercury (☿) is located in the seventh house on the 24th degree, 58 minutes, of the sign Scorpio. Mercury in secretive Scorpio suggests that the individual would rather listen than reveal his own thoughts. Maybe this person is a private investigator or a spy? Mercury in the seventh house further suggests that intellect and communication wield tremendous influence over the individual's relationships. It might indicate an attraction to especially secretive partners, or that the individual favors deep and challenging thinkers.

In the Kabbalistic Tree of Life, Mercury is associated with Splendor, the orange sphere of tricks and magic. The house that hosts Mercury/Splendor designates the area in your life in which you can absorb messages offered by synchronicities. If it falls in your house of career, then the universe communicates to you through synchronicities related to your career. If it sits in the fourth house, then God speaks to you through synchronicities related to your home or family.

Mercury represents your intellect and your ability to communicate. It acts as the ambassador of the sphere Splendor from the Tree of Life. The house that hosts Mercury highlights the area in your life in which you can balance talking and listening, as well as the giving and receiving of information.

Mercury in Aries or Mercury in the First House: Quick-minded, impulsive, and highly intuitive, you can be argumentative and aggressive with your intellect. You often receive sudden flashes of insights and knowledge. You can be an intellectual leader or an agile and fierce trader. Your Splendor comes from talking and writing about yourself. You can become the message you are trying to deliver.

Mercury in Taurus or Mercury in the Second House: You are a practical and pragmatic thinker. Your intellect manifests through art as well as financial transactions. You have great powers of concentration, and you can make money from writing, trade, and negotiations. Your Splendor lies in your talents. You can turn your intellect into a vehicle for wealth and abundance.

Mercury in Gemini or Mercury in the Third House: You are highly intelligent and talkative, wielding a fantastic talent with writing and the spoken word. You serve as a messenger that connects disparate people. You are an objective thinker, logical and reasonable. Try to cultivate relationships with siblings and neighbors. Your Splendor comes from writing and communicating. You are also a trickster. Just make sure the joke doesn't turn on you.

Mercury in Cancer or Mercury in the Fourth House: Your intellectual expression is linked to your emotions. You think what you are feeling and feel what you are thinking. You possess a good memory and communicate pleasantly with family. Creating an office or big library at home will help you to flourish. Your Splendor comes from your home and family and encourages you to find friendship and intellectual stimulation in the home. You can communicate with God through family members.

Mercury in Leo or Mercury in the Fifth House: You exhibit a dramatic form of intellect, roaring more than you speak. In other words, you can be an intellectual snob. Writing and speaking is often related to performance or standing in the center of attention. Your Splendor comes from children and playful people. You speak and sometimes think like a child. You can communicate to God through children or your inner child.

Mercury in Virgo or Mercury in the Sixth House: Highly rational and analytical, you pay attention to small details. You are a good editor and possess an efficient and effective style of thinking. You are a natural-born messenger. You need to be cleansed from any substances that might affect your nervous system, and your health issues often arise from the way you think or express yourself. Your Splendor comes from your work and service. You communicate with God in your workplace and when you serve others.

Mercury in Libra or Mercury in the Seventh House: Your intellectual expression is linked to relationships and partnerships. You work better with other people who can function as sounding boards for your thoughts. You have strong diplomatic abilities, and you express your artistic self through communication and writing. Your partner is the Splendor of your life. You need someone who is your intellectual equal.

Mercury in Scorpio or Mercury in the Eighth House: You exhibit a deep and intense style of intellectual expression. Blessed with a penetrative mind and fascinated with the unknown, you have a great facility with research and laying bare of hidden information. Your sexuality is linked with communication, and you possess a strong need to communicate intimacy. You can be successful as an agent (real estate, insurance, talent). Your Splendor comes from intimacy. You need to create intimacy in your life in order to communicate with God.

Mercury in Sagittarius or Mercury in the Ninth House: You have an optimistic and idealistic outlook on life. You need to connect to foreign sources of information as well as to alternate cultures and philosophies. You possess a conceptual mind that requires knowledge and more knowledge. Learning foreign languages will enhance your abilities. Your Splendor comes when you interact with foreign cultures. You can communicate with God while traveling inward or outward to different countries.

Mercury in Capricorn or Mercury in the Tenth House: You have a disciplined, structured, and strategic form of intellect. You might have experienced some difficulties with communication in early childhood, but that can change for the better after forty. Try to incorporate your writing talents into your life's work. Your Splendor comes from your career. You can communicate with God and shine your intellect to others via your worldly pursuits.

Mercury in Aquarius or Mercury in the Eleventh House: You are highly intelligent, scientific, and futuristic. You often think outside of the box. You enjoy beneficial communication with friends, groups, and random people. Your Splendor comes from your friends and community. God communicates with you through your friends and organizations. You have a message for humanity—speak it out loudly.

Mercury in Pisces or Mercury in the Twelfth House: You have a poetic and imaginative mind and possess heightened psychic abilities and perceptions. Dreams and daydreaming deliver a great deal of information to you. You probably lived past lifetimes as a writer and messenger. God is in constant communication with you. But don't think that you need to suffer in order to hear God's angels.

Your Eternity: Venus, Sensuous Mother Nature

The energy of Venus corresponds to pleasure, finance, art, law, and all of your most significant relationships. It is associated with the Kabbalistic sphere of Eternity. Venus reveals the type of person that you are attracted to. It also designates your mode of social and artistic expression. On your journey toward your destiny, Venus represents the way you form close relationships with other travelers as well as how you react to the scenery, smells, music, and food you encounter on the road. God, the ultimate artist, created us in God's own image, and therefore we all are artists too. We carry an artistic longing in our genes, deeply engraved in our DNA. The word *amen*, often used to sign and seal our prayers, is Hebrew for both

Mercury represents your intellect and your ability to communicate. It acts as the ambassador of the sphere Splendor from the Tree of Life. The house that hosts Mercury highlights the area in your life in which you can balance talking and listening, as well as the giving and receiving of information.

"faith" and "art." To be an artist, then, is to believe. And when you have faith, you are an artist. Artists create not solely for themselves, but to move others in their society too. And Venus in your chart signifies how you react to social situations and relationships. It also provides clues to your views on finance and art.

Venus, the ruler of Taurus and Libra, stands for your feminine side. In our sample chart (figure 2), Venus (♀) is located on the 7th degree of Sagittarius in the seventh house. This suggests that this individual's artistic expression (Venus) might be connected to foreign countries (Sagittarius). It also implies marriage (seventh house) to a foreigner or a philosopher (Sagittarius).

Venus represents pleasure, finance, and your tendencies in personal relationships. It also acts as the ambassador for the sphere Eternity in the Kabbalistic Tree of Life, the sphere of pleasure, nature, and art. The house that contains Venus highlights the area in your life that will call you to repeat certain actions and behaviors to propagate expansion and growth. This house demarcates the part of your life that can teach you about your relationship to God.

Venus in Aries or Venus in the First House: You are aggressive in relationships and social situations, and impulsive with finances and your artistic expressions. You likely are attracted to strong and masculine partners, generally preferring to take the lead in relationships rather than to compromise or follow. Your relationship to yourself stands as a good indicator of your relationship with God. Your Eternity, the archetype of pleasure and sensuality, comes from your own personality. You light your own path. You need to enjoy yourself.

Venus in Taurus or Venus in the Second House: You have a strong attraction to beauty, art, design, fashion, colors, music, and food. You create strong, practical, and enduring relationships. Luxury, pleasure, and pampering yourself are important for your well-being. You host Eternity, the sphere of the arts, in the house of talents. Make sure you attend to your artistic talents and treasures. You will find great pleasure in art and your own sensual gifts. Your relationship (positive and negative) to money and your artistic gifts hint at your relationship with God.

Venus in Gemini or Venus in the Third House: You are a social being at your core. Often flaky and unstable, you are nonetheless extremely charming. Your artistry usually expresses a message. You tend to connect communication to art, colors to words, music to information. Be careful of profligate spending. You carry Eternity (pleasure) in your mind, and thus you enjoy intellectually challenging genres of art. Your relationship to your brothers, sisters, relatives, and neighbors mirror the way you relate to God.

Venus in Cancer or Venus in the Fourth House: This position suggests deep familial love. Nurturing relationships is important to you, and your finances are often linked to your family and home. You view your home as your chief generator of pleasure. Watch out for unhealthy attachments and dependency on your primary partners. Your Eternity (pleasure) comes from your home and family. The quality of your relationships with your family will indicate the quality of your relationship with God.

Venus in Leo or Venus in the Fifth House: Art is a highly creative enterprise, and you often have financial interests in entertainment, sports, or speculation. To generate abundance, you need to connect to the child inside you. Generous and bombastic, you tend to fall in love with love rather than with your partner. Your Eternity (pleasure) comes from your creativity and from play. And your relationship to your children or to childlike people mirrors your relationship with God.

Venus in Virgo or Venus in the Sixth House: You are critical about your partnerships as well as yourself. Be careful of your tendency to overanalyze your relationships. You tend to edit your artistic projects before you finish creating them. With a personality that resembles that of a monk or nun, you can make money from service-oriented work. Your Eternity (pleasure) comes from work and service. Your relationships with employees or coworkers reflect your relationship with God.

Venus in Libra or Venus in the Seventh House: An excellent designer of sound and colors, you are attracted to beauty and symmetry. Armed with a strong sense of justice, you are fair in your dealings with others, and you generally require a strong partner in everything that you do. Your Eternity (pleasure) comes from your partners in life and in work, but you require a partner who enjoys similar interests and activities. Your relationships with significant others mirror your relationship with God.

Venus in Scorpio or Venus in the Eighth House: You have passionate and intense relationships that can border on possessiveness ("fatal attraction"). You gravitate to complicated and thoughtful people. You can be vindictive and hold grudges too long, but you can make money as an agent or manager of someone else's talents.

Your Eternity (pleasure) comes from intimate relationships as well as from magic and sexuality. Your intimacy with others echoes your intimacy with God.

Venus in Sagittarius or Venus in Ninth House: You have excellent relationships with foreigners, but your devotion to freedom often generates problems in long-lasting relationships. You spend too much money, but you are exceedingly generous. Travel can bring income. You are attracted to athletic people who are similarly adventurous and outdoorsy. You might marry a person from a different place or culture. Your Eternity (pleasure) comes when you teach, learn, or travel. Your relationships with foreigners or your in-laws parallel your relationship with God.

Venus in Capricorn or Venus in the Tenth House: A late bloomer in the areas of finance and art, you come off as reserved and aloof. You express a conservative or safe attitude toward relationships and your finances. Your partner could be older or more established. You should pursue a career associated with music, design, and art—anything that gives you pleasure. Your career thrives when you have a partner. Your Eternity (pleasure) comes from your career and professional life. Your relationships with bosses or other people of authority reflect your relationship with God.

Venus in Aquarius or Venus in the Eleventh House: You are friendly but also impersonal. You might enjoy too many social contacts to be able to focus on any one person in particular. You favor modern futuristic art and express yourself artistically alongside bands of friends. You are attracted to ingenious, unpredictable partners, and you often find them through clubs, organizations, or corporations. Your Eternity (pleasure) comes from friends and groups. Your relationship to your friends and community organizations mirror your relationship with God's angels.

Venus in Pisces or Venus in the Twelfth House: Ultra-artistic and sensitive, you need to use your psychic and intuitive gifts to make money. You often fall in love with mystical, elusive, or seductive people. You are tender and sympathetic with

Venus represents pleasure, finance, and your tendencies in personal relationships. It also acts as the ambassador for the sphere Eternity in the Kabbalistic Tree of Life, the sphere of pleasure, nature, and art. The house that contains Venus highlights the area in your life that will call you to repeat certain actions and behaviors to propagate expansion and growth. This house demarcates the part of your life that can teach you about your relationship to God.

partners and tend to absorb your partner's energy for good or bad. Be careful of addictions, dependency, and codependency. Your Eternity (pleasure) comes from mysticism and the stirrings of past lifetimes. You might have been an artist or great beauty who abused those gifts in a past incarnation, and thus Eternity is part of your *Tikkun* today.

Your Severity: Mars, the Great Warrior of Light

Long associated with passion, blood, war, and energy, the red planet Mars represents the relentless engine of the chart. Mars, the ruler of Aries and Scorpio, indicates the way you deal with conflicts and aversive situations as they arise on the journey to your destiny. It also suggests how well you distribute and deploy your energy and resources as your pursue your goals. In Kabbalah, Mars symbolizes the sphere called Severity, which stands as the fiery sword of God. Mars in your chart reveals how you express the warrior energy inside you.

Just as Jacob wrestled with God's angel for twenty-four hours (Genesis 32:22), you too engage in a special sort of spiritual training with God. The house that contains Mars designates the type of spiritual training you will receive as well as the area of your life in which you will undergo that toil. In Jacob's match with God, he suffered a dislocation of his hip. It was a brutal battle. But following this tenacious initiation, God granted Jacob his spiritual name: Israel, which translates as "wrestles with God." Your Mars house shows where your spiritual initiation might flower after a long struggle.

It also marks the place where you will encounter your own burning bush. Just as Moses received his call to action to liberate an entire people via the burning bush (fire/Mars), your adventure also begins with the fire of Mars. The house that contains Mars (Severity) holds in bondage the energy you have been called to liberate. Moses liberated the Hebrews from slavery in Egypt; you must liberate your house of Mars. If, for example, your chart shows Mars in the sixth house of work and service, you have been called to work in a position that allows you to free or to rescue others. You might pursue work as a firefighter, police officer, or even a school counselor who strives to liberate her students from drugs, gangs, and mediocrity.

Mars also dictates your desires and passion. It symbolizes the energy that drives you. How do you make love? What ignites you sexually? Additionally, Mars represents your masculine side. What would you fight for? On what principle would you go to war?

In our sample chart (figure 2), we find Mars (σ) at 10 degrees Pisces in the eleventh house. This position might indicate conflicts (Mars) with friends or groups (eleventh house) over religious issues (Pisces). Or it might suggest that you join groups (eleventh house) that practice a physical (Mars) form of mysticism (Pisces), like yoga or dance.

Mars represents your drive, energy, and temper under duress. It also serves as the ambassador of the sphere Severity in the Kabbalistic Tree of Life, the sphere of strength, aggression, leadership, and liberation. The house that contains Mars highlights the area of your life that calls you to action—an arena that might stand as a battlefield that you are driven to conquer. This house also reveals how and where you wrestle with God to attain a higher level of spirituality.

Mars in Aries or Mars in the First House: You are an action figure who boldly goes where no one has gone before. You are powerful, forceful, aggressive, outgoing, and charismatic. Often a daredevil, you might be prone to accidents. You prefer leading to being led and most often come out a winner. Aggressive sexually, you like it athletic and rough. You are a pure manifestation of the sphere called Severity. You tend to wrestle with yourself to understand the nature of the divine in you. You will benefit from practicing an aggressive sport such as the martial arts.

Mars in Taurus or Mars in the Second House: You direct action toward achievable and practical endeavors. You might find it hard to start new projects, but you will persist at all costs when you do. Moneymaking and art form the core of your passion and drive. You have to work hard for your money, but if you persevere, you will see results. You are sexually attracted to confident partners, and you prefer a more sensual style of sex. Your Severity comes from battles with your own self-worth. You wrestle with your talents or with money issues to connect to your inner divinity.

Mars in Gemini or Mars in the Third House: Your action is associated with intellect. You tend to talk about what you need to do. Your battlefields include emails, letters, words and communications. You might spread yourself thin among too many projects. You also might have an overactive nervous system. You think fast and arrive at solutions at the speed of thought. You like to be verbal during sex. You might experience conflicts with siblings or neighbors. Your Severity comes from your intellect. Be careful of your tongue. You wrestle with God intellectually. Doubt might plague you now and then, but when you overcome it, you will attain a higher level of faith.

Mars in Cancer or Mars in the Fourth House: You tend to be passive-aggressive unless you choose to funnel your energy toward people and projects that you feel strongly about. Your feelings drive your actions, which are generally directed toward achieving security. You might experience quarrels with family members. You have a need to please others sexually. You might experience Severity in your childhood home or in the home you create as an adult. By wrestling with emotional issues, you eventually connect to God.

Mars in Leo or Mars in the Fifth House: Courageous and full of valor, you express your energy and will with vigor. You have a tenacious ambition and drive to attain a position of power. You also demand a great deal of feedback and reinforcement from others. You gravitate toward sports, gambling, and risk-taking. And you enjoy creativity in the bedroom. Your Severity emerges in creativity and entertainment. Be careful to avoid becoming too severe with your competitors. You wrestle with God over your propensity to gamble and take risks.

Mars in Virgo or Mars in the Sixth House: You have a strong drive to succeed in work, but you can resent and criticize those who don't share your same tenacious work ethic. You also can become obsessive compulsive unless you direct your impulses toward your work and service for others. You direct your action toward efficiency and strive to be a leader at work. Conflicts with employees might occur. You benefit from working with your muscles, and you prefer clean and safe sex. You encounter Severity in the workplace or within your own body. Be careful not to judge God's work and creations.

Mars in Libra or Mars in the Seventh House: You direct your actions toward your significant relationships. You will fight only for peace, and sometimes you relinquish your own needs to avoid conflict. Your actions work best when directed in conjunction with a corporation or with other partners. You are attracted to strong and fit sexual partners, and you love to please them. You might experience Severity with your partners or in lawsuits. By wrestling for your own rights in partnerships, you get to know yourself and your divine nature. Remember that ultimate fighters fight for peace.

Mars in Scorpio or Mars in the Eighth House: You are extremely passionate and possess an intense sexual drive. Your actions are motivated by the pursuit of intimacy and success with joint financial affairs. You embody a powerful and purposeful warrior, but sometimes your actions go unnoticed. You tend to secret away all your feelings. This mystery leads to your Severity, which might appear as silent vengeance toward others. You wrestle with God via issues of sexual identity and intimacy. Remember that sometimes, often even, enemies can transform into best friends.

Mars in Sagittarius or Mars in the Ninth House: You embody Indiana Jones, the happy-go-lucky adventurer. You crave action and novel explorations. You possess an attractive personality that can infuse people with a sense of optimism and idealism. Innately moral and knightly, you will fight for what you believe in. You are a sexual creature, infused with a sex drive that pursues fun and adventure. Your Severity emerges when you camp out, travel, or venture to the academic arena. You wrestle with God as you struggle for moral justice.

Mars in Capricorn or Mars in the Tenth House: A ferocious manifestation of the martial energy, you possess a force similar to that of a unified and disciplined army. Your actions always are structured, purposeful, and effective. Like a tenacious CEO, you achieve impressive success in all of your worldly pursuits. Your Severity will emerge in the arena of your career because you can be ruthless to those that oppose your ambitions. You like to dominate in the bedroom, but you must take care not to use sex for material gain. You wrestle with God on the ground of discipline, persistence, and endurance. It might be a slow, long, but ultimately enlightening fight.

Mars in Aquarius or Mars in the Eleventh House: You are one of those idealists who believe in "power to the people." The paragon of a freedom fighter in the concrete jungle of modern life, you will fight for others and yet not for yourself. You are driven toward philanthropic work. Like Robin Hood, you require a beloved gang or group of friends to make a difference in the world. You enjoy experimental, even group sex, and you tend to express your sexuality in a friendly rather than intimate manner. Your Severity, however, emerges with these same friends. And you often wrestle with God on the battlefield of the groups and organizations that you join.

Mars in Pisces or Mars in the Twelfth House: Your actions are guided by dreams and imagination, which sometimes induce you to tilt at windmills and engage in imaginary wars. You work best within a peaceful environment. And your faith and belief in a cause allows you to move mountains. You lean toward tantric or mystical sex, and you possess the ability to reach a heightened state of mind while making love. Your Severity comes through mystical pursuits. In previous incarnations, you lived as a fierce warrior who likely inflicted pain on others. You wrestle with God as you seek to rectify that karmic debt. Try, in this lifetime, to avoid places that are beleaguered with war or conflict.

Mars represents your drive, energy, and temper under duress. It also serves as the ambassador of the sphere Severity in the Kabbalistic Tree of Life, the sphere of strength, aggression, leadership, and liberation. The house that contains Mars highlights the area of your life that calls you to action—an arena that might stand as a battlefield that you are driven to conquer. This house also reveals how and where you wrestle with God to attain a higher level of spirituality.

YOUR MERCY: JUPITER, THE LOVER OF WISDOM

By far the most popular of all the planets, Jupiter represents luck, expansion, benevolence, traveling, vacations, and abundance. It gives and gives and gives and gives. Always supportive and jovial (the latter word coming from *Jove*, the Latin name for the planet), Jupiter rules Sagittarius and Pisces. As you walk the road of life, Jupiter delivers the provisions and assistance in times of need. It demonstrates how well you receive the aid that the universe provides. A good-luck charm that opens new doors and opportunities, the house of Jupiter indicates the area in your life in which you can attract tremendous gifts and good fortune. Jupiter functions as your convenience store, always open, always fully stocked.

In Kabbalah, Jupiter symbolizes Mercy, the sphere of unconditional love. Mercy generates the grace of God, and your house of Jupiter highlights the arena in your life in which you will experience limitless abundance. According to the laws of Kabbalah, what you receive, you also need to give. This house reveals the qualities and traits that you ought to share unconditionally. In our sample chart (figure 2), we find Jupiter (♃) at 14 degrees Virgo in the fifth house, suggesting that this individual must pay attention to small details (Virgo) in matters of creativity (fifth house) in order to attract abundance and fame (Jupiter).

Jupiter represents luck, abundance, benevolence, and sharing. In the Kabbalistic Tree of Life, it acts as the ambassador of the sphere Mercy, the sphere of expansion and unconditional love. The house that contains Jupiter highlights the area in your life blessed with unlimited resources—like a tree bursting with fruit just waiting to be picked. This house underscores where you can give the most of who you are.

Jupiter in Aries or Jupiter in the First House: You are a benevolent person and a powerful leader, who always needs to save someone. You easily grab opportunities and plant new seeds. You serve as an envoy of Mercy—an envoy of giving and compassion. God rewards you so that you will give to others. Act as a clear channel without an overbearing regard for yourself, and you will enjoy all the treasures and benevolence available in this life.

Jupiter in Taurus or Jupiter in the Second House: You have been awarded an almost certain promise for material success. Practical philosophies about how to go about your daily activities interest you. You possess multiple talents and should pursue them all. Just be careful of gluttony. Your Mercy arrives through your talents and finances. If you tithe at least 10 percent of what you earn to charity, God will view you as a generous partner and help you to make even more.

Jupiter in Gemini or Jupiter in the Third House: You are incredibly intelligent—blessed with a facility for philosophy and logic. You also possess prodigious skills in writing and communication. However, you might need to talk less and listen more. Your Mercy comes across through your mind and communication. You can write, speak, and transmit God's grace to humankind. God consistently confers valuable ideas upon you.

Jupiter in Cancer or Jupiter in the Fourth House: You have a genuine love for wisdom. Giving comes naturally to you, but you will also need to practice receiving. You express your philosophies and ideals through your family or your roots. You will flourish most by inhabiting a big office and a big house. Watch out for obesity. Mercy and the love of God descend on your home and family. You are blessed with an auspicious genetic constitution, which suggests that the people in your family (either your descendants or ancestors) will be or have been touched by God themselves.

Jupiter in Leo or Jupiter in the Fifth House: You are a natural-born actor and performer. And you might possess a strong need to preach and vocalize your beliefs.

Abundance comes from creative projects, working with children, or speculative enterprises. Mercy arrives when you ask for it, especially when you ask in a childlike, innocent voice. Your job is to entertain and transmit your happiness to others.

Jupiter in Virgo or Jupiter in the Sixth House: You exhibit strong morals and a diligent work ethic. You tend to be critical of people who you perceive to be lazy. You might place too much emphasis on small details. Watch out for perfectionism. Abundance comes from hard work, service, and adherence to a strict healthy diet. Mercy flourishes as you pay attention to your diet and your physical, mental, emotional, and spiritual hygiene. Spread the word of compassion through your work.

Jupiter in Libra or Jupiter in the Seventh House: You enjoy abundance from partners and relationships. You also exhibit a gift for material success in the arenas of law, art, and beauty. You have a powerful sense of justice and fair play. You function best in harmonious work, social, and personal situations. Mercy comes via your partners and significant others. Develop compassion toward those closest to you.

Jupiter in Scorpio or Jupiter in the Eighth House: You are secretive about both your philosophies and abundance, and you possess a strong interest in other people's money and talents. You have a talent for research, and you know how to connect to the realm of the dead. Sexuality and intimacy are vital to your happiness. You express compassion when you feel it deep at your core. You exhibit intense emotions and must be careful not to drown others in that surge. Mercy comes to you when you dive deep into the ocean of wisdom.

Jupiter in Sagittarius or Jupiter in the Ninth House: You are an idealistic and philosophical person who is eager to share your belief systems. You acquire abundance by dealing with foreign countries and people from different cultures. You might be overly optimistic and unrealistically positive. Your Mercy comes when you teach compassion and study love. You will find it easier to connect to and receive from God in foreign cultures.

Jupiter in Capricorn or Jupiter in the Tenth House: Structure, endurance, discipline, and persistence are the keys to your success. You are a natural-born teacher and student. Conservative and sometimes narrow-minded, you must plan to generate abundance. You struggle for your goals and often they take time to come to fruition, but success in your career is assured if you persevere. Mercy arrives in your profession. Strive to make compassion and truth the integral messages of your career.

Jupiter in Aquarius or Jupiter in the Eleventh House: Friends as well as participation in groups and organizations can be the source of your abundance. You have a need to be surrounded with people. You enjoy working for all of humanity. You often receive unexpected help from a friend just when you need it most. Your compassion and Mercy should come from and be directed towards friends, groups, and organizations. Abundantly altruistic, you should take care to create some boundaries so that you won't be left dry and depleted.

Jupiter represents luck, abundance, benevolence, and sharing. In the Kabbalistic Tree of Life, it acts as the ambassador of the sphere Mercy, the sphere of expansion and unconditional love. The house that contains Jupiter highlights the area in your life blessed with unlimited resources—like a tree bursting with fruit just waiting to be picked. This house underscores where you can give the most of who you are.

Jupiter in Pisces or Jupiter in the Twelfth House: Imagination and visualization will help to manifest abundance in your life. Inventive and poetic, you have empathy and compassion for all sentient beings. Unfortunately, you tend to carry other people's burdens and sacrifice yourself. Be careful of addictions. You are Mercy—you embody the pure energy of compassion. You serve as a sort of breath of fresh air for everyone, clearing out the negative and introducing the positive. Be sure to take time out to recognize your vital contributions to everyone around you.

YOUR UNDERSTANDING: SATURN, THE LORD OF KARMA

Generations have viewed Saturn as the antagonist, the evil planet that causes strife and defeat. Astrologers often looked for Saturn in the natal chart to pin blame for mishaps and catastrophes. But no more. Now Saturn is the beloved teacher—the only planet blunt (and caring) enough to highlight our faults and challenges and compel us to deal with them. On our path toward our destiny, Saturn reveals how you cope with annoyance and limitations.

In Kabbalah, Saturn represents Understanding, the sphere that bestows the knowledge we need to survive and function. The house that contains Saturn/ Understanding marks the area in your life in which you have been struggling for many incarnations with reoccurring patterns of dysfunction that can be vanquished now. It also shows you where you must devote discipline and focus to achieve inordinate success. Saturn and the sphere of Understanding impart discipline, patience, persistence, and endurance. Just remember that these valuable lessons take time to master.

Saturn, the ruler of Capricorn and Aquarius, teaches us what we want by not giving it to us, forcing us to keep plugging away until we get it right. We have to prove that we really want it through determination and relentless work. If we do that, then eventually Saturn awards us the prize. And when we attain that reward, it lasts forever—unlike some of the other treasures that Jupiter (the "good") bestows effortlessly on us. Saturn highlights our karma. And when we fix it—with struggle, discipline, and dogged resolve—we can fix many lifetimes and even the world. If you pay attention to the lessons of Saturn, you grow in ways you never could have imagined.

In our chart, Saturn and the sphere Understanding also reveals where we store our fears and nightmares. Our real job on this planet, the reason we signed that astrological contract way back before our birth, is to face those fears, understand them, and learn how to utilize them to become (spiritual) superheroes. The movie *Batman Begins* illustrates this struggle. The protagonist's initial fear of bats transforms him into a superhero who derives his power from those very same bats (fears).

In Buddhist lore, we encounter the beautiful nun Uppalavanna, who sits alone under a tree, meditating on enlightenment. Suddenly, Mara, the devil, appears and attempts to distract her from her stillness. He searches for her darkest fear.

"Are you not afraid that someone will come and abuse you?" Mara asked. "Maybe you should head back home where it is safe."

Unmoved by Mara's scare tactics, Uppalavanna continues to meditate calmly.

"Though a hundred thousand rouges like you might come here to abuse me," she says, "I stir not a hair, I feel no terror."

The determined nun stands up to her fear of molestation. She recognizes it as a mere worldly nuisance that stands in the way of enlightenment, from connecting to the One. Your Saturn sometimes disguises itself as Mara in an effort to scare you. But your Saturn sign and house also marks the home of the Great Mother (in Hebrew, the *Shechina*), who emerges in times of darkness and delivers Understanding to your life—Understanding that banishes ignorance and fear.

In our sample chart (figure 2), Saturn (♄) is located at 13 degrees Cancer in the third house, perhaps suggesting a late bloomer (Saturn) in the resolving of emotional challenges (Cancer) with a sibling (third house).

Saturn represents discipline, focus, determination, fear, karma, and ultimately the opportunity for enlightenment. It serves as the ambassador of Understanding in the Kabbalistic Tree of Life, the sphere of the Great Mother, the ultimate teacher, and our soul's recurring patterns. The house that contains Saturn highlights your toughest challenges, the area in your life in which you will have to buckle down and persevere against all obstacles. This house demarcates the place in your life that you can grow the most, overcome fears, and attain union with God.

Saturn in Aries and or Saturn in the First House: You endure the lessons of patience and persistence. You might find it difficult to initiate projects, but Saturn confers the stability that will allow you to continue once you do. You might experience problems with masculine figures of authority because you might have lived a past incarnation as a warrior who abused his power. You fear your own power, and you fear not being recognized. You might also exhibit physical or emotional scars that require mending. Your body, scars, personality, and life embody the energy of Understanding. Pay attention to the location of your birthmarks and scars. They indicate stories from past lifetimes.

Saturn in Taurus or Saturn in the Second House: Your success with money-making and saving depends on discipline, persistence, and endurance. Late blooming in manifesting your talents, you are overly serious and materialistic. Your karma requires you to learn how to use values in conjunction with talents to make money. A past lifetime of super riches or extreme poverty might cloud your judgment about the value of money. You have a fear of being poor and of wasting your talents. Your Understanding (burning of karma) is accomplished via your talent and bank account. Make sure you understand that money is not indicative of your self-worth.

Saturn in Gemini or Saturn in the Third House: You need to master mental discipline. A late bloomer in the area of communication, you can develop admirable skills in logic and business. You fear being unintelligent or dull. In a past lifetime as a writer and communicator, you might have been punished for a miscommunication or for something you wrote that offended the authorities. Your challenges and

Understanding might come through your siblings, relatives, or neighbors. Your words carry much more weight than you suspect.

Saturn in Cancer or Saturn in the Fourth House: Family members are the source of much inhibition and frustration. Be careful not to project your problems onto other people, and avoid seeking too much advice or approval from the outside world. You fear not having a loving home, and you fear for your security. In past lifetimes you might have suffered difficult relationships with your mother or with motherhood. You might have karma with family members or your physical home. Understanding is delivered through family members and your physical home (such as trouble with plumbing or locks). Your home might be trying to teach you something.

Saturn in Leo or Saturn in the Fifth House: You might experience strife in matters of the heart, children, and creativity. Egotism, arrogance, and a false sense of pride—*hubris* from the enduring Greek tragedies—might be the source of your downfall. You fear never falling in love and not having children. You possess memories of your own royalty from past lifetimes, which often cause you to demand attention and admiration from everyone today. Late blooming when it comes to having children, you might also find your lost childhood and happiness late in life. Understanding comes from children, your greatest teachers, even if it might be difficult to have children of your own.

Saturn in Virgo or Saturn in the Sixth House: Karma and spiritual lessons manifest in health problems. You have fear of diseases that might result in hypochondria. Diets and purifications will help alleviate your frustrations and blocks. You probably spend too much time and energy on minute and ultimately insignificant details. You might have been a monk, hermit, or nun in a past lifetime, which brings karma about seclusion and isolation to this incarnation. Understanding comes through health problems or challenges at work. But it is through work and service that you can attain mastery over life.

Saturn in Libra or Saturn in Seventh House: Most of your partners in work and love have reincarnated with you before, but they might have been foes in previous lifetimes. You experience frustration in relationships and intrigues with close associates. You have a fear of relationships as well as a fear of aggression and conflict. You might marry late or choose an older partner. Understanding comes from developing and dealing with your significant relationships. You need to surround yourself with disciplined people who can help you develop discipline and structure.

Saturn in Scorpio or Saturn in the Eighth House: You approach difficulties by keeping everything to yourself. You need to learn how to reach out. You might have been abused in past lifetimes and now you mistrust others, especially if they threaten you with intimacy. You might experience some sexual setbacks. You tend toward paranoia. You fear your own sense of power, your sexuality, and perhaps you also fear magic. In a past lifetime, you might have abused some form of magic or the occult. Understanding comes from creating intimacy with another person. You gain power only after you learn to use it wisely.

Saturn in Sagittarius or Saturn in the Ninth House: You are attracted to traditional philosophy and morality, but you are a late bloomer in the area of higher education. Since this incarnation might be your first in your native country, you might carry memories from other nations and cultures. You might have fears of aliens, foreigners, and religions. You have to learn not to be too strict a moralist. Don't preach. Understanding comes through higher education and travel. Strive to be a student of life, ingesting as many subjects as possible so that you might put them all together into one grand Understanding of existence.

Saturn in Capricorn or Saturn in the Tenth House: You possess a prodigious ambition and drive to succeed. But that same ambition often generates obstacles to success. You might be overly pragmatic and calculating, enjoying success only late in life. You fear failure. You might have lived a past incarnation as a political or community leader who wielded an "ends justify the means" form of tyranny. Understanding comes through pressures and challenges in your career and professional life.

Saturn in Aquarius or Saturn in the Eleventh House: You approach difficulties impersonally, as if the trouble isn't really happening to you. Be careful not to project your problems onto others. You might have lived in the past as a rebel without a cause—someone who stirred

Saturn represents discipline, focus, determination, fear, karma, and ultimately the opportunity for enlightenment. It serves as the ambassador of Understanding in the Kabbalistic Tree of Life, the sphere of the Great Mother, the ultimate teacher, and our soul's recurring patterns. The house that contains Saturn highlights your toughest challenges, the area in your life in which you will have to buckle down and persevere against all obstacles. This house demarcates the place in your life that you can grow the most, overcome fears, and attain union with God.

up a revolution that made things much worse than before. You might suffer agoraphobia, fear of people. You can learn fortitude and discipline through friends or groups. Understanding comes through difficulties with groups and your society.

Saturn in Pisces or Saturn in the Twelfth House: You need to create boundaries with substances and other people. You might have had a past lifetime in which you drowned in water or despair. You fear mysticism and the mystic inside you, but you can learn much from overcoming these phobias. As you grow older, you will feel fewer and fewer limitations. Understanding comes from diving into your subconscious and retrieving lost memories.

The Myth of Our Celestial Family

This story helps to understand the logic of the relationship of planets with the twelve signs.

The sun was lonely. He stood fixed in the heavens, alone in his own brilliant light. He had so much to give but no one to give to. Though the entire universe could see him, he could not see himself. He could not know himself, he could gain no self-awareness. He craved company, someone to share with.

One day, at sunset, when his last ray was just about to sink below the horizon, he caught a glimpse of the most astonishing beauty he had ever seen. It was the moon.

The sun could not stop thinking about how gloriously the moon reflected his own light back upon him. It was a primordial love at first sight. And for the first time, the sun translated light into love. He anxiously waited twelve long hours to see if his love would be there when he rose. He spotted her again for only a moment, but that moment was sublime.

The relationship grew slowly, confined at first to dawns and sunsets, and then later expanded to include secret trysts in places no one knew existed, places so hidden and private even consciousness could not reach them. (Much later, humans named these magical unions solar and lunar eclipses.) The couple fell in love with each other and with themselves, as is always the case with true lovers.

Soon the moon became pregnant, and this fledgling family of light expanded across the heavens. First came Saturn, the eldest of the siblings. He was awfully serious and humorous too, a strange combination but nevertheless a mighty one. Then Jupiter was born, a joyous child with luck striding at his side. After Jupiter came Mars, the warrior, the athletic protector, the hero who always rode to the rescue. Venus arrived next. She was so beautiful that everyone spent most of their time just gazing at her. And last but not least came Mercury, the agile, always armed with a story and a trick up his sleeve.

The sun and moon ruled over twelve celestial domains, and they decided to divide up this kingdom among their splendid children. Saturn received the lands farthest away because, as the eldest and most responsible of the lot, they trusted him most of all. They gave him the windy land of Aquarius and the mountainous kingdom of Capricorn. Jupiter received the lands bordering his brother's domain, one realm on each side—Pisces, the mystical land of lakes inhabited by dolphins, and Sagittarius, the kingdom of the majestic horses. Mars was given the lands just adjacent to those of Jupiter on both sides, dominion over the volcanic lands of Aries as well as mastery over its energy wells. He was also given the territory called Scorpio, where the mighty eagle soared. Venus was bestowed the fertile lands of Taurus, where towering trees grow, as well as the cloud city of Libra and its sacred libraries. Mercury was bequeathed Gemini, the junction where roads from all the kingdoms meet, as well as the caves and mines of Virgo, from which the magic of service was unearthed. King Sun remained the ruler of the golden state of Leo, and the moon, the queen of life, continued her rule over Cancer, the compassionate realm of milk and sustenance.

The division of territory worked ingeniously, and this celestial family continues to rule in a graceful and melodious way. They teach us that the words *dysfunctional* and *family* do not always mean the same thing. They exemplify how brothers and sisters can thrive together in harmony and emanate that peacefulness to everything everywhere.

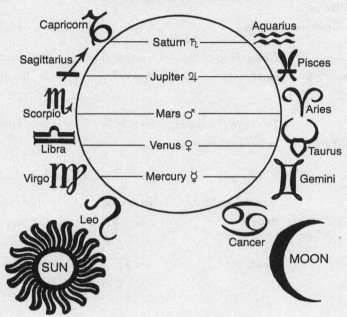

Figure 4: *The solar family*

Summary of Major Astrological Bodies and Signs

Astrological Body and What It Governs	Chakra	Sign	Area of Life
Mercury ☿ Intellectual expression	Crown (top of the head)	Gemini ♊ Virgo ♍	Communication, work, health
Moon ☽ Emotional expression	Third eye (forehead, between the eyes)	Cancer ♋	Home, family, mother
Venus ♀ Relationship expression	Throat (center of throat)	Taurus ♉ Libra ♎	Finance, talent partnerships, law
Sun ☉ Self-expression	Heart	Leo ♌	Vitality, creativity, love
Jupiter ♃ Abundance and luck	Solar plexus (just below the belly button)	Pisces ♓ Sagittarius ♐	Mysticism, higher education, travel
Mars ♂ Assertiveness and energetic expression	Sexual (genital area)	Aries ♈ Scorpio ♏	Personality, sexuality
Saturn ♄ Discipline and how one deals with limitations	Root (base of the spine)	Capricorn ♑ Aquarius ♒	Career, success, friends, groups

The Celestial Soap Opera

One quick aid in recalling the basic archetypal associations of the seven primary astrological bodies is to think of them as characters in a play that tells the adventurous story
of your life. The cast:

The hero, the protagonist, **you**, played by the **sun**, around which all the other
characters orbit.

The mother and/or **family**, played by the **moon**.

Your **lover** (whom you need to rescue), played by **Venus**.

Your best friend and **sidekick**, played by **Mars**.

Your **allies**—the wizard, fairy godmother, or the cavalry that saves you at last moment—
played by **Jupiter**.

The **comic** relief, played by **Mercury**.

Your **antagonist** (and the character that gives you purpose), played by **Saturn**.

The Days of the Week and Their Planetary Attributes

Another tip to remembering the planetary attributes is right on your desk calendar. The
names of the seven days of the week—many originally devised from Latin and adapted
through German to English—come from our seven visible celestial hosts. Sunday is
named for the sun, Monday for the moon, Tuesday (*Marti* in Latin) for Mars,
Wednesday (*Mercuri* in Latin) for Mercury, Thursday (*Jovis* for Jove in Latin) for Jupiter,
Friday (*Veneris* in Latin) for Venus, and Saturday for Saturn. A Kabbalistic interpretation
of the first chapters of Genesis tells us that God created the seven major archetypal
energies in seven days, one astrological planet per day. Applying the esoteric meaning

of each day can provide insights into the planets and how they work, and afford you a deeper understanding of events that occur on each day.

If your chart features a heavy dose of one or two particular signs, then the day associated with the planet attached to those signs—Leo = Sun = Sunday, Aries and Scorpio = Mars = Tuesday, for example—will stand as an auspicious day for you.

Also, when planning a certain kind of activity, regardless of your own astrological constitution, try to connect the event with an appropriate energy that flourishes on a particular day. For example, a public-relations gala would thrive on a Wednesday since Gemini and Mercury, the sign and planet of communication, oversee every Wednesday. A date with a lover, an activity associated with Libra, the sign of relationships, might enjoy extra juice when scheduled for Friday, the day of Venus, the ruler of Libra.

Day	Astrological Body	Sign	Example of Activity
Sunday	Sun	Leo	Sports, vacation, fun
Monday	Moon	Cancer	Family, nurturing
Tuesday	Mars	Aries, Scorpio	Competition, healing
Wednesday	Mercury	Gemini, Virgo	Communication, diets, editing
Thursday	Jupiter	Sagittarius, Pisces	Traveling, education, meditation
Friday	Venus	Taurus, Libra	Relationships, finance
Saturday	Saturn	Capricorn, Aquarius	The Sabbath, spirituality, structure

The Global Planets: Uranus the Fool, Neptune the Mermaid, and Pluto the Sinner Turned Saint

Modern astrology includes three additional planets: Uranus, Neptune, and Pluto. Astrologers have named Uranus, Neptune, and Pluto the global or generational planets because they affect entire generations rather than specific individuals. None of these distant planets can be seen from earth with the naked eye. They were assimilated into astrology as telescope-wielding astronomers discovered them over the past few hundred years. Since these distant planets feature long slow orbits around the sun, their movement across your chart is barely noticeable. While the moon moves through each sign every couple of days, and Saturn, the slowest of the personal planets, lingers in each sign for just over two years, Pluto can sit in the same sign for a decade. That means that every person in every country born within that span of ten years will show Pluto in the same sign.

Identifying the houses that contain these three planets will add richness to any comprehensive interpretation of your chart. Since the foundations of Kabbalah were set before the invention of the telescope, these planets do not represent any of the spheres of the Tree of Life.

URANUS: DON'T YOU KNOW THE JOKER LAUGHS AT YOU?

Uranus was discovered in 1781. Astrologers—by virtue of the law "as above, so below"—contend that once humans detect a planet, the energy it generates begins to describe and co-relate to events here on earth. Uranus, then, gives rise to revolutions and broad social change. The American Revolution, the French Revolution, the Industrial Revolution, and debates about slavery and then the U.S. Civil War to end slavery occurred in the immediate wake of the discovery of Uranus. This amazing era ushered in a new sort of empathy that begat a commitment to democracy and the Age of Aquarius notion of universal human rights, which Thomas Jefferson called "self-evident." Astrologers thus assigned Uranus to rule (with Saturn) Aquarius, the sign of the democracy, equality, and the future.

In your chart, the house that contains Uranus marks the area of your life in which you must think outside the box. It also stands as the house where the joker laughs at you. Life under the sway of Uranus can be unpredictable, hectic, strange, and funny. My client and friend, Ivana Milicevic, an amazing actress and comedian, has Uranus, the planet of jokes, right on top of her rising sign. When I told her that fact, she laughed and said, "it's funny that the planet of jokes has such a funny name. Uranus always sounds like 'your anus.'" I guess the joker laughs at himself.

Uranus is the planet of intuition and ingenious thinking. It attracts bright unpredictable ideas to that arena of your life. Uranus often signals a need to upgrade the system, to seek out innovations and futuristic techniques. It highlights where you possess an ability to change and where you might need to experiment with radical new approaches. In our sample chart (figure 2), we find Uranus (♅) in the eleventh house, suggesting that the individual has many unique or strange (Uranus) friends (eleventh house).

Uranus in Aries or Uranus in the First House: You are a joker. Humor holds the key to surmounting blocks in your personality. You appreciate technology and can implement it in all aspects of your life. You are spontaneous and need freedom.

Uranus in Taurus or Uranus in the Second House: Money can come and go very fast. You often devise unusual moneymaking schemes. Computers and technology can be the source of your income. Your talents are original and unique.

Uranus in Gemini or Uranus in the Third House: You are exceptionally bright but sometimes scatterbrained or absentminded. Your mind resembles a wild horse that is tough to tame. You might suffer accidents while traveling.

Uranus in Cancer or Uranus in the Fourth House: At least one of your family members is eccentric or a bit odd. Your house features a contemporary design and myriad state-of-the-art gadgets, but life in that home is often erratic. Sudden changes occur in your home or family life.

Uranus in Leo or Uranus in the Fifth House: Love can be unpredictable, and you might find yourself falling in and out of love frequently. You get bored fast. You are exceptionally creative but you demand many friends to help manifest your potential. You have uniquely ingenious children.

Uranus in Virgo or Uranus in the Sixth House: You gravitate toward unique work settings or schedules. You exhibit many talents and tend to jump from one to the other. An irregular or unpredictable diet might adversely affect your health. You are futuristic and innovative in your attitudes toward work.

Uranus in Libra or Uranus in the Seventh House: You are attracted to idiosyncratic people who need freedom. You possess an unorthodox attitude toward relationships. Expect unexpected changes in relationships and partnerships.

Uranus in Scorpio or Uranus in the Eighth House: You enjoy unique forms of sex. You often gain and lose money in a sudden way, especially when dealing in investments and other people's money. You have a strong facility with the occult.

Uranus in Sagittarius or Uranus in the Ninth House: Though you have many foreign friends, please be wary of accidents while abroad. You are talented with languages and philosophies. You are an exciting and funny teacher, and you can excel at teaching and studying science and technology.

Uranus in Capricorn or Uranus in the Tenth House: You might experience sudden changes in your profession and career. The more original and unorthodox your pursuits, the larger your chance for success. You possess abundant intuition that you should apply to your career. You need to work with many people or within large groups.

Uranus in Aquarius or Uranus in the Eleventh House: Your friends are unique and ingenious. You ought to belong to as many groups or societies as possible so that you can experience the full spectrum of the human experience.

Uranus in Pisces or Uranus in the Twelfth House: You are prone to gullibility

Uranus shows you in what aspects of your life it will be to recommended and somewhat safe to be different, unique, and innovative. It is the house that can upgrade you and push you toward the future

and adherence to dangerous ideologies. Watch what you choose to believe. Meditation, dance, and yoga can be transformative, especially when practiced with groups. You are highly psychic and intuitive. You have past-life karma with your close friends.

NEPTUNE: THE MERMAID WHO DANCES TO THE SOUND OF SILENCE

Neptune was discovered in 1846. In Greek mythology, Neptune is the god of the sea, and the planet was assigned to rule (with Jupiter) Pisces, the sign of the ocean and the collective unconscious. The discovery of Neptune, the planet of mysticism, coincided with a spiritualist movement that spread from India to England and then to the United States. Interest in yoga, Kabbalah, Sufism, the Gnostics, secret doctrines, and hermetic studies was resurrected around this time after many centuries of repression, in the wake of the Spanish Inquisition and the so-called Age of Reason.

The house that contains Neptune demarcates the area in your life in which you possess a mystical bent—a secret garden where you can find a sacred spring. Two trees bloom in that garden. The first, the Tree of Life, encourages you to eat. It brings mystical visions and a sense of oneness with the entire cosmos. The second, the escapist tree of drugs (high and low), induces addictions, dependency, and codependency. Neptune embodies both the ascent of the mystic and the self-destructive descent of the addict. The choice is always yours. Neptune represents your poetic self and your creative imagination. In our sample chart (figure 2), Neptune (♆) is located in the tenth house, the house of career, suggesting a need to implement mystical and spiritual (Neptune) tools to further career (tenth house) goals.

Neptune in Aries or Neptune in the First House: You are a natural-born mystic. You don't need to rely on charts, Tarot cards, or crystal balls because you already enjoy access to all that information. You are a dreamer, but watch out for dependency and a propensity to absorb other people's energy to the detriment of yourself.

Neptune in Taurus or Neptune in the Second House: Money feels like water you try to capture in your hand. It escapes. You spend too freely. Be careful of deceptions about what you are entitled to. You have talent in poetry, dance, yoga, and meditation. Use your imagination to create what you want. What you visualize will manifest in this reality.

Neptune in Gemini or Neptune in the Third House: A natural-born poet, you possess exceptional powers of imagination. Your dreams transmit information; write them down. You might share a psychic connection to your siblings, or one of them might have an addictive personality.

Neptune in Cancer or Neptune in the Fourth House: One of your family members is highly mystical or psychic and likely passed that gift to you. Or this person might be fighting that gift via an addictive or dependent personality. You might have suffered a lack of boundaries in your home life. It would be good for you to live near the ocean.

The house that contains Neptune demarcates the area in your life in which you possess a mystical bent—a secret garden where you can find a sacred spring. Two trees bloom in that garden. Neptune shows where in your life you can benefit the most from meditation, mysticism, and spirituality. It is the aspect of your life you are most sensitive about.

Neptune in Leo or Neptune in the Fifth House: Love can be an escape drug for you. Watch out for dependency and codependency. You also are susceptible to gambling addictions. Your children can be mystics or addicts. You can connect to the mystical by adopting a child's playfully creative attitude toward life.

Neptune in Virgo or Neptune in the Sixth House: You might have a weak immune or lymphatic system that requires a boost. Try to work in a profession that involves imagination, illustrations, dance, or music. Use your gut feelings instead of logic. Finding a workplace near the ocean is ideal. At minimum, place a fountain on your desk.

Neptune in Libra and Neptune in the Seventh House: Be wary of a lack of boundaries in relationships and partnerships. You could easily become the drug of choice for your partner or vice versa. You require a mystical, telepathic connection to insure a fulfilling relationship.

Neptune in Scorpio and Neptune in the Eighth House: A natural-born psychologist and healer of the soul, you are a shaman that can access secret information via dreams and visions. You also use sexuality as a form of mystical journey. Try Tantric yoga.

Neptune in Sagittarius or Neptune in the Ninth House: You travel a great deal, preferably by water. Try visiting religious centers or places along the ocean. You can enjoy mystical experiences in foreign cultures. Your studies ought to focus on faith, religion, and imagination.

Neptune in Capricorn or Neptune in the Tenth House: You are multitalented, but your career path might be confused and unstable. Try to find work that makes use of your intuition, mysticism, and your ability to see the unseen.

Neptune in Aquarius or Neptune in the Eleventh House: You have mystical, imaginative, and elusive friends, but some of them might deceive you or cause disruptions in your life. Connect to groups that practice healing, yoga, dance, or movement.

Neptune in Pisces or Neptune in the Twelfth House: You often long for escape from loneliness or isolation. You might have a memory of drowning or religious persecution from a past lifetime. Watch out for addictions. You possess a powerful potential for spiritual evolution.

PLUTO: THE CRIMINAL WHO TURNED INTO A SAINT

Discovered in 1929, on the eve of murderous World War II and the destructive nuclear age, Pluto is the lord of transformation and change. In Roman mythology, Pluto is the lord of the Underworld and death, and in astrology Pluto rules Scorpio, the sign of sexuality, death, and transformation. Pluto generates both the most ruthless criminals and the most powerful healers.

Pluto marks the power point of your chart. The house that contains Pluto highlights the area in your life in which you possess much authority and influence over others. It also shows what and where you can radically transform yourself for the better. Pluto might also signal enemies or hidden forces that obstruct your growth. In our sample chart (figure 2), we find Pluto (♇) in the eighth house—a potent configuration that suggests that the individual experiences profound transformations (Pluto) in relation to sexuality and intimacy (eighth house).

Pluto in Aries or Pluto in the First House: You can be a political figure or a prominent person of authority. You enjoy great influence over others. You desire power and dominance. You can sublimate these tendencies by becoming a healer.

Pluto in Taurus or Pluto in the Second House: You have great artistic gifts, and you can make money from other people's assets and talent. You possess a flair for managing large projects. Watch out for moneymaking schemes that involve illegality.

Pluto in Gemini or Pluto in the Third House: You excel at investigating crime as well as the deeper mysteries of the soul. You are a talented writer who can transform people with words. A neighbor or sibling might have criminal tendencies or exceptional healing abilities.

Pluto in Cancer or Pluto in the Fourth House: You enjoy deep connections to your family, but sometimes these bonds can fray and strangle. One of your parents dominates everyone in the home; he or she might act like a dictator. Your early difficult childhood was likely colored with power struggles.

Pluto in Leo or Pluto in the Fifth House: Be extra careful with your children. They are powerful people, but they must be protected in their early years. You might engage in dangerous love affairs. You are creative in a transformative way. You can gain power through speculative endeavors.

Pluto in Virgo or Pluto in the Sixth House: You are a healer who thrives with intimacy in the workplace. You might be subject to health risks at work unless you deal in service to others. You need to be the boss.

Pluto in Libra or Pluto in the Seventh House: You are attracted to commanding people. Your partner is likely to be immensely influential. You also might have powerful and obstructive enemies.

Pluto in Scorpio or Pluto in the Eighth House: Inheritance and legacies can be the source of income. You know powerful people from all walks of life. Fascinated with death, you enjoy an open rapport with the realm of the dead.

Pluto in Sagittarius or Pluto in the Ninth House: You can transform and influence people from or within foreign countries. You can be healed much faster in an alien culture or by using techniques that differ from those of your own background. You need to work in mass media or international companies.

Pluto in Capricorn or Pluto in the Tenth House: You desire power and influence in your career. You strive to dominate your field, but you can attract jealousy, power struggles, and enemies in your professional life.

Pluto in Aquarius or Pluto in the Eleventh House: You cultivate powerful friends and can influence many people either directly or through your association with your many acquaintances. You also have a bunch of secret friends or belong to secret societies.

Pluto in Pisces or Pluto in the Twelfth House: You desire privacy and isolation. You are mystical and might find yourself living as a hermit. You have been an authoritative and influential person in past lifetimes, and you might attract subconscious enemies as a result of some dirty dealings in those previous incarnations.

PART III

THE TWELVE KINGDOMS
OF LIGHT

CHAPTER 12

Spiritual Fitness: Working Out Your Twelve Energetic Muscles

THE ASTROLOGY OF BEING

Before you rush to check out your own sign or look into the sign of a potential lover, breathe deeply and read this part of this book first.

The best way to absorb and assimilate the teachings of the twelve signs is to dedicate one week to each sign. For one week, you become that sign. The first week, the Aries week, you will become an Aries in order to master leadership and the initiation of new projects. Then you will dedicate a week to Taurus and learn how to become a sensual Taurus. Then for a week you will be a Gemini, then a Cancer, then a Leo, and so forth. The section on Libra will strengthen the spiritual muscle that fosters harmonious partnerships. That of Scorpio will enhance intimacy, sexuality, and transformation, while Capricorn will help you to ascend your career ladder.

Over the course of twelve weeks, you will revivify every area of your life, invigorating the pursuit of your financial, romantic, familial, and health goals. This program will activate all of the mystical archetypes that we all carry inside and deliver a newfound resolve, purpose, and joy to every single life. Most importantly, stepping into the shoes of each sign will automatically teach you compassion. Money, love, and losing weight are admirable, wonderful aims, but I can think of no greater gift than developing a sincere and lasting compassion — both toward yourself and toward all other people. Strive diligently to become each sign. And the signs will award you this invaluable treasure.

In the next twelve weeks you will undergo a new training regime. You will view the signs as spiritual muscles that must be developed equally, symmetrically, in order to harmonize your aura and help you to create your authentic and rewarding path in life. While it is true that each of us has a destiny written by the stars of our natal chart, we still can choose how we enact and unveil that destiny. It is similar to the relationship between the influences of nature versus nurture, genetics and environment, in determining who we are. We now know from studies conducted by psychologists that our genes provide us with a range of possibilities and traits. Our environment then acts to support, develop, or hinder these potentials.

For example, you might be born with a genetic ability to be a professional basketball player. Tall, strong, and lightning fast, you can do magic with an orange ball. But if you sit on your butt all day long, then, with all due respect to your wonderful genes, you will not succeed. If you train hard, practice, and interact wisely with your environment, however, you will eventually enjoy the glory of being a celebrated player. Similarly, your natal chart provides you with "genetic" material. But if you want to maximize the full potential of that astro-DNA, you will have to exercise your free will and bushwhack your own path. This book is designed to help you unleash your potential by activating a different spiritual muscle each week, a different archetype, a different sign. It will pose challenges. It will confer myriad gifts. It promises to be an entertaining and wonderful journey that will grant you the opportunity to unlock all the propitious and unexpected possibilities the stars have prescribed for you.

In order for this system of self-improvement to work, you must first unlearn all that you have learned about the zodiac signs. You need to approach this part of the book with a baby's mind, open and free of all prejudice and precognition. Forget your own sign—I already have shown that you have within you all the signs of the zodiac. Now it is time to access and activate the hidden parts of your potential.

COMICS NAVIGATORS

For thousands of years, Kabbalists have scrambled the letters of names and words in order to find hidden meanings. If you shuffle the letters of the word *cosmic*, you find the word *comics*. I love comic books and graphic novels. They present a powerful take on life. Often they feature a superhero or heroine. You are that superhero, and I want you to start thinking like one.

Part III will prepare you for that role so that you will be able to attract whatever you need in life. We all have things we want to change in our lives—issues or flaws to fix, repair, or delete, strengths and dreams we wish to enhance or create. Part II helped you to identify the traits and tendencies you were born with—in other words, the energetic building blocks you received in this lifetime. Now you will learn how to reorganize these blocks to plot your own path and carve your own destiny. You will develop the ability to transcend the confines of your own chart, to fix your issues and flaws, to amplify your strengths, and to manifest your dreams.

PREPARATIONS

Before you begin the work on each sign, make a list of all the people you know from that sign and write two short paragraphs that describe each of them. One paragraph should delineate their positive traits, and the other should be dedicated to their less desirable characteristics. Circle all the traits or characteristics that are common among all the people in your list. The auspicious traits that repeat represent your positive plug into that sign's energy. The negative traits signify your *Tikkun* (rectification) and highlight what you need to fix within that archetype. If you cannot find people you know from any particular sign, refer to the list of famous people listed for each sign and write the paragraphs about one or two of them.

I highly recommend getting an astrology program that generates charts and helps with interpretations. I find this site to be the most helpful resource: *www.alabe.com.*

IDENTIFY THE SIGN IN YOUR CHART

When you arrive at each new sign, examine your own chart and determine whether you have any planets in this particular sign. If you do, those planets will facilitate your connection to the archetype.

Everyone has each sign in a particular house of the chart. If you discover that Gemini presides over your house of career, for example, then, during the week dedicated to Gemini, you will not only learn about the archetype of Gemini in general, but you also will be guided to direct the Gemini traits and tendencies toward advancing your career. You will be instructed, for example, to look for opportunities to communicate your ideas more clearly at the office and to act as a bridge—Gemini is the messenger—that brings people together around a common goal. If you find that Capricorn rules your house of marriage, then during the week of Capricorn you will work primarily on improving your relationships. This focus will personalize the cosmic navigator program and enable you to balance your chart—and your life—most efficiently.

Many people view free will as the opposite of, or at odds with, fate or destiny. The Cosmic Navigator takes a different view. As I see it, the day and hour of your birth predestine certain genetic tendencies. In your life, you will exercise your free will by activating (or not activating) these tendencies in various ways. The way your life unfolds, in other words, is the product of the interaction or marriage between you and your higher self.

Every sign displays a dark side, a shadow that must be managed and assimilated. Any unadul-

terated energy poses a danger. Even common electricity requires transformers, converters, adaptors, loops, fuses, and circuitry to harness its voltage for our practical use. Pure, unfettered electricity will shock, burn, and even kill. Pay attention to the "Dark Side of the Force" section for each one of the signs. Since we all contain all of the signs within our natal charts, we are all susceptible to deleterious nature of each archetype. Recognizing the negative traits of Aries, for example, will help you to unravel the blockages and disabling patterns you might encounter in the area of your life ruled by this sign.

Darkness, just like evil, does not exist. It is very childish to blame the devil or Satan for our transgression. The devil did not make us bad, our bad side created the devil. Therefore, there is no "dark side" to the signs. God did not create darkness, God created Light. Therefore, darkness by definition is the lack of light, the same way that hate is the lack of love and jealousy is the lack of trust. What is perceived as the shadow or the dark side of the sign is the unbalanced manifestation of that archetype in our lives, that is, lack or excessive use of the energy of the sign. The signs are frequencies of the Solar Light. Therefore, the same way there is no such thing as darkness, only the lack of light, the dark side of each sign is the lack of connection or the abuse of the sign. The dark side of Aries for example is violence. This shadow is manifested when the masculine penetrating energies of Aries are overused, yielding atrocities such as those found in wars and genocides.

SYNCHRONICITIES: THE RESIDUE OF GOD'S PRESENCE

During your journey through the signs, as you try on the costume of a different arche-type each week, you will learn how to surf the currents of the archetypes by paying attention to synchronicities. Each zodiac sign is represented by a bank of symbols that you will discover as you read about that particular sign. Aries' totems, for exam-ple, include the ram, the color red, Mars, the face, blood, muscles, fire, sparks, matches, the warrior, conflict, assertiveness, seeds, superheroes, the Tarot card called the Emperor, windows, Tuesday, Moses, Jesus, and Leonardo da Vinci. Attending to these signs and symbols each week will turn astrology—and life—into a magical game and can transform even the drudgery and setbacks of daily existence into amus-ing and meaningful moments of enlightenment.

So throughout these twelve weeks, and for the rest of your life if you like, look for these symbols out in the world and try to figure out what they might indicate. Let's say that the assertive hero of a movie or TV show you watch during the Aries week has to reconcile some past emotional problem before he or she can truly advance his or her hyper-imperative goal in the present. It's a common plot point to be sure. But if you find yourself moved and fascinated by this little story twist more than by the zippy action and fight sequences, maybe it stands as an important mes-sage. Perhaps you should look into some unresolved issues from your past before plunging ahead to conquer the world.

Synchronicities can be defined as incidents or situations that happen simultane-ously and independent from each other and yet display a strong link. You talk about a person you have not seen for a long time, and suddenly you meet him across the pump at a gas station. These synchronicities enhance our perception of the intercon-nectedness of all things. They represent a junction of energy in which individuals on different paths collide to exchange information and perhaps create a whole new path. This twelve-week astrological program is designed to generate these phenomena. The work you will be doing with the energies of the signs will make it easier for you to recognize synchronicities, interpret them, and then, finally, use them to further your goals.

First, pay attention. Notice everything. Even silly things like the appearance of the name of one of the planets on a billboard near your office. During an especially painful period of my life, I kept noticing billboards that read, "Saturn Is in Your Neighborhood." It meant nothing to me, but these signs persistently popped up everywhere I went. And then I would discover some new problem that had arisen in my apartment, my body, or my personal life. Finally, it dawned on me. The billboards, of course, were simply advertising the car brand named Saturn, but they eventually forced me to recognize that I was in my Saturn return—a stretch of life that comes around every twenty-nine years to highlight our *Tikkun* and force us to change our not-so-holy or -productive ways. As soon as I remembered that and faced up to this helpful challenge, the antagonism in my life ceased virtually overnight.

Once you begin to recognize synchronicities, the more often they will appear. Next comes the challenge of reading what these signs are trying to teach you. Sometimes they will appear nonsensical, while other times the interpretation will be obvious. Try asking yourself some questions. What did you feel when the synchronicity occurred? Did you have any bodily reaction—tightness in the gut or a twinge in your neck, for example? What were you doing when it happened? Is there a reoccurring theme? What are the results or ramifications of the coincidence? These queries can help in decoding the hidden messages in the synchronicity. Whenever great changes occur in your life, the more synchronicities will appear. Some mystics contend that synchronicities represent graffiti that says, "God was here."

Write down all the coincidences and synchronicities you experience during each sign and review them later. Often, time and distance will reveal new implications. For example, in the week dedicated to Scorpio, which is the sign of death and transformation, one of my students ran into a woman he had not seen in year. She was a good friend of a man he had known a decade before. She told him that their mutual friend had died and that his funeral was scheduled for the following day. My student attended the funeral and met his first love in the adjacent pew. She told him that she had just gotten divorced, and they ended up talking for hours, reconnecting on an intimate level (Scorpio is also the sign of intimacy). This interaction caused my student to recognize how much he had grown since his first love relationship and also how much work on his old patterns he still needed to undergo.

Colors and Hebrew Letters

Kabbalah offers an interesting teaching that declares, "There is no *Mazal* (constellation) for Israel." The rabbis assert that once you go directly to God (*Isra-el* in Hebrew means "direct to God") you can break free from the limitations of your astrological chart. Each of the twelve signs is represented by a Hebrew letter that can be used to awaken that particular archetype within your daily life. Using the Hebrew letters as portals to these celestial archetypes, you will be able to go directly to God. This is the work of the cosmic navigator.

During the next twelve weeks, you will discover the mystical powers of the Hebrew letters. You will also learn how to work with the color associated with each sign. Meditations with these letters and sprinkling your clothes and home with particular colors will help you to rectify and even alter the destiny inscribed in your chart. If you often experience strife or imbalances in your primary relationships, for example, find the sign that rules your seventh house of relationships. Then meditate with the Hebrew letter associated with that sign. If you determine that more communication might help, then wear orange, the color of Gemini, which will amplify your communication skills. If more fun in the bedroom would take the edge off your relationship woes, then decorate your bedroom with yellow or gold, the colors that belong to fun-loving Leo.

This technique works with a concept called sympathetic magic, which allows you to mimic an archetype in an effort to attract its particular energy into your life. It works on others too. If a friend suffers persistent money and debt problems, check for the sign that rules her second house of money and teach her to meditate with the appropriate Hebrew letter. Suggest that she add some reddish orange, the color of Taurus, the archetype of finances, to her wardrobe and office. These ancient potent symbols will help to focus and enhance the energy field surrounding that particular life issue. And like magic, they will stimulate the rectification of your problems.

It is crucial to mediate for at least a few minutes every day, using the appropriate Hebrew letter as a meditation aid. Each chapter will instruct you on the shape and meaning of each Hebrew letter.

Here's what that meditation means to you: Trace the outline of the letter on a card or a piece of paper and fill it in with the color that is associated with that particular sign. Sit in a comfortable position and place the card at eye level in front of you. (You can hang it on a white wall.) Stare at the letter with your eyes open for five minutes without blinking. It might be a challenge, but do the best you can. While you gaze at the card, try to envision the changes you want to make in your life that are associated with the energies of the sign. For example, while meditating on the letter *Zain* (associated with Gemini), focus on improving your communication with someone dear to you or on mending a business transaction that might have turned sour.

Signs and Their Corresponding Colors and Hebrew Letters

Aries	Hey הֵ	Red
Taurus	Vav ו	Red-orange
Gemini	Zain ז	Orange
Cancer	Chet ח	Orange-yellow
Leo	Teth ט	Yellow
Virgo	Yod י	Yellow-green
Libra	Lamed ל	Green
Scorpio	Nun נ	Green-blue/turquoise
Sagittarius	Samech ס	Blue
Capricorn	Ain ע	Blue-violet/indigo
Aquarius	Tzadik צ	Violet
Pisces	Kuf ק	Violet-red

After you have stared at the card for five minutes, close your eyes and take note of the images and thoughts that appear on your mind screen. Some of these shapes and ideas might be important messages and clues that will enhance your journey through the signs. It might be something you ought to do tomorrow. It might be some object you ought to notice when you travel out in the world. The more you meditate with the letters, the more adept you will become at deciphering the messages you receive.

Sit with your eyes closed for five to ten minutes. Let the image of the Hebrew letter and everything else slowly melt away. And then open your eyes.

Synchronicities force us to look out into the world for clues that will enhance our spiritual growth and spur us toward our worldly goals. Meditations allow us to look inside ourselves for the same things. The cosmic navigator harnesses both of these exhilarating powers.

Bon voyage!

♈

Aries: The Liberator

March 21 to April 19

Key Phrase: "I am"—identity

General Qualities: Leadership, initiative, the warrior, direct, powerful, liberating, strong sense of justice

Dark Side: Self-centered, aggressive, macho, blunt, pushy, inconsistent, accident prone

Element: Cardinal fire

Planet: Mars

Day: Tuesday

Theme: The spark

Parts of the Body: Head, blood, face, genital area, muscles

Color: Red

Gemstone: Diamond

Musical Note: C—the beginning of the scale

Hebrew Letter: Hey h.]

Kabbalistic Meaning of the Letter: The window of the soul and the abbreviation of the name of God

Path in the Tree of Life: Path 4, connecting Beauty and Wisdom

Tarot Card: The Emperor

Movies: Gladiator, 300, The Matrix, Henry the V, superhero movies, action films

Affirmation: "I am powerful and all conquering. I am grateful for all that I have accomplished and all that I will achieve."

Overview

Aries, the first zodiac sign, embodies the primal archetype of identity and knowledge of self. Since Aries signals the arrival of spring, it represents the process of liberation from the frozen grounds of winter. Aries bestows our sense of purpose and symbolizes the hero's call for action. It connects us to the ability to assert ourselves, find our direction, access our leadership skills, and free us from our limitations. In the week of Aries, you will practice assertiveness. You will learn how to be a shepherd, a leader, and a liberator. You will identify your oppressor and work with the archetype to break away from whatever holds you down.

The Territory of Aries

No man becomes a prophet who was not first a shepherd.
—Mohammad, an Aries

Aries initiates the astrological year and liberates life from the frozen bonds of winter. Like a dammed spring suddenly released, Aries surges with the energy of life, breaking the iron chains of the ruthless cold. Aries begins on the spring equinox, marking the time of the year when the day and the night are equal and balanced. From the beginning of Aries until the summer solstice (June 21), the amount of light each day grows and grows, outstripping the dark by a wider and wider margin. Aries leads the light into its triumph.

As a cardinal fire sign, Aries functions to push us forward. It creates change through action, action, and more action. Ruled by Mars, the god of war, Aries can be a difficult sign to deal with. It is easy to despise or fear its brutal force. Traditional astrologers regard Aries and the planet Mars as the root cause of all destruction, strife, violence, and war. Fire burns. But we must not forget that it also warms us throughout the winter. And by giving us the first spark of fire, Aries awarded us our advantage over the animals that once ate us for lunch. The eldest sibling of the zodiac, Aries for generations protected us when we were left alone by Mommy and Daddy (the moon and sun).

At the same time, people with the sun sign Aries don't really work for nothing. They feel compelled to remind us of all the times they risked their own lives to save us. They inevitably and sometimes aggressively make sure we know *who* they are as well as how very important they are. Their ranks include such leaders as Moses, Mohammad, and Jesus. (Jesus was most likely born in the Bethlehem manger during the annual spring Passover pilgrimage to Jerusalem.) They serve as the shepherds or as the alpha rams that guide us to our destiny. We salute them, and yet we hope too that they will develop enough self-confidence so that they quit reminding us how much we owe them.

Aries represents the commando of the zodiac, who is trained in the arts of war and capable of amazing physical and mental feats. The house in your chart that is ruled by Aries indicates the area of your life in which you harbor enormouos energy and strength.

YOUR OWN PRIVATE ARIES

Get out your chart and identify the house (or the area in your life) governed by Aries. Then determine if you have any planets in Aries. (You might want to refer to part II of the book to remind yourself of the interpretation of each planet in this particular sign.)

During this week, focus attention on the area of your life governed by the house ruled by Aries. For example, if Aries rules your second house, then direct your efforts toward your finances and talents. Look for synchronicities and opportunities that either emerge or can be applied to that part of your life. This sort of specific concentration will afford you a more personal and intimate connection to the wisdom of the stars as you progress through each of the twelve signs.

Aries in Your First House (Your Rising Sign): You are courageous, a daredevil who will jump into a new challenge without thinking twice. You tend to expend too much energy. So chill out! You can achieve more by delegating authority instead of doing it all by yourself. You are self-motivated as well as competitive, impulsive, and somewhat impatient. You are a natural-born leader, who is constantly pushed by life to take charge. During the week of Aries focus on your appearance, body, and health.

Aries in Your Second House: You are a go-getter when it comes to moneymaking and showing off your talents. Be careful not to burn your money with excessive spending. You need to expose and liberate your hidden talents. In order to make more money, you ought to assume a position of leadership and initiation. During the week of Aries, focus on your finances, talents, and self-worth. You might hear a call for adventure or a new moneymaking possibility.

Aries in Your Third House: You are a warrior whose weapon is intellect and words. You possess an aggressive mind that can turn sharp and blunt. Be careful not to make enemies through the way you talk, write, and communicate. Read your emails twice before you send them. You are rather argumentative and demand the final word. You need to liberate your mind from the bondage of old thought patterns. During the week of Aries, pay attention to your siblings, neighbors, communications, writings, and business ventures.

Aries in Your Fourth House: Your home life might feel like a battlefield, or you might have grown up in a family rife with competition and aggression. It will be best for you to live in a warm place, especially later in life. You need to liberate yourself from emotional bondage from your early childhood, especially from traumas that served to compromise or oppress your true identity. During the week of Aries, pay attention to your home life, family, and emotional well-being. You might be called to liberate one or more family members from some distressing issue that afflicts them.

Aries in Your Fifth House: Your life is filled with short-lived and dramatic love affairs. Your children will be boys or very masculine in nature. You usually get along well with children because you are playful yourself. You might be drawn to competitive or extreme sports. And you love to create projects, games, outings, and parties in an impulsive and spontaneous manner. You need to liberate yourself from your fear of falling in love. During the week of Aries, focus on ways to have more fun and to enhance your creativity. Pay attention to your children and your lover.

Aries in Your Sixth House: You should look for ways to work for yourself because you chafe when bossed or managed by someone else. You might suffer conflicts with your employees. Take precautions against head injuries, cuts, and mishaps, and make sure to monitor your blood pressure. Overall you enjoy a healthy disposition and will benefit greatly from a regular exercise routine. You need to liberate yourself from people who want to undermine your abilities and powers. During the week of Aries, focus on your health, diet, exercise, and your work.

Aries in Your Seventh House: You are attracted to strong, independent partners in both love and business. And these relationships often end up as battlefields. Your enemies might be ruthless and aggressive. You need to work on liberating yourself from relationships that are oppressive or from people who are intimidated by you and wish you ill. During the week of Aries, focus on your partners, significant others, and clients.

Aries in Your Eighth House: You might experience wars or conflict relating to sexuality, intimacy, joint financial affairs, or inheritance. You are sexually attracted to masculine, outgoing people. You have a powerful sexual drive, but you need to liberate yourself from desires that can be harmful or counterproductive. You possess a strong need to dive into magic and the healing arts. In the week of Aries, emphasize intimacy, sexuality, and the letting go of things you cling to too tightly.

Aries in Your Ninth House: You are adventurous both in travel and education. You have an active interest in foreign cultures, especially in countries located in warm climates. You might experience conflict with in-laws. You need to liberate yourself from cultural narrow-mindedness, rigid morality, and zealotry. During the week of Aries, pay attention to opportunities that emerge from foreigners, travel, and higher education.

Aries in Your Tenth House: You are a natural-born leader in your professional field. You thrive when you manage your own enterprise or business. You demand everything right here and right now, but you will have to learn patience in your career. You need to liberate your community from oppression. Find the underdogs and fight for them. During the week of Aries, focus on your career and your contributions to your community.

Aries in Your Eleventh House: You need your gang of friends—preferably masculine, outgoing friends—with you wherever you go. You always take an active interest in friends, groups, and organizations. You are open to new acquaintances and tend to be the leader of your circle. Humanitarian work and nonprofit organizations could serve as the arena in which you feel like a liberator. During the week of Aries, emphasize your friends, groups, and organizations.

Aries in Your Twelfth House: You probably lived as a powerful, aggressive leader in a past incarnation—perhaps a soldier or warrior who inflicted much bloodshed. In this lifetime, you likely need to reconcile with your victims from that past. Due to this history, you might be afraid to expose your powers and abilities. You need to reconnect to the leader inside and open up to a mission that is bigger than yourself. During the week of Aries, highlight your spirituality, mysticism, and the suffering of people around you.

ARIES AND THE GOD COMPLEX

As a musician, I love visiting Istanbul not only for its striking beauty, but also for the fact that you can enjoy fantastic music there for free, five times a day. I am referring to the muezzin's chant or call for prayer that resounds from the city's mosques. It always sounded to me like a call for action, a daily reminder of a higher realm of consciousness beyond the mundane. In Arabic, the call says: "*La Ilaha Illallah Wa Anna Muhammad Rasul Allah,*" which means, "I bear witness that there is no god but God and Muhammad is his messenger." I never understood why Muhammad had to insert his own name into the powerful mantra. Could he not resist the urge to append his identity and signature to the prayer? Why did he have to be such an Aries?

Then one day, while I was in the Byzantine Christian church Haghia Sophia (which stands opposite to the famous Blue Mosque in Istanbul), I realized Muhammad's true intent. It was not egotism that prompted him to force his name on his followers' daily lives, but his concern that his devotees might one day declare him a God—a la Jesus—and abandon his mission of uniting the Arab tribes under the banner of monotheism. It was as if he were saying to them: "There is no god but God, and if you think of making me a god, let me tell you something: I am just a messenger, not more."

Moses, another Aries, was called to liberate his people from slavery, introduce them to humanitarian laws, and transform them into a nation of warriors. He used moxie and magic and no shortage of Aries fierceness to accomplish this impossible task. Though he remains the unquestioned hero of Exodus, his name is mentioned only once in the Haggadah, the book read every Passover to retell the story of the emancipation of the Hebrews from slavery in Egypt. Some versions of this book don't mention Moses at all. The reason: the rabbis who compiled the Haggadah apparently feared that people would start worshipping the remarkable Moses as a God.

Jesus of Nazareth, who was later called Christ (meaning "the Anointed" in Greek), faced a similar Aries issue. Though we celebrate his birthday on December 25, Christ was not a Capricorn. The celebration of Christmas began around the fourth century, when the church elders moved his birthday from April 1 (his suggested date of birth according to Christian esoteric traditions) to the winter solstice in an effort to associate him with other savior deities of the old world such as Apollo, Horus, and Mithras. Christ's message was inner-monotheism—the godhead is inside all of us. The kingdom of God is not somewhere out there in heaven, Christ said, but right here with us every day. He tried to show through his own example that each one of us has the spark of God inside of us. After his death, his followers divided over the question of whether Jesus was a human or a god. When Constantine finally legalized Christianity, he demanded that the fathers of the Church make up their mind on this debate so that he could begin executing those who thought the other way. In the year AD 325, the famous Council of Nicaea devised the Christian formula: Christ is a god and a man combined.

Most Aries happily would subscribe to such a compromise for themselves. They all possess this irresistible feeling inside that they are here to accomplish a grand purpose, that they were born to save and liberate the world.

Aries in your chart (houses or planets) marks the spot where you are touched by God. It underscores the divinity in you. It represents the place where the spark of God inside can shine brilliantly. But a word of warning: don't take yourself too seriously. Being touched by God does not mean you are God.

It works the other way too, and so don't be afraid to be great, especially in the areas of your life influenced by Aries. For example, a man who had Aries in his first house (the house of personality) reported receiving many compliments during the week of Aries. I suggested that he probably received compliments all the time, but he ignored them because he feared that acknowledging his own potency would make him less humble and human. Unleashing his Aries energy for a week taught him to appreciate his own touch of godhead, and most crucially, to thank those around him who sweetly encouraged the "spark" in him.

IDENTITY: "I AM"

Each sign comes with one phrase that describes its archetype best. "I am" explains the Aries need to find their identity as well as helping the other signs to find theirs. Just as the date and hour of birth astrologically describe who we are for the rest of our days, Aries, which kicks off the astrological year, provides the identity for all the rest of the signs. When Moses confronted the burning bush, he heard the voice of God sending him on what seemed to be an impossible mission. As a blunt, fearless Aries, Moses immediately demanded God's name, God's identity. God's answer, "I am that I am," became the mantra of monotheism as well as the name of God for the first sphere of the Tree of Life.

"I am" is everywhere and nowhere at the same time. He/She is you, me, the flowers, and the trees. The Sufis, the mystics of Islam, reinforce this philosophy with their concept of the perfect man (or woman), who is able to see God in everyone and everything. Practice being a "perfect man" by seeing God in everyone you meet.

This week, pay attention to synchronicities that might hint at your identity and your true purpose in this lifetime. Look for these clues in the area of your life ruled by Aries.

In addition, investigate your own name. Nothing can tell you more about your identity and mission than your name. If you don't know what your name means, look it up via an Internet search engine, such as Google. You will find many baby-names websites that provide the origin and meaning of pretty much every name out there.

Just as the burning bush called Moses to action, you will encounter an inciting incident that will lead you on a mission. The clue to that call for action lies in the house ruled by Aries—and maybe in your name.

Aries in your chart (houses or planets) marks the spot where you are touched by God. It underscores the divinity in you. It represents the place where the spark of God inside can shine brilliantly.

THE SACRIFICIAL LAMB

Aries, the protector, the sign that stands in the front, confronting the dangerous and the unknown, is also the sign associated with sacrifice. Who is the sacrificial lamb? A baby Aries—a lamb that is sacrificed before he grows into a ram. Soldiers, representatives of Aries, march off to the front lines to protect us. They sacrifice their lives so that others might live freer, safer lives. In Hebrew, the word for "battle" is *krav*. Many know this word from *Krav Maga*, the martial art taught by the Israeli Defense

Force. *Krav* derives from the same root as the word *Korban*, which means "sacrifice." Battle, war, and sacrifice are linked in Hebrew as well as in the archetype of Aries. And in the Hindu tradition, the Brahmin, the elite caste of priests, are named for the fire (Aries) that consumes the sacrifice that they offer to God.

During the week of Aries, you will be asked to perform some sort of sacrifice. Pay attention to synchronicities. They will suggest what or who you need to relinquish.

This week, pay attention to synchronicities that might hint at your identity and your true purpose in this lifetime. Look for these clues in the area of your life ruled by Aries. In addition, investigate your own name. Nothing can tell you more about your identity and mission than your name.

MUHAMMAD AND THE BEAR HUG FROM GABRIEL

According to tradition, Muhammad was born somewhere in March or April, which would make him an Aries. He was a liberator, a warrior, and a leader. At the age of forty, he embarked on spiritual retreats in the caves of the desert. Like Moses and Christ before him, the fiery hot land of Aires, the desert, served as the place for his call for action. On the seventeenth night of Ramadan, AD 610, he climbed a mountain to unite with his creator. Muhammad tells us that the angel Gabriel visited him on the mountain and commanded him, "Recite!" Like any good Aries, he refused. (Most of you probably know already that it is pretty much impossible to tell an Aries what to do.)

Unaware that the angel already had much experience with argumentative Aries, Muhammad tried to quarrel with the angel. But, Muhammad says, the angel just "whelmed me in his embrace until he had reached the limits of my endurance" (Muhammad ibn Isma'il al-Bukhari, quoted in *Muhammad: His Life Based on Earliest Sources*). It took a bear hug and some wrestling moves on the part of the archangel to get the Aries to submit to God's will. Then the gates opened and Muhammad started channeling the Koran. "Surrender," not surprisingly, is one of the definitions of the word *Islam*.

You too wrestle with God wherever you have Aries in your chart. It marks a place where you might argue with God over your destiny. Some battling with God is permissible. Though Jacob permanently dislocated his hip during his match with an angel, don't push your battle to the death.

Aries in your chart also reveals the place in your life where you fight too much. Identify that part of your life and see if you can surrender, let it go, allow life to guide you, relinquish control, stop trying so hard.

During the week of Aries, you will be asked to perform some sort of sacrifice. Pay attention to synchronicities. They will suggest what or who you need to relinquish.

SOWING THE SEEDS

Aries begins the astrological year as well as the spring. It places the seeds in the ground. But Aries is not the most nurturing of the signs. It will not stick around long enough to watch the seed sprout. Restless and impatient, Aries would rather race off on a new adventure.

In his monumental work *Hero With a Thousand Faces*, Joseph Campbell, another Aries, writes that all myths are basically "the one, shape-shifting yet marvelously constant story." It took an Aries to show us that everything, every tale, is all one, all the same, all emanating from the same source—the seed. Joseph Campbell called this idea of unity "monomyth." Moses, Christ, and Muhammad all preached that that God's true name is Oneness. Who can blame them? They all belong to the first sign, the sign of identity encoded in the DNA of the seed.

Aries' attachment to the seed also explains why they seem to talk about themselves, and pretty much nothing else, all the time. Aries plants the seed in the ground. And it sits there, invisibly, until it eventually pushes upward and blooms months later in Taurus or Gemini or in the fall harvest. The delicious bounty arrives when Aries is long gone. Who will remember the Aries then? So the Aries remind us ahead of time: "I put the seed in the ground. I did that. It was me, me, and me." They can't help it.

You wrestle with God wherever you have Aries in your chart. It marks a place where you might argue with God over your destiny. Aries in your chart also reveals the place in your life where you fight too much and need to surrender.

How to Get Along with Aries

- Aries is a fire sign, and fire needs oxygen (air) in order to burn. Air means reinforcement, since we generally fortify people with words, which are ruled by the air signs. Don't be stingy with words of encouragement. Aries might look like they don't need praise and affirmation, but they do. Like little children, they constantly need you to remind them how great they are.

- Never ever tell an Aries what to do. The ram is the leader of the flock; his job is to lead and not to be led. When you want the Aries to do something, suggest it. Hint at it. But don't issue commands. You cannot boss the boss. Even God had a hard time telling Moses and Muhammad what to do.

- Let the Aries talk about themselves. "I" and "me" are by far their favorite subjects. And, most of the time, you will be entertained. If it becomes too much about "me," tactfully, slowly, try to divert the subject. Just don't jump down their throats about it—unless you want a war.

- Do not let the Aries conquer you. Aries tend to run from people who grovel at their feet or show too much need. Never surrender completely. The second the Aries feel that you are theirs, they will move on to the next person to conquer. As long as you are not completely available, the Aries will fight to win your heart.

- Give the Aries a mission, something to fight for, something to defeat, like an evil empire or an injustice. As long as Aries have a mission, they will live up to their full potential. When bored or aimless, they contrarily turn into tyrants or destructive soldiers. There are few things more dangerous than an unemployed warrior.

- Let the Aries enjoy their gang—their buddies or girlfriends who gather together regularly for games and fun. Let them play. Only then will they remain faithful.

- Be spontaneous and unpredictable. Act unexpectedly with them. They love the new and different.

THE DARK SIDE OF THE FORCE: ARIES

Aries can be pushy, demanding, selfish, aggressive, violent, and detached from feelings. Prone to a quick temper and little patience, Aries often begin a million projects and then give up on them before they take root. Like little children, they demand immediate gratification. The Aries obsession with self sometimes escalates to the point where nothing matters besides them. This view represents a rather distorted version of monotheism in which the Aries is God and the rest is irrelevant.

The darkest shadow emerges on a personal or social level. The unemployed-warrior syndrome strikes whenever the Aries energy has nothing to do. With an active, purposeful mission, the Aries thrives. But the minute the warrior faces some downtime, watch out. He will often turn his aggressive essence on whoever lingers nearby, and the result can be injurious, bloody, and catastrophic. The Emperor, the Tarot card that corresponds to Aries, portrays a powerfully muscular man poised to conquer new horizons. Once the Emperor conquers everything out there, however, he transforms into the tyrant of his neighborhood. Rome suffered this Aries-driven fate after Augustus, when bored and idle emperors such as Caligula and Nero ravaged themselves and the mighty empire.

You might harbor an unemployed warrior in the area of your life ruled by Aries. Make sure that you frequently initiate positive projects in this arena of your life, and that you renew the energy of the house of Aries by deliberately following all these projects through to completion.

THE HEBREW LETTER *Hey*

In the fifth chapter of the *Sefer Yetzirah,* the core Kabbalistic text that describes the creation of the cosmos, the author explicitly ties the Hebrew letters to the zodiac signs. And with these central energetic pieces, the book asserts, God then manufactured the entire universe. The Hebrew letter *Hey* radiates the energy of Aries, and Aries radiates the energy of the letter *Hey.* Even today, people who speak all sorts of languages will yell out, "Hey!" to draw someone's attention, mimicking God's understanding that the Aries energy always attracts attention.

Hebrew also uses *Hey* as an identifying article similar to the English word *the.* Affixed to the word *boy,* for example, the *Hey* transforms *a* boy to *the* boy—the one and only (such an Aries thing to do).

In the Bible, Abraham appended the letter *Hey* to both his and his wife's name to stimulate fertility. You can stimulate whatever you need in your life by meditating with the letter. Meditate with the letter *Hey* whenever you need to activate your inner superhero, who always wins and always, fearlessly, gets the job done.

Stare at the letter *Hey* without blinking for as long as you can and then close your eyes. You will then see the letter outlined in white hovering in a sea of blackness. To activate the energy of this powerful letter, juxtapose the *Hey* you see in your mind's eye with images from your life of the area in which you could benefit from more assertiveness and strength. For example, visualize yourself leading a productive business meeting or forcefully initiating a project you have been afraid to launch. To enhance the power of the *Hey,* you might want to paint the one on your card red (the color of Aries).

In ancient Hebrew, *Hey* is the word for "window"—a metaphor for the opening through which the pioneer and explorer can view the distant horizon. The eyes are considered to be

You might harbor an unemployed warrior in the area of your life ruled by Aries. Make sure that you frequently initiate positive projects in this arena of your life, and that you renew the energy of the house of Aries by deliberately following all these projects through to completion.

the windows to the soul, and this sort of visual meditation will not only activate your life, but also allow you to access the needs and impulses of your higher self. In reflection of that lofty notion, the letter *Hey* often stands as an abbreviation for *God*, just as *JFK* signifies President John F. Kennedy. Wherever you see a *Hey*, it suggests that God is there.

THE PARTS OF THE BODY

Aries governs the head, face, the two cerebral hemispheres, and muscles, and it co-rules (with Scorpio) the sexual organs. Aries is also associated with blood. In Hebrew, the word for "blood" is *dam*, the word for "red" is *adom*, and the word for "human" is *adam*. All share the same root. Humankind is a mixture of red blood and earth—quite a lot of Aries.

Aries look athletic and muscular, and they are generally quite robust and healthy. Since they often plunge headfirst into danger, they might have scars or birthmarks on their faces.

This week, work out to get your blood and muscles pumping. And eat a few extra helpings of leafy greens, which are rich in iron, the metal of Mars and Aries.

Mediate with the letter *Hey* whenever you need to activate your inner superhero, who always wins and always, fearlessly, gets the job done.

THE COLOR OF ARIES: RED

Think red, and you invoke Aries: the red rose that symbolizes passion, red blood gashing out of a wound, infrared light attached to a sophisticated weapon, the red of intoxicating wine, and, of course, the red planet called Mars. The color red serves both in defense and offense. For example, the red string that some who practice Kabbalah wear on their left wrists functions as a charm against the evil eye; the red energy of Aries, the logic goes, can ward off negative energies aimed at us from others.

A red alert signals an imminent attack, just as the sounding of the ram's horn (Aries) in ancient days served to gather a tribe's warriors for a fight. Red lights warn us to stop. If we don't obey the red stop light, a red siren on a police car will chase us down (or worse, we'll crash violently into cross traffic). We are genetically programmed to pay attention to red. If we don't sit up, take notice, and act fast when red blood pours from our body, we might die.

Wear at least a bit of red whenever you want to come across as a powerful leader, warrior, and initiator. If life in your bedroom lacks passion, try adding some red accents. (Think of the *Zona Roja* district in Mexico City, *Moulin Rouge* in Paris, and the red-light district in Amsterdam.) Try dressing in red this week and notice what this frequency brings to you. Just remember the warning: red can't help but attract attention—and perhaps a bit of aggression.

WHAT SHOULD I FOCUS ON IN THE WEEK OF ARIES?

Aries in your chart provides hints to your identity and how to go about achieving your destiny. Examine this particular arena of your life and stay alert for any clues that suggest a mission, a call to action, or underdogs that you might want to rescue or liberate. This week, wear red more often, initiate new projects, and exercise leadership, even in minor situations, such as deciding which restaurant or which movie your group should go to. Use your muscles. Start an exercise routine or work out more than usual. Aries like to run, jump, throw, wrestle, make love, and sweat. In addition, focus this week on the unity of all things. Notice how everything is connected and how you function as the center of all this interconnectedness.

You should also seek out synchronicities related to Aries, and try to interpret the symbolic and practical messages directed to you. The symbols of Aries include the ram, the color red, Mars, iron, the face, blood, muscles, fire, sparks, matches, the warrior, conflict, violence, war, assertiveness, passion,

This week, work out to get your blood and muscles pumping. And eat a few extra helpings of leafy greens, which are rich in iron, the metal of Mars and Aries.

leadership, seeds, identity, superheroes, the Emperor Tarot card, wrestling, leadership, liberation, slavery, windows, Tuesday, Moses, Jesus Christ, and Leonardo da Vinci.

Your Aries Week Checklist

- Identify where you have Aries in your chart and try to apply the lessons of Aries—leadership, initiation, action, and passion—to that area of your life.
- Be assertive.
- Search for clues to your identity.
- Write one sentence that can describe your identity.
- Plant a seed in your life—a new beginning. If you want, plant an actual flower or vegetable seed in a kitchen pot or your backyard.
- Be decisive. As master Yoda said, "Try not. Do or do not."
- Practice seeing God in everyone you meet.
- Exercise. You need to sweat this week. If you turn red from the effort, way to go.
- Meditate on the Hebrew letter *Hey*.
- Read or speak aloud the affirmation of Aries twice a day—once when you wake up and once before you go to sleep: "I am powerful and all conquering. I am grateful for all that I have accomplished and all that I will achieve."
- Wear red and note the results.
- Liberate yourself from any oppression you might be feeling.
- Perform a sacrifice—a letting go of something you do not need.
- Accept and acknowledge ("thank you") any compliment given to you.

THE RITUAL OF ARIES: THE BURNING WISH

Aries marks the beginning of the astrological year. To kick off the year that begins today, with a little help from friends in very high places, try this ritual that will invoke a little push from Aries. This ritual resembles the priestly sacrifice (often of animals) from ancient times.

Use a red pen to write down something you want to achieve this year—some vital mission you yearn to accomplish. Then burn the paper with the flame from a red candle. (Please take care not to catch anything else on fire.) As the paper burns, pay attention to what you experience. Does the paper burn completely? Was it hard for it to burn? Did anything else happen as you conducted the ritual? These clues and synchronicities can teach you much about your proposed ambition. Now it is up to you to make your mission happen.

This week, you also might want to reenact the story of Exodus from the Bible. Read chapters one through twelve of Exodus (the story continues beyond the twelfth chapter, but these chapters will suffice). Kabbalah views the story of Moses liberating the slaves and leading them to the promised land as a powerful metaphor. Before you read this timeless epic, meditate on the following questions: Who or what is oppressing you or preventing you from being true to yourself? (If you are sick, your oppressor could be an organ in your body.) What is your own promised land, the aspiration you yearn to attain? When you read Exodus, imagine that you are the enslaved Israelites and your oppressor is the pharaoh. Moses represents your inner spark of God, your liberator, your Aries. And the promised land represents your goal.

By inserting yourself, your dilemmas, and your aims in the place of the biblical characters, you will likely light upon clues that will propel your own liberation. After reading each paragraph of the Israelites' advance toward freedom, write down or think about how it relates to your predicament. What action might you take now that metaphorically matches the behavior of Moses and his tribe? What equivalent step might you enact to spur the realization of your goal?

For example, let's imagine that you feel enslaved to a tyrannical boss. First you need to recognize the oppression and figure out why you found yourself in this "land of Egypt." Even the Hebrews doubted Moses at first, preferring the known of slavery to the unknown of freedom.

Returning to the example of the tyrannical boss, try to identify what makes you suffer. Why are you feeling distressed? Yes, you may have to walk in the unknown, or maybe you will find yourself in a new work environment that is even worse. That is the leap of faith Aries prompts us to take, just as he did as he jumped through the vortex of fire to retrieve his gifts.

It is up to you to find the courage to overcome what Sigmund Freud called "the secondary gain," the weird benefit you enjoy from sticking to the oppressive situation. For example, your secondary gain might be the prestige of your position or the fact that you are happiest when someone tells you what to do. Finally, when you find yourself in the desert, struggling to maintain your faith, Moses, your liberator, brings you the Ten Commandments. So write your own contract with your higher self. List ten obligations—five positive actions you promise to take ("I will send out my resume," "I will further my education," "I will resolve other relationship conflicts," and so on) and five "thou shalt not" vows (such as, "I will not compromise on my salary," "I will not put myself down").

This entire exercise will not only assist your escape from pain, but it will also teach you how to view all the enduring ancient tales from every culture as allegorical and effective strategies for living today.

FAMOUS ARIES

Moses, Jesus Christ, The Prophet Muhammad, J. S. Bach, Leonardo da Vinci, Thomas Jefferson, J. S. Bach, Akira Kurosawa, Aretha Franklin, Robert Frost, Rafael, Vincent Van Gogh, Rene Descartes, Mother Hale, Billie Holiday, Russell Crowe, Hans Christian Anderson, Joseph Campbell, Marlon Brando, Bette Davis, Ashley Judd, Harry Houdini, Jackie Chan, Samuel Beckett, and Charlie Chaplin.

Harry Houdini, who could liberate himself from all forms of self-imposed physical bondage, was an Aries.

Taurus: The Artist and Financier

April 20 to May 20

Key Phrase: "I have"—from self-worth to a bank account

General Qualities: Artistic, affectionate, stable, reliable, patient, practical, financial facility, a knack for sensual enjoyment, and a love of nature

Dark Side: Materialistic, possessive, resistant to change, stubborn, fanatical, narrow-minded, gluttonous, and indulgent

Element: Fixed earth

Planet: Venus

Day: Friday

Theme: The sustainer

Parts of the Body: Throat, neck, thyroid gland

Color: Red-orange

Gemstone: Jade

Musical Note: C sharp—the second tone

Hebrew Letter: *Vav* ו

Kabbalistic Meaning of Letter: The hook or nail

Path in the Tree of Life: Path 5, connecting Wisdom and Mercy

Tarot Card: The Hierophant

Movies: *Chocolat, Like Water For Chocolate, Perfume*

Affirmation: "I am my own spiritual guide. I possess the ability to translate my inner wealth into material abundance. I am worthy of success and financial abundance."

OVERVIEW

Taurus, the sign of Shakespeare and Buddha, epitomizes the material life that Aries, the warrior, strives to protect. If Aries is the warrior, then Taurus is the princess he saves from harm. Taurus engenders sensual pleasure, art, luxury, assets, values, money, and finance. The teachings of Taurus are embedded in the concept of self-worth. If you value yourself, then you will uncover opportunities to use your innate talents to generate abundance. Taurus will teach you to raise your self-esteem in order to optimize your particular gifts and translate them to money. Taurus also represents our connection to nature and our capacity to relish the five senses and enjoy the little pleasures of life.

THE TERRITORY OF TAURUS

Situated in some of the most *valuable* energetic "real estate" around, smack in the middle of beloved spring, it's no wonder that Taurus rules money and finance. Taurus sees, hears, smells, tastes, and touches Mother Nature in her full bloom and ecstasy, and thus Taurus also oversees the pleasures of our own five senses, which includes food, art, sensuality, and music. The month of May marks the time of year when the people of the ancient world celebrated their fertility rites. Back then, men and women would gather around the maypole, for example, to consummate their love.

Taurus enjoys life like the rest of us enjoy the blossoming rush of spring, only it does so on a daily basis. Taurus connects us to the sweet fine things of life. It represents rich desserts, spas, gardens, luxurious hotels, decadent food, pampering massages, hikes in nature, cashmere socks, symphonic orchestras, heated car seats, cocktails on tropical beaches, and every other sumptuous gratification.

Those born under Taurus, the fixed earth sign, can be stubborn and obstinately hooked on their ideas, values, and pleasures. Who can blame them when such extravagant delights appear wherever they look? But Taurus is not as materialistic at its core as many traditional astrologers contend. The Hierophant, the Tarot card associated with the sign, represents the spiritual teacher—a person who truly perceives the beauty and opulence of the material world and yet chooses to pursue a more transcendent state of ecstasy. The Buddha was a Taurus. At the age of twenty-nine, he opted to renounce the comforts of his princely life in order to locate the source of human suffering. And because of his journey from luxury to a greater good, we enjoy the teachings of Buddhism to this day. Herman Hesse's novel *Siddhartha* presents a wonderful, pleasurable depiction of the spiritual path of the Buddha and the Taurus.

VALUES

Taurus presents us with the concepts of money, talents, values, and self-worth. The logic is simple: if you value yourself, others will be more likely to perceive that value too. You will be able to price your talents high and earn a larger salary. In turn, you will have more money to invest in other talents that will mature into even more money.

Imagine a talented hairdresser who suffers from low self-esteem. She does not value herself. She does not value her talents. And she winds up charging less for her services than someone less skilled but more self-confident—maybe $30 a haircut, while her rival insists on $100 or $150. Her diminished self-esteem also prevents her from talking herself up, from marketing her superb talents to expand her clientele. She dreams of renting her own shop and hiring many employees, but her depleted value of self barely allows her to pay her routine bills, much less ask the bank or investors for a loan to enlarge her business. Meanwhile, the confident hairdresser charges more, earns more, and then uses that money to market, multiply, and reap even more. Taurus teaches that appreciation of oneself generates a virtuous circle of success that results in greater and greater wealth. And, sadly, a lack of self-value builds a circular rut of financial limitation.

Money is not an end but a means. It represents a barometer of your self-worth, an indication of how much you appreciate the talents the universe has bestowed on you. Money cannot make you happy all by itself. But when you are happy with yourself and your work, then your bank account—and, more crucially, your general sense of inner and outer abundance—swells.

But don't forget the rub: if you take yourself too seriously, if you brag about or over-value your talents unrealistically, then people will accuse you of *bull*shitting them.

On Wall Street, a bear market signals a contraction of wealth, while the beloved bull market—a Taurus market—denotes soaring stock prices. (I told you astrology sneaks itself into everything.) A statue of the charging bull is located in Wall Street and has become one of the city's landmarks. Sculptor Arturo Di Modica created the 7,000-pound bull statue to infuse Wall Street with optimism after the 1987 crash. It's no coincidence that the logo of Merrill Lynch, one of the world's leading financial managers, is a bull. Appropriately, Taurus rules not only finance but also art.

Taurus in your chart highlights the area in your life in which you possess many splendid talents and bull-market opportunities. It also indicates where you likely need to work on your self-esteem. This week, make a list of all your talents as well as how much money and time you have dedicated to each of them. Then keep your eyes open for synchronicities that might offer support to any of these talents. These clues from the universe will help you to determine which of these talents can be translated into income.

For example, one woman I know persistently found herself fielding compliments for her baking. She loved to bake for her friends and family, but she doubted her own ability to use her talent as anything more than a delicious hobby. Simply writing down the sentence, "Everyone seems to love my cupcakes" amid a list of all her other many talents finally induced her to take the plunge. She invested a bunch of money to renovate her kitchen, and she opened an organic cake bakery. All of a sudden, her son asked to join the enterprise; he knocked on the doors of all the local cafes and restaurants, while the woman baked away back home. Within in year, she had earned enough to move from her kitchen to a beautiful storefront bakery of her own.

Taurus in your chart highlights the area in your life in which you possess many splendid talents and bull-market opportunities. It also indicates where you likely need to work on your self-esteem.

FIND YOUR VALUE: MISSION STATEMENT

The Taurus archetype impels you to spend a few minutes contemplating your mission statement. Grab a notebook and write the one sentence that best describes why God sent you down to earth. What are you all about? What are you here to accomplish? Aries conferred your identity, and Taurus gives you value, the talents that come with that identity.

Imagine God as an investor of Light. Now you must offer a business plan for your life in which God can invest Light and energy. For example, when I sat down with a financial adviser (a Taurus), she told me to craft one sentence that spelled out what I believe in and what I am all about. This clear and definitive purpose would allow me to choose from among all the many projects and ideas I might dream up on any given day. The financial planner showed me the mission statement of the Ritz-Carlton hotel company: "Ladies and gentlemen serving ladies and gentlemen." Any new scheme or thought that does not fit this premise is not part of the Ritz-Carlton enterprise and thus must be discarded.

This week, write your mission statement and place it in a conspicuous spot (on your desktop, car, or bedroom wall). My financial adviser told me that if your statement is backed by integrity—meaning that you walk the talk (Taurus is a practical earth sign, after all)—then abundance and money will pour in effortlessly. It worked for me, and it definitely worked for the Ritz Carlton. It can work for you as well.

YOUR OWN PRIVATE TAURUS

Your house of Taurus indicates where you possess a direct link to Mother Nature and sensuality. It marks the area of your live in which you can advance your goals by connecting to the stimulation of your five senses. It serves as an anchor that will help to support you both financially and emotionally. Taurus is the fixed earth sign, and so you too must exert a constant stream of effort toward the issues governed by this house. This area of your life also holds the key to making money and amplifying your talents.

Taurus in Your First House (Your Rising Sign): You are a patient and stubborn individual who displays a strong affinity towards the arts, finance, beauty, and comfort. You require stability in your life to manifest your full potential. Make sure you enjoy yourself as often as possible. During the week of Taurus, pay attention to your body, appearance, health, and your direction in life.

Taurus in the Second House: Blessed with myriad talents that can support you financially, you have a gift for moneymaking. You probably need to select one of these talents to guarantee a steady and secure income. You enjoy talents in finance as well as in the arts. In the week of Taurus, focus on your finances and make sure that you invest in your abilities.

Taurus in the Third House: You might be slow to learn, but the information that you absorb sticks with you for a long time. Sometimes stubborn and narrow-minded, you nonetheless possess robust powers of concentration. Your talented siblings likely are blessed with a gift for moneymaking or in the arts. During the week of Taurus, pay extra attention to your communication, neighbors, business plans, brothers, and sisters.

Taurus in the Fourth House: You enjoy a stable home life. You need to live close to nature or in a house filled with plants and animals. Make your home comfortable and luxurious. You can earn money from buying and selling property and real estate. During the week of Taurus, focus on your family relationships and the condition of your home.

Taurus in the Fifth House: You require a stable and secure love life to truly enjoy romance. You are attracted to refined, dependable, and artistic people. Extremely creative, you enjoy a special connection to female children. In the week of Taurus, place a special emphasis on your children, having fun, creativity, and happiness.

Taurus in the Sixth House: You generally enjoy good health, but please monitor your thyroid gland and throat. Financial burdens or insecurities can yield physical ailments. You are a steady and hardworking individual who is appreciated both as an employee and a boss. During the week of Taurus, focus on your diet, health, work, and service.

Taurus in the Seventh House: You are attracted to sensuous and artistic people who provide you with a sense of emotional and financial security. You require a partner in order to ground your finances and exploit your talents. In the week of Taurus, highlight your significant others, partners, and relationships.

Taurus in the Eighth House: Finding a partner in business or love will improve your finances and your sense of security. You also enjoy a strong chance to receive an inheritance or legacy. You excel at making money from other people's talents and money. In the week of Taurus, pay attention to your sexuality, intimacy, and your partner's abundance.

Taurus in the Ninth House: Your higher education relates to art and finance, but you ought to study subjects that you can use practically in life. Try to travel to countries that present a legacy of artistic and cultural greatness. Money will flow when you deal with multinational organizations or with foreigners. In the week of Taurus, focus on travel to foreign lands—via the Internet and books, if not in actuality— as well as on higher education and your in-laws.

Taurus in the Tenth House: You need to be highly compensated for your work, and you can enjoy success in the arts or the world of finance. You possess many talents that will attract material abundance. Try to use your five senses in your career. In the week of Taurus, pay attention to your reputation, destiny, and career.

Taurus in the Eleventh House: You might have many Taurus friends or friends with Taurus qualities and traits. Money can come through your engagement with groups, friends, and organizations. You need stable and reliable friends. You might especially enjoy the company of women. In the week of Taurus, focus on your friends and your professional or community groups.

Taurus in the Twelfth House: You link the mystical to the financial, enjoying income from spiritual pursuits and creative visualizations. You probably lived as an artist in a past incarnation, and you still have issues with money in this lifetime. You like to have money, but you might despise materialism. In the week of Taurus, attend to your spirituality as well as to the pain and suffering of others.

BAT KOL: THE DAUGHTER OF SOUND

Taurus rules music, intuition, and your inner voice. The Bible describes intuition with the phrase *Bat Kol*, which means "daughter of sound." The word daughter is appropriate to Taurus, a feminine earth sign, which combines the material substance of our world with the wisdom of the heavens. *Bat Kol* suggests that God communicates with us via a melodic voice. This idea explains why angels in popular culture always appear to be singing.

The question always arises: how do we differentiate between that celestial inner voice and our own fearful thoughts? According to Taurus, our true intuition ought to register like music. English adopts this same Taurus rule when it describes good counsel with the phrase *sound* advice. Good advice should vibrate like harmonious chimes and bells. Fear, on the other hand, roils and disturbs, often announcing itself with troubling or tense sensations in your stomach, neck, or brow.

Since Taurus represents Mother Nature, find a tree and sit beneath it. Close your eyes and focus only on the sounds you hear. Try to isolate each sound. Try to determine its origin. Practice this attention to the ambient sounds for a few minutes. Then try this same exercise with your own thoughts. Listen to them one by one. Slow them down until you can settle on just one thought. That final thought should ultimately end in an affirmation: "I am thankful to God for making me the way I am."

A man who lives in Manhattan undertook this exercise for thirty consecutive days under a tree in Central Park. A month later he got a raise. He never thought about his salary or his job during his tree meditations. He simply worked on escalating his self-worth, and the salary bump just followed.

How to Get Along with a Taurus

- To make a Taurus happy, you must address all five senses. It's vital to cook well, look good, smell sweet, sing well, and touch, touch, touch. For example, if you prepare a dinner for a Taurus, add music to background, light fragrant candles, and present the food artistically. The entire sensory experience matters.

- Never talk business when the Taurus is hungry or uncomfortable.

- Don't be cheap. Think luxury.

- Compliment the Taurus on how she looks and dresses, as well as the car she drives.

- If a Taurus insists on talking about a particular subject, don't try to persuade her otherwise. If she feels that you are trying to change her, the Taurus will stubbornly dig in and refuse to move.

- Help the Taurus see, appreciate, and invest in her talents. Support all of the Taurus's artistic endeavors.

The Dark Side of the Force: Taurus

Stubbornly fixated on the five senses, Tauruses can become overly materialistic. They stagnate amidst their comfort, refusing to move even when every other sign insists that they must. They also are prone to fixate on their ideas. Adolf Hitler, born on the first day of Taurus, zealously fixated on racism and aggression. Karl Marx, another Taurus, clung tightly to his own philosophies. He asserted that religion is the opiate of the masses. Though correct in many ways, he ended up creating a whole new religion called communism. Sigmund Freud, yet another Taurus, invented the first coherent system of psychology, but he obsessed on the notion that all our problems stem from sex and our bodily functions. His conclusions are not surprising when you consider that Taurus rules bodily sensations and stands opposite to Scorpio, the sign of sexuality. Freud eventually suffered from throat cancer. People often develop illness in an organ that they overuse. Taurus rules the throat, and Freud invented *talk* therapy. Perhaps his Taurus nature led him to over-activate this particular body part until it finally killed him.

THE HEBREW LETTER *Vav*

ו

According to *Sefer Yetzirah*, the Book of Creation, the Hebrew letter *Vav* was assigned to Taurus. *Vav* translates as "the hook" or "nail," and indeed the shape of the letter resembles a sharp nail. Like a nail, Taurus acts as the physical connector that binds any two objects together.

Taurus embodies the old alchemical formula "as above, so below." Alchemy viewed the Tree of Life as the symbol of this ancient formula—the nail that joined the heavens to the earth. Trees, of course, represent nature—another sign that Taurus operates as the yoke that physically joins the spiritual with the material. The word *yoga* comes from the Sanskrit word "to yoke," and the practice of yoga stands as a spiritual system designed to yoke the body to the soul. The letter *Vav* proves that Taurus is much more than a sign obsessed with luxury and stuff. Grounded firmly in the earth, Taurus serves as a ladder, a magical pea tree that leads to the divine. Even many atheists and agnostics, who admit to no belief in any religion or spiritual pursuit, will concede that they do believe in the awesome, inexplicable power of nature (Taurus).

In Hebrew, the letter *Vav* functions as a conjunctive prefix similar to the word *and*: boys *and* girls, black *and* white. Again Taurus nails two separate things into one. Additionally, the Bible uses *Vav* to transform verbs from future to past tense, indicating that Taurus (and the material world) not only unites objects in space, but also joins actions in time. This concept might prompt some to engage in a convoluted philosophical discussion, but the simple truth of *Vav* and Taurus is this: everything in our material world is One. All objects joined by the nail of Taurus, as well as all time (past, present, and future), are united. Taurus and this material world simply provide the vessel in which life and unity can thrive.

Meditate on the letter *Vav* whenever you want to connect to something or somebody. Use it too whenever you need abundance or an outlet for your talents. In addition, take at least two yoga classes this week and ask the teacher to show you the Tree Pose.

THE PARTS OF THE BODY

Taurus rules the neck, throat, and thyroid gland. It oversees one of the narrowest spots in our body—a place therefore vulnerable to energy blockages and disease. Many of us, for example, suffer sore throats whenever we overtax our immune system. If you imagine an energy flow from the crown of the head to the soles of our feet, the throat presents a bottleneck where traffic easily clogs. This peril explains why so many religious traditions call for the daily chanting or singing of prayers to help clear the traffic jam in the throat.

Throat ailments also indicate that you might not be communicating what you need. Perhaps you are not expressing your own self-worth. Make sure that you speak up this week. You might also want to chant some of the names of God associated with the Tree of Life (see chapter 10) or any other mantra you feel attached to. These potent vocalizations will open up a carpool lane in your throat that will permit the energy to flow smoothly.

In addition, many cultures consider the neck to be an especially erotic or sensuous area. Women often adorn their Taurus necks with jewelry and perfume as if to emphasize and enhance the part of their body associated with the sign of sensuality.

THE COLOR OF TAURUS: RED-ORANGE

The color of Taurus is red-orange. Taurus brings a lighter, calmer version of red, but a darker, richer version of orange. Check your wardrobe, office, and bedroom to determine if you have enough Taurus in your life. You can wear red and orange—either blended or adjacent to one another—to attract the energy of abundance and sensuality. If you like, color the letter *Vav* reddish orange and use it in your meditations.

What Should I Focus on in the Week of Taurus?

This week, make an inventory of your talents and strive to appreciate them. Taurus encourages you to value yourself. You should also indulge and pamper yourself. Go to the spa, book a massage, eat delicious desserts, and buy yourself a gift. Taurus teaches that you are worth it. Demonstrate to the universe that you are open to receiving benevolence and abundance.

In addition, spend time in your garden and out in nature. Stimulate Taurus by visiting museums, art galleries, and concert halls. Be sure to activate all of your five senses.

Meditate on the letter *Vav* whenever you want to connect to something or somebody. Use it too whenever you need abundance or an outlet for your talents. Take at least two yoga classes this week and ask the teacher to show you the Tree Pose.

As always, seek out synchronicities related to Taurus, and try to interpret the symbolic and practical messages directed to you. The symbols of Taurus include the bull, anything related to the five senses (smells, tastes/food, decadent desserts, music, noises, touches, bumps, caresses, art), nature, trees, dirt, the throat, voice, money, finance, the stock market, nails and yokes, self-esteem, talents, reddish orange, stubbornness or stubborn people, luxury goods, Friday, Venus, Buddha or Buddhism, Shakespearean plays, and pleasure.

Your Taurus Week Checklist

- Identify where you have Taurus in your chart and try to apply the lessons of Taurus—pleasure, sensuality, and self-worth—to that area of your life.
- Connect to the five senses. Play background music when you work, light a scented candle, hug and touch people, eat delectable food, and view art.
- Recite the affirmation of Taurus every day: "I am my own spiritual guide. I possess the ability to translate my inner wealth into material abundance. I am worthy of success and financial security."

- Pamper yourself.
- Make a list of all your talents and how much money and time you have invested in them.
- Write your mission statement.
- Go to nature. Hike in a forest. Lie on the ground and feel the earth.
- Sit under a tree and amplify your thoughts of self-worth.
- Practice yoga.
- Meditate on the letter Vav.
- Plant a tree.
- Wear red-orange clothes.

THE RITUAL OF TAURUS: PLANTING A TREE

Since Taurus rules the spring as well as Mother Nature, honor this archetype by planting a tree, your own Taurus Tree of Life. First, write down your most vital talent—one that you yearn to develop and expand. Dig a hole in your backyard and plant this piece of paper alongside the new tree. If you don't have room for a tree, put in a small bush or any kind of plant.

For the next two weeks, visit the tree/plant every day and meditate on the talent that you decided to nurture. The growth of the tree will reflect the growth of you talent.

If don't have the ability or space to plant a tree, you can instead contribute to our Tree of Life forest. Just go to *www.TreeofLifeGrove.org* (for trees in the United States) or *www.TreeOfLifeGrove.org.il* (for trees in Israel).

FAMOUS TAURUSES

John Muir, Rudolph Valentino, William Shakespeare, the Buddha, Sigmund Freud, Eva Peron, Barbara Streisand, Salvador Dali, George Lucas, Karl Marx, Vladimir Lenin, Duke Ellington, and Socrates.

John Muir was an amazing naturalist who invented the idea of national parks in the United States and inspired the entire world to preserve what we have not already destroyed.

♊

Gemini: The Messenger

May 21 to June 20

Key Phrase: "I think"—"I think, therefore I am."

General Qualities: Intelligent, informative, versatile, agile, adaptable, powerful communication skills, well-connected, adept networker, writer, speaker, and messenger

Dark Side: Overly talkative, prone to exaggeration, deceptive, propensity for lies and theft, emotionally detached, swings of moods, double personality, and overrationalism

Element: Mutable air

Planet: Mercury, the messenger of the gods

Day: Wednesday

Theme: Flexibility

Parts of the Body: Hands, lungs, nervous system

Color: Orange

Gemstone: Clear crystal

Musical Note: D, the Beatles' favorite key

Hebrew Letter: *Zain* ז

Kabbalistic Meaning of Letter: The sword of reason

Path in the Tree of Life: Path 6, connecting Understanding with Beauty

Tarot Card: The Lovers

Movies: *American Beauty, Sliding Doors*

Affirmation: "I am attracting the right relationships into my life. I surround myself with people who understand and love me. I effortlessly receive the information I need to give and share with the rest of creation."

OVERVIEW

While Aries represents the pure masculine force and Taurus embodies the feminine, Gemini symbolizes their union, as well as the merger of all opposing forces. Gemini, the sign of John F. Kennedy, Henry Kissinger, and Bob Dylan, is the communicator, the messenger of the cosmos. It is the sign that makes us think before we speak and speak before we act. Gemini uses intelligence and communication to bridge any gaps or dissonance we might find in our lives. It is the sign of business, negotiation, writers, marketing, and public relations. In the week of Gemini, you will improve your communication skills and stay alert to how you interact with others. Gemini will amplify your skills in negotiations and business. And you will learn how to bring people together for a common cause and how to identify your own vital messengers.

One last thing before we fly high with the energies of Gemini: you will find this chapter very chatty and long. The reason is that the book is based on my lectures, and I always find that when I teach on Gemini, the speed of the lecture as well as its length is prolonged.

THE TERRITORY OF GEMINI

Gemini is the sign of the messengers and communicators. Geminis manage the marketing and publicity of the zodiac. The widespread popularity of astrology—evidenced by the daily column in most every newspaper, the slew of astrological sites on the Internet, and the famously cliché "What's your sign?" bandied about in bars and cafes across the globe—illustrates the relentless handiwork of Gemini. Geminis are masters of branding.

The location of Gemini in the zodiac year explains the true meaning of this agile and talkative sign. Gemini arrives at the end of the spring, assigning Gemini, a mutable air sign, the task of kindly persuading Taurus to relinquish her tight grip over the spring so that the year can continue and grow into summer. Taurus, as we saw earlier, is the most stubborn and fixated sign. Gemini must marshal all the cunning, cleverness, and communicative skills he can round up to nudge Taurus from her seat of power. Each year, against all odds, Gemini succeeds.

The messenger job description also entails marrying or negotiating a deal between Aries and Taurus. While Aries, ruled by Mars, represents the ultimate man and Taurus, ruled by Venus, is the manifestation of a woman, Gemini enables the connection between them both. In recognition of this crucial task, the Tarot designates the Lovers as the card of Gemini. This archetype joins all opposites chiefly via the technology of effective communication. Gemini possesses mastery over language and with irresistible talk seduces the two back into the one.

How does Gemini do it? We can locate the key to this mysterious trick in the name of the sign. *Gemini* means "twins" in Latin. These twins share the same genes, and yet one twin is male and the other is female. Though they are the same—born simultaneously from the same womb—they are also opposite (masculine and feminine). And the ability to be both different and yet the same makes the twins the logical bridge between what the mystics call "the Oneness of God" and the "multitude of life." Gemini's paradoxical ability to be logical and illogical at the same time gives us the capacity to understand the dichotomy inherent in the axiom that all is One, even though that Oneness manifests in so many individualized and seemingly separate creatures.

Gemini—the twins, the two—embodies duality. Geminis wield the tools of logic and language to help us make sense of the universe. Geminis are rarely selfish with information, nor are they secretive. Whatever they learn, they share. Whatever they receive, they give. When my first book came out in Israel, I needed a way to reach many people in little time. My very good Gemini friend, Noa Tishby, offered to organize an event for the book. She is a fabulous celebrity in Israel and within less than forty-eight hours she managed to round up all the media and A-list stars in Israel to come to the book signing. Everyone knew that the beautiful Gemini had a message to deliver, and they showed up. They did not want to miss an opportunity to listen to her story.

THE MESSENGERS

Like all good messengers, Geminis never choose sides. They express loyalty to all, while maintaining the sense of objectivity demanded of a translator, a mediator, or a reporter on the battlefield.

Gemini is also the sign of business and negotiation. The first written documents of early civilizations did not focus on praise for the gods, laws to live by, or passionate love poetry. Instead, about 85 percent of the first written material features lists of commerce: "5 sheep, 3 sacks of barley." The rest of the documents from that time are dictionaries that explained how to write the words *sheep* and *barley* so that all the Gemini merchants would be on the same page—or in this case, the same tablet. Written communication from the start equaled business.

Today Gemini continues to rule over all the proliferating tools of communication and commerce including faxes, emails, phones, the Internet, letters, books, and trade. All the technology of today has enabled Geminis to connect virtually every corner of the globe. Emerging on the heels of Taurus, Geminis sell and promote the art created by the previous archetype. They also trade with the money and finances generated by Taurus. The Twin (Gemini) Towers in New York, of course, once housed the World Trade (Gemini) Center. The Twin Towers were destroyed in 2001 when Saturn (the planet of karma and challenges) was in Gemini.

This week you will become a Gemini. You will practice being a messenger. Open yourself to all forms of communication, and try to channel it to others. When you hear some news tidbit on the radio, think of someone who might need that information and make a note to pass it on. Be alert and flexible, and don't argue. Simply convey the news without emotional attachment or judgment.

LIES WE ENJOY BEING TOLD

You can recognize Geminis immediately. They talk fast, and they use their hands to express themselves. They often cut you off in the middle of a sentence because they know what you want to say and they already have formulated the reply. They scratch their faces when bored, and they continually offer to introduce you to people who can help further your goals. They are connectors. Just don't believe every little thing that pops out of the Geminis' mouthes. Sometimes they add extra details to the news they disseminate. They exaggerate to dress up the information, to make it more entertaining, or to facilitate the sale. Think of some of the wild promises proffered in late night infomercials. Think of the claims of just about any advertising at all. They all derive from the ingenuity of the Gemini. These are the world's storytellers—that's their calling. And if the story isn't strong enough to hold the listener's interest, well, the Gemini simply spices it up with some hyperbole. "Lose twenty-five pounds in two weeks." "Iraq has weapons of mass destruction that threaten our security." Sure it's possible. Sure it is.

This week you will practice being a messenger. Open yourself to all forms of communication, and try to channel it to others. Be alert and flexible, and don't argue. Simply convey information without emotional attachment or judgment.

In the age of information, when stimuli bombard all of us from all directions, getting noticed is tough. Gemini must resort to all sorts of tricks to slice through the clutter. I have a friend in Los Angeles who works for a prominent public-relations company that represents many famous actors and musicians. You have probably seen many of his clients smiling down on you from posters and billboards. He told me that his firm often hires computer-graphics designers to transform the publicity photos of their celebrity clients—making the celebrities thinner, more muscular, younger, smoother, tanner, and more attractive. They fit the buttocks to the frame, add a six-pack to a flabby stomach, and erase ungodly wrinkles. Yes, the photos are lies, but they are fabulous lies, the Gemini will say—lies that you enjoy being told.

Here is a tip on how to become a Gemini. It is called the law of three to five minutes. This week, make sure you go to a social event. It could be a gallery opening, a cocktail party, a networking event, or even a bar or club where you can interact with many people you do not know. When you arrive, start conversing with the first people that you see. Then obey the law that states that you should engage in conversation with a person you do not know for a maximum of three to five minutes. No more and no less. When you hit five minutes, respectfully terminate the conversation and move on to another person. Be sure that you are the one who ends the conversation and walks away. This will instill in the other person the feeling of wanting more.

Your Own Private Gemini

Gemini marks the spot in your chart where you can excel as a messenger. It also highlights the area in your life in which masterful communication can serve to unearth the energetic treasures that await you there. And finally, your Gemini house exposes the area where you might experience some form of duality. For example, a man who has Gemini in the tenth house of career might have two careers that compete for his attention. One woman with Gemini in her fourth house of home and family found herself continually traveling back and forth between Los Angeles and New York. The key to solving this sort of Gemini duality is not to choose one or the other, but to figure out how to unite the two into one. For example, the woman with homes in two places chose to marry the love of her life, and they decided together to move to Miami.

Look at your chart and find your Gemini. Once you identify the house that Gemini rules, try to link that house to an effort to improve communication, engage in public relations/publicity, or a need to unify a split.

Gemini in Your First House (Your Rising Sign): You are a very curious individual who finds everything and everyone fascinating. You talk and talk and find it hard to relax and sit still. You can be an intellectual leader and a powerful communicator. During the week you dedicate to Gemini, focus on your body, appearance, and how people perceive you. This is the time for your own personal public relations. Let everyone know who you are.

Gemini in the Second House: You have a great deal of talent with public relations, marketing, advertising, and negotiation. You also exhibit a unique way with words, which suggests that you can make money from writing and communicating. You might have two different talents or earning possibilities that require unification. During the week of Gemini, work with your talents and finances to identify how the universe supports your income.

Gemini in the Third House: You are a natural-born writer and messenger. Your job is to deliver messages to the rest of humankind. You are blessed with a quick and agile mind and have multiple interests. You are eloquent and witty, charming and social. You might need to learn how to bare down and deepen your understanding on a specific subject. You also generally maintain good relationships with neighbors and siblings. During the week of Gemini, pay attention to the way you think, talk, and write. Make sure you reconnect to your neighbors and siblings.

Gemini in the Fourth House: Your home reflects your intellectual interests. If you live in an apartment building, try living on the highest floor possible. A view could help you tap into the essence of Gemini. You might have two homes or two places you consider your safe haven. Communication between family members is extremely important for you. During the week of Gemini, spend time with family members and inside your home.

Gemini in the Fifth House: You enjoy a great deal of intellectual creativity, and you have a talent for communicating with children and playful, creative people. Sports that involve the hands, lungs (running), and mind (chess) are good for you. Your children are intelligent, and you can have a good rapport with them. You might have twins. Your love life fluctuates and might include two different lovers at the same time. During the week of Gemini, place emphasis on your love life and your creativity. This is also a great time to reconnect with your children, if necessary.

Gemini in the Sixth House: You excel in work when you act as a messenger: a writer, marketer, or trader. Writing can be a great way to serve humankind. You might work at two jobs at the same time, but it will be best to eventually unite them into one. Pay attention to your nervous system, hands, and lungs. The way you think and breathe can determine your overall health. Running can be a therapeutic activity for you. In the week of Gemini, focus on your diet, health, and work.

Gemini in the Seventh House: You are attracted to communicative, intelligent, and curious people. Your partner must stimulate your intellect, or else you will grow bored and start looking around. You might be interested in two people at the same time. Take pains to avoid telling lies. During the week of Gemini, focus on your partnership and also spend some time trying to communicate and make peace with your adversaries.

Gemini in the Eighth House: You excel in deals and negotiation that involve other people's talents and money. Your communication style is tied up with sexuality. It entails the physical as well as the verbal. Your partner might possess a talent for writing and communicating, and you can make money from his or her skills. In the week of Gemini, focus on communicating your sexuality and your need for intimacy.

Gemini in the Ninth House: You have a powerful need to speak foreign languages and perhaps to conduct business with foreign cultures. It is important to maintain good communication with in-laws. You are not only a philosopher, but you also apply that philosophy to your life. This week, try to travel, especially for business. Now is also a good time to correct misunderstandings with in-laws or foreign friends.

Gemini in the Tenth House: You might have two careers to choose from. You can excel in careers that involve putting things together, networking, writing, and communicating. You will be known as a negotiator and a connector. You harbor diverse interests, but you will need to integrate them into one coherent pursuit. In the week of Gemini, focus on communication in your career. You can further your worldly goals dramatically during this week.

Gemini in the Eleventh House: You interact with many interesting friends and diverse groups. Your friends tend to be younger and talkative. You are popular and well liked because of your humorous outlook on life. During the week of Gemini, focus on nurturing communication with friends who you might not have spoken to for a long time.

Gemini in the Twelfth House: Mysticism and spirituality are linked to your intellect and words. You tend to read about spirituality. In a past life, you might have been a writer who was severely punished for what you wrote, and so you might shy away from writing in this lifetime. Be careful not to slander or gossip about others because that can create powerful enemies. This week, focus on retreats, spiritual activities like meditation, and letting go of whatever you are holding onto but really don't need.

This week, make sure you go to a social event where you can interact with many people you do not know. When you arrive, start conversing with the first people that you see, but engage in conversation for a maximum of three to five minutes. When you hit five minutes, respectfully terminate the conversation and move on. Be sure that you are the one who ends the conversation and walks away. This will instill in the other people the feeling of wanting more.

GEMINI AND THE BINARY LANGUAGE

Computers all over the world—in China, India, Bulgaria, Europe, Brazil, the Netherlands, Dubai, and Zimbabwe—speak the same language. This language has only two symbols: zero and one. It is called the *binary* language, from the prefix *bi*, which means "two." A digital image of your mother, a digital recording of Beethoven's fifth, or a love letter you sent in the form of an email all find expression in the language of the twins.

For a long while, I did not understand why computers had not achieved independent consciousness. Why had the quest for artificial intelligence failed? But after thinking about Gemini, I recognized the problem. Computers break everything down into zeros and ones; they "see" the world divided into two and only two forces. This fixation on duality is not far from the way many mystical doctrines view the world as well. Kabbalah, for example, divides life into receiving and giving. Daoism asserts that life is a dance between yin and yang. Buddhism breaks life into Form and Emptiness. Alchemy sees the world as the relationship between above and below, and astrology explains life through the proportion of light and dark hours in the day. But while all of these spiritual doctrines provide us with techniques to unite these dualities into oneness, computers are confined by their everlasting logical loops of true/false, yes/no, closed circuit/open circuit, zero and one.

Humans, along with most sentient beings, are divided into two genders—feminine and masculine. The sexual organ of a man resembles the number one (1), while the sexual organ of a woman resembles the number zero (0). Through the act of lovemaking, human beings are able to put the one and zero together, and this union of the sexual organs of male and female yields new life. By making love, a man and a woman can create a new biological "machine" called a child. Although computer programmers from all over the world strive to make computers function more like human beings, in order to infuse the machines with "intelligence," computers, so far, can only place the zeros and ones next to each other. They do not have the capacity to merge them together. They cannot create a new intelligence, and that, I think, explains why they do not exhibit self-awareness or a soul.

The Tarot supports this analysis. In the Tarot, Gemini is represented by the card called the Lovers. This card informs the computer—or the humans developing the computers—that the endless string of zeros and ones that comprise the binary language must communicate with each other and then make love. Only then will computers develop a new kind of consciousness. Clearly, it will take an ingenious programmer to nudge two digits into falling in love. Perhaps it's time for computer technicians to learn more about matchmaking. Most likely, the solution will emerge from quantum theory that postulates that a single particle potentially can exist in two places at the same time (again the idea of opposition and sameness emblematic of Gemini).

Computers might not be able to fix this problem of duality, but you can. During the week of Gemini, make sure that you put all your own zeros and ones together. Find the duality in your life. Where are you caught between two oppositions that must make love or unite? How can you wed these opposing options rather than choosing one or the other? Searching for these dualities also will enable you to develop and improve your communication and negotiating skills.

ADAM AND EVE: THE FIRST GEMINI

In the first story of creation in Genesis, we read that God created Adam and Eve in his own image and that God created them simultaneously. "In the image of God created He him; male and female created He them" (Genesis 1:27). This story suggests that Adam and Eve were born as lovers and twins at the same time. Though this notion would appall many mainstream religious leaders, astrology as well as the pictorial system of the Tarot embraces the symbolic power behind this assertion. If you look closely at the Tarot card of the Lovers, you will see a scene from the Garden of Eden. Adam stands on the right and looks at Eve, who is on the left looking up at an angel. Between the two lovers/twins grows the Tree of Knowledge of Good and Evil. Good and evil, one and zero, yes and no—the dualities at the center of our Gemini world.

Adam represents consciousness, while Eve represents the subconscious. Adam, the emblem of our rational intellect, looks at Eve, the symbol of the subconscious or mystical aspects of our being, in an effort to understand and experience the divine higher self, which is personified by the hovering angel.

During the week of Gemini, find the duality in your life. Where are you caught between two oppositions that must make love or unite? How can you wed these opposing options rather than choosing one or the other? Searching for these dualities also will enable you to develop and improve your communication and negotiating skills.

One day, while driving down Sunset Boulevard in Hollywood, I realized the timelessness and universality of this symbolism. I saw a huge billboard that showed a man and a woman taking a shower side by side. Both were very sexy and wonderful to look at, but that was not really the billboard's message, since I knew that their perfect bodies had probably been fabricated, or at least tweaked, by PhotoShop. The deeper message came from the fact that the man, on the right, was looking at the woman, on the left, who in turn was looking up at the source of the water that was splashing down upon them. It was Adam and Eve all over again, suggesting that the masculine energy requires the feminine in order to get in touch with the ultimate divine source. This symbolism teaches us that the true mission of Gemini, and all forms of communication, is to link together the masculine and feminine, the active and receptive aspects of life.

Everyone, including you, has a masculine, Adam side and a feminine, Eve side. The masculine communicates, while the feminine listens. In order to be a gifted communicator, you must insure that these two energies complement each other inside of you. If you usually talk too much, this week try to speak less and listen more; and if you generally don't talk that much, try to speak more. Then note how much better your communication with other people—real, meaningful communication—flows.

About a year ago, I interpreted the chart of a powerful businessman in Turkey. He was dynamic and forceful and had his Gemini in the seventh house (the house of relationship). At fifty-eight, he still had not managed to enjoy a lasting, meaningful love relationship. He yammered on about that simple fact for ten straight minutes. His main complaint was that he gives too much and never receives. Eventually I tried to interject one sentence of information. Before the Turkish translator could finish telling him what I'd said, he interrupted with a brand new question. I forcefully told him to pay attention, that even in this session in which he had paid me to give him information, he was too busy giving his own words. I suggested that whatever happened in the session with me probably mirrored the occurrences in his life. He was too busy talking, talking, talking. He never listened. I asked him a simple question that finally sealed up his mouth: "Why are you so afraid of silence?" I counseled that he was so busy radiating energy that he allowed no space for God or people around him to give back to him. He asked so many questions without a break that he left no time for life to answer. For the last ten minutes of the session, he finally sat quietly and listened. He finally received.

Tree of Knowledge of Good and Evil

In the second chapter of Genesis, we read that God created a garden for Adam and Eve and that he planted two trees in the midst of the garden, the Tree of Immortal Life and the Tree of Knowledge of Good and Evil. With these symbols, the Bible introduces the concept of free will. (Remember, nothing is sealed in the stars; there is always room for free will.) God instructed Adam and Eve never to taste from the fruits of the Tree of Knowledge of Good and Evil. We all know how that turned out. The newly created couple took a bite from the forbidden tree, giving birth to our legacy and what the Christians call "the original sin." Personally, I don't think that it was all that original (just try telling any toddler not to touch something) or a sin. But the important part of the story is that from the Tree of Knowledge, Adam and Eve received all the information of the creation. Genesis tells us that their eyes opened. They suddenly knew all there is to know, and yet they never had experienced that knowledge first hand. It was akin to hearing about the intricacies and pleasure of making love but never actually doing it.

Genesis reports that after they tasted the fruit, Adam and Eve noticed that they were naked. For the first time, Adam and Eve realized that they belonged to different genders. The fruit of the Tree of Knowledge created this separation, the splitting of the masculine and feminine, the one and the zero. But dualities engendered by the Tree of Gemini did not end there. After they concealed their private parts from each other with fig leaves (and thus creating the first "haute couture"), Adam and Eve hid from God. This original game of hide-and-seek marks the separation between the higher self and the ego or between God and humankind. Separated from God, they had no choice but to descend from the Garden of Eden, and they descended to earth to experience all that they had downloaded from the Tree of

Everyone, including you, has a masculine, Adam side and a feminine, Eve side. The masculine communicates, while the feminine listens. In order to be a gifted communicator, you must insure that these two energies complement each other inside of you. If you usually talk too much, this week try to speak less and listen more; and if you generally don't talk that much, try to speak more. Then note how much better your communication with other people—real, meaningful communication—flows.

Knowledge. (I do not subscribe to the idea that God kicked Adam and Eve out of paradise. I believe that after the "high" that they surely experienced after tasting from the intoxicating fruits of the Tree of Knowledge, Adam and Eve suffered a hangover, or a "down," and that lowly feeling was experienced as the fall from heaven.)

This whole story—our primary Western creation myth—is a trick of Gemini, a story that gives the Gemini its mission. Gemini separates so that it can unite. With no separation—between man and woman or humans and God—there is nothing to be united. And there is no need for Gemini. We had to experience the fall or separation from God to provide us the chance to evolve and return to a heavenly state of enlightenment. It wasn't a sin to taste from the apple. It was a necessary stage of human development. We should not scorn Adam and Eve for their choice. Instead, perhaps, we ought to thank them for the opportunity that they and Gemini bestowed. Yes, we should be careful with our curiosity (your Gemini house highlights the place where you have to be extra mindful), but that curiosity leads humanity down the path of higher development.

According to Christianity, Jesus represents the second Adam, who holds the keys that will return us to heaven. Kabbalah, meanwhile, encourages us to study and therefore eat from the fruits (the spheres) of the Tree of Life in order to regain our lost oneness with God. Gemini divides to unite. It brought us here to earth, and now the archetype of Gemini and all its emissaries are doing their best to connect us all and show us the way back to Eden. In fact, Gemini governs this book and any other form of communication that delivers the message of unity. Today, we enjoy a new kind of Tree of Knowledge called the Internet. It offers us an endless stream of information about everything, but we must guard against spending more time tasting from this digital dualistic tree than we do living and experiencing the fruits of life.

THE CROSSROADS

As the archetype of duality, Gemini presides over all junctions. The crossroads or junction always has been associated with trade, commerce, the exchange of goods, and the transferring of ideas and philosophies. One reason the Middle East always figures prominently in the news of the day is that it has long served as a junction between the East and the West; between Europe, Africa, and Asia; between various religious traditions and attitudes toward life. The land now called Israel has always functioned as such a junction. But, alas, it is a junction without traffic lights, and for the last four thousand years, energies, philosophies, and people from myriad cultures have been colliding with a sometimes fierce velocity.

One beautiful scene in the Coen brothers' film *O Brother, Where Are Thou* depicts the three heroes meeting a guitar player in a remote junction. They discover that the passenger had encountered the devil at the same junction and had sold his soul for the ability to play the guitar. He played so well that they all conclude that he'd made a good bargain. This scene is loosely based on the legend of Robert Johnson, the grandfather of rock-and-roll, who supposedly met the devil at the inter-section of Highway 61 and Highway 49 in Clarksdale, Mississippi. Here we see evidence that in the junction, under the influence of Gemini, things, including souls, get traded back and forth. The myth of the crossroads also appears in the lore of the Yoruba tribes of West Africa. Elegua, this culture's trickster messenger god, often lurks at the junction, plying his trade.

This week, go back and review your life. At what point did you find yourself at a critical junction, forced to make a choice between two or more options that changed your life? Who served as the Elegua at your junction? Understanding your past and how it all played out at the crossroads before will help you to identify the vital junctions of today and tomorrow. From now on, whenever you find yourself at a crossroad, use the energy and tools of Gemini, including meditations with the Hebrew letter *Zain* (see "The Hebrew Letter *Zain*" later in this chapter), to help you make the best choice.

I vividly remember the junction that changed my life—that moment at the gates of the park in Mexico when the well-built young man offered to show me the real Guadalajara. My fear of muggings and black-market kidney rustling screamed at me to flee. But I also felt the energy of the crossroads urging me even more loudly to jump onto the new path. That moment triggered my unplanned two-year sojourn in Guadalajara, where I eventually discovered yoga, Kabbalah, and astrology. And this book is undoubtedly a direct result of that junction near the park and my encounter with the thirty-year-old Elegua I met that day in Mexico.

I don't mean to suggest that you should follow any stranger who walks up to you with a crazy offer. Sometimes not doing something can be just as good, if not a better path. I had a client who had a twin sister. When they were in college, a friend offered them both a chance to shoot heroin. My client refused, but her sister took the dare. Ten years later, the sister still struggles with her addiction, while my client is a psychologist who specializes in drug addiction. Gemini, twins—the same, but opposite.

How to Get Along with Geminis

- When you meet a Gemini for the first time, make sure you have valuable information to share. Deliver the information in a short and entertaining manner. Remember the three-to-five-minute law.

- If Geminis start scratching their head, playing with their hair, or fidgeting, it means one thing: you are boring them. Change the subject and let the Gemini do the talking.

- Try to address both sides of the Gemini's dual nature. For example, a Gemini who obsesses over superficialities like shoes, manicures, and which bar stands as the hottest this week might also harbor a deep interest in spirituality. Therefore, go ahead and play with her, but then invite her to a spiritual gathering. She will love the fact that you have acknowledged both sides of her personality.

- Introduce your Gemini friends to other people. Geminis value contacts and connections more than anything else.

- Flaunt your intellectual side. Share the knowledge you have. The Gemini needs to be stimulated.

The Dark Side of the Force: Gemini

The planet Mercury, the namesake of the messenger god in Greek and Roman mythology, rules Gemini. As the divine messenger, Mercury—Hermes in the Greek scheme—was the only god with access to both Olympus (heaven) and the Underworld (hell). Both the pure and the profane loved him. The Underworld accepted and honored Mercury because he also served as the god of thieves and liars. Why does Mercury, and by extension, Gemini, rule theft and lies? Simple. Geminis are the traders. They mark up prices to turn a profit. And sometimes they are forced to fabricate justifications for the increase. Business comes first. A successful deal makes a successful Gemini, and sometimes the Gemini will do and say anything to seal the deal.

Geminis love to talk, but they don't always listen. Their attention span is short, and that can offend those who don't feel heard. In addition, this attention deficit means that Geminis tend to know a tiny bit about everything and very little about any one thing. Geminis also must remain wary of their natural curiosity. The same curiosity that killed the cat can do the same to a Gemini, whose probing mind can easily lead him into uncharted and even dangerous territory (remember Adam and Eve and that little apple). The dual nature of the sign is also emblematic of the manic depressive. Watch out for sharp fluctuations in mood or energy.

This week, go back and review your life. At what point did you find yourself at a critical junction, forced to make a choice between two or more options that changed your life? Understanding your past and how it all played out at the crossroads before will help you to identify the vital junctions of today and tomorrow. From now on, whenever you find yourself at a crossroad, use the energy and tools of Gemini to help you make the best choice.

THE HEBREW LETTER *Zain*

According to *Sefer Yetzirah*, the Book of Creation, the letter *Zain* is assigned to Gemini. In Hebrew, *Zain*, like Gemini, has two meanings: "weapon" and "penis." Both meanings suggest the sword. We use the sword to cut, to separate objects in two. This weapon is also associated with the tongue (which is shaped like the tip of a sword). The tongue, of course, speaks; speaking is the Gemini's *raison d'être*, and a Gemini's speech can be sharp, just like a sword, if not more so. The pen, they say, is mightier than the sword. We use language to cut and slice life into groups, to categorize and understand other people and things. We separate chairs from tables and trees from rocks so that we can function in this world, even though at their core, all of these objects are comprised of the exact same tiny atoms.

The glyph that signifies *Zain* also resembles the contours of the male sexual organ. The phallus is used in the act of making love. It unites the feminine and the masculine, the mission of Gemini. *Zain* therefore represents a double-edged sword. It cuts and separates, but it then serves to unite.

Meditate with the letter *Zain* to rectify your communication skills, when you need to attract a messenger or some sort of agent, or when you need help with writing, opening business opportunities, or intellectual pursuits.

THE PARTS OF THE BODY

Gemini governs the hands, lungs, and the nervous system. People from just about every culture use their hands for communication. Those who can't speak with their tongues often use sign language—using their hands to verbalize their thoughts. The hands also represent the duality of Gemini, the two sides working together in the service of one person.

The nervous system, meanwhile, embodies the highest qualities of Gemini. The nervous system functions as the human body's messenger. It delivers all the commands from the brain to the organs, and in return it communicates sensations and pain back to the brain. Pain, for example, is the message that your body sends when something goes wrong. This week, take note of any pain. Listen to the messages of your body. It might be wise to find the part of your body that aches and use the other chapters of part III to identify which sign/archetype governs that body part. This sign is sending you a message that something is amiss. It also makes sense that the headquarters of the nervous system, the brain, like Gemini, is divided into two parts: the left and right hemispheres.

Meditate with the letter *Zain* to rectify your communication skills, when you need to attract a messenger or some sort of agent, or when you need help with writing, opening business opportunities, or intellectual pursuits.

THE COLOR OF GEMINI: ORANGE

Orange, the color of information ("look at me") and communication, is the color of Gemini. In fact, many designers consider orange to be the color of the new millennium—the color of the age of information. In the Kabbalistic Tree of Life, orange represents the sphere of communication (called Splendor) as well.

Orange is definitely the color of speed and tricksters. For example, in the TV series *Starsky and Hutch*, the heroes, who behave like (twin) brothers, zip around in an orange car. In another TV series, *The Dukes of Hazzard*, the two cousins create a great deal of havoc while racing their orange car that they call the General Lee.

In color therapy, orange is used as a stimulant and has proven effective in the treatment of depression. It is also used to treat lung problems such as bronchitis and asthma.

Wear the color orange when you want to be noticed for your trickster qualities and fun traits. This color can help you with communication and intelligence.

WHAT SHOULD I FOCUS ON IN THE WEEK OF GEMINI?

During the week you dedicate to Gemini, focus on your communication skills. Ask yourself, how do I serve as a messenger to others and who are the people that act as messengers for me? This is the best week to fix, mend, and expand your communication skills and your writing abilities.

Also pay extra attention to your siblings, relatives, and neighbors. Gemini governs all of these people, who you often need to communicate with. If you have little or no contact with your neighbors, now is the time to initiate a connection. The Sufis say that a close neighbor is better than a distant brother.

Most importantly, pay attention to how you speak about others. The rabbis tell us that

Wear the color orange when you want to be noticed for your trickster qualities and fun traits. This color can help you with communication and intelligence.

the worse thing we can do is to slander another. Gossip falls under this same category. Try to refrain this week from spouting negative things about your fellow human beings. This restraint will ensure that no one will say bad things about you.

In today's culture, your phone—so often a cell phone which is always with you—functions as your number one messenger. Pay attention to how you greet people when they call. How do you answer the phone? Most critically, what do people hear if they call and you are not available? Force yourself to listen to the greeting on your voice mail. First, make sure that you customize the message in your own voice. You want people to receive the message of you—energetically speaking—and not some digitized generic voice. Also, your message should be short, welcoming, and to the point. One woman listened to her own message and discovered for the first time the reason why friends and business associates had stopped leaving her messages. Her voice mail greeting lasted almost two minutes. It began with a recording of her favorite rock song and then continued with an endless stream of blessings. It was a nice gesture, but no one could stand waiting through it all, and she missed out on a lot of information. Don't stifle your messengers.

Gemini is represented by a broad bank of symbols, but remember, just about any form or communication—from billboards to a phone call from a telemarketer—can signal a vital synchronicity this week. Seek out these symbols, and try to find both the symbolic and practical messages directed to you. The symbols of Gemini include swords, pens, mail and the mail carrier, computers, the Internet, billboards, radio, media, TV, books, languages, commerce, trade, relatives, siblings, neighbors, writing, messengers, bills, twins, bridges, highways, dualities, intellect, hands, lungs, nervousness, the color orange, junctions, intersections, malls, stores, and phones.

Your Gemini Week Checklist

- Identify Gemini in your chart and try to apply the lessons of Gemini—communication, intelligence, and unifying dualities—to that area of your life.
- Convey information to others.
- Talk less, listen more.
- Look for your own messengers.
- Find your dualities and try to unify them.
- Meditate with the letter *Zain*.

- Say aloud the affirmation of Gemini: "I am attracting the right relationships into my life. I surround myself with people who understand and love me. I effortlessly receive the information I need to further my goals."
- Wear orange.
- Contact your siblings and neighbors.
- Eliminate slander and gossip.
- Do some cardiovascular activity to stimulate your breathing and exercise your lungs.
- Improve your phone messages and emails.

THE RITUAL OF GEMINI: THE BREATH OF LIFE

This exercise evolved from an ancient yoga breathing technique, and it can really change your life. Yoga is designed to connect the body with the soul. The breath of Gemini can make it happen.

Sit in a comfortable position and hold your right hand in front of you. Take your thumb and gently place it on you right nostril. Then place your index finger on your third eye, the point right in the center of your forehead. And finally place your middle finger on your left nostril. To begin, block off your left nostril with your middle finger and inhale deeply through your right nostril only. Keep the breath in your lungs as you block your right nostril with your thumb. Then release your middle finger and exhale through your left nostril. Now breathe in through your open left nostril. Hold the air in your lungs, close the left nostril with your middle finger, and breathe out through the right nostril.

Repeat this technique for ten minutes, breathing in and out slowly and deeply. Do this meditation right after you wake up in the morning and before you go to sleep at night.

According to Hindu tradition, our left side (left nostril) is connected to the *Ida*, the feminine, lunar side, and our right side (right nostril), *Pingala*, is masculine and solar. When we alternately breathe through each of the nostrils, we balance our inner duality and marry the masculine and feminine inside. If you feel sleepy or lethargic in the middle of the day, block your left nostril and breathe deeply for ten minutes through your right nostril only. This breath will activate your masculine energy. If you feel stressed or anxious, do the opposite; block your right nostril and breathe through your left, stimulating the feminine and cooling energies of the body.

How do you answer the phone? What do people hear if they call and you are not available? Listen to the greeting on your voice mail. First, make sure that you customize the message in your own voice. You want people to receive the message of you—energetically speaking—and not some digitized generic voice. Also, your message should be short, welcoming, and to the point.

FAMOUS GEMINIS

Laurence Olivier, John F. Kennedy, Marilyn Monroe, Arthur Conan Doyle, Queen Victoria, Bob Dylan, Miles Davis, Bob Hope, Walt Whitman, Angelina Jolie, Donald Trump, Clint Eastwood, Thomas Mann, Prince, Che Guevara, Adam Smith, Igor Stravinsky, Paul McCartney, Ralph Waldo Emerson, Henry Kissinger, John Paul Sartre, Tupac Shakur, and Salman Rushdie.

♋

Cancer: The Master of Compassion

June 21 to July 22

Key Phrase: "I feel" — unconditional love

General Qualities: Nurturing, natural-born healer, supportive, compassionate, family oriented, sensitive, homey, and maternal

Dark Side: Guilt, attachment, dependency, passive aggressiveness, and a deep need to be needed

Element: Cardinal water

Planet: The moon, the giver of light in our darkest moments

Day: Monday

Theme: Birth

Parts of the Body: Ribs, stomach, breasts, internal organs, womb

Color: Orange-yellow

Gemstone: Pearl

Musical Note: D sharp

Hebrew Letter: *Chet* ח

Kabbalistic Meaning of Letter: The wall

Path in the Tree of Life: Path 7, connecting Understanding and Severity

Tarot Card: The Chariot

Movies: *The Piano*, *Kundun*, and all family-related movies

Affirmation: "I am loved by my family and nurtured by the universe. I forgive those who have wronged me and ask forgiveness from those I have injured."

OVERVIEW

Cancer is the giver of life, the archetype of the Great Mother and the womb of creation. Cancer is also called the queen of the zodiac, while Leo, the next sign, is the king. Cancer, the sign of the Dalai Lama and Princess Diana, represents the family and home, the (crab) shell that provides security and shelter, protection and emotional sustenance. Of all the signs, Cancer is considered to be the most nurturing and caring, like the mother who nests her children under her wings. Cancer can help you to rectify and heal family problems, find security, and create a safe environment for growth. In the week of Cancer, you will learn to improve your familial relationships as well as how to enhance your emotional connections to your home and office. You will also develop your capacity for compassion and unconditional love.

THE TERRITORY OF CANCER

Cancer initiates summer with the summer solstice, the longest day and shortest night of the year. *Solstice* derives from the Latin words *sol* ("sun") and *sistere* ("still"). As the North Pole inclines closest to the sun in late June, like a pendulum that reaches the end of its swing, the sun appears to stand still, to stop momentarily before it reverses its direction. In astrology, June 21 is called "the gateway of mankind" because it marks the moment when light reigns in its fullest.

Perhaps the most distinguishing characteristic of humankind, the gateway to all of us, is feelings—our capacity to love, grieve, and empathize. And as the cardinal water sign, Cancer births emotions. Since water is the element necessary for all known life, Cancer also initiates life, which gives this archetype dominion over birth and motherhood. This sign forces us to confront and deal with our emotions and also with our mothers. Just as our mother once housed us in her womb, Cancer provides us with the container, our home, in which all of our early emotional experiences occurred. Ideally, our family and home offer a shelter in which we can feel safe and secure, a place of unconditional love and support. Without the security of home, we cannot hope to achieve our goals.

The Christian tradition associates the summer solstice with Saint John the Baptist. Cancer, in other words, gives rise to the man who baptized people in water—in empathy—as the crucial step in their spiritual evolution. Many Christians view Saint John as the initiator of the Christian faith because he prophesized the arrival of Jesus: "I baptize you with water but the one after me will baptize you with fire" (Matthew 3:11). John, the watery Cancer, heralded Jesus, the fiery Aries.

Modern mythologies make use of this same astrological metaphor. In the movie *The Matrix*, for example, Morpheus initiates the hero, Neo. Morpheus awakens him from ignorance by feeding him a pill and a glass of water (Cancer). These psychological metaphors suggest a loving mother who gives birth to a hero. Freud and many other psychologists espouse that most of our enviable traits, as well as our traumas and fears, were downloaded to us from our mothers and close family members. As you work with this archetype, you will have to confront the fears that obstruct your sense of security and safety.

Cancer rules motherhood, family, our home, and all aspects of our lives that contain our energy. It serves as our Holy Grail. Your car might represent Cancer if you spend many hours driving. Same for your office, if you work a lot. In the logic of the zodiac, Aries arrived first as the masculine archetype or Adam, and Taurus, the feminine archetype, or Eve, followed. They met and fell in love, suggesting Gemini, the connector and the Tarot card called the Lovers. In Cancer, Aries and Taurus decide to move in and create an emotionally secure home together. And in that Cancer home, Eve becomes pregnant. Leo, the next sign, will then represent the child born to this zodiac family.

Cancer in your chart highlights the area of your life in which memories from early childhood might hinder or advance your goals. It marks the place where you are most vulnerable and emotional, the area of your life that requires nourishment and protection. President George W. Bush, who established the department of homeland security, is a Cancer.

YOUR OWN PRIVATE CANCER

Identify your house of Cancer and focus this week on conceiving and giving birth to something new in your life. Cancer is the sign of nourishment and motherhood. Try to mimic nature by giving light to something within you, something that can grow and develop like your own baby.

Cancer in your chart highlights the area of your life in which memories from early childhood might hinder or advance your goals. It marks the place where you are most vulnerable and emotional, the area of your life that requires nourishment and protection.

Cancer in Your First House (Your Rising Sign): You are emotional and sensitive. You require emotional security to maximize your capabilities. Your strong maternal instinct means that you need to be needed. Influenced by the moon, you ought to pay attention to the moon's cycles so that you can manage your mood swings. This week, focus on your body, health, and physical and emotional self-nourishment.

Cancer in the Second House: You need emotional security to enjoy financial and emotional well-being. Saving for a rainy day will reduce your anxiety. You have been blessed with nurturing and healing talents that can make you money. You value family immensely. In the week of Cancer, nurture your finances, talents, and self-worth.

Cancer in the Third House: You possess a rare combination of intellect and emotionality. You could be a great poet or someone adept at communicating emotions and feelings. You have strong maternal instinct towards neighbors and siblings as well as an impressive memory. You need to open up and express yourself. This week, emphasize you communication skills and business, and pay attention to your relatives.

Cancer in the Fourth House: You connect strongly to your mother and your home and often feel protective of your family members. Living close to where you grew up or in similar surroundings will benefit your well-being. Try to live close to water. During this week, make sure you nurture your home and family. You also might encounter many coincidences involving your home, family, motherhood, and mother.

Cancer in the Fifth House: Children love you because your child within shines brightly. Your creativity lies in your subconscious. You don't always know what you will create, but that enviable invention just seems to flow through you. You are romantic and sensitive to your loved ones. This week, work on your creativity and happiness. Spend time around children. One other thing you can try is to practice some water sports.

Cancer in the Sixth House: You work well from home and perform best in a homey, comfortable workplace. You tend to nurture and support your employees and colleagues. You need to work with family, or in a field where you heal or take care of other people. Be sure that you avoid absorbing negative energy from the outside world. Stress and emotional problems can trigger disease. Watch your digestive system and internal organs. During the week of Cancer, pay special attention to your workspace, diet, and health.

Cancer in the Seventh House: You are attracted to nurturing and emotional people. Be careful of overmothering your partners in important adult relationships. Your marriage partnership centers on the need to create emotional security and stability. Make sure you place a fountain in your bedroom. During the week of Cancer, try to nourish, enhance, and protect your partnerships and significant others.

Cancer in the Eighth House: You might receive a family inheritance. Money also flows from relatives—your own or your partner's. Your emotional security greatly influences your sexuality and your ability to be intimate. Your family could have a connection to the occult or magic. This week, focus on joint financial and artistic affairs as well as sexuality and intimacy.

Cancer in the Ninth House: You can develop a potent emotional connection to in-laws. You also might live in a different country for a while. Your higher-education pursuits should be related to emotional subjects, because you are generally emotional about your philosophy of life. The week of Cancer represents a propitious time to travel, study, and enhance your understanding of truth.

Cancer in the Tenth House: You need to connect emotionally to your career and professional life. You cannot work solely for money; you require meaning too. Try to work with family members or in a profession that deals with families or homes. During the week of Cancer, focus on your career, your reputation, and your standing in your community.

Cancer in the Eleventh House: You are emotionally connected to your friends, community, and organizations, nourishing and supporting them with unconditional love. These people often serve as family for you. In addition, family members can become your close friends. During the week of Cancer, invest time in your friends, groups, and organizations.

Cancer in the Twelfth House: You might experience karma and difficulty with your mother, motherhood, or your family members. Your mother might have been your daughter in a past lifetime. Try to find a spiritual practice that highlights compassion and unconditional love. This week, focus on your ability to let go of old patterns that relate to home, motherhood, or your own mother. If possible, go on a spiritual retreat.

Isis, the Great Mother

Isis, the great mother goddess from Egyptian mythology, was revered by many other cultures, including the Greek and Roman. The ancient Egyptians worshipped her in the form of the Nile River (water) and as the goddess of birth. Many early depictions of Isis show her nursing her child, named Horus, in poses similar to those of Mary and Jesus in the subsequent Christian iconography. Most of all, the Egyptians saw Isis in the moon, the celestial body associated with Cancer. She always wore a crown made of two crescent moons surrounding a full lunar disk, which symbolized the three primary phases of the moon: new, full, and changing.

Isis generally sits on a throne, but it is not her own throne. The throne belongs to Osiris, her husband, who represented the pharaohs. Isis, then, signifies the power behind the throne. She contains or houses that power. She symbolizes form, while the pharaoh represents the essence (or invisible energy). Cancer, of course, functions as the home, the container of our emotional essence. It provides us with boundaries, the form required for our maturation and growth. From our earliest days, for example, we receive sustenance and a strengthening immune system from our mother's breast milk, which acts like a wall, a shell, to protect us from the microbic dangers of the outside world. Like the crab that carries its home on its back everywhere it moves, we carry our family's genetic and environmental influence everywhere we go.

This Isis archetype drives us to confront our mother issues. On the Monday of the week you dedicate to Cancer, call your mother for a regular "hello, how are you" conversation. Immediately after you hang up, sit down for a meditation. Visualize yourself sending light from the moon down to your mother. Forgive her for all the mistakes she might have made and request her forgiveness for any offense you might have committed. Then call her again. This time, tell her how grateful you are for everything that she has done for you. Note the difference between the two conversations. (If you do not have a living mother or mother figure, practice the meditation without the phone calls. If you like, you can invent and write down the dialogue of the two phone calls from your imagination.)

THE CHARIOT: *Merkavah*

The symbolism of the Chariot, the Tarot card assigned to Cancer, crosses space, time, and cultures. The earliest mention of the chariot in Judaism dates back to the sixth century B.C.E. In the wake of the destruction of the first temple in Jerusalem (586 B.C.E.), the royalty and intellectual leadership of the Jewish nation was exiled to Babylonia. There, on the rivers of Babylon (again, Cancer the symbol of water), the prophet Ezekiel experienced an extraordinary vision. He perceived a marvelous chariot descending from the sky. Early Kabbalists called this apparition the *working of the Merkavah* (Merkavah means "chariot" in Hebrew). For the Kabbalists, the revelation of Ezekiel solved a problematic issue. How could a mystic, who works with the powers of visualization, harness an image of God who is formless, limitless, and all mighty? Any image of God surely would be inadequate. Kabbalists balked at depicting God as man or woman, old or young, big or small, because they understood that God is One, all encompassing, everything. We cannot imagine an older, white-bearded man as God, as Michelangelo drew for the Vatican, because God is not masculine and most certainly the infinite God does not look like a stern, all-too-finite man. But the Chariot conferred a perfect image—the representation of the throne of God. The chariot evoked the place that contained the essence of God, a home of compassion, mercy, and unconditional love.

This depiction of God also seems to jibe with Tibetan Buddhist dogma, which considers the Buddha of Compassion as the highest manifestation of enlightenment. You might want to note that His Holiness the Fourteenth Dalai Lama, the man considered to be the reincarnation of the Buddha of Compassion, is a Cancer with a Cancer rising.

The Hindu epic Bhagavad Gita similarly portrays the god Krishna as a charioteer who advises Arjuna, the princely hero, on the mystical aspects of life. The instruction occurs in the chariot as the duo debate the merits of Arjuna's war against his relatives. Here again the chariot reveals its cross-cultural connection to God's wisdom in a story centered on family dysfunction. Cancer, of course, is the sign of family.

In modern life, the chariot of old has been transformed into your car. Connect this week to your personal chariot on a spiritual level. Take a look at the car's condition—

its paint, engine, and cleanliness. It mirrors the condition of your own body. What do you have piled up in the backseat? Junk, trash, piles of work, music? The stuff reveals much about how you conduct and approach life. Spend time this week tidying up your car inside and out. Treat it like you want to treat your higher essence or soul. The energy you invest in this task will return to you threefold.

As the first water sign, Cancer also governs all sorts of mystical journeys. Deep, wavering, and reflective, water is esoteric code for psychic visions. Amid their quest for the fourteenth reincarnation of the Dalai Lama, the Tibetan lamas camped on the shores of a crystal clear lake high on the Tibetan plateau, waiting to receive a vision that would direct their search. In the Native American traditions, some tribes gazed at waterfalls to access supernatural wisdom and predict the future. In the Western epic of King Arthur, the Lady of Avalon, the mystical lady of the lake, gives Arthur (the hero) the sword (the powers of Gemini) that initiates his journey to unify his kingdom. The access code for all these mystical powers conferred by water and Cancer is simple yet profound: we need to feel to open the gates of heaven. The password to the spiritual realm is spelled *compassion*.

Your Cancer house describes the area in your life in which you will locate your throne, the chariot that can carry you on your quest to self-realization and success. Place a fountain in the area that represents where you have Cancer in your chart. If Caner sits in your first house, then spend time immersed in water yourself. If it lies in your house of money, then place a fountain at work. If you find Cancer in your seventh house of relationships, then put a fountain in your bedroom.

Most crucially, deliberately extend four acts of compassion to others this week. By showing compassion, you will learn a great deal about forgiveness and acceptance.

This week, call your mother for a regular conversation. After hanging up, sit down for a meditation. Visualize yourself sending moonlight down to your mother. Forgive her for all the mistakes she might have made and request her forgiveness for any offense you might have committed. Then call her again and tell her how grateful you are for everything she has done for you. Note the difference between the two conversations. (If you do not have a living mother or mother figure, practice the meditation without the calls. If you like, you can imagine and write down the dialogue of the calls.)

Connect this week to your personal chariot. Take a look at your car's condition—its paint, engine, and cleanliness. It mirrors the condition of your own body. The stuff you have piled up in the backseat reveals much about how you conduct and approach life. Tidy up your car inside and out. Treat it like you want to treat your higher essence or soul. The energy you invest in this task will return to you threefold.

SURFING THE WAVES OF THE MOON

In many traditions, the moon represents the mother who awards us light and love in the darkest moment of our lives. New scientific theories argue that the moon's influence over the earth's great bodies of water facilitated life on land. The tides, the theory postulates, washed the earth's tiny organisms, which first evolved in shallow pools for about 2.7 billion years, up onto dry land and then sucked them back into the water. After awhile, these creatures evolved to survive in both places, and then finally, some branched out to live exclusively, like us, as air-breathing creatures on land. Astrologically, this theory fits because Cancer (moon and water) is the sign of birth and life.

With words like *moonstruck* and *lunatic*, humans have long associated emotions and moodiness with the moon. In Judaism, most of the holidays are determined by the moon. Passover is celebrated on the Full Moon that follows the Spring Equinox; Rosh Hashana, the Jewish New Year and the date of birth of Adam and Eve, fall on the New Moon in Libra. Under the influence of the moon, we reconnect to our more emotional and instinctual nature. We suppress our intellect and reason and become one with the nurturing, life-giving power of Mother Nature. The moon provides a definitive structure of twenty-eight days for fulfilling your wishes and manifesting what you need in life. As long as you learn to surf the ebb and flow of the moon's energies, they can help you to avoid mood swings. The three powers of the great goddess are reflected in three phases of the moon: the waxing moon (the beautiful Virgin), the full moon (the loving Mother), and the waning moon (the Sage).

At the new moon—a night when the moon is completely hidden by the shadow of the earth—start a project. It could be a new relationship, sending out a resume for a new job, writing a book or business plan, or embarking on a health regimen. As the moon grows, it will assume the shape of a capital D (☽), and during these two weeks, you will add effort to your project. When the moon becomes full, pull back and reflect. Take a rest and evaluate your progress. Then, as the moon wanes and takes the shape of a C (☾), edit, cut, or rearrange your project. This marks the time to let go of relationships or blockages that obstruct your progress. Working according to this schedule turns you into your own astrologer. It attunes you to the mechanics of the heavens. You add things to your life as the moon adds light, and you edit things from your life as the moon subtracts light. Since the moon also governs instinct and emotions, be sure to invest your project with feeling.

Place a fountain in the area that represents where you have Cancer in your chart. If Cancer sits in your first house, spend time immersed in water yourself. If it lies in your house of money, place a fountain at work. If you find Cancer in your seventh house of relationships, put a fountain in your bedroom.

THE JEWEL IN THE LOTUS: COMPASSION AND UNCONDITIONAL LOVE

Cancer embodies forgiveness. Just as our mothers ideally love us no matter what we do and our family ideally supports us without question, Cancer teaches us to give and forgive unconditionally. Tibetan Buddhism has made an art of compassion. For centuries the wise men and women of Tibet have formulated and perfected spiritual techniques to help the human race amplify this hallowed trait. *Tibet* translates as "the land of snow," and snow, of course, is composed of water (Cancer). The Tibetans chant *Om Mani Padme Hum*, which means "the jewel is in the lotus," to generate the energy of compassion. The jewel is the pearl, the gemstone of Cancer, and the lotus grows in water.

During the week you dedicate to Cancer and compassion, you might benefit from reading *The Art of Happiness* by the Dalai Lama. (Since Cancer governs your car, you might want to grab the audiobook version and listen to it while you pilot your chariot.) Unfortunately, many Tibetans, who so love their homeland, were driven from their home by the Chinese invasion fifty years ago. But that sacrifice led to the dissemination of the teaching of compassion to the rest of the planet. It's as if the Tibetans had to demonstrate to the world the authentic value of their teaching by forgiving the nation that stole their freedom and their land. As the Dalai Lama says, to give compassion towards another person, you must first experience suffering. That pain, the loftiest teaching of Cancer explains, will drive you to be kind, loving, and forgiving of another because you will understand the terrible cost of that pain.

One of my clients is a yoga teacher who always enjoyed perfect health. When her students came to her with backaches or any physical trouble, she brushed them off with some meaningless spiritual gobbledygook like, "You created that back problem yourself. You attracted it to compensate for some wrongdoing or spiritual lack." Then one day, she bent to pick up her yoga mat, and snap, her back went out. For two weeks, she could not teach. She could barely move. In the wake of this dreadful suffering, she changed her attitude toward others. Today, when someone complains of back pain, she sympathizes and nurtures them with extra attention and love.

Cancer Nelson Mandela suffered years in prison to secure justice for his people (his family).

I believe mothers suffer such intolerable pain during childbirth for this same reason. This agony not only helps them to give birth to the baby but also to compassion and unconditional love. Our salty tears, shed when we suffer, also remind us of the same lesson of Cancer, the ruler of the salty ocean, the esoteric symbol of emotion. The location of Cancer in your chart is the area in which you might suffer the pain of birthing your compassion. This suffering is not a curse. It makes you a deep and compassionate being.

How to Get Along with Cancers

- Cancers need to be needed. Don't be afraid to show your vulnerability. They will appreciate you when you bare your emotional side.

- Show patience with Cancers. They are notoriously slow. If you live with a Cancer, afford him or her enough time for preparation before you go out.

- Visit your Cancer friends in their homes. Bring something for their homes. Compliment them as hosts.

- Do not try to make Cancers feel guilty. Guilt is their job. They will react in a disproportionately distressing manner whenever you try to make them feel bad.

- If a Cancer friend or family member is moving his or her home or office, offer to help. Just as the hermit crab becomes most vulnerable when it is looking for a new shell, so does the Cancer.

- Try to get along with the Cancers' family members. Even if they complain about their family, respond with impartiality. No matter what, do not slander those family members.

- Nourish, feed, love, and listen to them. Cancers eat up emotional support.

- If a Cancer withdraws into his or her shell, drop everything to talk. Encourage the Cancer to discuss the issue that caused the emotional pain. Show compassion to these people who bring us compassion. Sometimes *they* need to know that they are loved and looked after.

The location of Cancer in your chart is the area in which you might suffer the pain of birthing your compassion. This suffering is not a curse. It makes you a deep and compassionate being.

THE DARK SIDE OF THE FORCE: CANCER

The dark side of Cancer stems from this heightened capacity for nurturing and compassion. I call it the Jewish mother syndrome, which can be described as a mixture of attachment to and overprotectiveness of the person you feel so much for. It can generate guilt and lead to a destructive codependency. Imagine a nurse who strives superhumanly to tend to her patient. Now imagine that she falls in love with the patient. That emotion might lead her to root against his complete recovery because a cured patient will result in his release from the hospital, and out the door will walk her love. Cancers must recognize that old ladies who do not want to cross the road should not be forced across just because the Cancer feels compelled to help.

Cancers can also fall prey to passive-aggressiveness. Like the hermit crab, the symbol of Cancer, they tend to scuttle about sideways. Instead of telling us what they need, they try to make us feel what they want, sometimes in convoluted and alienating ways. They tend to behave as if we are all telepathically connected, and when we don't automatically know what they want, they will withdraw into their shell and make us feel bad. Cancers often need to learn that most of us aren't psychic twenty-four hours a day. And they should take care to tell us directly what they want.

THE HEBREW LETTER *Chet*

According to Kabbalah, the Hebrew letter *Chet* radiates the energy of Cancer. *Chet* translates as "a wall" or "fence." This letter symbolizes the shell of the crab, the walls of the city that protect and secure the population, the fence around the family home. *Chet* is also the first letter of the Hebrew word *Chava*, which means "Eve"—the mother of life (a powerful parallel to Isis). Just as Cancer embodies the energy of the Great Mother, the letter *Chet* symbolizes birth.

Meditate with the letter *Chet* for help with fertility (of children, ideas, or projects). Use it too to acquire your dream house, to heal family issues, to generate compassion, and to calm mood swings.

THE PARTS OF THE BODY

Cancer governs all the parts of your body that house or contain any organ—your ribcage, for example, which protects and secures your heart. Interestingly, while the ribcage relates to mother Cancer, the protected heart corresponds to the next sign, Leo, the child. Cancer oversees the membranes of all our cells, which function as houses for the vital substances inside. Cancer also governs the stomach and the womb (the latter the organ that protects the fetus and gives it its first home). This association explains why we use the phrase "gut feeling" to describe inexplicable emotions or hunches. In other words, the organs tied to sensitive and psychic Cancer serve as a barometer for our intuition. Ulcers and stomach pain emerge from bottling up our emotions (Cancer). Try to avoid passive-aggressiveness and eating yourself up from within by expressing your feelings directly.

To maintain healthy Cancer energy, drink ten cups of water a day. Water will not only cleanse and heal your body, but it will also help you to become more psychic, intuitive, and compassionate.

THE COLOR OF CANCER: YELLOW-ORANGE

The color of Cancer is orangey yellow or a muted dark yellow. Wear this color when you want to emphasize the energy of compassion, nurturing, and motherhood. And make sure you place this color all around your home.

WHAT SHOULD I FOCUS ON IN THE WEEK OF CANCER?

The key phrase "I feel" defines Cancer. This week, focus on your emotions. Try this week to slow down so that you have time and space to feel. It is also a good time to remodel or spruce up your home and to spend time near bodies of water.

Our mother and family members often generate powerful emotions, both sweet and a touch bitter too. In times of trouble, we cry for help from Mother: *Mama Mia* (Italian), *Mommy* (English), *Ima'le* (Hebrew), *Annee* (Turkish). It might seem weird that we cry out for our mother for protection rather than for our father, the supposed strongman of the house. But astrologically it makes perfect sense.

As always, seek out synchronicities related to Cancer, especially those that occur in the astrological house ruled by Cancer, and try to interpret the symbolic and practical messages directed to you. The symbols of Cancer include the crab, shells, houses, family, mothers, mother figures, walls, fences, Tibet, compassion, feelings, tears, the stomach, the womb, birth, the chariot, your car, orange-yellow, pearls, water, ocean, rivers, lakes, the moon, suffering, guilt, gut feelings (intuition), memories, and unconditional love.

Your Cancer Week Checklist

- Look into the fears that prevent you from feeling secure.
- Do something special for your house.
- Apply feng shui principles to your house and office.
- Work on the affirmation of Cancer: "I am loved by my family and nurtured by the universe. I forgive those who have wronged me and ask forgiveness from those I have injured."
- Try to think back to your earliest memory. Picture that tiny you back then and imagine yourself hugging and nurturing that little kid.
- Call your mother, meditate on forgiveness, and call her again.
- Watch the changing light of the moon from night to night.
- Meditate on the letter *Chet*.
- Wear orange-yellow or a combination of the two colors.
- Clean your car.
- Commit four acts of compassion.
- Drink lots of water.

THE RITUAL OF CANCER: FENG SHUI, A SPIRITUAL MAKEOVER FOR YOUR HOME

The Chinese apply special attention to their homes and living environment. They developed a system called *feng shui*, a term that means "wind and water," to help them to live in harmony with their environment and to transform their living spaces into temples. I am not surprised that the culture that built the Great Wall (the letter *Chet*) also provided us with a spiritual science of spatial arrangement and home design. What follows is merely an elementary introduction to this complex and beautiful tradition. For more information, consult one of the many feng shui books designed to prompt a spiritual makeover of your life and home.

Feng shui places your house or office space on a *Bagua*, an eight-sided diagram (figure 5). Each of the sections of the *Bagua* represents an aspect of your life. For example, in the section that relates to relationships, you might want to place a painting of two people hugging or an object that was given to you by your lover. In the money corner, you might want to install a fountain, which will symbolize a constant

Figure 5: The Bagua

stream of abundance. The whole process simply attempts to accentuate the flow of energy that will deliver good fortune to that area of your life.

Overlay a plan of any space—for your entire house or office, your bedroom, for example—atop the *Bagua*. Position the main entrance of your space on the diagram so that it lines up the words *front door* on figure 5. If possible, use the room that falls in the "partnership" area of the diagram as your master bedroom, and the room that sits near "wealth" as your office. It is often impossible to move rooms to fit the diagram, but you can then work with the *Bagua* and add and subtract objects to any space to fix your spatial problems. One woman, for example, told me that she had not had any success with relationships since she moved into a new house. It turned out that the room she had dedicated to storing her junk fell smack in the corner of relationships. We cleared out the storage and moved her bed into that room. Six weeks later she started to date a new man. Within a year, she was engaged. Miracles do happen. Sometimes they just need a helping hand.

FAMOUS CANCERS

His Holiness the Fourteenth Dalai Lama, Alfred Kinsey, George Orwell, Helen Keller, Princess Diana, Hermann Hesse, Mel Brooks, George W. Bush, Bill Cosby, Tom Cruise, Harrison Ford, Jean Cocteau, Frida Kahlo, Gustav Mahler, Wole Soyinka, Rembrandt, Nelson Mandela, Ernest Hemingway, Carlos Santana, and Robin Williams.

♌

Leo: The King and Queen

July 23 to August 22

Key Phrase: "I will" — authority

General Qualities: Childlike, playful, fun-loving, generous, loyal, powerful, attractive, regal, authoritative, charismatic, and creative

Dark Side: Willful, dominating, egotistical, stubborn, controlling, and fixed in their opinions

Element: Fixed fire

Planet: The sun

Day: Sunday

Theme: The dynasty

Parts of the Body: Heart and spine

Color: Gold and yellow

Gemstone: Tiger's eye

Musical note: E

Hebrew Letter: *Tet* ט

Kabbalistic Meaning of Letter: The serpent

Path in the Tree of Life: Path 8, connecting Mercy and Severity

Tarot Card: Strength

Movies: *Braveheart, The Lion King, The Chronicles of Narnia, The Fifth Element*

Famous Personalities: Bill Clinton, Napoleon Bonaparte, Madonna, Alfred Hitchcock, Fidel Castro, and Carl Jung

Affirmation: "I feel strong, vital, and happy. I can create my own destiny and manifest all my wishes. I am ready to share my joy and love with all who surround me."

OVERVIEW

Like a king or queen who consolidates the power of many lords, Leo holds the zodiac together. The sign of former President Bill Clinton, Madonna, and Napoleon, Leo catalyzes many attractive aspects of life, such as love, romance, children, happiness, playfulness, sports, gambling, entertainment, and fun. The energy of Leo commands the center of attention and prods us to uncover the child inside all of us. Leo teaches self-confidence, creativity, and the connection to the spiritual. In Leo, you will focus on love, happiness, and playfulness. You will practice being creative and seeing with the innocent eyes of a child. You will learn to identify the beauty in life and find techniques to enhance your charisma. Leo also offers the opportunity to exercise your will while feeling like you deserve to receive all the gifts life can offer.

THE TERRITORY OF LEO

Life isn't about finding yourself. Life is about creating yourself.
—GEORGE BERNARD SHAW, A LEO

Just as the sun has shined its light upon us for billions of years, the fixed fire of Leo serves as a lighthouse to the rest of the zodiac signs. Leo is the fixed sign of summer. It represents the sustaining power of masculine heat, vitality, and pure energy. In summer, the solar disk, ruler of Leo, looks like a mane shining upon the earth, emanating its irrepressible radiance. The most powerful of all the signs, Leo possesses the capacity to contain the most light. This ability to channel light (both physical and spiritual) crowned Leo as the king of the astrological system. Arriving when school is out, Leo rules fun, happiness, and children, as evidenced by all the kids running around like tiny ambassadors of God, making sure that we don't take ourselves too seriously.

Leo's fixed fire represents the everlasting flame of God. In the old temple in Jerusalem, the seven-candlestick lamp, always burning, symbolized God's eternal presence on the earth. Gold, the metal of Leo, epitomizes perfection in many traditions. Alchemy endeavors to transmute lead into gold through a harmonizing of the four elements. First you take fire (Aries), then add earth (Taurus), then add some air (Gemini), and finally you dissolve the mixture with water (Cancer). They all blend seamlessly in Leo, the fifth sign—the fifth element. It marks the ideal accumulation of all the previous signs. This logic explains why Leo rules the heart, which has four chambers, one for each element. Leo arrives to impart the ultimate life lesson: it's all about love and Light (spirituality).

Leo, the king, personifies the father. Make an effort this week to connect to your father or some other authority figure, like your boss. Since the king demands respect from all his subjects, try to present your father with as much love and respect as you can offer without flattery.

YOUR OWN PRIVATE LEO

Your house of Leo indicates where you need to roar and show yourself. It marks the place in which you can act like a king or a queen. In fact, here you can actually be a king. You grow in this kingdom through spirituality and through giving and receiving vast amounts of love. Direct fun and creativity—act like a child—to the area of your life ruled by Leo.

Leo in Your First House (Your Rising Sign): You are a natural-born leader, blessed with charisma. You need to keep the child in you alive to express yourself most fully. You have a great deal of vitality and happiness to share with the world. In the week of Leo, focus on nurturing your self-love, your creativity, your personal development, and your health.

Leo in the Second House: You need to be proud of your income as well as your talents. Confidence in your own gifts and skills will lead to increased prosperity. You are an adept entertainer and a performer. Try to maintain a playful, childlike attitude when dealing with money and finance. In the week of Leo, pay attention to your finances, talents, and self-worth.

Leo in the Third House: You are proud of your intellect as well as your writing and communication skills. You express a dramatic and creative communication style that can either inspire or intimidate those around you. You also have a strong connection to siblings and neighbors. During the week of Leo, focus on your relatives, communication skills, and business.

Leo in the Fourth House: You ought to live in a big, spacious house—and decorate it like a castle. Your home serves as your fortress. You are proud of your heritage and loyal to your family members and your roots. This week, highlight your home, family, and mother.

Leo in the Fifth House: You have an enormous talent in entertainment and sports. You love to be the center of attention, and you get along well with children and creative, playful people. You possess the capacity to fall in love completely in a way that not many can. I think you invented the phrase "head over heels." In the week of Leo, make sure to experience love to the fullest.

Leo in the Sixth House: You do not take kindly to orders and commands, and so you had better be the boss or work for yourself. You need to be proud of what you do. In matters of health, take care of your heart and back. You tend to do too much, to overtrain or strain your body. This week, pay special attention to your workspace, diet, and health.

Leo in the Seventh House: You are attracted to colorful, entertaining, and creative individuals, but they can sometimes turn out to be self-centered and childish. You tend to be proud of your significant others and look up to them. During the week of Leo, make sure that you nourish and protect your partnerships and significant others.

Leo in the Eighth House: You attract bossy and powerful partners and business associates. You do well by dealing with other people's talents and money. In matters of sexuality, you are also attracted to strong and dominating people. In the week of Leo, focus on your sexuality, intimacy, and spiritual transformation.

Leo in the Ninth House: You are proud of your philosophy and outlook on life. Traveling to different cultures and countries can help you to find love. You are attracted to rituals and ceremonies from foreign traditions. During the week of Leo, try to travel or study other cultures.

Leo in the Tenth House: You need to be proud of what you do for your career. You can be an influential leader in your professional field. You also enjoy a talent for entertaining, and you relish standing in the center of attention. Focus your time and efforts on your career. You can achieve growth and success this week.

Leo in the Eleventh House: You have many entertaining and interesting friends, who unfortunately tend to be somewhat self-absorbed. You are a loyal friend and demand the same loyalty from others. You often serve as the leader of your community, and people admire you for your strength. During the week of Leo, focus on nurturing and developing friendships.

Leo in the Twelfth House: You might have been a celebrity or famous person in a past lifetime. But you probably took too much credit for your fame without realizing that you were simply channeling God's gifts. This lifetime, the road to success and recognition looks long and cluttered with obstacles. Your father might have been your child in a previous incarnation, and you might experience unresolved issues with authority figures. During the week of Leo, try to take time off work to focus on your spirituality and the letting go of old psychological and emotional blocks.

DRAMA QUEENS (AND KINGS)

Drama makes the Leo a Leo. (Leo also rules entertainment and movies.) When we approach the king or a queen, we are required to say, "Your highness." We bow, curtsy, and submit to innumerous formalities. Why bother? Doesn't the king know that he's a king and the queen know she's a queen? Why does he insist on a scepter, a throne, and a stretch limo? Why does she wear a bejeweled crown? Isn't a regular hat sufficient? And why a palace? What's wrong with a real big house? Don't they have enough confidence to know who they are?

No, and that's precisely the point. Leos, just like real-life celebrities (and some spiritual gurus too) constantly need to hear how great they are. From everyone. Like children, they demand constant reassurance and immediate reinforcement.

Kabbalistic astrology reveals a vital component of this entire spiritual system—and indeed of this entire life—in what I call the reverse theory. Leos might pretend to be confident, but they are not. In fact, souls who choose to reincarnate as Leos (or with a heavy Leo emphasis

Leo, the king, personifies the father. Make an effort this week to connect to your father or some other authority figure, like your boss. Since the king demands respect from all his subjects, try to present your father with as much love and respect as you can offer without flattery.

in their charts) do so in order to develop and acquire self-confidence. Remember the courage-seeking lion in *The Wizard of Oz*? Taurus is the sign of art, but do you think the Taurus is an artist? No. She is born a Taurus to learn how to become an artist. Are Capricorns patient? Hardly. They are actually the only sign deficient in patience. And so all of us opt for a particular sign to train ourselves in the archetype we lack most.

What is the color of grass? Let me give you a clue: it's not green. Colors—just like the signs—represent a certain frequency of light waves. Grass appears green because it contains all of the colors (or light frequencies) except for green. When the white light that contains the entire color spectrum hits the grass blades, the grass absorbs all of the colors it contains, but the green, which is not present and therefore not absorbed, bounces off to your retina. Same thing with a red apple—it represents all the colors besides red. Gemini, the sign in charge of communication, simply decided at some point that it would be easier to say "an apple is red" instead of "an apple is all the colors except red," even though it's not true (once again, Gemini and their lies).

Leo, then, embodies all the signs except for Leo. And because it is inefficient and tiresome to say "all the signs besides Leo," or "all the signs except for Virgo," we simply call them Leos and Virgos. Leos need all that attention—the pomp, drama, crown, and throne—because they lack self-confidence, the very quality that they are supposed to rule. Same goes for you. The characteristics of your sign highlight the qualities you have come here to master. You must work to assimilate those qualities because you were actually born without them. Your primary archetype—whatever it is—simply reveals your potential, your destiny. It is entirely up to you to reclaim it. Leo teaches that the cosmic navigator—no matter his or her sign—stands as a person who sails toward self-actualization and self-discovery. Now that every inch of the earth has been mapped and displayed on the Internet for all, navigators can't really sail off somewhere for novel adventure and new discoveries. Instead, we journey inward, back to the source, back to the One. Ideally, Leos help to show us the way by reminding us of the unifying and everlasting love they hold in their hearts.

Leo encourages us to become a king or queen of our kingdom. And most of all, a king requires a mammoth sense of entitlement. Speak out loud the affirmation: "I am a good person, and I deserve love, abundance, and happiness." Then act on the key phrase for Leo: "I will." What is your will? Make a list of the things you want from all the people around you. Instead of writing a will for your death, write a will for your life. What do you want from the universe?

LEO LOVE

Leo rules the heart and the spine. Kabbalists refer to the Torah as *Lev*, Hebrew for "heart," because it begins and ends with the Hebrew letters representing *l* and *v*. This nickname suggests that we must understand the wisdom of the ancient testament through the heart rather than the mind. The ancient Egyptian hieroglyphs always depicted humans with their chests facing forward and their faces turned in profile. This odd composition isn't a sign of the primitiveness of Egyptian artists but a poetic statement about the supremacy of a person's heart over his brain.

The spine also occupies a central place in the myths and spiritual doctrines of many cultures. In Exodus, God tells Moses that God's wonders will be channeled through Moses' shepherd rod. The rod, or staff, serves as the primary tool of wizards, while witches deploy a more practical staff, namely their broomsticks. The staff symbolizes the spinal cord. Kundalini yoga teaches that a sacred coiled serpent resides at the base of the spine. Through yoga and spiritual practice, we aim to awaken the serpent so that it travels up the spine to the crown chakra to create a state of enlightenment. In other words, Leo (heart and spine) functions to allow our access to the spirit of God. It required five signs—all four elements—before we enjoyed a clear channel to divine love. And when we channel that Light, when we love, the zodiac asserts, we become a Leo, the king of our destiny.

Nearly every spiritual tradition insists love is the way to know God. Rumi, the great Sufi and poet, describes his relationship to God as the longing for his beloved. In the enchanting mystical saga *The Chronicles of Narnia*, C. S. Lewis made his main protagonist a lion named Aslan (*Aslan* is Turkish for "lion"). And in this tale, Aslan the lion (the symbol of Leo) represents the spirit of love. Leo also represents the inner child and children in general. When we fall in love, we usually become more childlike and creative. Everything, even mundane walks down the street or grocery shopping, transforms into great fun. Leo is the king of love and enlightenment. Leo energy is transformative and magic. And for that reason Leo was granted dominion over all the other archetypes.

Leo in your chart highlights the area of your life in which you can become a beam of Light and a channel for Love. It indicates where an open heart and an open love will grant you access to strength, courage, and success.

THE GOLDEN CHILD

Leos are charming. They love to play, party, and have fun. Like little children, they relish attention, and they entertain endlessly, which explains why Leo oversees movies, theaters, all forms of performance, creativity, sports, and gambling. In his book *Thus Spoke Zarathustra*, Friedrich Nietzsche explicates the three stages of the soul. We all start out as a camel, a beast of burden, subject to the will of a master. Then we evolve into a lion (Leo), who is yet subject to his own will and desires. Though the lion is too proud to serve anyone, he is still enslaved to himself. Kabbalah provides us with a way to transcend our obsession with our own will, our self-imposed slavery to ego. When we place God's will before our own, Kabbalah assures us, we can then ascend to the next stage of development. Jesus, an adept Kabbalist himself, summarized this teaching, "Thy will be done."

Leo encourages us to become a king or queen of our kingdom. And most of all, a king requires a mammoth sense of entitlement. Speak out loud the affirmation: "I am a good person, and I deserve love, abundance, and happiness." Then act on the key phrase for Leo: "I will." What is your will? Make a list of the things you want from all the people around you. Instead of writing a will for your death, write a will for your life. What do you want from the universe?

The Tarot card called Strength represents Leo to underscore this core spiritual axiom. Only the strong, the truly brave and invincible, possess the courage to surrender their inner Leo, their own will. In Nietzsche's scheme, we move to the final stage the second we stop being slaves to our own will and ego. Then, out of the lion emerges what Nietzsche called "the Child"—the golden child, a perfect being subject to none and yet congruent with all. This child is not childish, but he or she is often childlike, laughing and playing with life. Many of the most eminent spiritual leaders laugh all the time. They are never afraid to look foolish or joke playfully with their devotees.

Leo marks the home of your inner child (your higher soul). And your Leo house can connect you most directly to God's will. You can become a spiritual master in this area of your life, shining most gloriously whenever you act like a child and cultivate fun. Success comes with creativity and playfulness. Be silly in this area of life, and you will be taken more seriously.

One woman who had Leo in her house of work realized that she had repressed her inner child and playfulness at work as she tried diligently to fit in with her stern coworkers. She also had failed to win a promotion or a raise. During the week of Leo, she brought a big stuffed lion puppet to her cubicle to remind her of her innate humor and goofiness. Suddenly everyone around her changed their mood too, smiling and joking with her about the silly lion. Six months later, she found herself promoted and given a large salary bump. The only drawback, she reported, was that she had to move to a new department, leaving behind all the lovable people she had so enjoyed entertaining with her funny puppet shows. As a parting gift, she left them her happy lion.

YOUR BIRTHDAY: YOUR LEO DAY

From this day forward, promise to celebrate your birthday, always, every single year. Forget about the whole "fear of aging" nonsense. Never keep your birthday a secret. It can actually be dangerous. At some point, nearly all of us begin to suffer issues with our advancing age. I once was asked to cast a chart for a woman who refused to give me the year of her birth. She was dumbfounded that I could not formulate her chart unless she confessed her age. She agreed only after I swore in the name of all the gods and goddesses alive and dead that I would never reveal her secret.

So why, with so much pride and pain at stake, should we celebrate another tick up on the age meter? Because your birthday represents your Leo day. On this date, the sun returns to the spot it occupied at your moment of birth. It lights up your chart in a primal and powerful way. Instead of having one sun, you metaphorically have two—the actual, present-day sun that travels through all of the signs each year on top of the sun etched in your natal chart. Astrologers call this the solar conjunction. Sounds great, right? Sunny and warm like the weather in San Diego. But it is also perilous. Too much sun—two fiery suns—can make it too, too hot.

From an astrological viewpoint, your birthday is one of the most challenging days of the year (regardless of your age). The two suns bake you like an oven and create unrealistic expectations. You become a double Leo, since the sun rules Leo, doubly in need of attention, adulation, and deference to the king (you). Therefore, many traditions since our earliest days have constructed rituals (again Leo) to help us cope with this harsh day, rituals that nudge you to feel accepted and loved, special and regal. You receive gifts (homage to the king). Your friends call to wish you a happy birthday or buy you dinner, lunch, breakfast, drinks, and snacks (off with the heads of those who forget!). You stand in the center of the room as your loved ones present you with a flaming cake. Everyone snaps your photo as if you were a celebrity. On this day, you are a celebrity. So don't get burned by the heat of double sun. Celebrate.

Even if your birthday does not fall during this week of Leo, you need to become a Leo anyway. Buy yourself a gift. Send a message to the universe that you are special and deserve to receive. The universe will acknowledge your entitlement and soon present additional gifts as well.

How to Get Along with Leos

- Be happy and playful. Being interesting and nurturing don't account for much with this sign. Leos value fun.

- Love Leos, adore Leos, and make them feel as if they are royalty.

- Give the Leos as much attention as you possibly can. They beam when they feel they are the center of your universe.

- Offer as many compliments and affirmations as possible.

- Initiate adventure and risky activities. These outings do not have to be as extreme as jumping off Niagara Falls, but they should be exciting.

- Leos need ritual. If possible, establish habitual activities with them. These rituals might include anything from calling at 1 P.M. every Tuesday or going to yoga class together the first Sunday of every month.

- Be a loyal friend. Leos cannot stand and can rarely forgive a traitor. Throughout history, betrayal of your king or queen has resulted in severe punishment. Leos tend to make the best friends and the worst enemies.

- Allow Leos to assert their will. Try to offer your help with *their* projects and enterprises.

THE DARK SIDE OF THE FORCE: LEO

Now I take a big risk. Daring to mention the flaws of Leo is akin to high treason, at least in the eyes of all the Leos out there. But, with all due deference to our regal friends, their fragile confidence means that they can't take criticism. Remember the Queen of Hearts from *Alice in Wonderland?* Whoever dared to defy her will received the typical Leo response, "Off with his head!"

Additionally, Leos tend to overgive, and they sometimes have difficulty receiving from others. Sure, they love to receive adulation, but their pride—their propensity to hide their inner self-doubt and inadequacy (a king can't show weakness after all)—makes it hard for them to reveal that they actually need something. They often can't receive help without feeling that they now owe you something in return. In the first scene of *The Godfather*, a man visits the Don and asks for a favor. He gets his wish but for a price. One day in the future, the Godfather will ask him to do something in return. It's not a great bargain. You never know what the payment will entail or when the debt will be called in. It's like the lord of old who received land and wealth from the king, yet he knows that someday he will be obligated to fight in the king's battles, whether he believes in them or not. Leos give but with a condition. And that condition is loyalty. Since they exact this dicey deal from others, they squirm a bit when receiving. They don't relish the idea of ceding some power over them to you. It therefore is best to give to a Leo

Even if your birthday does not fall during this week of Leo, buy yourself a gift. Send a message to the universe that you are special and deserve to receive. The universe will acknowledge your entitlement and soon present additional gifts as well.

unconditionally, so they don't suspect your motives. And Leos, more than anyone, need to work on doing the same.

As the sign of children, Leos can also be childish, self-centered, demanding, and controlling. They want it—usually praise, love, and attention—right now. In a fit of anger, one Leo I knew called me up to tell me that I was not to call her. I hadn't even called, but she needed to be the one to issue the final command. Leos also display the childish propensity to fall in love with love rather than with the person they supposedly love. The feeling of love so intoxicates that they actually forget about their partner. If you happen to be that partner, well, you need to remind the Leo that you exist.

One last little childish chink in the crown, I promise, and then we can go back to adoring the Leo as he and she deserves. Napoleon syndrome represents a Leo-based neurosis that occurs when an individual perceives himself as physically, spiritually, intellectually, or emotionally small. This person then attempts to compensate for that inadequacy by aggressively conquering and controlling every environment, as if to say, "I'll show you who's small." Napoleon succeeded for a while, crowning himself emperor and conquering most of Europe, until the world grew weary of his antics and locked him up on a small island. The cure: give the Leo some praise and affirmation. And, on a personal note to all Leo readers, I thank your royal highness for leaving me with my head.

THE HEBREW LETTER *Tet*

The Hebrew letter *Tet* represents Leo. The glyph of the letter is supposed to resemble a coiled serpent, also known as the kundalini in Sanskrit. Both Eastern and Western esoteric teachings place the ambassadors of God in symbols associated with Leo. Kabbalistic tradition contends that we can decipher the true power of the Hebrew letters by examining the first word in the Bible that starts with that letter. The first word beginning with *Tet* is *Tov*, which means "kindness," "good," or "beauty." In other words, Leo rules kindness and goodwill. This sign loves to provide us with joy and comfort. The word *Tov* appears right at the start of Genesis. God creates Light, and the verse states that God saw "that it was Good (*Tov*)." In other words, God saw that it was Leo. No wonder Leos are prone to such outsized egos. And no wonder they function as kings. They describe and embody God's Light.

Leo in your chart highlights your potential to shine kindness and beauty. The house with Leo in it is the area of your life in which people will appreciate and love you. Meditate with the letter *Tet* whenever you want to attract love, romance, playfulness, and benevolence.

THE PARTS OF THE BODY

Since Leo rules the heart, spinal cord, back, and chest, Leos (and Leo risings) tend to have large chests. They are a bit more susceptible to heart problems probably because they tend to be type-A personalities. When we have a heart attack, it is as if we are having a Leo attack. Either we don't have enough Leo energy (love, spirituality, playfulness), or we are trying to channel too much. Either way, fixing it requires a balancing of the Leo archetype. This week, put yourself on the A-list without stressing your type-A personality. Walk slowly, wait patiently in lines, and breathe deeply. The heart benefits also from aerobic workouts, so go for runs, swim, or hike at least three times.

THE COLORS OF LEO: YELLOW AND GOLD

The royal color gold is associated with Leo. Gold glimmers brilliantly to attract the eye, just as Leos like to attract attention. Wear gold jewelry and clothing to help you channel the energies of Leo. Yellow, a cousin of gold and the color of the sun and the lion's coat, also represents Leo. Make sure that you sprinkle enough yellow or gold in your house. It will attract love, happiness, and vitality.

WHAT SHOULD I FOCUS ON IN THE WEEK OF LEO?

In the week of Leo focus on having fun. Spend time with children and playful people. Take a risk and go on an adventure. (Just don't harm yourself or others.) Step into the spotlight and act, perform, or behave like a child. In addition, try to create something new in your life. This creation could fall in your work, family, love life, sex life, or wherever Leo sits in your chart.

Look for synchronicities that might direct you towards being able to express yourself and your creativity. The symbols of Leo include lions, the sun, children, celebrities, royalty figures, courage, strength, love, sports, gambling, risks, spirituality and spiritual totems, Sunday, rituals, manes of hair, gold or yellow, heart, spine, serpents, egotism, childishness, birthdays, fun, adventure, compliments, happiness, and creativity.

Your Leo Week Checklist

- Become a king or queen. Work on your sense of entitlement.
- Speak the affirmation of Leo twice a day: "I feel strong, vital, and happy. I can create my own destiny and manifest all my wishes. I am ready to share my joy and love with all who surround me."
- "My will be done!" Write your will for life. What do you want?
- Meditate on the letter *Tet*.
- Wear yellow or gold.
- Call your father, your boss, or any other authoritative person who you love.
- Let your inner child loose. Play.
- Buy yourself a birthday gift, even if it is not your birthday.
- Spend time around children.

THE RITUAL OF LEO: FINDING SOMETHING BEAUTIFUL IN EVERYTHING YOU SEE

I have been living in Hollywood for nearly a decade and have met many actors both before and after they attained fame and recognition. All of these performers share the traits of charm and energy. It seems as if the Leo inside them made them famous. How do they do it? A famous singer told me the secret. Whenever he meets someone, at a party, an interview, or on the set, he always finds "something beautiful in them that I can compliment without lying." I played devil's advocate and asked, "What happens if there is nothing beautiful about them? Not everyone is a star." He cut me short. "There is something beautiful in everyone," he said. "Some gold that shines through." I watched him do it. One day, we met a not-so-attractive man at a social gathering. After shaking his hand, the singer pointed at the man's shoes.

"These are great shoes. Where the hell did you buy them?" It was true. The shoes were unique. And the compliment worked like magic. The guy opened up to my friend, and they spent a long time talking business and shoes.

Just remember: this spell works only if you do not lie. Try this magical technique this week with every person that you encounter. Start with yourself. Use it on your partner, friends, and strangers. It will open the heart of every person that you deal with. Why? Because it makes them feel like Leos—royal, special, and majestic.

FAMOUS LEOS

The list of celebrated Leos could fill this entire book because Leos innately strive for fame and recognition. Here are but a few: Stanley Kubrick, Henry Ford, C. G. Jung, Mick Jagger, Amelia Earhart, Arnold Schwarzenegger, Jennifer Lopez, Barry Bonds, Percy Bysshe Shelley, Neil Armstrong, Lucille Ball, Mata Hari, Dustin Hoffman, Whitney Houston, Cecil B. DeMille, Alfred Hitchcock, Fidel Castro, Magic Johnson, Lawrence of Arabia, Madonna, Robert De Niro, Robert Redford, and Bill Clinton.

Leo in your chart highlights your potential to shine kindness and beauty. The house with Leo in it is the area of your life in which people will appreciate and love you. Meditate with the letter *Tet* whenever you want to attract love, romance, playfulness, and benevolence.

Virgo: The Fixer and Doer

August 23 to September 22

Key Phrase: "I analyze" — authority

General Qualities: Modest, honest, humble, discriminating, orderly, analytical, logical, responsible, altruistic, hardworking, and possessed of healing and diagnostic powers

Dark Side: Perfectionistic, obsessive-compulsive, overly critical, and paying excessive attention to small, insignificant details

Element: Mutable earth

Planet: Mercury

Day: Wednesday

Theme: Making things happen

Parts of the Body: Intestines, colon

Color: Yellow-green

Gemstone: Agate

Musical Note: F

Hebrew Letter: *Yod* י

Kabbalistic Meaning of Letter: The hand of God

Path in the Tree of Life: Path 9, connecting Mercy and Beauty

Tarot Card: The Hermit

Movies: *Elizabeth: The Virgin Queen, Elizabeth: The Golden Age, Mary Poppins, As Good as It Gets, The Sound of Music, The Name of the Rose*

Affirmation: "I am dedicated to serving humanity and to God's will. I am purified and healthy, and I am thankful to my body for helping me to manifest my potential."

OVERVIEW

Virgos fix all the snags and glitches of the zodiac. In a way, they are God's technical-support crew, ever ready to serve us all. Following childish and attention-seeking Leo, Virgo's job is to clean up the mess created by the lions and make sure the cycle continues to function smoothly. Virgo, the sign of Queen Elizabeth I and Mother Teresa, is the archetype of work, service, health, and purity. Virgo reminds us of the importance of the physical body. Diet, order, and hygiene are paramount for Virgo. This archetype also helps us to be analytical, methodical, organized, and precise. In Virgo, you will improve your work ethic and your health. You will pay attention to what you eat and find tips for improving your physical well-being. This sign will encourage you to become more self-sufficient and to release yourself from dependency and codependency.

THE TERRITORY OF VIRGO

Virgos confront an exacting toil. They must persuade King Leo, a fixed sign who is superglued to his throne, to cede his crown and relinquish power. A perpetual state of Leo would prove deadly. With the scorching sun, he would transform the world into a desert. Virgo must marshal all her cleverness to nudge the Leo aside and allow the cooler seasons to emerge. The planet Mercury, the trickster and the messenger of the gods, abets this thorny task. Ruling both Gemini and Virgo, Mercury affords these two mutable signs the eloquence and intelligence to trick Empress Taurus and King Leo into letting go of their precious domains. The Virgo must be tenacious enough to withstand the ferocious fits and roars of the lion, who inevitably resists the surrender of his throne like a recalcitrant child who refuses to go to bed. Virgo functions as the super nanny of the zodiac, firmly hustling the Leo off to sleep, and Virgo also serves as the detail-oriented editor of the Book of Life. As editors, they must ensure that one paragraph harmoniously flows into another. Without the Virgo, even the greatest story ever told would devolve into unreadable anarchy.

Some beginning astrologers find it difficult to distinguish between Virgo and Gemini since they both radiate the persuasive communicative powers of Mercury. To put it most simply: Gemini is the writer, and Virgo is the editor. Gemini, the air sign, creates the message that travels through the air like a radio wave, while Virgo, the solid earth sign, functions as the radio that makes it possible for us to hear the message.

My father, a Virgo who knows little about astrology, once offered me the most succinct summary of this dichotomy. He said that the world is divided into people who know nothing about everything (Gemini) and people who know everything about nothing (Virgo). Geminis deploy the energy of Mercury to collect a little bit of information about every possible subject (which makes them very interesting), and Virgos harness Mercury to burrow into one little slice of life (which makes them very thorough). Gemini is the telescope. Virgo is the microscope. Science needs both.

Locate your houses of Virgo and Gemini in your chart. Do you function as a microscope in the area of your life ruled by Virgo? Do you employ a telescope in the area ruled by Gemini? Some people seem to have this configuration reversed, focusing on knowing a tiny bit of everything in their house of Virgo and not much about any one subject. This disharmony with the ruling sign makes it difficult for them to attain success in that area of their life. One woman, for example, noticed that she had Virgo in her sixth house of health and diet, and yet she functioned in that house more like a Gemini. She sampled innumerable diets, jumping from one to the next to the next after just a couple of weeks. That was the wrong approach for the Virgo energy, and predictably none of these diets ever paid dividends. Then she switched to Virgo mode. She chose one diet, studied it thoroughly, and stuck with it and it alone for a long time. It proved an enormous struggle for her, but three months later she managed to fit herself into her ten-year-old jeans.

VIRGO AND HEALTH: LIFE UNDER THE MICROSCOPE

Virgos view life through a microscope. And what do you see when you look through a microscope? You likely won't notice the awesome beauty of a big Renaissance painting, but you will remark that one corner of the frame is a little bit crooked. You won't see how perfectly your newly painted wall blends with your décor, but you will notice a tiny drop of paint splattered on the carpet behind the lamp. Mostly, what you detect when you peer through the microscope are germs.

Locate your houses of Virgo and Gemini in your chart. Do you function as a microscope in the area of your life ruled by Virgo? Do you employ a telescope in the area ruled by Gemini? Or do you seem to have this configuration reversed, focusing on knowing a tiny bit of everything in your house of Virgo and not much about any one subject? If so, this disharmony with the ruling sign can make it difficult for you to attain success in that area of your life.

It was Virgo Ernest Rutherford who zoomed in closely enough on the atom to see its structure. This obsession with analyzing and dissecting everything makes the Virgo remarkably adept at locating the cause of diseases, uncovering the flaws in our diets, and cleaning and fixing all that is wrong in our lives. Virgo makes us read the fine print on our food packaging to find out if the product contains trans fats. Naturally, Virgo rules health and hygiene. Virgo's supreme organization and attention to minute details compel us to clean up our acts after the unruly, messy party of Leo. It's not always fun. But Virgo keeps us from drinking and playing ourselves to death.

My good friend Dr. Julian Neil, a psychoanalyst and a naturopath, has been on my case to change what I eat for breakfast. Before I met him, breakfast for me consisted of a cappuccino and a chocolate biscotti (which I have to admit, I do miss every so often). That changed when he explained the detailed and rather mind-numbing biology of my diet's effect on my body. In short, he proved to me that my organs would soon begin to rebel. He encouraged me to make my own organic oatmeal for breakfast every day. It took much getting used to, but this new regimen worked miracles for my health, energy, and disposition. (And here I'd always thought chocolate made people happy.) Try to eat this breakfast every day this week. You will notice wonderful changes immediately. (If you have any medical issues stemming from mental, emotional, psychic, or spiritual problems, then please check out Neil's website *www.DrJulianNeil.com*, where you will find many valuable articles and health tips.)

Try eating Virgo Organic Oatmeal every day this week. You will notice wonderful changes immediately.

Virgo Organic Oatmeal

Items needed:

A short, wide-mouthed thermos

Five organic whole grains (no rolled, processed, or flaked grains): millet, barley, rye, amaranth, and flaxseeds

Organic raw sesame and sunflower seeds

Dr. Bernard Jensen's Rice Bran Syrup

Dr. Bernard Jensen's Black Cherry Juice Concentrate (Jensen's Grape or Apple Concentrate may be substituted.)

Two organic fruits; no citrus except kiwi (You may substitute organic dried fruit with no nitrates or sulfides.)

Directions:

1. Grind 7 tablespoons of each grain (barley, millet, rye, amaranth, and flaxseed) in a (clean) coffee grinder.

2. Grind 2 tablespoons of each of the seeds (sesame and sunflower).

3. Mix the ground grains and seeds together.

4. At night, place about 3 tablespoons of the ground mixture in a wide-mouthed thermos.

5. Add boiling water to mixture while stirring it with a spoon. The mixture should be soupy in consistency, as the grains and seeds will absorb the water.

6. Seal thermos and let stand overnight.

7. In the morning, remove the cereal from the thermos and add:

    2   fruits of your choice (If you use dried fruits, you will need to add more water.)

    1   tablespoon of rice-bran syrup

    1   tablespoon of black cherry juice concentrate

Cinnamon or spice to taste (No sugar or honey. If you want the cereal to be sweeter, use more rice-bran syrup.)

Eat this cereal every morning. Over time it will balance hormones, rebuild bowel function, strengthen the nervous system, and purify the blood.

PURIFICATION

Virgo arrives as the anticlimax of the zodiac. After thirty days of our dissolute Leo vacation, Virgo forces us back to reality. The kids go back to school. And many adults go to rehab. Since I work in Los Angeles and New York, I constantly meet people in treatment centers, Alcoholics Anonymous, or similar twelve-step programs. They proudly declare, " I am three years, five months, and twenty days sober." (It amazes me that these people remember to the hour how long they have been clean of drugs and drink, and yet they don't remember how long they've been married or how old their daughter is.) Virgos generate this precision, accounting, and attention to details. These details enable the Virgos' purification. It also reveals how long recovering addicts have been married to the helpful—and sometimes life-saving— influence of Virgo.

Virgo also insures that someone actually works and brings home some food. While Leo commands everyone "to do this and do that," Virgo actually makes things happen. Virgo works and serves. This archetype cuts the expenses, accounts for all the resources, cleans up every mess, and allows things to survive and function. Though Virgo appears as the most humble sign, we must never underestimate the Virgo clan. Without them, nothing would come into fruition. No child would grow up, no movie would be released, and no organization would actually accomplish its goals.

Virgo derives from a Latin concept that means "self-possessed." Such independence and self-reliance allows Virgos to advocate for what they believe is necessary for the zodiac wheel to continue to turn. They don't need anyone's help to do their job. Most of the time it is actually easier when no one else is around to interfere. Virgo, which is associated with the Tarot card called the Hermit, thus represents monasteries, nuns, monks, and hermits. The Virgin Mary, for example, did not even need a man to conceive her child.

Virgo represents the servant, but Virgos are not the slaves. Virgo gave birth to one of most powerful rulers Europe has ever known—a woman who reigned for forty years, transforming England into an empire and supporting the likes of Shakespeare. Queen Elizabeth I was not only a Virgo, but she was also called the Virgin Queen. She declared herself a virgin to skirt the responsibility of marrying and subduing herself to a man. Like any true Virgo, self-possession won out. Her public "virginity" did not mean that she did not have sex. She apparently enjoyed many lovers. But she kept her ultimate energy to herself and remained true to her own creed. And she helped to tame and raise her unruly empire.

Practice independence and self-reliance in the area of your life ruled by Virgo. Focus on doing things on your own and in your own way.

Your Own Private Virgo

Virgo in your chart underlines the area of your life that probably demands more efficiency and precision. It marks the arena that might require a touch of editing, reorganizing, and cleansing. This area of your life also affords you the opportunity to serve others. In the week of Virgo, focus on your work, diet, and service. And pay attention to small details that will produce practical results.

Virgo in Your First House (Your Rising Sign): You are modest and feel best when you serve other people. Blessed with a brilliant and analytical mind, you always attend to tiny details. Watch out for your tendency to criticize yourself and your loved ones. During the week of Virgo, highlight your health, your leadership skills, and your direction in life.

Virgo in the Second House: You have a talent for accounting and editing. You can make money by focusing on small details and deploying your gift for analysis. You benefit from a detailed budget in business and in your personal life. In the week of Virgo, pay attention to your finances, talents, and your self-worth. It is important to give yourself some credit.

Virgo in the Third House: You have a sharp and discriminating mind. Try not to intimidate others with what you say and write. Your communication style is precise and businesslike. Avoid criticizing your siblings and neighbors. This week, focus on your relatives, communication skills, and business.

Virgo in the Fourth House: You grew up in a family in which someone criticized too often. Your family holds high expectations for you. You keep a tidy, organized home, and you will do well in work when you set up an office at home. This week, emphasize your home, family, and mother.

Virgo in the Fifth House: You might be overly critical of your lover and children. You need to work on being more romantic and creative in love. You do not enjoy taking risks or gambling. During the week of Virgo, pay attention to your children, lovers, happiness, and fun.

Virgo in the Sixth House: You enjoy much success in work and service. You have a strong work ethic and excel in statistics, service-related professions, and accounting. Pets and animals are important to you. This week, highlight your work, diet, and health. Pay attention to what you eat. Your system cannot handle all types of food.

Virgo in the Seventh House: You tend toward seclusion, and so you need to work on cultivating close relationships. You love to serve your partners, and you are attracted to hard-working individuals. Be careful not to criticize your partner or relationships. During the week of Virgo, focus on your partners and significant others.

Virgo in the Eighth House: Your marriage or business partner has a talent for accounting and orderly management of finances. You can be critical of sexual or intimate partners. Try to reduce your attention to details, especially when it comes to sex. This week, focus on your sexuality and intimacy.

Virgo in the Ninth House: You are attracted to practical philosophies and outlooks on life. You benefit from higher education, and you also tend to enjoy foreign cuisines. You might find your in-laws to be overcritical and judgmental. During the week of Virgo, focus on traveling, higher education, and finding your inner truth.

Virgo in the Tenth House: You can excel in careers associated with accounting, editing, service, or any profession that demands accuracy, precision, and analytical skill. You are known as an efficient, orderly, and effective individual who can bring order from chaos. During the week of Virgo, pay attention to your career and your status in your community.

Virgo in the Eleventh House: You might be critical with your friends and groups. However, you can serve your community as a watchdog over the creeds of the society. Your coworkers might be your closest friends. You tend to serve your friends. During the week of Virgo, focus on your friends, groups, and organizations.

Virgo in the Twelfth House: You might have been a monk or a nun in a different lifetime who worked on purifying yourself to attain a higher state of consciousness. In this life, you tend to withdraw from society. Remember that you are not a monk any longer. This week, focus on letting go of perfectionism, criticism, and self-doubt.

THE SUPER NANNY

Virgo represents the super nanny, hired by Aries and Taurus after they meet via Gemini and give birth in Cancer to the child Leo. Virgo raises, tames, puts boundaries on, and purifies that ebullient and wild Leo child. For you, Virgo arrives as the week to purify and clean up after that boisterous Leo child inside.

The cheerful, chaste, and impeccably dressed Mary Poppins personifies this archetype. She descends to the earth with an umbrella as a parachute and brings order, magic, and structure to the lives of the family she joins. Her name is Mary, just like the ultimate Virgo, Mary, the virgin mother, an icon who functions as a second or substitute mother to us all. Maria (whose name is the Latin version of *Mary*) from the *Sound of Music* also personifies this Virgo superhero. She is a nun, pure and humble, who drops into a large, motherless family and helps to save the gaggle of children from the Nazis.

Practice independence and self-reliance in the area of your life ruled by Virgo. Focus on doing things on your own and in your own way.

All three of these women named Mary serve. Specifically, their mission is to serve children. And Virgos excel whenever and wherever they have someone to serve. Mother Teresa, herself a Virgo, became revered worldwide because of the service she provided to the homeless, sick, and impoverished in Calcutta. She reminders us that while Leo oftentimes feels the need to be famous in order to serve, Virgo can become famous by serving.

Super nannies often have to say no. No to mess. No to over-indulgence. No to idleness. No to impurity. And no is the primary teaching of Virgo. Many people say no all the time, and yet they have not mastered the true teaching of Virgo. Saying no in the right manner creates high magic. If you say no in a way that sets boundaries in the appropriate spots, then you are actually saying a silent yes to growth and achievement. Virgos function as gardeners who say no to weeds, no to too much sun, no to bugs that might eat the delicate roots, and no to children who want to run on the newly sown grass. How else do you think a virgin remains a virgin if not for her ability to say no to inappropriate suitors?

No also affords Virgo reign over what and how much we eat. If you want to lose weight, you must say no to sugar, white bread, and cakes. You set limits. You do not say no to food entirely. You simply say yes to health.

This affinity for no also gives Virgo rule over accounting and budgets. A producer of a big, dramatic Leo movie must say no whenever the director exceeds the allocated funds. If not, then the movie might not ever be completed. Editors also say no when they cut a certain scene or chapter that does not serve the whole.

Virgo in your chart highlights the area in your life in which you need to practice saying no. It does not mean that you must turn negative or limit yourself. It implies only that you need to set tighter boundaries. Where do you need to set some boundaries in terms of time or spending?

VIRGO AND PETS

Scientific studies have shown that keeping a pet around house reduces our stress and improves our overall health. If nothing else, our dog forces us to get off the sofa to walk him around the block a few times each day. This finding jibes astrologically since Virgo rules both pets and health. We also nanny our pets, cleaning up after their mess and satisfying our Virgo urge to serve.

Pets also supply a profound Kabbalistic purpose. Most city dwellers divide into cat lovers or dog people. Dogs tend to love their owners unconditionally. They jump and wag their tails happily whenever we walk in the door. They teach us how to receive love because they give us no choice. Meanwhile, cats, aloof and hyper-independent, often ignore us. They generally don't care if we overtly love them or not as they strut to the other side of the room or hide in the closet. Most veterinarians say that cats are attached to their home itself rather than to the people that live there. Yet we have to care for and love our cats in the face of this impassiveness. They teach us how to give. Our pets help to highlight our innate imbalances. Like Kabbalah, they charge us to balance giving with receiving.

Sixty-three percent of American households have pets. Forty-four million have dogs while thirty-eight million have cats. Does that mean that Americans overall need to learn how to receive love?

The Detail-Oriented Accountants that Took Down Mighty Al Capone

Before his arrest in 1931, Al Capone, the infamous Chicago gangster, wielded so much power and influence that no one could touch him. You want to know who brought down this sinister evildoer? Was it Superman? Batman? Spiderman? Nope. It was the Virgos: the accountants at the Internal Revenue Service. They nailed the big bad wolf on tax evasion. These charges resound petty and irrelevant compared to the murders and terrors Capone inflicted on his community. But they worked. His ugly reign was stopped because he failed to file his taxes correctly. The Virgos calculated that he owed the U.S. Treasury $215,080.48, to be precise. Thank God for Virgos.

Virgo in your chart shows the area in which you need to pay more attention to small details. Do it. You don't want to be brought down by sloppy oversight like Al Capone.

Virgo is the most humble sign. The word *humble* derives from the Latin *humilis*, which means "earth" (Virgo is an earth sign) or "lowly." While Leo resembles Tarzan, roaring and pounding his chest to announce his presence, Virgo accomplishes the job quietly on her own.

To prove this point, let's play a little game. Name three famous directors. Now come up with three famous actors. Easy, right? Now name three famous film editors. What happened? Why are you so silent? Anonymous film editors toil under the energy of humble Virgo, while directors and actors stand in the spotlight of Leo. Yet any knowledgeable film buff will remind you that in most cases, editors influence a movie's quality far more than actors and often directors too. I once attended an editing session for a blockbuster movie. It was hilarious. The editors sat together poking fun at the miserable acting and the stupid script. As ambassadors of the energy of Virgo, they are, of course, paid to locate all the flaws and clean them up by saying, "No, that's out." They change and shift shots and reactions around to compensate for the inadequacy of the actors and directors. Music producers and engineers—Virgo editors themselves—fix the faltering voices of pop stars with astute electronic tweaks, boosts, and distortions. Sometimes they hire ghost singers to hit notes that the fabulous famous star cannot reach. Virgos repair things behind the scenes. They don't get that much credit, but they are indispensable. And they love to serve.

Virgo in your chart shows the area in which you need to pay more attention to small details.

How to Get Along with Virgos

- Cross all the *t*'s and dot all the *i*'s. Then choose your words wisely, as if they were a scarce resource. If you send an email, spell-check twice.

- Ask Virgos for advice. If they refuse and claim that they're no expert (though they probably are), tell them that you value their insight anyway.

- Be clean and tidy. Dress up to code, appropriate to the occasion. They don't really approve of a casual or sloppy style.

- When Virgos shift into argument mode, gently change the subject. It is hard to keep up with their logic and thoroughness. You can't win an argument with a Virgo.

- They love dining but prefer not to spend too much money on themselves. When you go out, select restaurants that are delicious but inexpensive.

- Don't get upset if Virgos are stingy with compliments. But if you ever do receive a compliment from a Virgo, then you will know that you really deserve it.

- Help Virgos serve and be useful. That is all they want.

The Dark Side of the Force: Virgo

Inchworm, inchworm,
Measuring the marigolds
Seems to me you'd stop and see,
How beautiful they are.
   —"Inchworm," Frank Loesser

Like the inchworm, Virgos are so busy classifying and categorizing, analyzing and differentiating, that they forget to experience the flowers or whatever life presents to them. We all fall prone to this sort of obsession in the area of our chart ruled by Virgo. I interpreted a chart for a man who had Virgo in his house of relationships.

He demanded that the entire reading focus on his mate. He yearned to understand everything about his partner. After a while, I rebelled and told him that he was so busy classifying her and criticizing her that he forgets to simply enjoy her. This Virgo propensity drives a man who loves butterflies to start killing them and pinning them up on the wall so that he might examine and catalog their every little spot.

It is sometimes easier to categorize an experience than to surrender to it and feel or savor it. This logical and distancing behavior gives us a sense of control over life. The inchworm syndrome causes Virgos to zoom in and obsess on a small slice of life to the exclusion of the larger, richer, and often more uplifting whole. They cut and cut and cut, trimming down to the smallest unit. But when they find it, they often forget what they were looking for.

Virgos' attention to detail and to cleaning up messes also leads to perfectionism. If you zoom in on anything, of course, you will find some defect or flaw. And that leads to another Virgo issue: criticism. They generally are not cruel-hearted people who relish putting us down. They usually criticize themselves far more severely than they criticize others. Still, the closer you are to a Virgo, the more criticism you will have to parry. Why? They want to be perfect. And they want you and everything in their lives to be perfect too. Virgos frequently need to permit themselves to experience life and all its flaws without judgment just a little bit more.

Like the character in the movie *As Good as It Gets*, Virgos' quest for order and routine makes them susceptible to obsessive-compulsive disorder. For example, I send out a biweekly email newsletter called *SpiriTalk*. I am not a Virgo, and therefore I don't really care about spelling mistakes. For me, the message is more important than the form it takes. (Alas, at the same time, to make this book possible, I had to hire an editor. If only I had more Virgo in me.) One late night, I made several horrendous spelling errors in the newsletter, and I forgot to spell-check it before I sent it out to thousands of people. The next morning, I received a phone call from a concerned woman who informed me that I had misspelled the word *please*. I apologized, but she demanded that I correct it. I told her that such a correction was not possible because I had sent the email and could not retrieve it. "Oh, my God!" she gasped. I was shocked by her shock. I asked if she was a Virgo. "Yes," she said and then hung up the phone.

The Puritans from early American history represent another example of this Virgo energy gone crazy. They were indeed hard workers and heavily oriented toward service. But they took the saying "no" thing too seriously, which resulted in rigidity, sanctimony, and atrocities such as the Salem witch hunts of the seventeenth century.

THE HEBREW LETTER *Yod*

י

Kabbalah assigned the Hebrew letter *Yod* to Virgo. *Yod* is the smallest letter in the Hebrew alphabet, and yet Kabbalah asserts that all the other letters are made of different configurations of *Yod*. It represents the humble energy of Virgo. It is small and attracts little attention. But all the rest of the letters owe their glory and shape entirely to the letter *Yod*. *Yod* and Virgo are like the atom, the microscopic unit that comprises and animates everything. *Yod* translates as "hand." Metaphorically, Virgo serves as the hand of God—the sign busy always doing God's work.

The tiny glyph of *Yod* also stands for the sperm of God. Centuries before the invention of the microscope, the Kabbalists associated the shape of the letter *Yod* with the invisible components of semen. At first it seems strange that the sign charged with the safekeeping of God's sperm is Virgo, the virgin. (The Hermit, the Tarot card assigned to Virgo, similarly represents a person purified from our normal carnal temptations.) But it makes some sense. If a sexual sign like Taurus or Scorpio enjoyed rule over God's sperm, we probably would not have too much of it left. In the Eastern tradition called Tantra, it is the monks and the nuns who practice the sacred yoga of sexual union in the service of mysticism. The symbolism of the letter explains that Virgo takes the potential (the DNA in the sperm) and transforms it into something actual. It accomplishes this crucial task by paying attention to small details and by staying clean, orderly, and dedicated to service.

Virgo in your chart reveals a place of vast potential. It houses the sperm of God that can yield a great deal of abundance as long as you take care to direct it toward the service of the greater good. Meditate on the letter *Yod* to amplify the energy you need for work, service, health, cleanliness, purification, and order.

The Parts of the Body

Virgo rules our colon and intestines. This sign basically oversees all the assimilating systems that are responsible for discharging toxins and waste. Our Virgo mechanisms extract, analyze, and differentiate the good from the bad in the food we ingest. Cleanses, fasts, detoxifications, and a consistent attention to hygiene will bolster your inner Virgo. Help Virgo help you. Try some sort of detoxification program this week, even one as simple as eliminating alcohol or sugar from your diet.

The Color of Virgo: Yellow-Green

The color of Virgo is yellow-green. Wear this color combination—yellow adjacent to green—whenever you want to attract the energy of purification and health.

What Should I Focus on in the Week of Virgo?

In the week of Virgo, focus on improving your diet and health. Try to detoxify from any substances, chemicals, or even people that you feel are draining or abusing you. Reorganize and edit your life to eliminate any obstructions that hold you back. Also identify how you can be of service to those close to you, your community, and the world as a whole.

Look for synchronicities, especially those that relate to your work, pets, relationships with coworkers, and your health. The symbols of Virgo include virgins and virginity, the Virgin Mary, nannies, hermits, nuns, Mercury, diets, detox, rehab, cleanliness, order, the digestion and excretory system, employees, obsessive compulsions, hands, sperm, humility, work, service, criticism, tiny details, cleaning, self-reliance, and the word *no*.

Virgo in your chart reveals a place of vast potential. It houses the sperm of God that can yield a great deal of abundance as long as you take care to direct it toward the service of the greater good. Meditate on the letter *Yod* to amplify the energy you need for work, service, health, cleanliness, purification, and order.

Your Virgo Week Checklist

- Purify yourself for a week: no alcohol, fried foods, white bread, white sugar, coffee, or sweets.
- Speak the Virgo affirmation twice a day: "I am dedicated to serving humanity and to God's will. I am purified and healthy, and I am thankful to my body for helping me to manifest my potential."
- Start eating Virgo Organic Oatmeal for breakfast.
- Meditate on the letter *Yod*.
- Wear yellow-green or a combination of yellow and green.
- Practice saying no as well as setting healthy boundaries.
- If you can, travel for one night to a remote place without your cell phone, books, or computers. Try to feel what it's like to live as a nun or monk for a day.
- Do something of service behind the scenes.
- Find your spiritual name.

THE RITUAL OF VIRGO: YOUR SPIRITUAL NAME

Virgos label and categorize through their naming of objects and situations around us. I did it earlier in this chapter by accusing Virgos of having the inchworm syndrome. While your birth name represents your Aries label, your spiritual name reflects Virgo. The continually popular names *Mary* and *Maria* embody the Virgo energy. *Maria* comes from the ancient Hebrew name *Miriam*, the name of the sister of Moses in the Old Testament. The New Testament promoted the energy surrounding this name by giving the name to the mother of Christ. In both cases, Miriam/Mary/Maria is closely related to a savior figure. She seems to exist to serve the hero, to support him in his efforts to liberate others. The Aries hero needs the Virgo to protect him from those he aims to serve, as well as from himself.

The old nursery rhyme "Mary had a Little Lamb" expresses the relationship between Aries (the lamb or young ram) and Virgo (Mary): "'Why does the lamb love Mary so?' the eager children cry 'Why, Mary loves the lamb you know,' the teacher did reply." In Hebrew, the name *Miriam* is composed of two different words, *mar* ("water") and *yam* ("bitter"), which means *Miriam* translates as "bitter sea" or "bitter water." In other words, the Virgo washes away the bitterness of suffering with the water or compassion. Service stings a bit as the Virgo confronts the pain of those she serves. If we Kabbalistically shuffle the letters of *Miriam* to decode the name's hidden message, we find the word *Yam-ram*, which means "elevated water." Virgo, through devoted service, transforms the bitter water of Miriam or Mary into elevated or holy water.

The Sikh tradition of India emphasizes the powerful mantra *Sat Nam*, which translates as "the Name is Truth." Your job now is to find the higher truth embedded in your name. It might come to you in a dream, during meditation, or after you scramble the letters of your everyday name. Once you discover your spiritual name, keep it a secret. Use it as your power word whenever you need to access God and your higher self. My brother tried this exercise after attending a class I led on the Virgo archetype, and he kept his spiritual name secret. Then he went on a trip to Ecuador, where he was violently threatened by several muggers. During the attack, he refused to panic, and he instead spoke his power name to locate advice from Above about how to handle the danger. He survived without a scratch—and without losing his money.

Sometimes, when it comes to our name, we need to venture across the world to find what is right beneath our noses. A woman named Angela, who always warred with her parents (she had Virgo in the fourth house, the house of family), hated her given name. She longed for a spiritual moniker that reflected her true nature, and she traveled to India to visit a guru. He christened her with an exotic Sanskrit name that she then tried to force on her friends and family. To her profound disconsolation, they all resisted. In one of my workshops, I asked her the meaning of her Sanskrit name, and she proudly replied, "messenger of love." Then I asked her for her given name, and she frowned and said, "Angela." I remained silent for a minute, and everyone else in the class started to giggle until she understood. We then discussed how angels in the Bible are synonymous with messengers. They serve as messengers for God's love. For the first time, she recognized that the wise guru had awarded her with the same name that her parents had given her back at her birth. She had traveled to the other side of the world to find the spiritual name that was always hers.

Another interesting example of how our name provides us with a roadmap to our destiny was made known to me when I was on a book tour in Bulgaria. On the front page of one of the biggest newspapers of Sofia, 24 *Hours*, was an image of a jackal who had apparently escaped in the dead of night from the Sofia zoo. Well now, whoever named the jackal *Houdini* should have known better. Sooner or later the jackal of all trades will escape even the most fettered and chained cage. So be careful how you name your business, your children, even your pets.

FAMOUS VIRGOS

Mother Teresa, Sean Connery, Charlie Parker, Leonard Bernstein, Johann Wolfgang von Goethe, Mary Shelley, Ernest Rutherford, Queen Elizabeth I, Peter Sellers, Leo Tolstoy, D. H. Lawrence, Agatha Christie, B. B. King, Greta Garbo, Sophia Lauren, Stephen King, and Kobe Bryant.

Libra: The Beauty and the Lawyer

September 23 to October 22

Key Phrase: "I balance" — harmony

General Qualities: Logical, friendly, polished and refined, easygoing, social, possessed of aesthetic good taste, diplomatic, and having a strong sense of justice

Dark Side: Superficial, indecisive, self-serving, hypocritical, indulgent

Element: Cardinal air

Planet: Venus

Day: Friday

Theme: The mirror of relationships

Parts of the Body: Kidneys, waistline, ovaries

Color: Green

Gemstone: Opal

Musical Note: F sharp

Hebrew Letter: *Lamed* ל

Kabbalistic Meaning of Letter: Learning and teaching

Path in the Tree of Life: Path 11, connecting Severity and Beauty

Tarot Card: The Lady of Justice

Movies: *Beauty and the Beast, Gandhi, Kramer vs. Kramer,* and any film about relationships or lawyers

Affirmation: "I am balanced, in harmony with life. Justice will prevail, and I will be rewarded for all my efforts. I generate peace and tranquility with all my relationships."

OVERVIEW

Libra stands in the middle of the zodiac, and its scales symbolize balance and justice. The sign of John Lennon, Gandhi, Eleanor Roosevelt, Libra represents the archetype of harmony and beauty. It also governs relationships, partnerships, and close associations. Libra teaches that our relationships represent mirrors that reveal who we truly are. Libra is also associated with the law, courts, enemies, design, fashion, art, and lifestyle. In Libra, you will focus on your relationships and partnerships and connect to your sense of fashion and design. Libra also will familiarize you with universal justice and karma.

THE TERRITORY OF LIBRA

An eye for an eye makes the whole world blind.
—M. K. GANDHI, A LIBRA

Libra begins on autumnal equinox—when the balance between night and day, light and dark reaches a perfect equilibrium. This archetype therefore emanates justice, fairness, balance, and the harmony of relationships. Here, in the middle of the astrological year, we encounter the true beauty behind any relationship, whether it is a partnership of man and woman or dark and light. Relationships thrive on equality. When both sides give as much as they receive, nourish as much as they take nourishment, and heal as much as they enjoy healing, then the relationship blossoms and radiates harmony. From the fall equinox forward, the story turns a little sad, because the days begin to shorten and the darkness rises. This diminution of light affects our mood. And we tend to confine ourselves inside more and more to escape the harshening conditions. We look increasingly into our subconscious, our insides. Libra inaugurates this more introverted half of our year.

As the cardinal (initiator) air (communication) sign, Libra also initiates communication. In order to conduct any conversation, you need a partner who will listen and reply. Relationships—at least most human relationships—demand communication. Libra arrives as the "Hello, how do you do?" sign.

Why did this responsibility for relationships fall to Libra? Well, way back when, God, the ultimate real estate mogul, decided to give his twelve children some territory on the sacred mountain of life. He shaved off the top of the mountain and sliced the circular plot into twelve lots of equal size. He offered Aries, the eldest, the first choice, and he selected the most strategic spot with the broadest view. Then Taurus settled in the acreage adjacent to Aries because she loved to be close to the big strong brother who would protect her if anything went wrong. Then Gemini set up shop next to Taurus, alongside the main road that leads to center of the mountain, scheming all the while about building a toll booth in the middle of the highway. Cancer then built her house in the next plot, right atop a well. Leo, nestling near his mother Cancer, then erected a huge castle with the tallest towers, and Virgo, who surely would need to help out Leo when she could, constructed her humble adobe in the lot beside his.

Overlooking it all, Aries ignored all this construction because none of it really blocked his primary view out to the horizon. But then Libra marched into the plot directly opposite of Aries. And as the archetype of beauty, architecture, and design, he began construction on a gorgeous mansion. Aries scanned the scene and perceived trouble at once. This Libra compound would obscure his view of the world. It would obstruct his ability to see any enemies coming at him and diminish his ability to protect himself and his clan. And before Libra could finish pouring the foundations for his project, Aries, red with anger, charged onto his territory, hollering, "You must stop all this madness and leave while you still can!"

The Libra calmly approached the intruder and politely inquired, "Hi, neighbor. What seems to be the trouble, bro?"

Furious at his ignorance, Aries countered, "You cannot build in front of my house. You are blocking my view!"

The Libra smiled his irrepressible smile and said, "I cannot block your view, dear friend, because I am your view."

A stunned Aries fell silent for a few seconds. He did not expect such a profound reply. "Listen," he said, "I am the sign of exploration and new horizons. I cannot permit you to block my path."

"Well, then you will explore yourself through me," the Libra parried. "I am your mirror. And you will see yourself through me."

Aries wasn't really sure how to handle this novel experience. And for the first time in his life, he retreated to think it through.

As the first sign that falls directly opposite another on the circle, Libra represents the first sign that actually necessitates a relationship. Aries was created as a stand-alone archetype. And while the subsequent signs interacted with the others alongside, each enjoyed its own pure energy. Nothing opposed it directly. But Libra, plopped down directly in Aries' vital line of sight, had no choice but to deal with Aries. Therefore, Libra initiates relationships, tact, diplomacy, and compromise. How does Libra do it? By acting as a mirror. Our relationships reflect our true nature back to us. What we hate about our partners is what we loathe about ourselves. And what we love in our partners echoes what we appreciate in ourselves. Mirrors reflect to us our own image but reversed. Same with the opposite signs. If you want to know about Libra, simply examine the attributes of Aries and reverse them. If Aries is the warrior, then Libra will be the peacemaker. If Aries is all about himself, then Libra will be all about his partner. If Aries relates to Mars, then Libra nuzzles up to Venus. All the opposing signs (Taurus-Scorpio, Gemini-Sagittarius, Cancer-Capricorn, Leo-Aquarius, and Virgo-Pisces) work this same way. If Taurus represents "my money," then Scorpio represents "my partner's money." If Gemini deals with lower education, then Sagittarius deals with higher education. If Cancer is the family, then Capricorn is about standing outside the family in career. If Leo symbolizes the king, then Aquarius evokes democracy. And if Virgo embeds itself in reality, then Pisces swims toward fantasy.

Libra in your chart indicates the area in your life in which you require a mirror, a partner who will enable you to understand yourself more fully.

Your Own Private Libra

The area in your life governed by Libra highlights the place where you ought to exercise diplomacy and balance to advance your goals. Relationships and significant others are enormously valuable here. Strive to cultivate harmony, peace, and beauty in this area of your life. And expect to encounter many moments when you will have to think of the needs of other people and compromise your own wants and inclinations.

Libra in Your First House (Your Rising Sign): Blessed with an affinity for beauty, symmetry, and harmony, you are physically attractive yourself. You tend to avoid confrontations at all costs, although sometimes the cost is to your own interests. You have good taste in clothes and art. During the week of Libra, pay attention to your body, health, and your emotional and physical nourishment.

Libra in the Second House: Watch out for imbalances between your expenses and earnings. You might experience swings and fluctuations in your income. You are talented in art and possess a strong sense of fairness and justice. You could be a great lawyer or mediator. You require a partner to make more money, or you will do well when you allow your partner to manage your money. This week, focus on your finances, talent, and self-worth.

Libra in the Third House: You enjoy harmonious relationships with siblings and neighbors. You speak and write in a diplomatic and calm style. You might relish the company of your brother- or sister-in-law. This week, highlight your relatives, communication skills, and business. Listen to the advice of your partners in work and in life.

Libra in the Fourth House: You live in a beautiful, tastefully designed home. Harmony holds the key to a successful household. Your mother is a beautiful person, but she might be overly influenced by her surroundings. You enjoy good relationships with family members. During the week of Libra, take note of coincidences relating to home, family, motherhood, and your mother.

Libra in the Fifth House: You possess the potential for having beautiful children, and you will enjoy a harmonious relationship with them. You need a love partner. Just make sure that your neediness does not influence the choices you make. Don't accept just anyone who presents him- or herself. During the week of Libra, focus on your creativity, children, and happiness. Try to find a partner to play sports with.

Libra in the Sixth House: You enjoy harmonious relationships with coworkers, employees, and your household pets. It is important to nurture relationships with people and clients in your workspace. Watch your kidneys and ovaries. Problems in relationships might translate into diseases. This week, pay special attention to your workplace, diet, and health.

Libra in the Seventh House: You have the potential to enjoy a beautiful and harmonious relationship with your significant other. Your partner functions as a mirror to you. You are attracted to good-looking and refined people. Blessed with a natural diplomacy, you can resolve conflicts in a peaceful way. During the week of Libra, make sure to nourish and protect your partnerships and significant other.

Libra in the Eighth House: You might enjoy an inheritance from your partner's family. You are sexually attracted to attractive and charming people. You require a balanced relationship to create intimacy. This week, work on your intimate relationships, sexuality, joint artistic and financial affairs, death, transformation, and letting go.

Libra in the Ninth House: You enjoy many foreign friends and connections to foreign cultures. Your life or business partner might be a foreigner or someone you encountered while traveling. You are interested in higher education that involves law, fashion, or art. You can enjoy harmonious relationships with in-laws. During the week of Libra, try to travel and study.

Libra in the Tenth House: You need a partner to fully attain your potential. Your career can be linked to law, art, music, fashion, or design. People perceive you as peace-loving and diplomatic. This week, pay attention to your career, reputation, and standing in your community. You can shine and radiate in your career.

Libra in the Eleventh House: You enjoy good relationships with your friends and groups, although some of your friends might be shallow or superficial. You can meet new friends through your business or life partner. During the week of Libra, focus your energy on your friends, groups, and organization.

Libra in the Twelfth House: You have unresolved karma with your partners in work and in life. Subconscious psychological issues seem to surface whenever you interact with your significant other. I recommend couples counseling, even during good times. This week, try to go on a spiritual retreat and focus on letting go of old patterns in relationships, law, and justice.

LIBRA: BALANCE AND HARMONY

The test of a first-rate intelligence is the ability to hold two opposing ideas in the mind at the same time, and still retain the ability to function.
— F. SCOTT FITZGERALD, A LIBRA

While Gemini, the other air sign, taught us how to identify dualities in order to unite them, Libra instructs that all oppositions, no matter how extreme, are equal and therefore the same. The scale, the symbol of Libra, reinforces this lesson. We place one object on the left side and a seemingly different object on the right. When we note the same weight—the same importance—we can deduce that these objects radiate the same essence. Libra insists that any extreme will generate the opposite extreme. For instance, if you encounter four or five planets clustered in Leo, then you probably will have located not a super-Leo owner of this chart, but an Aquarius, the opposite sign to Leo. Moses, who served as a super Aries in liberating his nation, is actually most known as a lawgiver (law, of course is ruled by Libra, the opposite sign to Aries.) Meanwhile, Genghis Khan, the warrior who conquered half the world, was a Libra, the sign of peace.

How can this be? Well, just as the Tree of Life is composed of spheres, our existence can be found on wheels or globes too. We live on a round planet and interact with our environment according to the laws of a round zodiac wheel. Oppositions make themselves known within the confines of the two sides of a sphere. If these oppositions turn more extreme, if they walk further away from each, they eventually will convene at the same point. What lies east of the east? The west. What lies west of the west? The east. California, for instance, is known as the Wild West, firmly

Libra in your chart indicates the area in your life in which you require a mirror, a partner who will enable you to understand yourself more fully.

affixed to the western part of the United States. But if you stand in Los Angeles and move further west, you will eventually hit China and Japan, which are considered to be the Far East. This confusion is the magic of Libra. Every extreme is actually the same thing. Saint Paul, who compiled and wrote parts of the New Testament, was a Jewish zealot who endeavored to persecute and destroy the early Christians. His extremism eventually led to his conversion to Christianity and his spreading the teachings of his once-hated nemeses all over the world.

You will experience wild swings and fluctuations in the area of your life ruled by Libra. You might have to choose between two opposing options or possibilities. It might prove difficult to decide. Libras are often indecisive. Just remember that Libra exists to show you that all dualities are illusions. Both options hold equal value.

COMPROMISE: THE NECESSITY OF RELATIONSHIP

We all need a relationship. Having a significant other means we are significant to another, and that's a wonderful thing. But to remain significant, to insure the endurance of any relationship, at some point, no matter what, you are going to have to compromise. In 1977, Jimmy Carter, a Libra, brokered a peace treaty between archenemies Israel and Egypt. It didn't seem possible that anything or anyone could bring these hardened antagonists together. But he accomplished the impossible by forcing each side to make concessions. And out of those compromises large and small, harmony emerged out of perpetual war.

All relationships demand compromise. Sometimes they even require sacrifice. The key is to realize that the sacrifice is made not for our partner, but for the sake of the partnership. When you give up your free day better spent on the beach to help your husband move his office, you sacrifice not for him but for your marriage. And the truth is that you benefit from a happy harmonious marriage too. The sacrifice profits your husband in the short term as you lug file box after file box to the car. But in the long run, the pleasure of a companionable and delicious marriage serves you even more than that simple chore benefits him. Keeping that commitment to partnership foremost in mind whenever you compromise will reduce the chance of generating passive-aggressive guilt.

You will experience wild swings and fluctuations in the area of your life ruled by Libra. You might have to choose between two opposing options or possibilities. It might prove difficult to decide. Libras are often indecisive. Just remember that Libra exists to show you that all dualities are illusions. Both options hold equal value.

Also, whenever you long to change something in your partner, make sure that you commit to changing something in yourself. You might promise to talk less about yourself, if your partner commits to stop smoking in the car. Write a contract that outlines the consequences if either of you violate the rules. For example, the transgressor agrees to wash all dishes for a month. The planet Saturn, the lord of karma (associated with the sphere Understanding in the Tree of Life) is considered to be exalted when it falls in Libra. Though Saturn officially rules Capricorn, it functions most comfortably in Libra. Saturn orbits the sun every twenty-eight or twenty-nine years. Every seven years (Libra is the seventh sign), this planet touches one of the corners of your chart. When a relationship hits the seven-year mark, the first kiss from Saturn, it produces much hardship and strain that forces the partners to reflect and reevaluate their union. It creates what we call the seven-year itch. In the wake of this challenge, the partnership either emerges more robust and durable, or it crumbles apart.

Some individuals might deduce that their partner has become a scratched mirror that has ceased to reflect their true image and then go looking for someone new. Many cultures also perpetuate the superstition that a broken mirror brings seven years of bad luck, a variation of this astrological dance between Libra (the mirror sign) and Saturn (the planet of the seven-year-itch). Some Kabbalistic tales and rituals acknowledge the adversity brought on by this Saturn-Libra test of seven and attempt to mitigate the consequences of its sting. Saturday—the day of Saturn and the seventh day of the week—commands a day of rest devoid of any work. Many people spend this day in devotion to God and their partner and family. In the Bible, Jacob, the eminent patriarch and father of the twelve tribes of Israel, had to work seven years to marry Leah and seven more to marry Rachel—a toil designed to make him appreciate and hold fast to his prizes. And in Jewish marriages, the bride circles her groom seven times to bind him in her love and break down the walls around his seven chakras.

Be aware that every seven years, perhaps every seven months too, your partnerships (both personal and professional) undergo some scrutinizing and need reevaluation. Try to use these challenges to grow closer to your partner. Use Libra-inspired compromises and sacrifices to solidify the relationship.

LAW, BEAUTY, ART, AND DESIGN

Ruled by the planet Venus, Libra symbolizes the Venus energy devoted to beauty, art, music, design, fashion, and aesthetics. Librans enjoy a profound understanding of space and symmetry, as well as an innate sense of justice—of what is right and appropriate for others. The Lady of Justice, the Tarot card associated with Libra, is always portrayed as a beautiful, blindfolded woman who carries the scales of justice. It is said that justice is blind because it must adhere to impartiality above all. A Chinese client of mine remarked that in China, the birthplace of sunglasses, judges were instructed to wear sunglasses so that others would not see their emotional response to a case, and thus the judges would appear impartial. But the astrological rationale for this blindfold comes from Libra's devotion to beauty. We cannot trust Libra to dole out the same justice to a handsome knight as she would to an ugly slob. We blind the sign of justice to eliminate her attachment to aesthetics.

Fairness or balancing every element of a situation finds a home in beauty as well as law. Design and art depend on symmetry of color, objects, and composition. Music relies on the harmony between tones. In fact, Pythagoras, the father of the Western musical scale, insisted that music can be described as the mathematical relationships between the different tones. That is why there are seven white keys in the scale. Meanwhile, the earliest written law—the tablets of Hamurabi from the nineteenth century B.C.E—declares, "an eye for an eye, tooth for a tooth." But another Libra lawyer, Gandhi, remembered the vital Libra imperative of compromise to attain a loftier level of beauty, justice, and peace. He said, "An eye for an eye makes the whole world blind." Apparently, Mahatma ("great soul") Gandhi was not blinded by that crude ancient take on justice.

Libra in your chart highlights the area in your life in which you can excel in law, art, music, design, and all aesthetic pursuits. Strive often to be creative and artistic in this area of your life.

Every seven years, perhaps every seven months too, your partnerships (both with your spouse or work) will undergo some scrutinizing and need reevaluation. Try to use these challenges to grow closer to your partner. Use Libra-inspired compromises and sacrifices to solidify the relationship.

PARTNERS AND ENEMIES

Libra rules relationships in the positive sense, but it also governs your known enemies—a negative sort of partnership. Like your partners, your enemies also serve as mirrors that reflect your true identity. While your spouse might reflect all that is good in you, your enemy reveals the traits and situations that you have yet to master. And sometimes you will need a Libra lawyer and a Libra court to duel it out with your known Libra enemies.

Libra teaches justice here on earth and justice in the cosmic, universal sense too. Karma—the name for your personal cosmic justice—translates as "action and reaction." For every action in your past lifetimes, you will confront a correlated consequence here in this life. And for your every act in this incarnation, you will encounter a corresponding reaction in some future lifetime. Ecclesiastes (11:1) advises and warns: "Cast your bread on the waters; for you shall find it after many days." (I wonder if this saying represents some coded message for modern society cautioning us against casting our pollutants into the rivers and oceans because "after many days" we will have to deal with the consequences.) This verse mirrors the Eastern lessons of karma. Everything you do—good and bad—will come back in some way in your future. Sir Isaac Newton adapted the cosmic laws into his groundbreaking laws of motion. He discovered that for every force, there is an equal and opposite force. These powerful laws launch spacecrafts as well as our own life.

Libra in your chart highlights the area in your life in which you can excel in law, art, music, design, and all aesthetic pursuits. Strive often to be creative and artistic in this area of your life.

Karma instructs that your enemies in this lifetime might in past lifetimes have been your partners, who decided to reincarnate as enemies to teach you lessons they failed to inculcate as your ally. Similarly, your lovers in this lifetime might have functioned as your enemies in a past lifetime. Maybe your current spouse once served as your enemy—an enemy you could not tolerate or forgive. Maybe now, via your love affair, you will heal all that past anger and advance a step closer to the Light. These are your soul mates—your lovers and enemies alike. They are the equals, the same, under Libra.

And perpetuating the antagonism against your enemies only hurts yourself. Libra encourages us to compromise, to avoid violence, and attend fervently to diplomacy. Only that tack—and tact—will break the cycle of karma, of action and subsequent reaction. Gandhi, for example, invented the modern-day version of passive resistance and brought the formidable British Empire to its knees without firing a shot. And John Lennon, another eminent Libra, sang, "Give peace a chance." Sadly, both these Libra titans of peace were shot and killed by enemies.

Your Libra house might harbor enemies who come at you to teach you a valuable cosmic lesson. They might be filled with aggression and irrationality. They might not be aware themselves of the vital lesson they aim to bring to the fore. They might be difficult to handle with tact and forgiveness. But if you view them as more than enemies, if you do your best to unveil the lesson in their hostility, you will then be able to prevail. And you will be able to transcend your karma.

How to Get Along with Libras

- Libras are fairly easy to befriend and enjoy. They are outgoing, social, and tactful, so it should not be that hard to get along just great with them.

- Dress nicely around Libras—in fine clothes and pretty, coordinated colors.

- Make sure that you smell good. Brush your teeth and hair. Libras love to be seen around attractive and well-groomed people.

- Try to avoid confrontations. They do not appreciate aggression.

- Be social and open. Introduce them to others. Invite them to parties and social events.

- Use words such as we, us, and together rather then I, me, and alone.

- Compliment them on their looks, clothes, jewelry, and other aspects of their appearance.

- Ask about their partners and always share news about your own relationships.

- Avoid gossiping with them about other people. They are tempted easily, and gossip will harm you both.

- Don't tell them things that you don't want broadcasted to the world. They are not good at keeping secrets.

- Always present both sides of the story. They like to examine both points of view, both options. Don't slant too heavily in one direction.

- Go ahead and lead them. They love strong and determined people.

THE DARK SIDE OF THE FORCE: LIBRA

Libras are notorious for their indecisiveness and for flip-flopping. Well, this last sentence is true, and it is not. Do I sound like a Libra now? Libras see both the good and bad in every option. They weigh everything on the scale. That is their job. And sometimes it freezes them, disabling their capacity to pick one option from another. Lawyers work like this too. Sometimes they know that their client is guilty, but they defend him anyway. One of my good friends is a beautiful and incredibly intelligent lawyer who managed to procure acquittal for someone who shoplifted by claiming that the fact of the perpetrator's obesity made her unbearably depressed at the time of her crime. The woman was guilty, but the lawyer tipped the balance with her sympathetic rationale.

As the initiator of communication, Libras naturally tend to talk too much. They squirm and bristle in silence. In weighing their options on the scale, they also often swing wildly to one extreme and then the other before finding the point of equilibrium. This manic extremism can drive their partners batty. And as the sign of relationship, Libras often grow too dependent or codependent on others. They encounter difficulty balancing their own interests with their partners, or they too dramatically disregard their own needs in their quest to satisfy their significant other.

Finally, Libras must rectify what I call the mirror-on-the-wall complex. Snow White is a Libra. How do I know? Well, how many dwarfs did she live with? Seven. Her stepmother was also a Libra. How do I know? Well, who else would stand in front of a looking glass all day asking, "Mirror, mirror upon the wall, who's the fairest of them all?" The stepmother committed myriad atrocities because she yearned to be the most beautiful woman in the kingdom. She was overly obsessed with superficial beauty.

Your Libra house might harbor enemies meant to teach you a valuable cosmic lesson. If you view them as more than enemies, if you do your best to unveil the lesson in their hostility, you will then be able to prevail and transcend your karma.

And this trivial concern generated another notorious Libra affliction: comparison. Libras constantly measure themselves against others, and this propensity causes them grave pain. They obsess over what other people might think of them. "What is he thinking that I am thinking?" They lock themselves in these endless speculative loops like the image of a mirror that is reflected through a mirror of a mirror. As highly intelligent air signs, they actually savor the convoluted mental gymnastics birthed by such speculations. But these thoughts too often will cause the rest of us to throw up our hands in befuddlement and frustration.

THE HEBREW LETTER *Lamed*

The Hebrew letter *Lamed* is unique. It sits smack in the middle of the Hebrew alphabet, just like Libra marks the center of the zodiac. *Lamed* stands as the tallest Hebrew letter, the only glyph that extends up beyond the requisite height limit. It resembles a mountain peak, overlooking everything like a flag that signals the invaluable center-piece of the entire territory. Lamed serves as the root for the Hebrew words meaning "learn" and "teach." According to Kabbalah, teaching and learning are one and the same. To achieve balance and harmony in any Libra relationship, each party must give and receive, learn and teach, in equal measure. Any partnership that skews to one side—where one partner always teaches and the other simply learns—will not last.

Examine all your close relationships this week, both in love and business, and try to determine whether they are balanced between giving and receiving, teaching and learning, healing and being healed. Meditate with the letter *Lamed* whenever you wish to rectify, heal, or create harmonious relationships. This letter can also help to balance your body's energy.

THE PARTS OF THE BODY

Libra energy oversees the kidneys, waistline, and ovaries. Low-back pain often signals a kidney problem. Drinking lots of water will bolster your kidney function. Since Libra rules relationships, investigate this week the balance between your masculine and feminine sides. Within your own body, the feminine represents the left side and the masculine represents the right. Identify where you have scars, injuries, aches, and pains. Which side is stronger or more flexible? If you find more problems on the left, it might signify a need for you to amplify feminine traits like love, service, and kindness. It suggests that you need extra work with the energies generated by the six feminine signs. If you suffer more on the right side of your body, then you probably ought to energetically address the six masculine signs.

THE COLOR OF LIBRA: GREEN

Green, the color that falls in the middle of the visible spectrum, is the color of Libra. Green evokes peace and calm. Hiking in a green forest, for example, often serves to eradicate stress. Wear green to generate more harmony in your life, and place green in your home to insure a relaxed and peaceful living environment. Pay a visit to your garden or to a park or a forest to help balance your own energy. Lately there has been a great deal of media attention and consciousness around turning "green"—in other words, becoming ecofriendly. Seen through astrological glasses, this new necessary trend is here to help us fix our relationship (Libra) with earth.

WHAT SHOULD I FOCUS ON IN THE WEEK OF LIBRA?

In the week of Libra, focus on art and design. Move your furniture around and try to discover some new possibilities hidden in the spaces you inhabit. Spend extra time with your partner. If you don't have a partner, capitalize on the support of this archetype of harmonious relationships to begin a conscious search for your true love.

Follow the synchronicities related to your business partners, lovers, perceived enemies, lawyers, designers, and artists. The symbols of Libra include scales, balance, seesaws, Venus, middles, seven, relationships, marriage, teaching and learning, green,

Examine all your close relationships this week, both in love and business, and try to determine whether they are balanced between giving and receiving, teaching and learning, healing and being healed. Meditate with the letter *Lamed* whenever you wish to rectify, heal, or create harmonious relationships. This letter can also help to balance your body's energy.

interior decorating and décor, peace, diplomacy, compromise, kidneys, ovaries, mirrors, indecisiveness, multiple options, wild fluctuations to the extreme, personal grooming, beautiful clothes or furniture, attractive people, law, justice, opals, superficiality, and nonviolence.

Your Libra Week Checklist

- Clarify and nurture your relationships. Identify how your partners in work and in life mirror who you are.
- Speak out loud the affirmation of Libra: "I am balanced, in harmony with life. Justice will prevail, and I will be rewarded for all my efforts. I generate peace and tranquility with all my relationships."
- Meditate on the letter *Lamed*.
- Wear green.
- Pinpoint oppositions in your life (such as two friends who dislike each other) that you ought to balance or harmonize.
- Surround yourself with beauty. Wear luxurious clothes. Attend an art or fashion show.
- Compromise. Let go of your ego in relationships. Be a diplomat. Avoid conflicts.

THE RITUAL OF LIBRA: COUPLES MEDITATION

This partner exercise from Tantric yoga will allow you to view your companion as a mirror. It might also reveal your connection from past lifetimes. Try to practice this technique with someone you share at least some intimacy with. This person does not have to be a lover. He or she could be a close family member or friend of either gender.

Each partner should take a shower before you begin to wash away any negativity and strain from the day. Also, don't eat for a few hours before you start the meditation, and never try it while under the influence of drugs or alcohol.

Meet at sunset, the hour of Libra. Dress in white from head to toe. Sit cross-legged on the floor (or on chairs) facing each other. Your knees should slightly touch your partner's. Each of you should then hold your hands up in front of you, palms toward your partner. Your palms should line up and almost touch your partner's palms. For the next five to ten minutes, hold your hands up and look straight into the eyes of your partner. Try to not blink the whole time.

At first, you might giggle from embarrassment. That reaction is common. Stick it out, palms almost touching, through the initial reaction. The energy and intensity will begin to increase. Soon you will see your partner's face darken as a result of your own neuron's fatigue from staring at the same spot. To amplify this effect, try not to blink. You will then begin to view images on his or her face. Sometimes these images will relate to your shared past lifetimes. Show patience. It takes time for your normal vision to tire and the ritual's special effects to take root.

Repeat this meditation three different times with the same partner. After each attempt, write down your experiences, feelings, and images that you might have detected. Share them with your partner. You will glean much insight into the nature of your relationship. This exercise might also stimulate strange and powerful dreams. Share these with your partner as well. If you like, you might decide together to focus the exercise on a particular problem or issue between you. Think about this intention for a moment before you open your eyes to gaze at your partner. The meditation likely will help to provide clarity on this problem for you both.

FAMOUS LIBRAS

Mohandas Gandhi, Ray Charles, John Lennon, Catherine Zeta-Jones, Bruce Springsteen, F. Scott Fitzgerald, George Gershwin, Ivan Pavlov, Samuel Adams, Brigitte Bardot, Euripides, Matt Damon, Sting, Eleanora Duse, Susan Sarandon, Miguel de Cervantes, Lenny Bruce, Oscar Wilde, Arthur Miller, Dizzy Gillespie, and Eleanor Roosevelt.

Scorpio: The Lord of Transformation

October 23 to November 22

Key Phrase: "I desire"—the drive

General Qualities: Intense, sexual, intimate, passionate, driven, powerful research abilities, skilled at healing, secretive, drawn to the occult

Dark Side: Possessive, vindictive, emotionally self-centered, possessed of criminal urges, paranoid, and destructive

Element: Fixed water

Planet: Mars

Day: Tuesday

Theme: Regeneration

Parts of the Body: Sexual organs, reproductive organs, and the nose

Color: Turquoise/green-blue

Gemstone: Topaz

Musical Note: G

Hebrew Letter: *Nun* נ

Kabbalistic Meaning of Letter: The fish and the serpent

Path in the Tree of Life: Path 13, connecting Beauty and Eternity

Tarot Card: Death

Movies: *Children of Men, Angel Heart, V for Vendetta*, all spy and horror movies

Affirmation: "I am passionate and sexual, creating intimacy with everyone I encounter. I accept death, knowing it will lead to a rebirth. I am open to being a vehicle for God's healing powers."

OVERVIEW

Scorpio is one of the most difficult archetypes to comprehend—probably because it governs some of the more intense and mysterious aspects of life: death, sexuality, magic, the occult, intimacy, and transformation. Because of this sign's ability to generate transformation, Scorpio long ago became known as the sign of healing. Scorpio (sign of Pablo Picasso, Martin Luther, and Hillary Clinton) teaches us how to let go and dispose of what we no longer need in order to create space for the new. In Scorpio, you will learn about the energies of transformation, magic, death, and reincarnation. And you will work to enhance intimacy (both sexual and nonsexual) with people around you.

Leo, the child of Aries and Taurus, who met through Gemini and gave birth in Cancer, grew up with the help of his Virgo nanny. He married in Libra, and here, in Scorpio, the new pair consummates the marriage by making love and transforming from two individuals into one united couple. On a recent trip to Bulgaria, I was invited to a national radio program called *The Other Side of the Moon*. The interview happened to coincide with a full moon in Scorpio. The first question asked of me was, "Are you aware of the Satanist Church of America?" The second question was whether I knew any Satanists. I was shocked at the direction of the inquiries. I'd thought I was there to talk about Kabbalah. But then I remembered it was a show named for the dark side of the moon on the night of the full moon in Scorpio—a time when people might be driven to project some of their ugliest fears. It reminded me about how some fundamentalist Christians demonize Hillary Clinton (a Scorpio) by calling her the anti-Christ (in other words, Satan). Under the influence of Scorpio, we sometimes can't help but obsess on the dark.

THE TERRITORY OF SCORPIO

Dying, dying, the world is dying.
But no one dies in such a way,
That they don't have to die again.
—KABIR, THE GREAT SUFI (FIFTEENTH CENTURY)

Scorpio arrives in the middle of autumn. At this time of the year, the leaves begin to transform from green to shades of orange, red, and yellow. The trees cast off their leaves just as the serpent, one of the symbols of Scorpio, sheds its skin. It is a gorgeous time of year, but a melancholy one too. The trees turn naked. They appear to die. They pretend to die. And that is the secret of this sign that rules death. Scorpio is not really concerned with death. Death actually delivers rejuvenation. It destroys only to transform.

The concept of death as a vital part of life is beautifully depicted by the biological process called *apoptosis*. Apoptosis, which means "falling leaves" (appropriate for a Scorpio process), was coined by Kerr, Wyllie and Currie in 1972 and explains how cells die in order to promote life. In fact, cancer is caused by the uncontrollable growth of cells. These cells do not die and, because death is not part of their cycle, they end up killing the organism upon which they host. Apparently, you cannot cheat the Angel of Death. You just have to realize it is a necessary part of life.

Scorpio is also the sign of sexuality and intimacy, which explains why the trees end up naked and exposed. This sign oversees the magic of sex. It generates the magic of healing and change into something better. It rules all kinds of secret magic as well as the afterlife, the most secret location of our ultimate transformation from one life to the next. Halloween and the Day of the Dead arrive during this mysterious month to underscore this archetype's spooky power. According to the Celts, the veils that separate the realm of the living from the dead thin dramatically at this time of year, allowing us to cross from one to the other with relative ease.

As you become a Scorpio this week, you will be asked to destroy the parts of your personality that you do not need. Ask the universe to reveal what traits, tendencies, or things are obstructing your development. They could include a substance, a relationship, an attitude, a fear, or some false hope.

THE SCORPIO MANTRA: "DEATH IS NOT THE END"

As the fixed water sign, Scorpio is both intensely emotional and overwhelmingly stubborn. Scorpio rules two of the most complicated and mysterious human experiences: death and sex. Kabir, the renowned Indian Sufi, asserts that we all reincarnate again and again—live and die, die and live—not to learn how to live better but to master the art of dying. When we truly know how to die, we don't have to return to live again. But in order to die well, you must live well. We must love life. Otherwise, death becomes just another escape. Legends state that when Kabir passed on at 120 years of age, both his Muslim and Hindu followers argued over his death rites. The Muslims wanted to bury him, while the Hindus insisted on cremation. Though Kabir had died, he nonetheless settled the argument with a stunningly ameliorative lesson of Scorpio. When his devotees lifted the shroud that covered his corpse, they found that his physical body had transformed (Scorpio) into flowers. The Muslims buried some of the flowers, and the Hindus burned the rest.

Most types of yoga emphasize *Shavasana,* or "corpse pose meditation." At the end of the practice, after you have worked hard to perfect a variety of challenging poses, you lie flat on your back, close your eyes, and pretend to die. This instruction is not merely a benevolent gift of rest and relaxation. It vitally affords you the chance to practice death. It prepares you to remain calm and still at the end of life's journey so that you will be able to join God without anxiety or resistance.

I like to view death as a rebooting of your soul. When we add a new software program to our computer, we often must restart the entire system to incorporate the new information. Death permits our soul to shut down and reboot, allowing us to assimilate all of the lessons we installed during our lifetime. It simply wouldn't work to live forever without earning a chance to truly utilize all the information and magic that we've absorbed. Our system would clog from enormous files that never integrate with the primary motherboard. Death reorganizes and amalgamates all our experiences so that our soul can grow more adept and formidable.

As you become a Scorpio this week, you will be asked to destroy the parts of your personality that you do not need. Ask the universe to reveal what traits, tendencies, or things are obstructing your development. They could include a substance, a relationship, an attitude, a fear, or some false hope.

Before you go to sleep each night this week, dedicate a few minutes to the corpse-pose meditation. Lie on your back, close your eyes, and imagine a calm beautiful place — a spot you would like to visit when you die. It could be a beautiful tropical cove, the shade beneath a giant redwood, or a luxurious living room with a magnificent view. This location will serve as your retreat following your death, your own Garden of Eden in which you will wait peacefully for your spirit guide.

THE ANTI—PUBLIC RELATIONS

Scorpio is a grueling, obstreperous sign for many people. In couples' readings, when I point out that one of the partners has moon in Scorpio or Scorpio rising, the other partner usually mumbles, "That would explain everything." Explain what? It explains their intensity.

Scorpios suffer from the worst public relations of all the zodiac signs. They carry a disquieting shadow wherever they go. I'll tell you a secret about Scorpios (since secrets are governed by Scorpio too): their rotten image is their own desire. They relish this repellent impression. They have cultivated it for millenniums. They actually want the rest of us to tremble and flee. The whole fun of Halloween—the Scorpio holiday—is for us to be scared to death.

Scorpios hold the secrets of the occult and the afterlife—the mysteries of the shadow. Unlike Leos, they cannot function under the spotlight. They need and relish a veil of privacy, intimacy, and darkness. Scorpio rules all of the components of life that most of us prefer to experience out of public view: sexuality, healing, confessions, death, transformation, espionage, sorcery, the occult, revenge, inheritance, and investigations. And this list represents just the facets of life Scorpio will admit to ruling. Imagine what they govern in secret. How can you tell if a person is a Scorpio? Just ask her for her sign. If she ignores you or counters with "Why do you want to know?" then she's a Scorpio.

This week, peer deep into your soul and identify your own darkest secret. What is the skeleton that you conceal in the closet? Your hidden shame? Then, if possible, meet in a confidential situation with someone you trust (or go to a session with a trustworthy professional—therapist, doctor, religious leader), and expose yourself and the secret. After you reveal the secret, write down how you feel—relieved, uplifted, terrified, criticized, accepted, loved. And also record any synchronicities and experiences that ensue from your revelation.

You might want to search for your secrets in your house of Scorpio, because this area of your life usually harbors many intense secrets and untold tales. A man with

Scorpio in the house of sexuality finally decided after ten years to call his mother and tell her that he was gay. Hiding his intimate life from his mother, who had always been a close friend, had tormented him severely. When he told her, she rejoiced, revealing that she had known (secretly) since he was thirteen. This man's unburdening transformed everything. Now free to introduce his partners to his mother, he soon met the love of his life.

Before you go to sleep each night this week, dedicate a few minutes to the corpse-pose meditation. Lie on your back, close your eyes, and imagine a calm beautiful place—a spot you would like to visit when you die. This location will serve as your retreat following your death, your own Garden of Eden in which you will wait peacefully for your spirit guide.

THE LORDS OF TRANSFORMATION

Scorpio people are deep and often dark—not because they radiate evil, but because they are saturated with energy. Their gaze penetrates. Their intensity makes us change. Often they don't have to do anything to effect our transformation. You simply live next door or sit beside a Scorpio on the bus and the alteration begins. Scorpios possess a kind of x-ray personality. They can see right through you—deep into your well of secrets. This sort of penetration makes most of us uncomfortable. And often we don't even notice the changes they trigger except in hindsight. Only in retrospect can we trace the transformation to a Scorpio or a Scorpio-oriented event. For example, we exude the famous morning glow after a powerful sexual experience (Scorpio). The virgin ceases to be virgin after sex. Witnessing the death (Scorpio) of someone profoundly alters and matures our outlook on life. A witch (Scorpio, magic) turns a frog into a prince.

The symbols of Scorpio reveal this archetype's transformative essence. While the rest of the signs have only one animal or totem that personifies their energy, Scorpio has three. The first, the scorpion, describes the vast majority of all Scorpios. This aggressive creature lashes out and stings for no reason. Next comes the serpent, which represents a much lesser percent of all Scorpios. These more-evolved creatures, which shed their skin to renew themselves, reveal the Scorpios' potential to regenerate and heal. But they also bite with vicious fangs and that bite can be poisonous and lethal. The final, extremely small percent of all Scorpios find representation in the eagle or phoenix. These rare and fortunate few serve as the utmost shamans and healers, wizards and witches, who secretly enhance all of our lives.

This week, peer deep into your soul and identify your own darkest secret. You might want to search for your secrets in your house of Scorpio, because this area of your life usually harbors many intense secrets and untold tales. Then meet with someone you trust (or go to a session with a trustworthy professional), and expose yourself and the secret. After you reveal the secret, write down how you feel—relieved, uplifted, terrified, criticized, accepted, loved.

Scorpios can be the worst or the best. They might start out as devilish scorpions, but as lords of transformation, they also retain the capacity to evolve into a serpent and even an eagle. Since Scorpio rules death and regeneration, Scorpios sometimes enjoy the privilege of several lifetimes (transformations) within the span of one human life. They can die without dying, and like the phoenix, resurrect as a new person. They sometimes transform from a criminal to a healer—like a murderous gang-banger who eventually metamorphoses into a crusader to keep others out of gangs.

Scorpio in you chart indicates where you possess the ability to transform profoundly. In this area of your life, you can become a whole new person.

YOUR OWN PRIVATE SCORPIO

Scorpio signals your potential to regenerate and transform. You will experience many episodes of death and resurrection, rebirth and change in your house of Scorpio. Letting go and flowing with the everlasting river of change will benefit this area of your life. Here's another trick of the Scorpio trade: this archetype grants access to this magnificent potential for renewal and rejuvenation whenever you create intimacy with others.

Scorpio in Your First House (Your Rising Sign): You are a passionate, complex, and intense person. Many find you intimidating and hard to handle. In this lifetime, you have chosen the path of the healer and transformer. You have a talent for research and finding the authentic root causes of all processes. In the week of Scorpio, focus on transforming your body and cultivating intimacy and sexuality.

Scorpio in the Second House: You enjoy a gift for identifying the talents of others and in working with their money. You can be a successful agent or manager. You also enjoy a rare talent for healing and research. This week, pay attention to your finances, talents, and self-worth.

Scorpio in the Third House: You are a deep and powerful thinker with a flair for research. There is no subject too hidden, dark, or intense for you. You could be a great investigator or spy. This week, pay attention to what you write and how you communicate with others.

Scorpio in the Fourth House: You need to live close to the ocean or a lake or spend time in the water. Untold secrets haunt your family, which might make your family life turbulent and emotional. One of your family members enjoys a potent gift for healing. During the week of Scorpio, focus on your family relationships and your home.

Scorpio in the Fifth House: Your love life might be shrouded in secrecy. You tend to fall for complicated and intense people, and you are passionate in love and in your creativity. Your children need a great deal of emotional support. This week, emphasize your children, love life, and creativity. Now is the time to heal the child inside you.

Scorpio in the Sixth House: You undergo periods of intense transformation in your diet and health. To attain better health, you might need to let go of certain foods that you enjoy. You are vulnerable to hernias, genital problems, and sexual diseases. During the week of Scorpio, focus on your diets, health, work, and service.

Scorpio in the Seventh House: You are attracted to deep and complicated people who might instigate turbulence and strife as a substitute for positive intensity. Creating intimacy and engaging in an active sex life will foster a satisfying partnership. This week, focus on your significant others, partners, and relationships.

Scorpio in the Eighth House: You are a passionate and sexual individual who needs to walk on the wild side every so often. Be careful not to abuse sexuality or magic. In a past incarnation, you most likely lived as a wizard or witch but misused your powers. You possess a rare gift for healing and transforming people. In the week of Scorpio, pay attention to your sexuality, intimacy, and your partner's abundance.

Scorpio in the Ninth House: You should study finance, investment, the healing arts, or any other subject that involves transformation. You are secretive about your life philosophy and religious beliefs. This week, try to travel to foreign lands as you pay attention to higher education and your in-laws.

Scorpio in the Tenth House: You could shine as a producer, healer, or investor. Creating intimacy with people in your professional arena will amplify your success. You are determined and passionate about your career. This week, focus on your career, your reputation, and your destiny.

Scorpio in the Eleventh House: You don't need many friends—just a few intense and intimate friendships. You can also create intimacy with groups, organizations, and corporations. You enjoy a great deal of influence over other people, or you know many influential people. In the week of Scorpio, focus on your friends and groups.

Scorpio in the Twelfth House: In a past lifetime, you experienced a difficult death, which has transmitted residual issues about death, sexuality, and transformation into this incarnation. You need to learn how to let go and permit change. Don't be afraid. Change leads to rebirth. You also might have trouble accepting your own strength and influence over other people. This week, highlight mysticism and letting go of what you do not need.

PROJECTIONS

Most of us will solicit trouble when we attempt to pinpoint what a Scorpio thinks or feels at any given moment. They keep it all secret, which makes them adept spies and private investigators. This secrecy, however, often proves dangerous both to Scorpios and to those of us who interact with them. Not knowing what a person thinks or feels induces us to guess. And often these conjectures are wrong. Usually we simply project our own fears and insecurities onto the other person.

For example, many therapy patients, who don't know anything about their therapist's thoughts or feelings, will fall in love with him or her and feel crushed when the therapist doesn't reciprocate their desires. The practitioner deliberately manufactures a safe, confidential environment to encourage the patient's experience of intimacy. After awhile, the patient might pitch his or her longing onto the therapist, mistaking the intimate environment for the therapist's feelings. This sort of projection (transference and countertransference) occurs with others in our business or personal life too. Sometimes, we might interpret an individual's poker face as negativity toward us. We suppose that our boss, an acquaintance, or even our spouse, dislikes us because they don't tell us otherwise. We begin to believe that they don't respect us or that they don't find us fun or fascinating. It might not be true at all. They might be Scorpios, who simply hold all their cards close to their chest. But the next thing you know, we have picked a nasty fight with them.

You might project false hopes and emotions, or you might fall prey to the projections of others, in the area of your life ruled by Scorpio. The best way to combat this phenomenon is to reveal your feelings openly. Don't wait for people to inflict their own problems on you.

One woman, who had Scorpio in the twelfth house of hidden enemies, realized that many of the women she knew hated her for her success. They projected their own failings and self-loathing onto her. I advised that whenever she encountered a woman who seemed threatened, she ought to offer that person a feminine type of compliment. For example, she should praise the woman's

Scorpio in you chart indicates where you possess the ability to transform profoundly. In this area of your life, you can become a whole new person.

clothes or the scent of her perfume. This technique instantaneously eliminated much negativity from her life, and it transformed her business too. She now works with more female clients than she does men.

THE SECRET SERVICE OF THE ZODIAC

Ruled by Mars, the god of war, Scorpio is nonetheless a water sign, which enables this sign to blend in seamlessly. They function as the deftest spies. They also excel at research, delving deep into secrets to unveil the source of any problem. Scorpios are the Secret Service agents of the zodiac. They expose the true essence behind any phenomenon. Their job, to put it most simply, is to expose. A healer, for example, lays bare the source of your ailment. In any intimate relationship, such as with a friend or a therapist, you reveal your secret self. You might find yourself proclaiming, "I've never said this to anyone before." In sex, you strip off your clothes to expose your body, and often your emotions too. Exposure of your hidden self generates intimacy, and that revelation makes you naked—and vulnerable. Now that person who saw you holds some power over you. He or she might turn around and betray your secret. In my travels in Eastern Europe, I met a powerful man (who happened to be a Scorpio) who was trained by the KGB. We talked about secret societies, and we could find parallels between Freemasons and the KGB. He concluded that the source of the power of these closed organization was their secrecy, which created a sense of intimacy among its members.

You might project false hopes and emotions, or you might fall prey to the projections of others, in the area of your life ruled by Scorpio. The best way to combat this phenomenon is to reveal your feelings openly. Don't wait for people to inflict their own problems on you.

Scorpio also rules the secrets of the occult and magic. We often fear witches and shamans because we don't understand how they do what they do. Humankind has ruthlessly murdered thousands of so-called witches. We projected our trepidation of the unknown and of change—and, I think, of death, the ultimate change—onto these mysteriously powerful women, and we punished them for our own fearful shortcomings. The word *occult* means "hidden," and the study of occultism (including astrology and Kabbalah) represents a systematic attempt to expose the underlying laws of the universe. Scorpios root around on the dark side of the moon not because they are evil, but because they simply gravitate toward the shadows to expose the secrets buried there. Therapists help to reveal our subconscious. Police investigators uncover criminals. And sex, we hope, discloses our love.

Scorpio in your chart highlights the area of your life in which you can add to the collective effort to reveal and expose. The secrets you lay bare can help all of humankind. Scorpio also reveals where you can shine as an investigator and healer.

How to Get Along with Scorpios

- Never lie. They can see right through you. Honestly attempt to reveal as much as you can without endangering your privacy. It is better to expose some of your secrets than to wait for Scorpios to send in their own "private investigator."

- Scorpio resembles a whirlpool in the ocean. You can't swim against the current. The only way to escape is to dive all the way down to the source and then move out of the narrow bottom. If you encounter trouble with Scorpios, you need to go all the way down with them. Be emotional. Dig deep into your inner core. There are no shortcuts. Go to the heart of the issue. And don't brush off their feelings or insights.

- Be intimate and real. Spend time one-on-one with your Scorpio buddies. Quality time is more important than the quantity of time.

- Scorpio governs sexuality and any other drive that evokes passion. Identify what drives the Scorpio and encourage that enthusiasm. A crazily successful Scorpio car dealer I know, in an intimate moment, revealed the secret of his success. He climbs in the car and drives it to the nearest highway. "I hit the accelerator," he said. "If I get an erection within ten seconds, then I know that I will sell the car for a huge profit." He paid no mind to the car's mileage or luxury features. He relied solely on his deep-seated Scorpio reaction. Remember, Scorpio equals *drive*.

- Don't try to expose Scorpios. They are private people, and you need to respect the "no trespassing" signs they erect around their personalities. They will eventually reveal themselves.

- Many astrologers contend that Scorpio is the only sign that gets along best with members of its own sign. That's not because no one else can stand Scorpios. It's just that few other signs can handle their intensity. If you want to get along with a Scorpio, practice becoming a Scorpio yourself. Be intimate, sexual, and mysterious.

Scorpio in your chart highlights the area of your life in which you can add to the collective effort to reveal and expose. The secrets you lay bare can help all of humankind. Scorpio also reveals where you can shine as an investigator and healer.

THE DARK SIDE OF THE FORCE: SCORPIO

Some people contend that Scorpio has no dark side. The whole thing, they say, is dark and problematic. This opinion represents more false projections. Still, from a more objective viewpoint, Scorpios do bear a host of issues that lurk deep within. They harbor many dungeons and cobwebs in their subconscious. Many suffer from a well-known sea-diving sickness that prevents a diver from telling which way is up to surface and which is down to the bottom of the ocean. This problem emerges when a person plunges so deep into the water that the sunlight cannot penetrate. Everything around the diver appears as the same dark color. He might believe he is swimming toward the surface, but he is actually heading deeper into the sea. This mistake can cause death. Scorpios sometimes dive so deep into their souls, into their subconscious, that they lose sight of the sun. This immersion in the dark can cause depression, disillusionment, and chronic pain. It might also create paranoia, because they believe that anyone who ventures in so deep after them must be out to get them. Without sunlight to distinguish the bright from the menacing, they—like a scorpion— simply assume the worst and sting everything, including themselves. To ameliorate this propensity, I recommend humming the Beatle's tune "Dear Prudence": "the sun is up, the sky is blue, it's beautiful, and so are you." Scorpios sometimes need to be reminded to come [up] to play.

Possessiveness and jealousy also plague Scorpios. As a fixed water sign, they often find it difficult to let go of their intense emotions toward a particular person, project, or idea. They cling maddeningly. Or they sting in retaliation without warning. Sometimes they sting seemingly for no reason at all. As a water sign, Scorpios are impressively psychic. And as the super private eyes of the zodiac, they perceive all of your hidden insecurities. They feel your hot buttons, even if they are not overtly aware of them, and when jealous or insecure they will press them viciously where it hurts most. A Hindu tale reminds us of a yogi who watched a scorpion accidentally fall into the Indus River. The yogi felt distressed at the scorpion's anguish and reached into the river to save him. The ungrateful scorpion promptly stung him. A second scorpion fell into the river. The yogi saved him too and received a second sting. It happened again, and the third rescued scorpion delivered a third hostile wound. A woman washing her laundry down the stream witnessed this remarkable and remarkably stupid scene. She approached the yogi and asked why he persisted when the scorpion not only failed to appreciate his selfless act, but also punished him for it. "The scorpion stings because it is in his nature to do so," the yogi said. "I rescue the scorpion because it is my nature to help the distressed." It might hurt, but you might try next time to forgive Scorpio. Their nature, after all, is just awarding you the chance to express yours.

When I was three years old, I shared a bedroom with my sister, who was about three years older than me. Thirty-six years later, after my sister had reprimanded her oldest daughter for unjustified nastiness toward her younger brother, my sister confessed to torturing me a bit too. She said that when I slept, I presented a sweet, naïve, and angelic expression (I used to suck my thumb), and she felt a compulsion to see if she could alter that tranquility. Scorpio will be Scorpio, and so she would crawl into my bed and pinch me, escalating this mischief with more and more force as she sought the threshold of pain that would wake me up crying. To be honest, I do not remember any of this, which is, of course, not a good sign. If my brain decided to repress the abuse, it was probably pretty traumatic. I do, however, remember waking as a small child from a recurring nightmare in which I was stranded on my bed amid a floor teeming with scorpions. You might have guessed that my sister is a Scorpio.

Many people asked me how it is possible that Scorpio rules both killing and healing. Think about how certain drugs or medicine can kill or heal depending on the dosage. This is why the serpent is the symbol of the medical field but is also known to possess a deadly venom. According to recent national statistics, each year hospital-related errors kill more people than car accidents or breast cancer. In addition, hospital infections kill five times more people than does the AIDS virus. Even today, we can see that killing and healing walk hand in hand.

And her (Scorpio) pinches were translated in my psyche into a nightmare of scorpions (a.k.a. my sister). It was not malice that compelled her to sting me in my sleep. It was her nature—a nature that she has transformed into that of an adoring mother and big sister. Of course, at that time I had no idea what astrology was or that my sister's sign was a scorpion. It is interesting how our subconscious knows much more than we do.

THE HEBREW LETTER *Nun*

נ

Kabbalah assigns the Hebrew letter *Nun* to Scorpio. In Aramaic, the root language for Hebrew, *Nun* translates as "fish of the deep." It signifies the Scorpio's tendency to dive deep into the ocean of emotions and the subconscious. *Nun* and fish in the Bible further suggest fruitfulness and reproduction, which corresponds to the sexual nature of Scorpio. *Nun* also represents the Hebrew word *Neshamah*, which means "soul." *Nun* thus radiates the quality of rebirth since our soul stands as the eternal part of us that never dies. *Nun* is also the first letter in the word *Nahash*, which means "serpent."

Mediate with the letter *Nun* to increase intimacy and healing in your life. This glyph can also help to facilitate any transformation you are going through.

THE PARTS OF THE BODY

Scorpio oversees the reproductive organs, genitals, and the nose. We generally uncover and expose our genitals only when we enter into an intimate encounter. There's a reason we call them our "private parts." After eating from the Tree of Knowledge of Good and Evil, Adam and Eve first realized that they were naked. And they hid their genitalia behind fig leaves. The verb "to know" in ancient Hebrew actually signifies "to have sex." The Tree of Knowledge informed them of their nakedness, while simultaneously awarding the ability to know each other sexually, to research each other's bodies. The Bible story then tells us that Adam and Eve went into hiding from God, but they probably simply sought out a private place to have sex. Scorpio energy drives us to have sex too. Enjoy. Just remember that if you don't know enough about your partner's secrets—where he or she has been and with whom—you open yourself to debilitating or even potentially fatal sexual diseases.

Mediate with the letter *Nun* to increase intimacy and healing in your life. This glyph can also help to facilitate any transformation you are going through.

Scent, detected by the nose, functions in animals as a prime instinct for assessing the environment. While the human nose doesn't hold that same supremacy, we do use the nose-inspired expression "to sniff out information." We symbolically rely on the nose to investigate and expose. Honor Scorpio this week by practicing some kind of aromatherapy. Visit a store that sells essential oils, and research what sort of scent would benefit your life. Remember that scientific studies have shown that certain odors—created by pheromones—activate sexual attraction.

THE COLOR OF SCORPIO: GREEN-BLUE

The color of Scorpio is a mixture of green and blue. Green comes from Libra, the preceding sign, and blue derives from the next sign, Sagittarius. The union of these colors makes turquoise. Many traditions—including those of ancient Egypt, Tibet, Native America, and Anatolia (Turkey)—use the stone and color turquoise to amplify shamanistic magic, power, influence, and healing. Wear this color to magnify your connection to the energy of Scorpio.

WHAT SHOULD I FOCUS ON IN THE WEEK OF SCORPIO?

Focus on change. Let go of anything that you do not need—stuff, relationships, and attitudes—to create space for new opportunities. Like the leaves on a tree, allow whatever blocks new growth to die. Also, strive to create intimacy with the people in your life. Open up. Tell secrets. Be sexual.

Identify and follow the synchronicities of Scorpio. This archetype's bank of symbols include sexuality, intimacy, doctors, healers, shamans, taxes, insurances, healing, death, transformation, magic, occult, secrets, spies, research, Mars, turquoise, paranoia, jealousy, deep-ocean fish, scorpions, snakes, eagles, and inheritance.

Your Scorpio Week Checklist

- Speak the Scorpio affirmation out loud twice a day: "I am passionate and sexual, creating intimacy with everyone I encounter. I accept death, knowing it will lead to a rebirth. I am open to being a vehicle for God's healing powers."
- Meditate on the letter *Nun*.
- Wear green-blue.
- Allow the death of whatever you don't need in your life.
- Practice the corpse-pose meditation.
- Tell someone close to you (or a psychologist) your darkest secret. Expose!
- Create intimacy. If possible, have sex (safely, of course).

THE RITUAL OF SCORPIO: YOUR INITIATION TO DEATH AND SEXUALITY

According to the wisdom of Scorpio, we all undergo three major initiations—three moments that profoundly change us forever. The first involves our understanding that we are mortal, that we won't live forever. Our first stab at sexual intercourse triggers our second initiation, and the moment of our death delivers the last. This exercise stimulates all three stages of Scorpio transformation.

Sit in a comfortable position and focus on your breath. If you like, you can use the Gemini breath ritual to instill a sense of deep tranquility. Once you feel relaxed, try to remember all the events that have occurred since you woke up that morning. You got up, brushed your teeth, grabbed a piece of toast, ran into your boss in the company parking lot, and so on. Then catalog the sequence of experiences from yesterday and then the day before. Now try to recall what you did on your most recent birthday.

Then slowly go back in time until you were approximately thirteen years old. Recall two moments from that year: a pleasant experience and also an aversive one.

Then retreat further through time to your first memory of death. What happened to trigger your realization that you will die and your parents will die? We are born with no concept of death. But at some early point, usually following the death of a relative, a grandparent, or a pet, we confront the Scorpio truth. Once you have identified the event that incited your recognition of mortality, leave your meditation and begin a "journal of death." Write all your memories of this episode. Interview people, especially your parents or siblings, for information about how you reacted to the news. What was the true story? Conduct a personal and private investigation into your relationship with the Angel of Death.

Since Scorpio also rules intimacy, you might want to ask your partner or a close friend to open this same type of investigation into his or her first encounter with death, and then share all the information with each other. This mutual revelation will enhance your intimacy tremendously.

Stage two requires you to recall your first sexual experience. In your journal of death, write everything you can recollect about that day and that moment. Where were you? Who were you with? How did it happen? What were your emotions before and after? It might not have been a perfect experience, but it holds a heavy significance over your ability to develop intimacy with another human being. Then try to remember your first memory of anything sexual, such as an early childhood fantasy or a person you found attractive. Then compare your early fantasies and longings with your actual sexual experience. How would you change you first actual sexual encounter? Write down your ideal first sexual experience. How would you have wanted it to be? Add colors, scents, and conversations. Change the setting and the identity of your partner, if you like. By rectifying your first connection to sexuality, you might heal any bitterness or disappointments that shadow you to this day. You might be able to defuse any negativity that blocks you from creating intimacy now. If you recall your first sexual experience with fondness, jot down every single detail that made it so memorable. These distant particulars might help you to remember how to enjoy your present sex life even more.

We cannot replicate the third stage of the Scorpio metamorphosis, your actual biological death. But we can prepare. Practice the corpse pose. Write down the feelings and thoughts that these exercises engender. I also recommend reading the *Tibetan Book of the Living*

Thank you, Rock Hudson, for bringing the AIDS epidemic into world consciousness.

and Dying by Sogyal Rinpoche. This book lays out the fundamental teachings of the *Tibetan Book of the Dead.* It will allow you to help others die with comfort and dignity and ease your own process of letting go when your time comes. Remember, Scorpio rules death but also guarantees transformation, renewal, and rebirth.

FAMOUS SCORPIOS

Pablo Picasso, Hillary R. Clinton, Niccolo Paganini, Theodore Roosevelt, Ted Turner, Bill Gates, Richard Burton, Julia Roberts, Fyodor Dostoevsky, Auguste Rodin, Saint Augustine, Lee Strasberg, Voltaire, Bjork, Jodie Foster, and Rock Hudson.

Sagittarius: The Traveling Prophet

November 23 to December 21

Key Phrase: "I see" — prophecy

General Qualities: Optimistic, lucky, free-spirited, wise, enthusiastic, seekers of knowledge, natural teachers, athletic, adventurous, and deeply moral

Dark Side: Overly optimistic, gluttonous, irresponsible, and lazy

Element: Mutable fire

Planet: Jupiter

Day: Thursday

Theme: The ember and the torch

Parts of the Body: Liver, thighs, and hips

Color: Blue

Gemstone: Turquoise

Musical Note: G sharp

Hebrew Letter: *Samech* ס

Kabbalistic Meaning of Letter: Trust and support

Path in the Tree of Life: Path 14, connecting Beauty and Foundation

Tarot Card: Temperance

Movies: *Raiders of the Lost Ark*, *Indiana Jones and the Temple of Doom*, *Indiana Jones and the Last Crusade*, and any other adventure films and documentaries

Affirmation: "I am lucky and optimistic, at one with synchronicities. I create alchemy between giving and receiving. I trust God to provide me with all I need."

OVERVIEW

Sagittarius arrives as the most optimistic and happy-go-lucky sign in the zodiac. It rules travel, higher education, truth, teaching, philosophy, religion, wisdom, foreign cultures, and adventure. Characterized by the archer shooting an arrow to the sky (this sign aims for the heavens), Sagittarius aspires always to understand the truth behind the cycles of the universe. Sagittarius (sun sign of Mark Twain, Ludwig van Beethoven, and Walt Disney) allies us with our sense of optimism and the positive attitude required to embark seamlessly on the journey of life. In the week of Sagittarius, you will learn about the healing properties of optimism and how to attract and create your own luck. You also will receive tips on how to locate and then teach your personal truth about the meaning of life.

THE TERRITORY OF SAGITTARIUS

Sagittarius falls in the worst energetic neighborhood of the zodiac. It rules some of the darkest days of the year, a span in which the daylight diminishes to its lowest point. In addition, Sagittarius sits smack in between Scorpio, the sign of death, and Capricorn, which is represented by the Tarot card called the Devil. What's up with that? How did Sagittarius, one of the most powerful and auspicious archetypes, find itself squished into such a sketchy neighborhood? Did Sagittarius have some kind of spat with God? Was he disinherited from his rightful and fortuitous legacy?

No. In truth, Sagittarius chose this spot. Sagittarius is a fire sign, and fire is the only element that can automatically banish darkness. The carrier of the fiery torch, the bearer of truth, Sagittarius (the mutable fire sign) delivers the adventurous prophets who venture into darkness, ignorance, and the unknown to spread wisdom and light. To accomplish this hazardous task, God armed these bold travelers with luck and optimism. Sagittarius represents the traveling fire, the Olympic torch that has been passed for thousands of years from one town to the next. (The original Olympic Games were dedicated to the chief god Jupiter, the ruler of Sagittarius.) Sagittarius brings the Truth, the whole Truth, and nothing but the Truth. He gallops all over the world as the knight on the white horse that slays every dragon.

Sagittarius highlights the area in your life in which you can locate and share wisdom and truth. For example, a woman with Sagittarius in her house of work used this archetype to identify the reason for her misery at work despite her success as a marketing executive. The fast-food products she peddled for money did not live up to her personal sense of truth. She would never use them herself, and she refused to allow her children to touch them. During her week of becoming a Sagittarius, she decided to quit her job, and she moved to a firm that promoted products that she did not have to lie about.

Poets William Blake, author of *The Marriage of Heaven and Hell*, and Emily Dickinson, who never left her house but adventured deep inside herself to locate profound truths, were both Sagittarians. You'll recall that one of Dickinson's notable poems said, "Tell all Truth but tell it slant." Sagittarius highlights the area in your life in which you can locate and share wisdom and truth. Sai Baba, spiritual teacher to people all over the world, and Baruch Spinoza, the philosopher who dared to say that Moses did not write the Torah, were both Sagittarians.

THE SLAYER OF DEATH

Like all mutable signs, Sagittarius must break the hold of the stubborn fixed sign that precedes it in order to propel change and progress. Gemini employed cunning to persuade Taurus to let go, and Virgo followed a meticulously detailed plan to force Leo off his throne. How does Sagittarius manage to oust Scorpio from power? How can Sagittarius kill Scorpio, the ruler of death? It seems an impossible task to kill something that is already dead.

Sagittarius, the sublime archer, slays death with an arrow made of a particularly lethal idea. With his arrow dipped in truth (this archetype also rules the various subsets of truth, such as philosophy and religion), Sagittarius cheerfully teaches us that death is not the end. It banishes death by spreading the truth of reincarnation, thereby vanquishing Scorpio's most formidable hold over us, our fear of death. Sagittarius carries the optimistic message of cycles, transmigration, and traveling from one culture to another and one state of being to the next. The truth of Sagittarius kills death. And the death of death is life.

But we must not look at Scorpio and Sagittarius, or any other two signs for that matter, as enemies. They are siblings, after all. While Scorpio teaches us about death and resurrection, Sagittarius offers the wisdom and philosophy (both Sagittarian traits) of reincarnation and the transmigration (traveling) of the soul. Sagittarius teaches us that we will come here again and again (Sagittarian cycles) until we learn (Sagittarian higher education) all that life on earth has to teach us. Then, our Sagittarian prophets assert, we will attain enlightenment and join the One.

A high-profile fundraiser who has become a very good friend of mine is a true Sagittarius. She will raise money only for candidates and companies she believes in. From an early age, she once told me, she had reoccurring issues with snakes. She even once had a snake drop down on her from the sky (it was actually from a high tree). She never understood why she had these issues until I explained to her the fact that her spiritual clan, the Sagittarians, is the slayer of serpents and dragons. And that is why she needs to confront them, but that does not mean she has to date them.

What one thing scared Indiana Jones, the fierce and brave Sagittarian? Not the Nazis; he could handle them. No. His worst nightmare was snakes, which he had to encounter again and again. Maybe the snake symbolizes a Sagittarian fear of intimacy (Scorpio) and that's why Indiana Jones had a different girlfriend in each movie!

Your Sagittarius house and planets underscore your connection to truth and integrity. This week, practice speaking the whole truth and nothing but the Truth. Pledge to avoid all lies, even the little white lies that we all love so much.

The Immortal Wounded Healer

The centaur, half-horse and half-human, symbolizes Sagittarius. In the Harry Potter series, a centaur rescues the young wizard in the dark woods from the malevolent Lord Voldemort. The centaurs always arrive in the darkest period of the year to save us from our enemies—depression, doubt, hopelessness, and all of our myriad fears. In mythology, both gods and mortals alike cherished the centaur above all. One beloved centaur named Chiron served as the magnificent healer and teacher of Hercules, Achilles, and many other gods and demigods. According to one version of the myth, Hercules had returned from slaying a poisonous monster (Scorpio), and his sword, still stained with venomous blood, accidentally nicked Chiron's ankle.

The majestic centaur should have died from this clumsy mistake, but the gods could not afford to lose his enormous store of wisdom. Unable to cure him, they opted to grant him immortality to keep him around. And Chiron, the wisest of all, the master doctor, became known as the wounded healer. He could heal everyone else, but he could not heal his own terrible pain.

In 1977, astronomers discovered an asteroid in our solar system that they named Chiron. Wherever you have Chiron in your chart highlights the area of your life in which you suffer from an incurable wound. But it is also in this area that you hold the potential to teach and heal others so wondrously that you can become immortal. This concept is also beautifully Sagittarian: it is your wound, the place where you are most injured, that holds the potential for your immortality.

Your Sagittarius house and planets underscore your connection to truth and integrity. This week, practice speaking the whole truth and nothing but the Truth. Pledge to avoid all lies, even the little white lies that we all love so much.

Locate Chiron (⚷) in your chart. It flags a deep personal wound. But it also signals your capacity to teach the wisdom of the Sagittarian centaur and achieve immortality in this lifetime. Chiron in the first house, for example, represents an immortality that stems from developing your personality and leadership skills. Chiron in the second house brings immortality via your talents; in the third house it brings immortality by way of your businesses or writings, and so forth.

Where is the Wound that will Make You Immortal?

Look at your chart and identify in what house—in other words, in what aspect of your life—you have a wound or an imperfection that can transform into your immortality.

Chiron in Your First House: Your wound is your personality or you might carry a wound from a past lifetime that affects your physical body. You are a wounded healer. Your values will remain long after you are gone.

Chiron in Your Second House: Your wound has to do with self-esteem or finances. Your own family or your ability to heal can become your immortality and how you will be remembered.

Chiron in Your Third House: You might have a relative or a sibling who is wounded and needs your help. You might be prone to being wounded through words, letters, email, or misunderstanding and miscommunication. Your words, business, and communication will leave a mark on humanity.

Chiron in Your Fourth House: You might feel a sense of rejection from your family. One of your family members or your mother might be wounded. Your own family can leave a strong impression on the rest of your community.

Chiron in Your Fifth House: Your creativity was somewhat blocked and your inner child is wounded. Your children might also be wounded healers. You can leave a mark through your creative talents.

Chiron in Your Sixth House: You might be physically wounded or have a wound relating to your diet or work. You can leave a permanent impression on your community through serving others.

Chiron in Your Seventh House: You attract wounded people to your life and you are already in pain from a past relationship. Past partners remember you in a powerful way. They will carry your legacy forever.

Chiron in Your Eighth House: You are wounded in your sexuality or from some past abandonment. You will be remembered as someone who pushed forward other people's talents. You are a healer.

Chiron in Your Ninth House: You are a wounded teacher, teaching people what you need to learn the most. You can leave a strong impression that will outlast your physical body.

Chiron in Your Tenth House: You are wounded in your career life or feel you don't get enough recognition from your professional life. You can be remembered through your endeavors in your career.

Chiron in Your Eleventh House: You have a great many wounded friends or you might be hurt by a group or an organization. Your influence over your friends will make them remember you and your work long after you die.

Chiron in Your Twelfth House: You had a difficult past lifetime and you are refusing to let go of it. You might have been imprisoned or in confinement. This lifetime you can be immortalized through compassion, helping the underdogs and underprivileged. You can be remembered as a mystic.

Locate Chiron in your chart. It flags a deep personal wound. But it also signals your capacity to teach the wisdom of the Sagittarian centaur and achieve immortality in this lifetime.

Your Own Private Sagittarius

Your Sagittarius house marks the area of your life in which you will experience a heavy dose of truth, a huge helping of genuine meaning. You can also excel as a teacher here. As long as you hold fast to optimism and conviction, Sagittarius can help you to manifest anything you want.

Sagittarius in Your First House (Your Rising Sign): You are a traveler who is fascinated by foreign cultures, wisdom, and philosophy. Idealistic and enthusiastic, you are blessed with an adventurous free spirit. During the week of Sagittarius, focus on your appearance, body, and health. Identify where the universe calls you on a quest or adventure.

Sagittarius in the Second House: You are lucky with money. Take care to avoid excessive generosity with yourself and others. You may make large amounts of money and then lose it or spend it. You possess a talent for teaching and higher education. You can be successful in a foreign culture and make money by traveling. This week, pay attention to your finances, talents, and self-worth.

Sagittarius in the Third House: You are intelligent and adept in the field of philosophy. You write and speak in a fluent and instructive manner. You might also enjoy a gift for languages. You exhibit generosity to your siblings and neighbors. This week, highlight your siblings, neighbors, communications, writings, and business ventures.

Sagittarius in the Fourth House: Your home benefits from foreign ideas and cultures. You likely have artifacts or décor from all over the world installed in your house. It actually might be good for you to live in a different culture for a spell. You probably moved homes quite often while growing up. This week, pay attention to your home life, family, and emotional well-being.

Sagittarius in the Fifth House: You are attracted to exotic people. Blessed with a passion for traveling, you will benefit from visiting exotic places around the world. You excel at sports and need to keep active. You can be lucky with gambling and taking risks, but only when you bet on educated guesses. During the week of Sagittarius, focus on having more fun, being more creative, and attending to your lover and children.

Sagittarius in the Sixth House: Your work might involve traveling, teaching, or foreigners. You make a difficult employee, and so you would flourish better as your own boss. Avoid excess with food and drink. Your liver, hips, and thighs are vulnerable to problems. This week, emphasize your health, diet, exercise, and work.

Sagittarius in the Seventh House: You require an adventurous partner. You might have two major loves or marriages in this lifetime. You might also meet your partner while traveling, or your partner could be from a different culture. This week, focus on your partners, significant other, and clients.

Sagittarius in the Eighth House: Attend to your business or life partner's financial dealings. They likely spend way too much. You are sexually attracted to exotic people, and you might enjoy a heightened level of passion or intimacy while traveling. In the week of Sagittarius, highlight intimacy, sexuality, and letting go of the ideas, attitudes, and people that you cling to.

Sagittarius in the Ninth House: You are a natural-born teacher of philosophy and truth who can excel in mass communication. You might live in a different culture for a while. During the week of Sagittarius, pay attention to opportunities stemming from foreigners, travel, and higher education.

Sagittarius in the Tenth House: You can attain success and recognition in foreign cultures. Your career likely deals with philosophy, teaching, and mass communication. The more optimism you display, the better your chance for prestige and accomplishment. You are blessed with a high sense of morality. Let those ideals guide your career. This week, focus on your professional life and your dealings with your community.

Sagittarius in the Eleventh House: You have many foreign friends, and you easily befriend travelers or people from different cultures. You require enthusiastic and optimistic friends who will lead you on adventures. This week, pay extra attention to your friends, groups, and organizations.

Sagittarius in the Twelfth House: You likely have unresolved karma with foreign cultures. You might have been persecuted for your beliefs in a different lifetime. Watch out for being overly optimistic and depending too much on luck. During the week of Sagittarius, focus on your spirituality, mysticism, and the suffering of people around you.

CYCLES ANALYSIS

For years people have asked me to explain what I do for a living, and I have never felt comfortable defining myself as an astrologer. Unfortunately, I know of too many astrologers who misuse and mislead. One day, while studying my own natal chart, I experienced an epiphany. Sagittarius rules my house of career. I remembered that I had started out hoping to become a psychologist, perhaps a psychoanalyst. So I decided to call myself a "cycle-analyst," since Sagittarius perpetuates the cycle of life and death. Sagittarius made me realize that astrology, at its core, analyzes cycles. It attempts to understand the future by studying the cyclical events of the past. That is the simple secret of the prophet. By noting the events of history and pinpointing how often these similar events recur, the Sagittarius seer can predict the future. For example, a Sagittarius can proclaim in the summer that all the lush green trees you see around you will stand naked half a year from now. It's a silly prophecy, but it demonstrates the cyclical logic of all soothsayers. They study the cycles and project the wisdom of their experience and knowledge into the future.

It takes about twelve years for Jupiter, the planet of Sagittarius, to orbit the sun. Jupiter also brings expansion and abundance. If you want to predict or prophesy in what area of your life you will experience good fortune this year, go back twelve years and identify the area in which you grew the most back then. If, for example, you enjoyed a promotion and a raise twelve years ago, you are likely to encounter a similar advance this year as well.

"IT'S ALL GOOD": THE MANTRA OF SAGITTARIUS

The fact that Sagittarius rules prophecy, optimism, and truth prods me to feel sanguine about the future of humankind. Since the sign that oversees prophecy (in other words, our future) also radiates unfettered optimism, the future is therefore supposed to be good. If the prophets of the zodiac, these wise centaurs that arrive at the darkest time of the year, gaze into the future and still retain hope and cheer, it leaves no doubt that (as Bob Marley said) "everything is going to be all right." Sagittarius marries truth and optimism. It teaches that when you are hopeful, you more easily see the truth. Teaching falls under the domain of Sagittarius too. If you want to teach well, this archetype instructs, you need to be optimistic. Sagittarius, the traveler, is on a quest for truth—a quest for nothing less than the meaning of life. Sagittarians venture everywhere—to every culture, philosophy, religion, and creed. They travel outside and then inside themselves as well to find the truth and then teach it to all of us.

An optimistic view of the future will benefit the area of your life ruled by Sagittarius. This arena—such as communication, family, relationship, career—also affords you access to the true meaning of life. Practice optimism this week. Speak the mantra of Sagittarius, "It's all good," as often as you can.

THE INDIANA JONES OF THE ZODIAC

Indiana Jones, the charismatic archeology professor, personifies the Sagittarius energy. Highly educated, athletic, and optimistic, he believes in and respects a multitude of religious truths. In his first movie, *Raiders of the Lost Ark*, he searches for a revered

Jewish relic, the sacred receptacle for the Ten Commandments that was built by Moses. In the second movie, *Indiana Jones and the Temple of Doom*, he retrieves the scared stones of the Hindu tradition, and in the third film, *Indiana Jones and the Holy Grail*, he locates the Holy Grail of the Christian faith. Sagittarius reconnects us to higher wisdom. He accomplishes this marvelous quest by adventuring into the world like Indiana Jones. He realigns us to the truths that reside in other cultures and traditions. Jewish lore says, "There is no prophet in his own village." To spread truth, a person must depart the comfort of his or her community. Christ, Muhammad, and Moses all left their homes before they could preach and teach their truths. Imagine if Jesus had wandered into the market in Nazareth and told the adults of his hometown what to think and do. They would have immediately laughed him off the pulpit, jeering, "What business is it of Mary's little boy to tell me what's what? I remember when he couldn't even recite his ABCs."

It takes about twelve years for Jupiter, the planet of Sagittarius, to orbit the sun. Jupiter also brings expansion and abundance. If you want to predict in what area of your life you will experience good fortune this year, go back twelve years and identify the area in which you grew the most back then.

Sagittarius tells us that we need to travel, like the hero who wanders into the unknown, to retrieve the gifts available to all humankind.

The house of Sagittarius marks the area of your life that can be optimized through travel and meeting foreigners. You might have to go on a quest to fulfill your potential. Take risks, seek adventure, and above all, remain optimistic. This week, watch a foreign movie or a documentary on a different culture.

How to Get Along with Sagittarians

- Challenge the Sagittarius. Give him a mission, a call for adventure. Dare her to excel and spread her fire.

- Be optimistic and pay respect to luck. Sagittarius understands the magic of fortune. The more optimistic you are, the more you focus on the positive events in your life, the more luck you will attract. Start simple: imagine that you will find a convenient parking spot with money already in the meter, for example. Optimism does beget luck. Try it. And play this kind of game whenever you are with your lucky Sagittarius friends.

- Travel with Sagittarians. At a minimum, travel with them to lectures, art exhibits, or movies about foreign lands.

- Don't argue with a Sagittarius about morality, philosophy, and religion.

- Give them as much freedom as possible. They are social creatures, beloved, like the centaur, by all. Let them travel to clubs, events, or odd daily adventures as they wish. Since they are half-horse and half-human, they need some space to run around.

The house of Sagittarius marks the area of your life that can be optimized through travel and meeting foreigners. You might have to go on a quest to fulfill your potential. Take risks, seek adventure, and above all, remain optimistic. This week, watch a foreign movie or a documentary on a different culture.

THE DARK SIDE OF THE FORCE: SAGITTARIUS

What happens when these prophets and preachers think they know the truth when they really don't? What happens when their ego poisons the works? The Bible labels these determined moralists as "false prophets." Unfortunately, false prophets never consider themselves false. In this mode, when they enshrine their own truth above all others, Sagittarius can become overzealous, preachy, and self-righteous. It produces missionaries, the "holy" Inquisition, holocausts, witch burning, and all other forms of religious tyranny. Without temperance and a respect for all traditions and truths (Temperance is the Tarot card associated with Sagittarius), Sagittarius transforms from a holder of the torch to the bearer of the raging bonfire that it uses to incinerate the heretics.

Jupiter, the ruler of Sagittarius, delivers abundance and luck, but when it expands too far it encroaches on excess. In Greek mythology, Jupiter, also known as Zeus, lusted without restraint for anything and everyone: women, goddesses, beautiful boys, and animals too. He probably would have had sex with a plant if he could have figured out how to make it work. Sagittarians are susceptible to such surfeit as well. They sometimes experience difficulty harnessing themselves to one person in a long-term relationship. Sagittarians also might fall prey to gluttony with food and drink.

THE HEBREW LETTER *Samech*

Kabbalah assigned the letter *Samech* to Sagittarius. *Samech* means "to trust" or "support." When we trust in life, when we flow with the synchronicities we encounter, we access the Truth. Trust brings optimism. Sagittarius demands that we trust.

Samech also translates as "adjacent" or "close by." By following Sagittarius's teaching of truth and optimism, we move closer to our higher self—we travel adjacent to God.

The shape of the letter *Samech* resembles the wheel of fortune, which is shown on the Tarot card of the same name and associated with Jupiter. The round letter epitomizes the concept of cycle analysis. The wheel always turns. Everything changes. And under the influence of Sagittarius, it changes for the good.

Meditate with the letter *Samech* to attract optimism and luck into your life. This letter also will amplify your prayers for support from God. Use it, too, whenever you travel. For example, before you land in a new country, imagine the letter *Samech* surrounding you and pray for synchronicities and adventures.

THE PARTS OF THE BODY

Sagittarius rules the liver, hips, and thighs. In mythology, many teachers and prophets had to sacrifice their liver to deliver their message. Somehow the liver seems to contain our inner truth. In some ancient civilizations, priests used the liver for divination. By examining the liver of a sacrificed animal—an art called hepatomancy—they uncovered the will of the gods. Prometheus, one of the Titans who supported the ascension of Jupiter, also presented fire to humankind. (In the language of fiery Sagittarius, he gave us truth.) He stole that fire from the chariot of the sun (practically, from the sign Leo), and, as punishment for this gift that brought humanity closer to God, he was perpetually chained to a rock. Every day, an eagle (one of the symbols of the previous sign, Scorpio) arrived to eat the liver of the defenseless hero. And every night, his liver would grow back (our livers do regenerate after surgery), allowing the eagle to return at dawn to feast all over again. When Odin, the supreme god of the Norse mythology, hung himself upside down from the Tree of Life, he punctured his liver with a spear. Following this Sagittarian ritual, he discovered the runes, which are used for divination (prophecy) to this day. And as Christ hung on the cross, a Roman solider punctured his liver to determine whether he had actually died. These mythologies suggest that the opening of the liver allowed the inner Sagittarius truth to pour directly to all of humankind.

Take care of your liver, the container of your inner truth. Alcohol, drugs, and most prescription medications tax the liver severely. Lay off a bit this week.

To activate the energy of Sagittarius, you can also work to strengthen your thigh muscles. Any form of squats will do the trick. If you wish, try the yoga chair pose. Basically squat into an invisible chair with your back straight. Hold the pose for three minutes. If this position proves too difficult, do it with your rear end and straight spine pressed against the wall.

Meditate with the letter *Samech* to attract optimism and luck into your life. This letter also will amplify your prayers for support from God. Use it, too, whenever you travel.

THE COLOR OF SAGITTARIUS: BLUE

Blue, the color that everyone loves and the color that blends impeccably with all others, is the color of Sagittarius. It symbolizes the popularity enjoyed by nearly every

Sagittarian. Blue also represents vastness and unbounded opportunity—as in, "the sky's the limit" and "as vast as the deep blue sea."

Wear blue when you aspire to attract the qualities of optimism, truth, wisdom, and trust.

WHAT SHOULD I FOCUS ON IN THE WEEK OF SAGITTARIUS?

In the week of Sagittarius, focus on your truth. What is the meaning of your life? What is your creed, your belief system? Ask the universe to reveal what you are supposed to teach to the people that surround you.

Focus too on cultivating an optimistic outlook on life. If possible, travel. At the very least, travel within your own hometown by seeking out other cultures and traditions.

As always, look for synchronicities that can help you on your journey to the Light. The bank of symbols for Sagittarius includes fire, torches, higher education, religion, philosophy, knowledge, traveling, foreigners, adventure, quests, in-laws, blue, Jupiter, liver, thighs, horses, centaurs, prophets, sages, teachers, wounds, truth, morality, cycles, religious zealotry, gluttony, luck, optimism, the wheel of fortune, temperance, trust, and wisdom.

An optimistic view of the future will benefit the area of your life ruled by Sagittarius. This arena also affords you access to the true meaning of life. Practice optimism this week. Speak the mantra of Sagittarius, "It's all good," as often as you can.

Your Sagittarius Week Checklist

• Find your truth, and for a whole week do not fib. Avoid even tiny lies that you think will help people.

• Use the affirmation of Sagittarius: "I am lucky and optimistic, at one with synchronicities. I create alchemy between giving and receiving. I trust God to provide me with all I need."

• Meditate on the letter *Samech*.

- Wear blue.

- Identify your area of immortality.

- Travel back twelve years to predict the expansion and growth that you can expect this year.

- Express optimism. Say, "It's all good," and it will be so.

- Rent a foreign movie or a documentary about a distant land.

- Read some books this week, go to lectures and book signings (Sagittarius is the sign of wisdom and education). If you happen to be driving long distances or flying, get some books on tapes. This is not as good as reading a book, but it's not as bad as not reading at all.

THE RITUAL OF SAGITTARIUS: THE KABBALISTIC CROSS

Kabbalah teaches an old Hebrew prayer designed to balance your body and your life: *Atah Malchut VeGevurah VeGedulah LeOlam Amen* ("To You is the Kingdom, the Power and the Glory Forever, Amen"). This prayer evokes what is known as the

Wear Sagittarian blue when you aspire to attract the qualities of optimism, truth, wisdom, and trust.

Kabbalistic Cross because it unites the four corners of the Tree of Life, which are represented by the spheres Crown, Kingdom, Mercy, and Severity. This cross symbolizes the four components of the universal spiritual force field: divine and mundane, masculine and feminine. As a sign that is half-beast and half-human, Sagittarius epitomizes the balance between earthly life, or the mundane (the lower, animal body of the centaur), and the divine (the upper, human body of the centaur). As the archer, who holds the curved bow (feminine) and the linear shooting arrow (masculine), Sagittarius evokes the other points of the spiritual cross as well. Working to harmonize these four corners, which are all contained within this archetype, delivers the Truth.

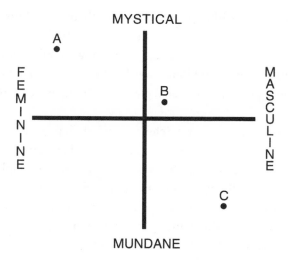

Figure 6: Sample locations on the Kabbalisitic Cross

Locate yourself on the graph shown in Figure 6. If you are an active, outgoing, and energetic go-getter, you will fall on the right, masculine side. If you are a receptive, more passive person who flows with whatever life brings, then you will place your-self on the left, feminine side of the cross. Now decide how mystical or earthly you are. If you are reading this book, interested in meditation and higher truths, then you most likely will land in the upper half of the picture. On the other hand, if you tend to skeptical, believing only in what you can touch, hear, and see, then you likely sit on the lower, more mundane half of the graph. The trick of the exercise is to figure out how to balance the masculine and feminine as well as the divine and mundane so that you move yourself smack into the nexus of the cross.

In the example above, the person labeled A sits in the feminine, mystical quad-rant of the graph. To move to a place of balance at the nexus of the cross, this person will have to become a little more grounded and earthly (mundane) as well as a little more assertive (masculine). Person C, the CEO of a junk food company, needs to do the opposite. Bossy and argumentative (masculine) and dismissive of everything besides making lots of money (mundane), she is prone to some serious heart trouble. She ought to cultivate some trust, mysticism, and compassion to move closer to the center of the cross. Meanwhile, person B has mostly balanced his mundane animal nature with his trust in the mysteries of the universe. In fact, he teaches a spiritual form of martial arts (mystical) while also organizing Brazilian jujitsu tournaments (mundane). However, he is too tilted toward the masculine. He needs to learn how to receive a bit more instead of his usual planning and taking care of things for everyone else.

Place yourself on the cross and determine what changes you might implement to push yourself closer to the point of equilibrium and harmony. You might also want to locate your family members, partners, and friends on the graph. Where do they land? Most likely, you will have to situate most of them near your own position. As the Sufis say, "Show me your friends, and I will show you who you are." You are all likely traveling together on this journey to the center of the cross. Help them out. Teach them your Sagittarius truth about how to get closer to the truth.

FAMOUS SAGITTARIANS

Sai Baba, Baruch Spinoza, Billy the Kid, Scott Joplin, Joe DiMaggio, Jimi Hendrix, Bruce Lee, William Blake, Winston Churchill, Mark Twain, Bette Midler, Woody Allen, Jean-Luc Godard, Walt Disney, Emily Dickinson, Frank Sinatra, Ludwig van Beethoven, Steven Spielberg, Edith Piaf, and Frank Zappa.

The Indiana Jones film trilogy was directed by Sagittarian Steven Spielburg.

♑

Capricorn: The Achiever

December 22 to January 19

Key Phrase: "I use"—winning with what I have

General Qualities: Persistent, ambitious, successful, career-oriented, disciplined, responsible, reliable, funny, and mature

Dark Side: Pessimistic, opportunistic, greedy, overly skeptical, cynical, fearful, having a willingness to step over bodies to achieve a goal, holding the view that the end justifies the means

Element: Cardinal earth

Planet: Saturn, ruler of karma and understanding

Day: Saturday

Theme: The business plan

Parts of the Body: Skin, teeth, skeleton, knees

Color: Indigo

Gemstones: Garnet, black onyx, hematite

Musical Note: A

Hebrew Letter: *Ain* ע

Kabbalistic Meaning of Letter: The all-seeing eye

Path in the Tree of Life: Path 15, connecting Beauty and Splendor

Tarot Card: The Devil

Movies: *The Devil Wears Prada, The Advocate, Fiddler on the Roof*

Affirmation: "I can achieve all my ambitions; success sits in the palm of my hand. I am a proof that discipline, persistence, and endurance can make my dreams come true."

OVERVIEW

Capricorn provides us with structure, discipline, and the plans necessary for the attainment of our worldly goals. It arrives at the start of bleak winter as the most pragmatic of the signs, an archetype designed to set us on the right track and help us manifest our potential. Capricorn (sign of Elvis Presley, Richard Nixon, and Martin Luther King Jr.) rules the areas of career and social status. It is the sign of tradition and the past. It teaches us persistence, endurance, and determination. In the week of Capricorn, you will focus on how to advance your career and identify your purpose in life. You will work to overcome your fears and frustrations and learn to see the benefits inherent in all the obstacles that you encounter.

THE TERRITORY OF CAPRICORN

Capricorn begins on the winter solstice, the shortest day of the year, the day we encounter the least amount of light. Capricorn, the cardinal sign of earth, initiates winter as well as all processes governed by the element earth, such as structural, power, political, financial, health and physical, disciplinary, and planning processes. The winter solstice has proven to be rather traumatic for many cultures in the Northern Hemisphere. As we progress toward the winter solstice, the days are stripped of their light. Everything becomes dark and gloomy. Early stargazers and shamans recognized this phenomenon and its deleterious effect on human mood and behavior. For example, in pre-Columbian Mexico, some cultures sacrificed people in a macabre effort to appease the sun god. They speculated that the sun, which slowly diminished around winter solstice, demanded the blood of human sacrifice in order to grow strong again.

Contemporary psychologists have dubbed the winter blues S.A.D., which stands for seasonal affective disorder. They recognized that humans, animals, and plants react to the changing seasons, a conclusion that astrologers from all over the world have been aware of for thousands of years. The symptoms of S.A.D. include oversleeping, a need for a nap in the afternoon (as in a siesta), a craving for carbohydrates that contribute to weight gain, grouchiness, melancholy, and antisocial behavior. Bears have found a practical solution to winter depression. They just go to sleep. Psychologists devised a different remedy. They expose the patient to light. They call it light therapy.

All over the world, wise elders, storytellers, religious teachers, and astrologers lit upon another solution. I am sure that you and your family have already practiced this same preventive medicine many times before. It's called the holiday season, or to be more specific, Christmas, Hanukkah, Kwanza, Saturnalia, and Yule, just to name a few. Our astute ancestors, like modern day psychologists, could not help but notice that people's moods sour as the days grow shorter. Versed in the practical applications of the ancient alchemical axiom of "as above, so below," they figured that as the light slowly disappeared above, people's energy levels declined correspondingly below. In order to enliven their communities, these ancients decided to concoct holiday festivities to crown the winter solstice with special significance. During the darkest time of the year, they created the holidays of light. You can call holidays the real *light therapy*. Hanukkah, also known as the Festival of Lights, was created to counter the growth of darkness both outside and in. During this holiday, Jews from all over the world spend eight days lighting candles. Hanukkah evokes a kind of sympathetic magic designed to abet the growth of light. We light eight candles (eight is the symbol of infinity), and once we reach eight candles on the eighth day, it seems as if the light has achieved a critical mass that will enable it to shine thereafter on its own. The Celts similarly ignited bonfires on the mountaintops during Yule for this same purpose: to beckon light into a darkening world. During Christmas, we drape the treetops in sparkling lights. When you visit any mall or city center around Christmas, you will see light therapy in action. The shops and front yards sparkle with so much light that you barely notice the burgeoning darkness of the night.

More recently, humankind has invented another technique to fight the winter blues. It's called shopping therapy, but its efficacy is short lived. Shopping's invigorating boost usually lasts until the first credit-card statement arrives in January. Shopping therapy derives loosely from Kabbalistic spiritual principles, but I have to say that in the last two centuries it has spun a little out of control. Kabbalah works on the principle of giving and receiving, and in the times of darkness we are encouraged to generate love and happiness by giving and receiving gifts. We bring a green tree (the Tree of Life) into our living room and surround it with presents. Jewish tradition calls on us to give chocolate golden coins (called Hanukkah *gelt*) to children. The chocolate, of course, contains enough sugar to make the kids high enough to forget the dreariness of winter.

In the week you dedicate to Capricorn, you might feel a diminishing sense of optimism and hope. That's normal. Some astrologers dub Capricorn the archetype of suffering. It is not an easy sign to channel. Allow two or three days for this mood to lift, and don't be afraid to reach rock bottom.

THE GATEWAY OF THE GODS

The winter solstice heralds the darkest day of the year. But it also heralds a marvel. What do Jesus Christ; Apollo and his lovely twin, Artemis; Marduk (the Mesopotamian Jupiter); Cernnunos (the horned Gallic god); Mithras (the Babylonian sun god); Baal (the Canaanite god); Bel (the Celtic sun god); Balder (the Norse god); Attis (the Phrygian savior); and Horus (the Egyptian sun god) all have in common? They were all born on the same day. Their birthdays land on the winter solstice, which means they are Capricorns. (Jesus Christ, as we noted in the chapter on Aries, is a Capricorn by proxy.)

This shared birthday teaches us a profound spiritual truth: in the moment of bleakest darkness and despair, when all seems lost, our higher self, the spark of god and goddess within us, is born. When we hit rock bottom, our savior—our genuine divine nature—comes to the rescue.

Astrology views the longest night of the year as the great womb of the Mother Goddess, who gives birth on that day to the god of Light. Spanish uses the phrase *dar luz*, which means "to give light," to describe any birth. In the wake of this astrological birth, the womb of the goddess—code for

In the week you dedicate to Capricorn, you might feel a diminishing sense of optimism and hope. That's normal. Some astrologers dub Capricorn the archetype of suffering. It is not an easy sign to channel. Allow two or three days for this mood to lift, and don't be afraid to reach rock bottom.

the all-encompassing darkness of the night—begins to contract. Like the night from this day forward, it shrinks smaller and smaller, while the baby called Light expands and grows. The winter solstice, according to esoteric astrology, therefore equals the gateway of the gods.

As you practice becoming a Capricorn, understand that the road to success and achievement often detours through a patch of darkness and despair. Capricorn teaches that anyone who has experienced the high of success first confronted the low of failure. Failure is OK, but being discouraged or giving up because of a setback is not. Human development sits on a seesaw of trial and error. And these errors push us toward victory. Capricorns, symbolized by the goat, are mountain climbers. This week you will climb. But first you must ascertain the mountain that you wish to climb. If you crave success, Capricorn insists that you answer one question without a doubt: what do you want?

This week you will decide on your goal for the next year. Allow the synchronicities you encounter to help you to identify what you really truly want. Capricorn in your chart likely indicates the area in your life in which you will encounter suffering and some hardships. These experiences should not be viewed as bad karma or punishment, but as a way for you to learn how to overcome frustration and deal with failure. After all, a gardener often uses manure, which might smell terrible, to prepare the garden for fragrant and fruitful plants. Your Capricorn house highlights where you will eventually enjoy your own fragrant and fruitful success.

THE COOL OF WINTER

Capricorn ushers in the coldest span of the year. It is the refrigerator of the zodiac, and as such, it arrives as the most conservative of all the signs. Capricorn conserves food and sustenance and it conserves ideas and ways of thinking. In the past, before the invention of refrigerators, if you did not heed the message of Capricorn, if you were not structured and disciplined with your food supply, you and your family would starve before you had the chance to grow new crops in the spring. Capricorns are therefore stingy and calculating with their resources. It's their job. It keeps them, and the rest of us, alive. Capricorn teaches us to be disciplined and careful with what we have so that it lasts and lasts. They animate this survival mechanism that has worked for thousands of years. Developing compassion toward your Capricorn partners and acquaintances will command a respect for their conservative (some might label it stingy) nature. Next time a Capricorn says, "Let's not spend on that. Let's leave the money in our 401K," don't argue. Just say, "OK."

I once learned a valuable lesson from an Israeli Arab who was training next to me in a gym in Tel Aviv. I had one shekel in my pants and was busy doing my abs routine inbetween benching. The shekel escaped my pocket and rolled onto the floor. I just figured that if it dropped it was on a journey and I should let it go its way, and besides I had 100 more crunches and did not feel like losing my groove. The guy who was curling next to me put his weights down and picked up the coin. He looked at me and said, "My father always said that if you don't pick up one shekel you are not worth one shekel (about 25 cents)." The man was a Capricorn and I learned my lesson.

This week you will decide on your goal for the next year. Allow the synchronicities you encounter to help you to identify what you really truly want. Capricorn in your chart likely indicates the area in your life in which you will encounter suffering and some hardships—and where you will eventually enjoy your own fragrant and fruitful success.

This week, focus on the preservation of your finances, resources, time, and energy. Make sure that you don't purchase anything without comparing prices. Keep a detailed log of all your expenses. How much do you earn each month? How much do you spend? For example, ditching your daily five-dollar coffee from the corner chain can save over $1,800 a year. Your Capricorn planets and house highlight the places where you have been blessed with bountiful resources that must be handled in a disciplined manner. Capricorn marks the area of your life in which you ought to be a bit more conservative and responsible.

SIGN OF THE TIME

Capricorn is the sign of structure. It represents a vessel, the container of all the other energies. While Cancer, the opposite sign, symbolizes the holy water, Capricorn epitomizes the Holy Grail, the cup that contains the water. If Cancer is the ocean, then Capricorn is the solid bedrock that supports it. Capricorn not only represents the structure of the three-dimensional physical world, but it also brings us the structure of time. Saturn, whom the ancient Greeks called Chronos, the lord of time, rules Capricorn. Why did Capricorn bind us to time? Why did this complex archetype give rise to old age, maturity, and other unyouthful things? Time allows us to evaluate our progress. Without time, we would not be able to measure our development. We would never know whether we have mastered any lessons. Activating the Capricorn energy within you demands that you make peace with time. You must begin to appreciate the fact that time ticks as the greatest healer and teacher that we enjoy on earth.

As a whole, Western society has declared war on time. We spend money and resources on creating faster airplanes, lightning-fast Internet connections, quicker workouts, speedier cars, and faster food. Yet with all these attempts to override time, we end up working more hours than ever before. And we end up with less free time. Obviously, we can't beat time. So why not surrender? Capricorn emerges to slow us down. Both Judaism and the Sufi tradition speak the adage, "Haste is of the devil." Capricorn reminds us that there are no shortcuts to genuine spiritual growth.

Matter does matter. To master the teachings of the material world, we must spend time on the earth. Why rush through the experience? Sometimes we look back on our life, and we wish we would have spent more time appreciating the moment—our first love, first kiss, college, pregnancy, the move to a new home. Like metal car chassis on an assembly line, we tend to move from one thing to another without stopping to savor the experience and fully assimilate it. In the week of Capricorn, make sure that you slow down enough to value each and every experience. Walk, think, speak, and eat more slowly.

This week, focus on the preservation of your finances, resources, time, and energy. Make sure that you don't purchase anything without comparing prices. Keep a detailed log of all your expenses. Capricorn highlights the places where you have been blessed with bountiful resources that must be handled in a disciplined manner. It marks the area of your life in which you ought to be a bit more conservative and responsible.

Capricorn delivers many tools that help us to appreciate time and actualize our potential. The Capricorn paraphernalia include discipline, persistence, perseverance, and endurance. All of these attributes relate to time, and all, when used wisely, beget success and accomplishment. If you have a goal that you aim to achieve (goals and achievements are ruled by Capricorn), you need to formulate a plan (plans are ruled by Capricorn) and diligently focus on it (focus is ruled by Capricorn). You will encounter some trials and errors, obstacles as well as frustration (all ruled by Capricorn) along the way, but you must maintain your determination and exhibit discipline and persistence (Capricorn again) until you reach the finish line—no matter how long it takes. Capricorn governs our career. And we must deploy all of these qualities to thrive in our chosen career.

Before setting out on your next little journey to the grocery store or to work, try to guess how long it will take to arrive at your destination. Once you settle on your estimated time of arrival, do not check the time until you get there. This rule will prevent you from driving extra fast or stopping to slow down to meet your estimate. Whenever I feel the need to fine-tune my relationship to time, I play this little game myself. The goal is to come as close to your guesstimate as possible. For example, one man tried this exercise on a trip from Dallas to an appointment that same day in Hollywood. And he arrived within two minutes of his estimate. His success in this game—despite all that could have gone wrong to slow him down—made him so happy that his meeting proved even more beneficial than he could have dreamed. The whole escapade awarded him a feeling of mastery over time and space.

THE LITTLE GIRL ON MAIN STREET

Some people recoil and grouse at the suffering we have to endure before we reach the top of the mountain. Capricorn shrugs and says, "Too bad. This strategy always works. And it teaches you what you need most in the process."

Imagine a happy little girl, about ten years old, vibrant and enchanted by life. She avidly looks forward to her weekly Saturday walks down Main Street with her father. They hold hands, share jokes, and gaze at all the gleaming goods and toys in the shop windows. One week, they stroll past a music store.

The girl points at the window and says, "Daddy, Daddy, look at that guitar. Please, Daddy, will you buy me that guitar?"

Her patient father already has heard similar pleas about a pink dress, a red bicycle, and a three-layer chocolate cheesecake in the past hour alone.

"Come on, Mommy is waiting for us," he answers.

A week later, they walk by the same store, and the little girl stops and begs, this time with tears, for the same guitar.

"Come on, dear, your little brother is all alone at home."

The girl contains her frustrations and plods silently home. The same scenario recurs again and again for years. Sometimes the girl tears loose from her father and enters the store to test out the guitar, but her father never agrees to let her take it home.

Around her thirteenth birthday, the girl informs her father that she plans to window shop one Saturday on her own. Her father doesn't buy her anything that she wants anyway. The father respects her wishes, but concerned for her safety, he secretly follows her. The girl heads straight to the music store to play the guitar. The shop owner knows her by name, and everyone there loves her cute smile and beautiful voice. She even has a group of fans, who know that she often arrives to play and sing most Saturdays around noon. Her father beams at the sight of his daughter and her appreciative audience. He is not stingy or cruel. He simply does not have any more room in storage for all the toys, bikes, and other accessories he has purchased for his little girl over the years. But on her thirteenth birthday, moved by her joy and persistence, he surprises her with the guitar. She jumps up and down with glee. It is the happiest day of her life. She sleeps with the guitar, dances with it, and she practices, dedicating every free moment to playing her precious gift. Within seven years, she has becomes a successful and acclaimed singer/songwriter. And she still owns and uses her guitar from Main Street.

The moral of the story is simple: You are the girl, and the father is God. In order to prove our commitment to ourselves and to God, we must demonstrate determination, especially when life does not grant us what we want (or what we think we want) immediately. Capricorn is the sign of the late bloomer. It represents the part of you that needs to focus and mature before it can flower. But when it finally does blossom, the magnificent flower will thrive for a long time. Sometimes the universe tests us to certify how much we really want something. If we show tenacity and endurance, we usually get exactly what we crave—and more. Unfortunately, most of us give up right before God is about to grant us our wish. To remedy that little human flaw, God created the persistent, resolute sign called Capricorn. This archetype delivers the superglue that adheres us to our dreams.

Capricorn in your chart marks the area in your life in which you are a late bloomer—the place where you will pay respect to time and appreciate the teachings of patience. You might have to push through frustration, suffering, obstacles, and inhibitions. But like the little girl, with persistence, focus, and resolve, you can triumph and attain much recognition. It takes millions of years of intense pressure to turn a lump of coal into a diamond. Your house of Capricorn marks the area of your life in which you too can turn coal into diamonds. Many astrologers associate Capricorn with the Jewish nation. For two thousand years, Jews all over the world concluded their Passover prayers with the sentence, "Next year in Jerusalem," asserting their wish to rebuild their ancient capital. It took close to two millenniums, but their prayers eventually were answered.

Before setting out on your next little journey to the grocery store or to work, try to guess how long it will take to arrive at your destination. Once you settle on your estimated time of arrival, do not check the time until you get there. This rule will prevent you from driving extra fast or stopping to slow down to meet your estimate.

THE DEVIL

The final three signs of the zodiac—Capricorn, Aquarius, and Pisces—are the most complicated and difficult to understand. According to Kabbalistic astrology, each sign represents the accumulated energies of all the signs that came before. Aries, the first sign, embodies the purest energy because it does not contain anything besides itself. Taurus is a composite of the energies of Aries and Taurus. Gemini represents Aries plus Taurus plus Gemini, and so forth. By the time we arrive at the final three signs, all the energies swirling around together obscure and confuse the issue.

Because of the impediments to grasping the true nature of these signs, we tend to project our fears onto them. We call Capricorns devils, nickname Aquarians weirdoes, and accuse Pisceans of being insane. Projections, as we know from psychology, say more about the accuser than the person being accused.

Nevertheless, I have pondered hard and long why the Tarot assigns the Devil to Capricorn. The creators of the Tarot might have thought that since Capricorn is the most skeptical sign, it would not take much offense at this moniker. This sign doesn't often take astrology or the Tarot too seriously anyway. But Capricorns' pragmatic, earthly natures (Capricorn is the cardinal earth sign) doesn't automatically make them nonbelievers. Sir Isaac Newton, a prominent Capricorn who directed his immense intelligence to deciphering the laws of the material world, also delved into alchemy and astrology.

I believe that what the creators of the Tarot noted is that Capricorn equals the Devil by virtue of fear. Capricorn channels the energy of fear because Capricorn represents the sign of survival in the harshest of times. And our fear of dying—from wild animals, from lack of food in winter—is what insures our survival. The Capricorn's responsibility, planning, and cautiousness keep us alive during the inhospitable months of winter. In the traditional depiction of the Tarot card of the Devil, we find an image of a man (Adam) and a woman (Eve) chained to the Devil. They are enslaved to their fear. When we become shackled to our fears, we sever our connection to the divine inside us. According to Kabbalistic astrology, evil does not exist. The Devil does not exist either. But fear of the Devil does.

The image of the Devil in the Western tradition reveals what we are most afraid of. The animal associated with the Devil is the goat, the symbol of Capricorn. The goat also evokes the Greco-Roman god Pan, who was actually a fine musician and a pretty nice chap overall. The lower half of his body was a goat, while his upper half was human. His only crime against Christianized civilization was his overactive sex drive. The collective Western fear of sexuality caused the god Pan to morph into the Devil. The term *panic*—meaning a manic manifestation of fear—derives from *Pan*.

Capricorn in your chart marks an area in your life in which you house many fears and inhibitions. These innate obstacles explain why it takes time to succeed in this arena. This week, confront your fears. Most likely, the fear of success as well as the fear of failure will pay you a visit. These two fears represent two sides of the same coin. Please don't panic when fear arrives. If fear overwhelms you, rest assured that you are successfully channeling the Capricorn. Don't brush fear away. Welcome it. Your job this week is to assimilate fear, to understand it. Humor is the antidote for fear. Laugh at yourself or your fear. Don't forget that fear's greatest fear is that it won't scare you anymore. Laughter will neutralize your fear. Remember that some fear is beneficial, but be careful not to get stuck or frozen in place.

Capricorn in your chart marks an area in your life in which you house many fears and inhibitions. These innate obstacles explain why it takes time to succeed in this arena. This week, confront your fears.

YOUR OWN PRIVATE CAPRICORN

Capricorn highlights the place where you ought to courageously face your fears. It is in that house that your inner Devil lurks. It is also the area of your life in which you experience doubt and karma from past lifetimes. More optimistically, it signals the area in your life that will bring you tremendous accomplishment and recognition as long as you focus, discipline yourself, and persist. You might encounter frustration, but this house highlights the path to your greatest triumph.

Capricorn in Your First House (Your Rising Sign): You are a thorough, disciplined, and methodical individual. The first forty years of your life are not easy, but you are a late bloomer and much success is promised to you in the future. You have a gift as a politician or as someone who knows how to use other people in a greater cause. You merely need a deliberate plan and much persistence. During the week of Capricorn, pay attention to your body, your direction in life, and your health.

Capricorn in the Second House: You are a late bloomer in connection to your finances, talents, and self-worth. You probably struggled with your self-esteem growing up or lived under someone who repressed your genuine talents. You are conservative with money and will do better under a meticulous financial plan. This week, work with your talents and finances and take note of how the universe supports your income.

Capricorn in the Third House: You have a conservative outlook on life and exceptional powers of concentration and focus. You might suffer issues from past lifetimes in relation to your siblings, relatives, or neighbors, but your relatives likely influence or guide your professional path. This week, pay attention to the way you think, talk, and write. Make sure to reconnect to your neighbors and siblings.

Capricorn in the Fourth House: You likely endured an arduous childhood or home life. You might have felt confined or inhibited by your family. You require structure and discipline in your current home. It might take you time to find the home you really desire or to create your own family. This week, connect to family members and to your home. It marks a good time for renovations and changes in your house and office.

Capricorn in the Fifth House: You might have children later in life. You enjoy a genuine appreciation of love, and you usually are quite serious about romance. Children can help to ground you. Cultivate more creativity in your chosen career, and try to be more playful in general. During the week of Capricorn, focus on your love life, your children, and your creativity.

Capricorn in the Sixth House: You experience karma related to your health, diet, and work. It will take time for you to locate your career path. You might find your true work and service close to the age of forty or when you feel matured. You might also be at risk for chronic diseases. Monitor your skin, bones, knees, and teeth. In the week of Capricorn, pay attention to your health, work, and service.

Capricorn in the Seventh House: You are attracted to older or more mature partners, who have their feet firmly planted in the ground. It might take time to find your partner. You do best with a more traditional partner or relationship. This week, focus on your partnerships. Spend some time trying to identify repeating patterns in relationships so that you might learn to avoid those past mistakes.

Capricorn in the Eighth House: Your partner might be a little tight with money, but he or she has a good grasp on finances. You are rather conservative sexually, and you might harbor fears about sex and intimacy. This week, focus on communicating your sexuality and your intimacy needs.

Capricorn in the Ninth House: You might encounter issues with your in-laws, who might appear too traditional, conservative, or aloof. You also experience past life karma with a foreign culture. Your career could be associated with foreigners. This week, plan a journey and focus on higher education to advance your career.

Capricorn in the Tenth House: You are a late bloomer in your career, but you will enjoy much success if you focus on one particular path. Your reputation and status in your community are vitally important to you. This week represents a time when you can dramatically advance your worldly pursuits.

Capricorn in the Eleventh House: You harbor unresolved issues with friends, groups, and corporations. You might experience pain generated by your friends, but as you grow older, your problems with groups and friends will diminish. You ought to follow a career that involves corporations, groups, or clubs. During the week of Capricorn, try to restart communication with friends or groups that you might not have spoken to for a long time.

Capricorn in the Twelfth House: You likely have been a politician or famous person in a past lifetime, but you abused your power and mistreated others. In this lifetime, success comes slowly to insure that you do not repeat those same errors. You need to overcome skepticism and doubt to find your spiritual path. You also might have to reconcile fears and phobias to find happiness. This week, focus on retreats, spiritual activities, and letting go of the fears and tendencies that hold you down.

SATURN RETURN

Kabbalah associates Saturn, the planet that rules Capricorn, with Understanding, the third sphere of the Tree of Life. Both astrology and Kabbalah revere Saturn, whose name is phonetically connected to the word *Sabbath*, which is the name of the holy day that the Ten Commandments directs us to dedicate to God. In Hebrew, Saturn is called *Shabtai*. It shares the same root as the word *Sabbath*, which means "to sit in peace or to rest." Kabbalah instructs that on the Sabbath, the bond between the above and the below is more solid than on any other day. Saturn, therefore, grants the ability to contact our divine self.

Locating this connection is not easy. The pinnacle of this powerful link between the above and the below occurs roughly every twenty-nine years, since Saturn takes about twenty-nine to thirty years to orbit the sun (as well as your chart). Every twenty-nine years, we all experience our Saturn Return. Instead of having one Saturn etched in our chart, which presents hardship enough, we have two. Saturn Return forces us to mature, assume responsibility for our actions, find our identity, and practice discipline. If you refuse, then the turmoil of Saturn will strike you hard.

Traditional astrology calls Saturn the malefic planet, in part because of the effects of the Saturn Return, which hits between the ages of twenty-seven and thirty-one and again between fifty-six and sixty. Unfortunately, some people do not survive this astrological earthquake. Individuals who eschew discipline or neglect to practice "becoming" Capricorn might find themselves in peril. Saturn is a harsh teacher. He reminds me of *Shaulin* masters, who will stop at nothing to transform their disciples into ideal warriors. Jimi Hendrix, the legendary poet and guitarist, died only two months before his twenty-ninth birthday. Jim Morrison, another rock icon, died at the age of twenty-eight, and Janis Joplin, the wonderful singer, passed away just three months before her twenty-eighth birthday.

Saturn Return is not always that deadly. Don't forget that Saturn and Capricorn rule career, focus, and success. Jesus of Nazareth left his hometown and began his spiritual quest at the age of twenty-nine. Siddhartha, who later became known as the Buddha, abandoned the comfort of his kingdom and family for a similar journey during his Saturn Return as well.

If you go back to the ages of twenty-seven to thirty-one, you will see that there was (or will be) a vast amount of upheaval in your life. Regardless of an individual's sun sign, anyone between the ages of twenty-seven to thirty-one and fifty-seven to sixty-one becomes a Capricorn for a few years, compelled to channel the energies of Saturn. If you know anyone who is going through a Saturn Return, lavish him or her with compassion because one day you too will be subjected to these challenging energies. The zodiac places Cancer, the sign of compassion, opposite Capricorn. Compassion was invented to ease us through these turbulent moments.

These astrological cycles also apply to businesses, relationships, and countries. For example, the state of Israel was born in the spring of 1948. The state was baptized with blood, war, and hardships. The young state had to prove to its allies and foes alike that it could survive and prosper in spite of continuous aggression from neighboring nations. Egypt, the strongest and biggest Arab nation, constantly threatened the new state from the south. It even rallied the rest of the Arab world to war with Israel. But Israel's destiny changed during its first Saturn Return. On November 7, 1977, when the state of Israel was twenty-nine years old, a miracle transpired. Anwar Sadat, a Capricorn and the president of Egypt, at the age of fifty-nine (during his second Saturn Return) came to Jerusalem on a mission of peace. At that time, this visit meant suicide. No leader in the Middle East ever had exercised such courage. And in return, Israel had to show maturity, discipline its people, and pull out of Sinai, an area that was taken from Egypt in 1967 and comprised about two thirds of Israel's total territory. This Saturn Return exacted much determination, focus, persistence, and endurance on the part of Israel to agree to the peace treaty. I remember watching the news as a little boy and witnessing the sight of soldiers evacuating their brothers and sisters by force from their villages in Sinai.

Sadat received the Nobel Peace Prize for his audacity and open-mindedness in 1978. In 1981, he paid for this peace with his life when he was murdered by a member of the Egyptian Islamic Jihad. In 2005, Israel entered its second Saturn Return and the political climate had changed. Egypt no longer represented the prime threat. The primary challenge to Israel's security now came from terrorist attacks carried out by the Palestinians. By the time of this second Saturn Return, Israelis faced a moral dilemma in the wake of the growing suffering experienced by the Palestinians. While the majority of Israelis felt that the Palestinians should enjoy their own state in the occupied territories, the Israeli settlers in Gaza and the West Bank refused to accept the territorial concessions such a compromise for peace demanded. Ariel Sharon, the prime minister of Israel at that time, took an unprecedented step. He decided to unilaterally disengage from the Gaza strip. This time, just like in the first Saturn Return, Israel evacuated its own people from the land they called home, agreeing to relinquish a portion of the territory they had been dreaming about for two thousand years. That concession represents their karma—the collective *Tikkun* of the Israelites. And it explains why the country is asked to cede territory in the name of peace on its every Saturn Return. I, along with all people in the Middle East, can only pray for another brave Sadat who could lead us to peace instead of war.

These world events mirror what happens to each of us. Every twenty-nine years, Saturn, the planet of *Tikkun*, arrives to remind us about our true mission. If you want to know what you came here to fix, then examine the most taxing and enduring lessons you experienced between the ages of twenty-seven and thirty-one and from fifty-seven to sixty-one. These lessons are your karma.

Israel was born under the sign Taurus, the fixed earth sign, who always finds it wrenching to give up her land. Saturn works through harsh coaching. It brings understanding, burns karma, and underscores *Tikkun*, and in the end, Saturn heals.

During Israel's first Saturn Return, Anwar Sadat died soon after negotiating the peace treaty. In the country's second Saturn Return, Ariel Sharon, the architect of the Gaza pullout, suffered a stroke and fell into a coma just a few months after turning over the land to the Palestinians. Israel's exact moment of Saturn Return arrived in August 2006 when it moved its armed forces into Lebanon to fight Hezbollah. I was born and raised in Haifa, the city where many of the Hezbollah rockets hit. During this time, my grandmother, who had lived in Israel for seventy years, told me that she had never seen such fear and aggression in the streets. She confirmed Saturn's tendency to compel change through its abrasive lessons and emotions.

At this same time, Iran underwent its first Saturn Return since its religious revolution in 1979. Many analysts and politicians believe that Iran acted as the primary force behind Hezbollah and the war in Lebanon. Astrology suggests that the crises in the Middle East arise from Saturn and Capricorn. (Cynics and statesmen alike often gripe that the conflicts in the Middle East are all about oil, another Capricorn commodity.) This astrological influence suggests that quick fixes and impulsive reactions will not resolve the problem. And indeed, the Israeli reactionary strike into Lebanon in pursuit of Hezbollah proved costly and fruitless. Saturn and Capricorn always demand long-term solutions that respect time, patience, and discipline.

At the age of twenty-eight, I almost drowned in the Pacific Ocean. In fact, I did die. When I surrendered and accepted my death, I stopped fighting the waves, and after a while I found myself washed ashore. A few months after this intense initiation, I was introduced to yoga, Kabbalah, and astrology. When I was twenty-nine years old, at the peak of my Saturn Return, I moved to Los Angeles with $600 and the telephone number of one person in the entire U.S.A. God knows it was a hard slog, but that Saturn-driven move helped me to create a rich new life. Saturn Return allows us to reset our goals and reboot our lives. Sometimes it kicks us so that we actually buckle down and revamp our ways. Sometimes we can take the initiative, enforce a little discipline on ourselves, and reboot with a bit less turmoil.

And sometimes Saturn Return is anything but onerous and gloomy. It promises great and sometimes unexpected rewards. For example, Sean Connery waited fifty-nine years, until his second Saturn Return, to be called "the sexiest man alive" by *People* magazine. Al Gore on his first Saturn Return was elected to Congress and started talking about global warming, and on his second Saturn Return, at the age of fifty-nine, received the Oscar for his film *An Inconvenient Truth*. When we choose to make love with time rather than fight it, we will benefit from Saturn's propensity to crystallize fortune in our career and public standing.

This week, you will exercise a mini, self-induced Saturn Return. By assuming the energies of Capricorn, you will be able to redirect your life by focusing on what you want to achieve. Capricorn and the planet Saturn highlight the places in your chart where you will deal with buried issues stemming from challenges that you failed to overcome in past lifetimes. The house of Saturn and Capricorn shows you the area in which there will be slow and tough learning. But these lessons will endure forever. Try to view your Capricorn house as the place in your chart where you store some of your most vital long-term investments.

How to Get Along with Capricorns

- Be punctual for your appointments with Capricorns. Always know what you want to accomplish from the meeting. Don't beat around the bush. Get down to business.

- Make sure that the Capricorn perceives your worth. If the Capricorn does not know you, bring letters of recommendation or any other proofs of your legitimacy.

- Capricorns love results; provide them with as many as you can. They also like to utilize whatever talents, assets, or ideas you might have. The more the Capricorn finds you useful, the better you will get along.

- Deliver whatever you promised and live up to what you say. Make sure that you back up your words with action, your proposals with money, and your plans with dedication.

- Capricorns are very cautious, and so don't try to rush them. You cannot impress a Capricorn by acting the daredevil.

- Respect the status quo and introduce new concepts slowly. Make sure these new ideas are based on precedent or strategies that have worked in the past.

- Show compassion towards Capricorns. They need more emotional support than nearly any other sign. They sometimes appear cold or indifferent. It is a façade. They really want to be touched.

Capricorn and the planet Saturn highlight the places in your chart where you will deal with buried issues stemming from challenges that you failed to overcome in past lifetimes. That house shows you the area in which there will be slow and tough learning. But these lessons will endure forever.

THE DARK SIDE OF THE FORCE: CAPRICORN

Capricorn assumed the unwanted chore of containing the collective fear of the entire zodiac. All our phobias, both individual (like fear of success) and societal (like homophobia), represent the shadow of Capricorn. All forms of prejudice and racism (skin is ruled by Capricorn) fall under this archetype. Martin Luther King Jr., a proud Capricorn, dedicated and gave up his life to helping us to see beyond the color of our skin. Capricorn also rules humor, which is a sweet remedy for all trepidations. Laughing at our fear often pushes us to overcome it. The old adage tells us that laughter can drive away demons where holy water fails.

Because of their conservative natures, Capricorns can stagnate and fall comfortably numb whenever they achieve a goal. They tend to mistrust change and innovations. They ascribe to the mantra "no news is good news." They too readily lock into the status quo, especially when the current moment—no matter how debilitating long term—feels OK. Impressively ambitious, Capricorns might also fall prey to an "ends justifies the means" sort of opportunism, stepping over and atop bodies to reach their personal aspirations. And as a sign frequently confronted with fears, frustrations, and obstacles, Capricorns sometimes turn pessimistic. Most Capricorns need to trust life just a bit more.

THE HEBREW LETTER *Ain*

Kabbalah assigned the Hebrew letter *Ain* to Capricorn. *Ain* means "an eye," reflecting Capricorn's skepticism and disbelief of anything he cannot see with his own eyes. However, the letter harbors a profound spiritual secret. In the ancient lore of Judaism, the eye symbolizes the whole cosmos: the white part represents the sea, the iris stands for the land, and the pupil signifies the temple of God. The rabbis tell us that if you want to see the holiest of holy, the place where God resides within that temple, then look at the image reflected on the pupil. That image—in other words, whatever you are looking at—represents God. Go to a mirror and stare into your own eyes. You will find your own self reflected in God's temple called your pupil. This beautiful metaphor instructs that we can see God only when we see God in each other. People who kill in the name of God need to work on mastering the higher truth of *Ain*. Maybe then they will realize that they never kill an enemy, but instead they murder God. Look people in the eye this week. Try to glimpse your own reflection on their pupils.

Sages report that the eye is the mirror of the soul. Capricorn and *Ain* reveal the area in your life in which you can catch a glimpse of your soul. It shows how God is reflected in your life.

Meditate on the *Ain* whenever you want to amplify discipline or ambition, fix problems with your career, or find a sense of direction in your professional life.

THE PARTS OF THE BODY

Capricorn is the sign of karma. Therefore, the body organs of Capricorn can be used to identify your karma and messages from past lifetimes. Capricorn rules the skin, bones, knees, and teeth—all body parts that give us structure. Capricorn also governs chronic diseases. Chronic implies that the ailment heals only after time, patience, persistence, discipline, and determination.

The skin, the biggest organ of our body, ensures that our internal organs remain in their place. In Genesis 3:21, right after God sends Adam and Eve to mortal life on

Meditate on the *Ain* whenever you want to amplify discipline or ambition, fix problems with your career, or find a sense of direction in your professional life.

earth, he gives them skins to wear: "God made leather garments for Adam and his wife and He clothed them." The traditionalists interpret this verse as nothing more than animal skins to keep the couple warm. But Kabbalah informs that before the fall from heaven, Adam and Eve existed as spirits at one with God. They had no mortal body. Their punishment entailed mortality, and for that they needed a body covered in skin. (In Hebrew, *leather* and *skin* are the same word.) In other words, God gave them the energy of Capricorn to provide them with a structure and the ability to survive on earth.

Take care of your skin this week. Go for a dermatological checkup. You also might want to book an appointment for acupuncture, which heals via the energy points on the skin.

The skin reveals much about our past lifetimes. Birthmarks, moles, or variations in color indicate a spot on your body where you might have experienced trauma or karma in a previous incarnation. Tattoos also tell a past-life tale both in the image and location on the body. Take care of your skin this week. Go for a dermatological checkup. You also might want to book an appointment for acupuncture, which heals via the energy points on the skin.

Your bones and skeleton are also ruled by Capricorn, the sign of structure and fear. Halloween deploys the skeleton to generate a fun-loving reaction of fear. After we die, our skeleton is all that remains visible here on earth. Archeologists dig up bones dating back millions of years, which fits Capricorns' energy of endurance, persistence, and time. Archeologists also find teeth, and they use these teeth to determine the age of the skeleton. The pain we often experience from our wisdom teeth, which emerge as we mature, symbolizes the growing pains of old age as well as the wisdom acquired by time and experience.

The Color of Capricorn: Indigo (Blue-Purple)

The color of Capricorn is indigo, a mixture of blue and purple. Wear dark blue or indigo whenever you want to be more responsible, reliable, serious, or disciplined. It is not surprising that business suits often come in this color.

What Should I Focus on in the Week of Capricorn?

Focus on focusing. In the West, we begin our year in Capricorn, admonishing ourselves to formulate New Year's resolutions (goals). Capricorn asks you to highlight your career, your status in society, and your commitment to manifesting your potential. Practice discipline and perseverance. Take note too of any karmic issues that might arise so that you can begin to resolve them. These challenges often appear as recurring patterns in a particular area of your life.

Seek out synchronicities. Capricorn's bank of symbols include goats, time, clocks, discipline, Saturn, the devil, saviors or sun gods, Saturday, career, ambition, focus, skin, bones, teeth, knees, indigo, pessimism, skepticism, determination, goals, business plans, conservatives, mountains, caves, oil and all things that come from beneath the ground, fear, panic, frustration, politics, humor, the winter holidays, New Year's Eve and Day, traditions, late bloomers, structure, patience, public recognition, hierarchy, older or more mature people, and opportunism.

Your Capricorn Week Checklist

- Undertake a discipline or commitment for the week. For example, commit to no desserts, no alcohol, cleaning out your closets, or going to yoga class every other day.
- Focus on a goal that you want to manifest this week and make a detailed plan of how you will make it happen.
- Speak the affirmation of Capricorn: "I can achieve all my ambitions. Success sits in the palm of my hand. I am a proof that discipline, persistence, and endurance can make my dreams come true."
- Meditate on the letter *Ain*.
- Wear blue-purple or indigo.
- Make friends with time. Walk slowly, eat slowly, and talk slowly. Take your time.

- Make a list of all your expenses and income.
- Practice the estimated time of arrival game.
- Try to laugh at any fears that crop up.

THE RITUAL OF CAPRICORN: THE CYCLE OF SATURN

This exercise will help you clarify your challenges and issues from past lifetimes that trickle into your current experiences. Saturn, the lord of karma and understanding, functions on cycles of about twenty-nine years. If you are younger than twenty-nine, then this exercise will not prove salient, but you will be able to implement the information in the future. Or you can share it with someone who might benefit from it now. Every twenty-nine years, Saturn teaches us the same lesson, but the lesson is not precisely the same. It's like reading a book when you are young and then again years later. It's the same book with the same information, but with each new read you learn different things.

A fine example of the twenty-eight- to thirty-year cycle of Saturn is the life of Governor McGreevy of New Jersey who, after being married for twenty-eight years, stood by his wife and in front of the whole nation said he was gay. The Saturn cycle, which put in motion a series of events, forced him to be true to his sexual identity.

Identify the primary challenges of your life today. Write them down in a paragraph that describes the frustrations and impediments and how you feel about them. Include as many stories and examples as you can. What area of your life do these challenges hit most often? Who is involved in them? Then go back twenty-nine years, and try to pinpoint an incident or situation that reflected these same hindrances. For example, a woman who was contemplating divorce from her husband of fifteen years discovered that twenty-nine years before her own parents had divorced, destroying her sense of security. Armed with this realization, she went with her husband to couple's counseling, and through diligence and hard work, she managed to bolster her sense of security with her husband. They worked on their problems, and they remained married.

Saturn's lessons are not always arduous and negative. Sometimes they simply push you to a higher level of accomplishment, prodding you to reach your true potential.

Famous Capricorns

Martin Luther King Jr., Muhammad Ali, Joseph Smith, Nostradamus, Mao Ze-dong, Josef Stalin, Isaac Newton, J. R. R. Tolkien, Richard Nixon, Henry Miller, Rudyard Kipling, Anthony Hopkins, Henri Matisse, Isaac Asimov, Mel Gibson, Sir Isaac Newton, Johannes Kepler, Stephen Hawking, Elvis Presley, David Bowie, Albert Schweitzer, Joan of Arc, Edgar Allen Poe, Federico Fellini, Jim Carrey, and Moliere.

Aquarius: The Joker

January 21 to February 18

Key Phrase: "I know"—awareness

General Qualities: Intelligent, ingenious, original, inventive, innovative, rebellious, reformative, humanistic, friendly, altruistic, sociable

Dark Side: Impersonal, require too much freedom, rebels without a cause, scatterbrained, irresponsible, and emotionally detached

Element: Fixed air

Planet: Uranus

Day: Saturday

Theme: Friendship

Parts of the Body: Ankles, shins, and the circulatory system

Color: Purple

Gemstone: Sapphire

Musical Note: A sharp

Hebrew Letter: *Tzadik* צ

Kabbalistic Meaning of Letter: The righteous and the saint, the fish hook

Path in the Tree of Life: Path 17, connecting Foundation and Eternity

Tarot Card: The Star

Movies: *Star Wars*, the *Star Trek* movies, all science-fiction movies, *Powder*, *Hair*, *Rebel Without a Cause*

Affirmation: "I attract beneficial friends and organizations to my life. I am a beacon of awareness and hope to the rest of humankind."

OVERVIEW

While Capricorn embodies tradition and the past, Aquarius arrives as the sign of the future and reform. Aquarius is a sign symbolized by a human being (the water bearer). It therefore represents fraternity, equality, democracy, groups, corporations, nonprofit organizations, clubs, and friends. Aquarius (sign of Oprah Winfrey, Franklin Delano Roosevelt, and James Dean) generates an individualistic and sometimes odd energy, yet one focused on friendly interaction with all other people. Aquarius also rules outer space, aliens, technology, gadgets, wireless, hope, and freedom. By connecting to the archetype of Aquarius, you will improve friendships and your relationship to the entire community. You also will assimilate the importance of helping your fellow human beings.

THE TERRITORY OF AQUARIUS

This is the dawning of the Age of Aquarius.
— GEROME RAGNI AND JAMES RADO, "AQUARIUS," FROM *HAIR*

We have landed in the futuristic cyberland of Aquarius, the water bearer. For thousands of years, the glyph representing Aquarius featured two wavy horizontal lines. Most people misunderstood this icon, believing that it portrayed water pouring from a bucket and figured Aquarius for a water sign. Spiritual astrologers and Kabbalists argued that these waves represented frequencies that travel—often invisibly—through the air. For millenniums, no one truly bothered to resolve this paradox. It loomed simply as another strange feature of this innately weird sign. Then, in 1900, Max Planck discovered that light travels through the air in waves. He called his theory of light waves electromagnetism. And from that point on, Aquarius should have been dubbed "the electromagnetic bearer." This vital scientific breakthrough served as one of the many signs of the dawning of the Age of Aquarius, and it verified Aquarius as the sign that governs information that traverses the air. Electromagnetism (scientific advances are also ruled by Aquarius) gave birth to radio, TV, satellites, microwave dishes, wireless technologies, and many other forms of conveying information. It heralded the age of information and fabricated the phenomenon called the global village.

While Capricorn managed the excess accumulation of energy delivered by all the previous signs by emphasizing structure, Aquarius dealt with the same befuddling overload by inventing a new idea called democracy. To Aquarius, all the signs are equal, all deserve civil rights. Aquarius originated the U.S. Constitution, the "all [humans] are created equal" passage of the Declaration of Independence (the United States' moon sign is Aquarius), and the right of each sign to exercise free speech and free energy emanation. Aquarius delivers the United Federation of all the signs—the U.S.A., or the United States of Aquarius. Capricorn devised a stern hierarchy to keep all the signs at bay. Aquarius, the sign of revolution, rebelled against that hierarchy and created an amazing new paradigm. *Viva la revolution!*

Aquarius in your chart signals the area in your life in which you must think outside of the box. You also benefit in this arena through incorporating the ideas and suggestions of friends. Allow democracy to reign here.

POWER TO THE PEOPLE

While Leo, the king, embodied the monarchy, Aquarius, which sits opposite to Leo, is the sign of equality and democracy. We replace the courtyard mantra, "Long live the king," with the invigoratingly egalitarian, "Power to the people!" Aquarius is considered to be the most evolved of all the archetypes. In Ezekiel's vision of the four creatures of the chariot, Aquarius appears alongside the other fixed signs—Taurus (a bull), Leo (a lion), and Scorpio (an eagle)—as a winged angel (Ezekiel 1:10). This representation suggests that Aquarius stands for our higher self, or Freud's superego, which explains the Aquarian fascination with all human beings, humanitarian work, and altruism.

Aquarius in your chart signals the area in your life in which you must think outside of the box. You also benefit in this arena through incorporating the ideas and suggestions of friends. Allow democracy to reign here.

Did you ever meet people who are infatuated with dogs? Those who live with several dogs, travel to dog shows, and advocate for the rights of dogs? These people harbor one desire more than any other: to be a dog. But it doesn't matter how avidly they pamper and adore their furry friends, these humans will never become a member of the canine family. Aquarians exhibit a similar complex, but instead of dogs, they are consumed with humans. They love us, obsess over us, and they create an infinite number of nonprofits to help us out. They indulge this rather selfless impulse because—and please indulge my admittedly quirky theory about this sign that governs quirks and eccentricities— because they are not human themselves. They are aliens. I don't mean that they come from another planet, although some of you who know or live with an Aquarius might argue the point. They are earthlings, born and raised here like you and me, but they possess an alien soul—a soul that has reincarnated many times on different planets. The Tarot card assigned to Aquarius, the Star, the sole major arcana that depicts extraterrestrial energies, bolsters this "legal alien" hypothesis.

In other words, Aquarians generally appear odd and idiosyncratic. They often behave as if they were sent to earth from their mother ship to study us and, more crucially, assist in our evolution to a higher spiritual plane. They continually push us forward in science (Thomas Edison), social responsibility (Abraham Lincoln, Franklin D. Roosevelt, and Oprah Winfrey), and in art (W. A. Mozart and Virginia Woolf). Aquarius is the sign of genius, and Aquarians are revolutionaries who yearn to make us assimilate the ideas of liberty, equality, and fraternity so that we stop fighting and killing each other.

Aquarius marks the place in your life where you can leap into the future and update and upgrade not only yourself but those around you too. You will benefit immensely here from groups, friends, and all sorts of other people. It is the area in life where you too can be called a genius.

THE JOKERMAN'S SONG OF FREEDOM

Fools rush in where angels fear to tread,
Both of their futures, so full of dread.
—BOB DYLAN, "JOKERMAN"

Aquarians exhibit a wonderful sense of humor and a unique take on life. Capricorn invented humor to cope with the devil and fear, but Aquarius perfected the jester archetype to combat Leo, the lion king. Living opposite to Leo, the most powerful sign, is a complex and thorny chore. How do you bend the will of the king? Aquarius does that by personifying the joker and the fool. *Fool* comes from the Latin word *Follis*, which means "a bag of air." We often mistake the phrase "wind bag" for nonsense or tomfoolery. But that dismissal flounders as a gross underestimation. This archetype resonates with extraordinary muscle. It can inform the emperor and everyone else too that the emperor is naked without losing its head. Every king tolerates and protects his court jester. Every King Lear has his fool. And every Leo

Aquarius marks the place in your life where you can leap into the future and update and upgrade not only yourself but those around you too. You will benefit immensely here from groups, friends, and all sorts of other people. It is the area in life where you too can be called a genius.

stomachs and nurtures an Aquarius. Through his ribbing and juggling of words and ideas, the fool underlines the foibles of the ruler and advises him to do better.

Evidence of the enduring potency of the fool can be found in our playing cards. The strongest card in the deck is not the Ace of Spades, King of Clubs, or Queen of Hearts, but the Joker. The Joker's effectiveness rests in freedom—freedom to become any card, freedom to criticize without recrimination. The fool enjoys freedom of speech—the liberty to say any daring and crazy thing at all—because everyone thinks that he is mad. Aquarius guards his freedom ferociously, even at the risk of acting the fool or the lunatic. It enables his capability to think outside the norm and advance society (the king). Science and technology—propelled by such characters as the nutty professor, the mad scientist, or even Thomas Jefferson's declaration of independence from King George—requires innovative and Aquarian thinking.

To quote the popular pop song: "Free your mind and the rest will follow" ("Free Your Mind," En Vogue). Express your funny side, without inhibitions, in the area of your life ruled by Aquarius. The world needs you to act the fool. Growth in this arena also necessitates freedom from inhibitions and tradition. For inspiration, go to a stand-up comedy show this week or watch the funniest movie you know.

Your Own Private Aquarius

Aquarius in your chart highlights the area of your life in which you ought to express your uniqueness and oddest ideas. You also must upgrade and update yourself here. Think about bringing the future into the present moment. This archetype also governs friends, organizations, and corporations. You need to join groups or enlist your friends to succeed in your house of Aquarius.

Aquarius in Your First House (Your Rising Sign): You are a unique individual who constantly conceives new ideas and innovations. You belong to the future, and your journey in this lifetime calls on you to update and upgrade us all. You require a great deal of freedom. During the week of Aquarius, pay attention to your body, your appearance, and your path in life. New horizons are opening for you.

Aquarius in the Second House: You can make money from innovative and unique schemes and ideas. You enjoy a talent with technology and computers, and you will be successful by incorporating the Internet and other space-age tools into your moneymaking plans. You possess an original attitude towards money, and you can make money more easily when surrounded by other people. This week, focus on your finances and invest in your talents.

Aquarius in the Third House: You possess an ingenious and brilliant mind. Share it with others. You might feel ahead of your time and sometimes misunderstood. Your siblings and neighbors often serve as your best friends. This week, highlight your communications, business plans, and siblings.

Express your funny side, without inhibitions, in the area of your life ruled by Aquarius. Growth in this arena also necessitates freedom from inhibitions and tradition. For inspiration, go to a stand-up comedy show this week or watch the funniest movie you know.

Aquarius in the Fourth House: Someone in your family is a unique or eccentric individual. Your home life might be erratic. You need to create a home that resembles a club or a salon, a place where many people gather. If you reside in an apartment, try to live on an upper floor. This week, pay attention to the relationships within your family unit and to your home.

Aquarius in the Fifth House: Your children are unique, funny, and idiosyncratic, and they can become your best friends. You are a funny, entertaining person who needs to play around with friends. You also benefit from laughter in romance. In the week of Aquarius, emphasize your children, fun, creativity, and happiness.

Aquarius in the Sixth House: Your workplace might be subject to sudden changes. You need to laugh more at work. You will benefit by working with computers, technology, electronics, and large groups of people. Fostering friendship with work colleagues brings excellent results. Pay special attention to your ankles, shins, and blood flow. This week, focus on your diet, health, work, and service.

Aquarius in the Seventh House: You need your partner to be your best friend because your path to a harmonious relationship is paved with backslapping and camaraderie. You thrive with a funny partner who loves freedom and allows you freedom as well. This week, pay attention to your significant others, partners, and relationships.

Aquarius in the Eighth House: Your passion, sexuality, and intimacy necessitates a partner who is first and foremost a friend. You need to experiment with your sexuality. You will benefit from joint artistic and financial affairs with friends. This week, highlight your sexuality, intimacy, and your partner's abundance.

Aquarius in the Ninth House: You enjoy many foreign friends. You ought to pursue an advanced education in science, computers, or any subject that can benefit the human race. You have high ideals, and your in-laws can become your good friends. This week, try to travel to a foreign land or pay attention to your higher education and your in-laws.

Aquarius in the Tenth House: The odder, more futuristic your career, the more success you will generate. You need to work with large groups of people or with your friends. You constantly seek to upgrade and update your career to keep up with a changing future. In the week of Aquarius, focus on your reputation, destiny, and career goals.

Aquarius in the Eleventh House: You have tons of friends, but you need to work on developing intimacy with at least some of them. You also belong to many groups, clubs, and organizations. You gravitate toward nonprofit and humanitarian outfits. This week, highlight your friends and group associations.

Aquarius in the Twelfth House: Your friends or community betrayed you in a past lifetime, and this karma makes you rather cautious or timid with other people. Your friends might become enemies or your groups might turn against you. You might be overzealous about your freedom and individuality. This lifetime calls you to update and upgrade spirituality and mysticism. In the week of Aquarius, try to let go of things that you do not need, go on a retreat, and practice spiritual rituals.

MODERN-DAY WATER BEARERS

I never understood the true meaning of the water bearer until I found myself living with an Aquarius. We got along just great but constantly disagreed on one issue—water. As an Aries (a fire sign), I warred unreasonably with water. Though I grew up in the arid Middle East, I had never learned how to preserve water. The Aquarian, meanwhile, was obsessed with saving water. His mantra, which he wanted to hang above the toilet, was, "If it's yellow let it mellow, if it's brown, flush it down." I thought he was crazy. But he urged me to ponder it, and I realized why the Aquarians, the water bearers, preoccupy themselves with saving water. While it is true that Aquarius is not a water sign, Aquarians are or were always the water bearers.

Let me explain. If we travel back in time, to an era before modern pumps, pipes, and desalination plants, the water bearers had to lug one bucket of water after another from the distant river. Eventually these water bearers got tired of the laborious work and started developing technologies and inventions that facilitate the bringing of water.

Though I loved my lush tropical garden, I listened to my partner and began to grow succulent plants that sucked up less water. A week after I planted the succulents, I met another Aquarius, who told me he had just purchased a new dishwasher—even though he could not afford to fix his car—because he'd heard that these new machines save a few drops of water. These Aquarians function as the modern-day water bearers, and we ought to listen to them about conservation. Make an effort to save water this week and note whether the total on your water bill declines.

THE AGE OF AQUARIUS

Aquarius is the sign of the future. And we experience the same difficulty in predicting and forecasting the future as we encounter when we attempt to categorize and understand Aquarius people. Aquarius is the most unpredictable and fluctuating archetype. The fact that they fall under no category is the only category that they fall under. A remarkably gifted Aquarian, Igor Orlovsky, who works as a standup comedian, told me he hates history.

"I could never ever remember all the dates of the battles and events," he said. "It was so boring. Every history class I took, I ended up falling asleep only to be woken up by the teacher who was bothered by my snoring. I just cannot understand who cares about the past."

I immediately recognized the problem. Aquarians, the people of the future, view the past as nothing more than a chain that ties us down. They see the past as redundant, done, and gone. Instead, they proclaim, let's focus on what is to come. Let's see what we can do about making the future better. Your house of Aquarius functions like this too. It marks the area of your life in which you harbor great hope for the future.

At the risk of alienating the Aquarians, I need to write a bit about the past, if only to illuminate the future—the Age of Aquarius that the hippies rejoice over in the wonderful musical *Hair*. Astrology divides history into ages that last about two-thousand years. Each age is named after a sign—only the progression of the ages move counter to the normal procession of the signs through the calendar year. For example, the Age of Aries started in the year 2000 B.C.E. The Age of Pisces lasted from the year 0 to about A.D. 2000, and so forth. We now stand at the crossroad between the Age of Pisces, which is the age of faith and religion, and the Age of Aquarius, or the age of knowledge and science. This transition, which has been occurring for about the last four hundred years, is fraught with turmoil. You can see it in the world around us. While some parts of the world become more Aquarian— more computerized, scientific, and modern—other groups of people cling to the dying age of religious fanaticism and narrow-mindedness. Even within the most advanced, egalitarian, and futuristic societies like the United States, religious fundamentalism battles against scientific advances like the theory of evolution and stem-cell technology. While scholars such as Samuel Huntington contend that wars around the globe erupt as a result of clashes between civilizations, I believe these wars spring from the fault lines that divide Aquarius and Pisces—between Pisces-based religious philosophies and those that venerate Aquarian-ruled science and equality. For thousands of years, astrologers have prophesied that the Age of Aquarius heralds the Age of Humankind, the era when our species will evolve to a higher spiritual state. Kabbalah has dubbed this period the Age of Sabbath. And the Mayan prophecies dictate that a new age of timelessness will begin in 2012. Great shifts—including war and scientific and medical revolutions—have cropped up with terrifying speed as the world embraces the unpredictable energies of Aquarius.

From the discovery of the planet Uranus (ruler of Aquarius) in 1781, we have dived deeper and deeper into the Age of Aquarius. The *liberte, egalite, fraternite* of the French Revolution, the American Revolution, the Industrial Revolution, and the information and cyber revolutions represent just a few blips on the radar screen of this new epoch. In alchemy, the symbol of Aquarius (≈) signifies the vital assimilation of substances. We witness a similar process of assimilation in the realities of globalization, political free-trade zones like the European Union and North American Free Trade Agreement (NAFTA), and the merging—often through corporate expansion (McDonald's, *American Idol*, Nintendo) or the transfer of spiritual rituals from the East to the West (yoga in Iowa) and the West to the East (Jesus in Korea)—of people from different races and cultures. Cell phones, computers, the Internet, satellites, and many other Aquarian inventions have fused humans together on every inch of the globe. Tokyo, Shanghai, and Singapore in the Far East have built western-styled skyscrapers, financial institutions, casinos, and Starbuck's shops, while Eastern-born yoga, Zen, and martial arts flourish in Europe and the United States.

Electromagnetic waves, the prevailing symbol of this burgeoning archetype, deliver the Aquarian message of union, equality, and fraternity by wireless technology. Today, mobile phones connect billions of people, groups, and ideologies. About 2.8 billion cell phones are in use worldwide with about 1.6 million added every day. By 2011, an estimated 4 billion people will carry a mobile phone. Not so long ago, technology was reserved for the rich, powerful, and elite. But democracy-loving Aquarius has ushered in a democratization of technology by drastically dropping the costs. Just a few years back, musicians had to wait for major labels to fund recordings in expensive analog studios. With today's relatively economical digital gadgetry, musicians from all over the world can record and then market their tunes right from their own bedrooms. Amateur video and filmmakers similarly share their artistic endeavors with sympathetic audiences everywhere via free Internet sites like You Tube. And financial traders buy and sell fortunes in London or Hong Kong while lounging with their laptops on the beach in Maui.

Aquarius, the ruler of all this futuristic technology, has also worked to create fraternity among the machines themselves. An iPod, for example, can now link up to your running shoes and adjust the tempo of the music to the pace of your jog. It takes no great prophet to predict that electromagnetic crime, consisting of cyberpirates, a digital mafia, and computer viruses, will follow these Aquarian trends. And the next big terrorist attack likely will emerge from and within the wireless skies.

National Public Radio recently interviewed an Israeli woman who had been relocated from her former home in the Gaza strip (see Capricorn discussion on Saturn return, p. 284). She despaired that her financial lot had tumbled badly because she no longer inhabited the land on which she used to grow Christmas trees for the European market. How funny and Aquarian that a Jew had sold trees to Christians farmed on territory that belonged to Muslims. The Oscar-winning *Brokeback Mountain*, a movie about the illicit love affair between two American cowboys, was filmed in Canada, directed by an Asian (Ang Lee), written by a woman (Annie Proulx), and starred heterosexual actors portraying gay men. This conglomeration of nations, genders, and subject matter mirrors the energy of assimilation Aquarius has preached for the last many years. This mutual cooperation and respect—rather than M-16 machine guns and Bradley fighting vehicles—will bring about world harmony and peace. This unification of ideas, resources, and people from all over the globe will give rise to the Age of the Aquarius.

Aquarius in your chart indicates where you can facilitate the painful transition from the Age of Pisces to the Age of Aquarius. You must change what you "believe" into what you "know." Back your faith with reason, facts, and information. And share it with us all.

How to Get Along with Aquarians

- Be spontaneous. Don't plan too much before hand. Allow for and honor synchronicities.

- Give Aquarians freedom. They need many people and acquaintances. Agree to go out with them, and invite them to group gatherings and clubs.

- Think outside the box and stay open to unusual ideas and new ways of looking at life.

- First and foremost, be their friend. It doesn't matter whether the Aquarian is your spouse, child, or student. Friendship is paramount to them.

- Stay abreast of the trends and buzz of the moment. Aquarians love to hang out with people who are aware of what's "in."

- Introduce the Aquarian to as many people as possible. And try to get along with his or her friends.

- Subscribe or become a member of the Aquarian's groups and clubs.

- Keep Aquarians on their toes. Do something outrageous now and then. Surprise them.

- Make sure to laugh at the Aquarians' jokes and try to make the Aquarians laugh too. Laughter is the door to their heart.

- Never call them selfish. They work hard to give to everyone, and they just might snap if you question their altruism.

THE DARK SIDE OF THE FORCE: AQUARIUS

The other signs often grumble about the Aquarians' impersonal nature and detachment from their feelings. Aquarians often find it tough to express their emotions. They harbor a strong group mentality. Like a deft party host, they yearn for everyone to feel good and have a good time. They wander from one person to the next to check that he or she is faring well. They rarely zero in on any one person with any depth or intimacy. This apparent superficiality often results in disappointment both in the Aquarian, who rues her missing out on a more intense one-on-one experience, and in the Aquarian's loved ones, who might feel neglected deep down.

Aquarians usually know many people from many walks of life. And they often fail to invest in one person and his or her emotional needs. It leads others to label them flaky, weird, and even cold. They can't really help it. To the egalitarian Aquarius, every person is equal. None takes precedence over another. The welfare of the group seems more important than the welfare of the near and dear. And that can frustrate the dear and near.

This phenomenon describes the force behind corporations, which are ruled by Aquarius and have been on a prolific ascendancy for about the last fifty years. When you call AT&T because they overcharged your phone bill, for example, you will locate no one to whom you can really complain. First, you can't even get a human being on the line. You sift and click through a recorded message designed specifically to send you and your individual troubles away. When you finally encounter a live human voice, you swiftly realize that you are merely talking to a screw in a much larger machine. She likely earns minimum wage, trying hard to make ends meet, and inhabits a life difficult enough without you complicating it with your gripes and ire. Not to mention she is probably talking to you from India. Corporations are designed to serve the corporation, not the individual. They rarely have a face. Can you tell me the name of the individual at Nike who ordered that the company's shoes should be manufactured by near-slaves in some remote third-world country? Does he have a name? We might finger the corporation, the board of directors, the shareholders, or for all I know we could finger you if you just happened to buy some Nike stock. Impersonal Aquarius is a far cry from Leoland where we encounter a singular king who can be blamed for whatever goes wrong.

Aquarius in your chart indicates where you can facilitate the painful transition from the Age of Pisces to the Age of Aquarius. You must change what you "believe" into what you "know." Back your faith with reason, facts, and information. And share it with us all.

Devoted to rebellion, Aquarians sometimes behave like rebels without a cause. They aggressively press forward with their revolution without realizing that they might be substituting one tyrant for an even worse situation. During the French revolution, the insurgents beheaded the king, then turned on each other and beheaded just about everyone in a short-lived reign of terror. A few years later, another rather tyrannical Leo named Napoleon stepped into the void and created a whole new era of havoc. In the current war in Iraq, we find an aggressive Aquarian effort to oust a murderous dictator and enforce democracy. But the result, at least so far, has been chaos, Abu Ghraib, and violence that arguably has made life even more dangerous for the average person. And if you are inclined to complain or pin blame for this mess, where do you turn? You might rail at George Bush or Dick Cheney, but as in an impersonal corporation, they deflect responsibility to others in a long looping chain—the Iraqi government, Shiites, Sunnis, Moktada al-Sadr, Ahmed Chalabi, Al Qaeda, Donald Rumsfeld, George Tenet, Condoleezza Rice, Stephen Hadley, Paul Wolfowitz, Douglas Feith, L. Paul Bremer, the nattering media, meddling Iran, Syria, so on and so on—until you throw up your hands and call AT&T to deal with your bill.

Aquarius must learn to pay respect to reform or slow e-volutions rather than to electrical re-volutions that end up electrocuting everyone. This all or nothing propensity often leads to what I call the dehydrated water bearer. In the early 1990s, I attended an enormous rave in the Negev Desert. Many of the partygoers took ecstasy, LSD, and other drugs, and each person soared, whirling and dancing on his or her own trip. Amid all this benevolent individuality, I saw a friend of mine, an Aquarius, tripping out in his own Aquarian way. He sprinted from dancer to dancer with a big bottle of water and urged them all to drink. He delivered water for hours, his own energy buoyed by the drugs he'd ingested himself. He brought water to people who asked for water, and he lugged water to people who never thought about water. He shared with people that he knew and with total strangers too. But he forgot to drink himself. And he eventually collapsed. This problem afflicts Aquarians and all do-gooders. So concerned with the well-being of every other person, they forget to recharge and replenish themselves. This self-neglect not only contributes to health problems, but it makes them no longer of water-bearing service to anyone else as well.

Aquarius in your chart signals the spot where you might give too much while forgetting to receive. Make sure that you stop, breathe, and refuel your own tank.

THE HEBREW LETTER *Tzadik*

Kabbalah assigned the Hebrew letter *Tzadik*, which is also known as *Dli*, or "the bucket," to the sign Aquarius. In ancient Hebrew, *Tzadik* means "a hook," the fisherman's tool that lands the fish. It signifies meditation, underscored by the image of the fisherman sitting serene and still on the bank of the river, fishing in his subconscious for insight and enlightenment. *Tzadik's* meditative pose explains the Aquarian connection to the New Age, the spiritual movement that began last century and delivered yoga, organic lifestyles, transcendental rituals, and esoteric spirituality into the mainstream. In

Aquarius in your chart signals the spot where you might give too much while forgetting to receive. Make sure that you stop, breathe, and refuel your own tank.

modern Hebrew, *Tzadik* translates as "a righteous man or a saint," reflecting the giving, altruistic essence of Aquarius.

Meditate with *Tzadik* whenever you want to attract more friends, bolster your humanitarian work, glimpse the future, or receive help and hope from unexpected sources.

THE PARTS OF THE BODY

Aquarius rules the ankle, shins, and circulatory system. If you have a good deal of Aquarius energy in your chart, make sure that you don't stand on your feet for too many hours a day.

Since Aquarius governs friends above all, allow these lovely allies to heal all that ails you. Forget about your body this week, and instead spend time laughing with all of your friends.

THE COLOR OF AQUARIUS: VIOLET

Violet is the color of Aquarius. Violet represents the highest frequency of light that we can detect with the naked eye. Aquarius, an air sign, thus strives to reach the highest point of the energetic spectrum. Wear or use violet to amplify the energies of friends, humanity, organizations, corporations, technology, the future, and your own uniqueness.

Above Aquarian violet, we find ultraviolet (UV), which can damage our living tissue by creating DNA lesions. This radiation can cause cell death, mutations, skin cancer, and other maladies. UV radiation has increased in the past decades as the Age of Aquarius triggered the Industrial Revolution, pollution, and the misuse of

Meditate with *Tzadik* whenever you want to attract more friends, bolster your humanitarian work, glimpse the future, or receive help and hope from unexpected sources.

earth resources by corporations. These abuses likely contributed to a hole in the ozone layer that had protected us from ultraviolet radiation for millions of years. It seems that Aquarius, by means of technologically induced pollution, has managed to make the planet more violet, more Aquarius. Ultraviolet light has been proven to cause DNA mutations, which can lead to cancer. But with some of these mutations, who knows how they will turn out? Perhaps Aquarius is simply altering the human genome to better cope with a future of polluted air and water. Who knows Aquarius? Who knows the future?

WHAT SHOULD I FOCUS ON IN THE WEEK OF AQUARIUS?

Focus on your friends, humanitarianism, and organizations. Join a gym, a club, or a spiritual group, then nurture and develop friendships. Make an effort to get closer to the people in your second and third circles of friends.

Valentine's Day falls during the month of Aquarius. Send cards to your friends this week, even if Valentine's Day itself is a long way off. Do some of that humanitarian work you have been thinking about. Help out at a nonprofit organization. And it might also be a good week to back up your computer, update and upgrade your programs, buy a new apparatus, or create your own website.

Aquarius loves synchronicities. Use them attentively this week. This sign's bank of symbols include friends, corporations, groups, clubs, the water bearer, space aliens, outer space, technology, the future, humanitarian work, saints, violet and ultraviolet, meditation, the New Age, revolutions, fools, genius, insanity, weirdness, impersonality, shins, ankles, democracy, freedom, independence, inventions, rebels, laughter, Uranus, *Star Wars*, *Star Trek*, and electromagnetism.

Your Aquarius Week Checklist

- Think outside of the box. Do not be afraid to be a little wild and crazy (as long as you don't harm others or yourself).

- Speak the affirmation of Aquarius: "I attract beneficial friends and organizations to my life. I am a beacon of awareness and hope to the rest of humankind."
- Meditate on the letter *Tzadik*.
- Wear purple or violet.
- Go to a stand-up comedy performance.
- Spend time with your friends. Invite a group over to your house or initiate an activity with more than four people.
- Save water.
- Join a group and work on a humanitarian cause.
- On a clear night, lie down on your back and stare at the stars for at least twenty minutes. Try to identify the images of the skies by connecting lines between the individual stars.

The Ritual of Aquarius: Show Me Your Friends, and I Will Show You Who You Are

Make a list of five of your best friends or close associates (not family members). Write one paragraph for each of these friends that describes what you like about them, and then compose a second paragraph that outlines their more challenging traits or the problems in your relationship. Be honest and offer examples to support your judgments. Then merge all five of the positive paragraphs into one. Pretend that you are describing an imaginary friend who possesses all the finest qualities of your dearest friends. Do the same with the five negative paragraphs.

Here's the twist: you have just described yourself. The long description of positive attributes you have generously ascribed to your friends is really a list of the beautiful parts in you. You are attracted to these friends simply because they reflect the splendid parts of your personality. The negative description lays bare what all your friends have come to teach you. These challenges are your challenges. Now that you perceive them in your friends, you can begin to monitor and overcome them in you.

Wear or use violet to amplify the energies of friends, humanity, organizations, corporations, technology, the future, and your own uniqueness.

We change over time. Our friends change over time. And usually we fall away from friends when they cease to reflect who we are. Perhaps you grew substantially, and your friend no longer serves as a good teacher. Or maybe they changed and don't accurately reflect you any more. Your lifelong friends ideally evolve and grow right along with you, continuing to mirror your genuine essence for years and years.

FAMOUS AQUARIANS

Oprah Winfrey, Paul Newman, Franklin Delano Roosevelt, John Belushi, Lord Byron, Charles Darwin, Wolfgang Amadeus Mozart, Thomas Edison, Abraham Lincoln, David Lynch, Charles Dickens, James Dean, Virginia Woolf.

Pisces: The Mystic

February 19 to March 20

Key Phrase: "I believe"—the leap of faith

General Qualities: Mystical, poetic, sensitive, compassionate, multitalented, psychic, emotional, perceptive, receptive, intuitive, graceful, imaginative, and creative

Dark Side: Confused, prone to addiction, frequent inferiority complexes, dependent and codependent, escapist, self-pitying, lacking boundaries, lethargic, indolent, submissive, and unrealistic

Element: Mutable water

Planet: Neptune, ruler of the oceans

Day: Thursday

Theme: Mysticism

Parts of the Body: Feet, immune system, and lymphatic system

Color: Red-violet

Gemstone: Amethyst

Musical Note: B, the last tone in the musical scale

Hebrew Letter: *Kuf* ק

Kabbalistic Meaning of Letter: The back of the head

Path in the Tree of Life: Path 18, connecting Victory and Kingdom

Tarot Card: The Moon

Movies: *The Little Mermaid, Harry Potter, The Golden Compass, Finding Nemo, Dancer in the Dark,* Bollywood films, and all fantasy movies

Affirmation: "I am at one with the flow of the universe, effortlessly attracting all that I need."

OVERVIEW

Pisces represents the final stage of human evolution: enlightenment and assimilation into the world beyond. Pisces, the sign of Albert Einstein and Dr. Seuss, is the sign of mysticism, poetry, sacred dancing, chanting, shamanism, dreams, and psychic abilities. The most sensitive and delicate archetype, it teaches us to transcend the illusion of the material world and unify with the divine. Pisces is also the sign of imagination. It shows us how to use the power of visualization to actualize our needs in the here and now. In the week of Pisces, you will connect to the mystic inside by practicing creative visualizations that will expedite the manifestation of your dreams.

THE TERRITORY OF PISCES

At last, we enter the mystical realm of Pisces. Though Pisces arrives as the final sign of the zodiac, the core qualities of this archetype negate any logical conclusions we might be tempted to draw based on its position in the astrological year. Pisces stands as the most nonlinear archetype.

The Moon, the Tarot Card associated with this sign, emphasizes the ever-flowing energies of Pisces—New Moon, full Moon, back to New Moon, etc. It defies the concept of beginning and end. Take a look at your chart. What shape do you see? The central symbol of astrology is a wheel, a circle, with no particular beginning and no specific end. Like the serpent that bites its own tail—an iconic spiritual symbol that defines the endlessness of spiritual life—Pisces signifies a beginning and a middle as much as it marks the end. Pisces is a mutable water sign, leading us from the frost of winter to the thaw of spring. Its watery flow induces the frozen rivers to crack open, thus announcing the proximity of spring.

The symbol of Pisces reiterates the fluid essence of the archetype. It features two fish, one swinging upward to symbolize a union with God, and the other diving toward the bottom of the sea in a gesture of self-destruction. To make the story even more tragic (tragedy is ruled by Pisces), the pair are linked by a silver cord. The mission of the fish—and Pisces too—demands a happy equilibrium. If we do not accomplish that balancing act, then the two fish will find themselves tugging and aggravating one another for eternity. These fish, which are sometimes portrayed as dolphins, insinuate the dualistic nature of the sign. Pisces is just as much the first archetype as the last, just as elevating as depressive. In other words, it is not easy being Pisces.

CONFUSION

When I first discovered that I have Pisces rising, I could not bear that my rising sign, my flagship, was this lazy, addicted, escapist, delusional, self-pitying couch potato of a sign. At first glance, Pisces resembles the garbage bin of the zodiac. Whatever junk the other signs didn't want was left to Pisces. This couldn't be me, I whined. I don't want to spend my life washing the soiled laundry of every other sign.

And so I rushed to call my mother from Mexico; I didn't care what time it was for her in Israel.

"Are you absolutely sure I was born in early morning?" I pleaded. "Please try to remember."

My mother mumbled sleepily, "Oh, I remember when you were born, and I also remember that it was so strange for everyone that you popped out precisely at four in the morning. You are always waking me up at four in the morning."

She was right; it was four in the morning in Israel. And I was crushed. Ten more minutes in the womb would have made me an Aries rising, which to me, a novice astrologer, sounded far more active, decisive, and fortuitous. Now that I am more familiar with the signs and how they interact, I am grateful that the infant me possessed the good sense to emerge into the world as a Pisces rising. If I had been an Aries rising as well as Aries sun, well, who knows what I might have been? A mercenary? A boxer? I almost certainly would not have delved into Kabbalah, mysticism, or astrology, and, for better or worse, this book would never have been written.

So why is Pisces such a disfavored and complicated sign? For starters, Pisces stands as the energetic mixture of all the archetypes that came before. Pisces, in fact, contains a little bit of Aries, a touch of Taurus, a sprinkle of Gemini, and dashes of Cancer, Leo, Virgo, Libra, Scorpio, Sagittarius, Capricorn, Aquarius, and, of course,

Pisces. The Aries in Pisces people leaps to wage war, but their inner Libra demands diplomacy. The Leo yearns to be king, while the Aquarius crusades for democracy. It is very confusing to be a Pisces. The characteristic Pisces inertia and sleepiness derives not from an innate lack of energy, but from a surplus of possibilities. Pisces harbor a multiplicity of talents. In fact, they possess every talent. However, each of the archetypes skirmishes within every Pisces, pushing and pulling them in countless directions.

This wealth of choices can cause Pisces to feel stuck. And sometimes they deal with this energetic deluge by escaping through drinking, taking drugs (addictions are ruled by Pisces), or, most commonly, by simply going to sleep. At least in slumber, in what the Australian Aborigines call dream time, they can fly from one project to another, accomplishing all, fulfilling every aspiration. Just as Scorpios cannot help stinging, Pisces cannot help dreaming. It is imprinted in their DNA. The other signs, which don't suffer such a perplexing overload, often spot this behavior—the sleeping through the alarm or drifting into a daydream—and accuse the Pisces of being lazy, delusional, or unrealistic. They underestimate the Pisces, and consequently many Pisces suffer from an inferiority complex. But none of this is fair. Pisces simply require a life coach to help them structure and organize their unlimited and yet disabling potential.

Though some astrologers accuse Pisces of laziness, the truth is that they work more hours each day than any other sign. They are so active in their dream life that when they wake up they sometimes feel like they need a nap to recover from the hard night's work. Throughout the centuries, Kabbalistic rabbis have used dreams as a means of divination. They called this type of divination a dream quest. In order to practice becoming Pisces, start with your dreams.

As you are going to sleep, focus on your breath. Take long deep breaths and imagine the air traveling all the way down to your feet, which are ruled by Pisces. Repeat this breathing exercise until you feel relaxed. Then think of one problematic issue in your life and let yourself drift off to sleep. The minute you wake up, write down whatever you remember from your dreams. If you do not remember the dreams, jot down whatever you feel or any thoughts, sensations, or synchronicities. Often these residual effects of your dream will provide insight into your dilemma. Repeat this exercise every night until you light upon some images or answers.

We all have to recognize that the true symbol of Pisces is not the fish but the dolphin, the most intelligent creature on earth. Einstein was a Pisces, and so obviously this archetype's foibles have nothing to do with a lack of intelligence. Pisces simply have a different job than many of us. They have been tasked with dreaming, imagining, and fantasizing a better future for us all. Their mission is to "imagine all the people living life in peace," as John Lennon said. Their agenda lies beyond the here and now, far above in the astral plain. Our job is to help them out instead of patronizing them.

Many mystical and religious traditions around the globe (religion and mysticism are ruled by Pisces) agree with Pisces' need to see and live beyond the bounds of the everyday. A multitude of doctrines purport that we live in a matrix of *maya* or illusion. So how can we take serious the indictment that Pisces live in illusion when the reality we call real actually is an illusion? Logically speaking, we are actually paying Pisces a terrific compliment when we call them delusional, conceding that they represent the only tribe that truly understands the nature of a reality that isn't real at all. Sounds confusing? Well, now you know how it feels to be a Pisces.

Pisces also teach us the vital lesson of flow, to let go and join the current of life. Remember the old nursery rhyme that says, "Row, row, row your boat gently down the stream, merrily, merrily, merrily, merrily, life is but a dream." This is the hymn of Pisces. They swim effortlessly with the current, and that habit of being effortless and flowing affords them the freedom to dream.

WHO ARE YOU? THE PISCEAN QUEST FOR IDENTITY

Lewis Carroll's *Alice's Adventures in Wonderland* owes a great debt to Pisces. Alice herself exhibits a host of Piscean tendencies. She eats funny food (magic mushrooms) laced with who knows what. She falls asleep under a tree (the Tree of Life), and she (dream/drug) travels to Wonderland, which is really a metaphor for her subconscious. In Wonderland, she encounters a hookah-smoking caterpillar (a version of the inchworm of Virgo, the opposite sign of Pisces). The first question the caterpillar asks is, "Who are you?" And in prototypical Pisces confusion, Alice replies that she doesn't know. She knows who she was, but, she says, she has changed many times since then. The caterpillar demands a better answer, but Alice can't help him.

In order to practice becoming Pisces, start with your dreams. As you are going to sleep, take long deep breaths and imagine the air traveling all the way down to your feet, which are ruled by Pisces. Repeat this breathing exercise until you feel relaxed. Then think of one problematic issue in your life and let yourself drift off to sleep. The minute you wake up, write down whatever you remember from your dreams. If you do not remember the dreams, jot down whatever you feel or any thoughts, sensations, or synchronicities. Often these residual effects of your dream will provide insight into your dilemma.

"I can't explain myself, I'm afraid, sir, because I am not myself," she says. "And being so many different sizes in a day is very confusing."

In the wake of her crazy experiences of growing huge and then tiny, traveling up and then feeling terribly down, Alice (Pisces) does not know who she is. Who are you? looms as the most difficult question for any Pisces. Aries, the first sign, represents the sign of identity, and yet here we are, eleven signs later, and we already have forgotten who we were. High or low? Happy or sad? Small or big? Aries, Libra, Taurus, or Scorpio? Pisceans suffer from the chameleon syndrome, which induces them to change their identity according to their surroundings. If they meet a writer, they suddenly feel the need to become a globetrotting journalist. When a businessperson wanders their way, they suddenly assume the personality of a CEO. This shapeshifting impedes the Pisces' ability to decide where to focus and what to do. The answers change too often, limiting their ability to act with resolve or self-assurance. Fortunately, Pisces don't have to answer the caterpillar's question. Who am I? isn't a Piscean concern. Their muddled identity serves them, propelling the Pisces to a more transcendent realization.

Pisces in your chart highlights the area in your life in which you enjoy the ability to see beyond the illusion of reality. This house also holds access to your strongest connection to God and the unity underlying all of creation. Pisces also reveals where you possess multiple talents and might find yourself pulled and pushed in different directions.

Go Mystic!

Nearly every spiritual tradition espouses the concept of unity or oneness as its core underlying principle. A mystic can see the oneness in all diverse and seemingly different things. Pisces have no singular identity. Instead they contain every identity in order to apprehend that these identities are all the same—all one, all unified in this archetype called Pisces. By becoming a mystic and recognizing the oneness inherent in all diversity, the multitalented and bemused Pisces can find peace. Their task, like that of the mystic, is to focus on the oneness behind all the singular signs, to shatter the illusion of separation. When they accomplish this horribly difficult task, they override their bewilderment. They perceive no conflict between the ego of Aries and the dependency of Libra, no opposition between high and low, poet and stock trader. Healing the rift between individuals and between opposing dogmas is one of the most ambitious and beautiful missions in the zodiac. Einstein said, "Reality is merely an illusion, albeit a very persistent one," and the illusion of division is just as persistent. Even the schism between the paradigms of science and religion can be mended with a mystical approach. The book *The Tao of Physics* by Fritjof Capra stands as a great example of this sort of blending of dichotomous ideas.

Repeat this vital Pisces teaching to yourself as often as you can: there is no distinctiveness peculiar to any sign, person, plant, thing, tradition, religion, or idea. Pisces' muddled identity nudges the Pisces in all of us to evolve toward unity, toward oneness with God. Rather than remaining stuck in the separation of our precious I/me selves, Pisces, with its clear, crispy waters, dissolves it all into the One. Pisces shoves us toward enlightenment. It blurs the differences between all the other signs, declaring them to be like water, which has no color or taste. Everything is therefore empty, egoless, and void. It is the state of enlightenment described by the Buddha.

No form. No ego. Easy, right? Not usually, and that is why the zodiac cycles through again. If we don't make it to the Buddha state just yet, the wheel of twelve

Pisces in your chart highlights the area in your life in which you enjoy the ability to see beyond the illusion of reality. This house also holds access to your strongest connection to God and the unity underlying all of creation. Pisces also reveals where you possess multiple talents and might find yourself pulled and pushed in different directions.

signs starts anew to award us another shot. Pisces smudges all identities into the One, into nothingness, so that the first sign Aries can be born afresh and search for his or her identity all over again.

This week, you will become a mystic. Try to embody the perfect man/woman. Greet every person you meet with smiles and loving energy. Imagine that everyone you encounter was sent by God to present you with a gift, a crucial challenge, or a message. Meditate each day for twenty minutes and attend at least three yoga classes. Visit a church, temple, or mosque, or, if you'd rather remain nondenominational, go to a park or a garden and walk among the trees. Find a place of peace and tranquility. In other words, search not for yourself but for Oneness.

REFLECTIONS

As Pisces switch identities in response to those in their vicinity, they resemble the water of a lake that reflects its surroundings. The movie *Zelig* by Woody Allen demonstrates this phenomenon rather splendidly, but this mirroring of the environment buttresses a purpose far greater than comedy. Since Pisces contain all of the signs within, they naturally possess the capacity to extend empathy to anyone no matter his sign or her problem. More than those of any other archetype, Pisces are able to walk in the shoes of other people, which might explain why Pisces rules the feet. This capacity to feel the pain and suffering of others makes Pisces adept healers. Feeling for others also fogs the distinctions between individuals, amplifying the priceless realization that we are all One.

This emotional talent, however, frequently seduces the Pisces into carrying other people's burdens. I had a client who was a double Pisces (with both her moon and sun in this compassionate sign). Wherever she went, she found herself assuming other people's problems and taking responsibility for things that had nothing to do with her. Her boss loved that. He'd spend hours chronicling his woes. And because of her vast empathy for everything he endured, he felt free to call her in the middle of the night for advice, or even worse, to ask her to cover for him while he ventured out on trivial excursions. Since she felt so much compassion for his plight, she found it impossible to tell him no. I counseled her to draw some boundaries. She had to stop carrying his cross. She could still be nice. She could still wipe his brow and offer him a bottle of water, but she had to allow him to shoulder his own cross on his Via

Delarosa. For two months she wrestled with the idea of setting boundaries. And a strange thing happened: her boss was fired, because for the first time since she went to work for him, he was forced to tackle all of his own assignments instead of relying on her to back him up. My client was promoted, and now she is soaring up the corporate ladder, offering water to others instead of hauling their load.

Identify three people in your life who would benefit from your empathy and compassion. You might commence the process by reflecting their energy back to them. This will enable you to step into their shoes and then extend compassion to them. For example, if your friend appears happy and enthusiastic, make an effort to match her vitality, even if you feel down. As you proceed with this assignment, look too for places where you ought to set boundaries. This dance of compassion and detachment will present you with a wonderful opportunity to learn about the upward soaring and downward diving fish within you.

This week, you will become a mystic. Greet every person you meet with smiles and loving energy. Imagine that everyone you encounter was sent by God to present you with a gift, a crucial challenge, or a message. Meditate each day for twenty minutes and attend at least three yoga classes. Visit a church, temple, or mosque, or go to a park or a garden and walk among the trees. Find a place of peace and tranquility. In other words, search not for yourself but for Oneness. The most famous American psychic, Edgar Cayce, was a Pisces.

YOUR OWN PRIVATE PISCES

Pisces in your chart highlights the area in your life in which you can locate your self-sabotage (downward swimming fish) as well as where you retain the greatest chance to become one with God (upward swimming fish). Pisces also underlines the area in which you enjoy manifold talents, but also much confusion and disillusionment. It is a challenging arena that can be rectified by adopting mystical techniques such as yoga, meditation, creative visualization, imagination, dance, and chanting. Your Pisces house usually contains an issue from which you might yearn to run away, dodge, or escape. Fight that urge, and you will experience astonishing results. Make sure that you allow other people to help you with your Pisces challenges. Don't be afraid to show vulnerability and share what you feel.

Pisces in Your First House (Your Rising Sign): You are a natural-born mystic with a prodigious capacity for feeling other people's pain. This energy might overwhelm you at times, and you will have to learn how to protect yourself with smart boundaries. You are appealing to other people, but few really know you. Like a slippery fish, you seem to slither through their hands. During the week of Pisces, focus on your body, appearance, and how others perceive you.

Pisces in the Second House: You are multitalented but might find it hard to concentrate on any one skill. You tend to spend money fast. Avoid allowing your money to drip through your fingers like water. You possess a marvelous imagination, and you can use your psychic or mystical gifts to attract moneymaking opportunities. This week, work with your talents and finances to identify how the universe supports your income.

Pisces in the Third House: You have an active imagination. Writing poetry or fantasy stories might prove to be auspicious forms of self-expression. Because you often expect others to communicate with you on a telepathic level, they might find it hard to understand you. Make sure that you explicitly explain what you think and feel. This week, pay attention to the way you think, talk, and write, and try to reconnect to your neighbors and siblings.

Pisces in the Fourth House: Somebody in your family (most likely on your mother's side) is psychic or a genuine mystic. You need to live close to the water. You expect your home to resemble a temple, a scared private space. You might have experienced a difficult childhood because of dependency or codependency in your family. This week, focus on your family members and your home. It might also be a good time for renovations or for buying and selling a house.

Pisces in the Fifth House: You tend to seek out secret love affairs as a means of escape. You enjoy a strong connection to children, but make sure that you create clear boundaries when raising them. Be extra careful that your children do not fall into drugs or any other addiction. During the week of Pisces, highlight your love life, your children, and your creativity.

Pisces in the Sixth House: You are extremely sensitive to your workplace and coworkers, and you need to make sure that you work in a spiritually and physically clean environment. You excel when you implement creativity and imagination in your work. Monitor your immune and lymphatic systems because health problems might arise from absorbing the negativity of others. This week, emphasize your work, pets, diet, and service to humanity.

Pisces in the Seventh House: You might have two marriages or two major loves. Be careful with dependency and codependency. You require at least some boundaries with your partners. You thrive in a mystically inclined relationship with someone with whom you share a strong telepathic connection. During the week of Pisces, focus on your partners, contracts, and relationship with your significant other.

Pisces in the Eighth House: Attend to how your partner in life or work deals with money or joint assets. You enjoy a strong link between sexuality and mysticism, and Tantric yoga will enhance this propensity. You can also excel in the study and practice of the occult. In the week of Pisces, communicate your sexuality and intimacy needs.

Pisces in the Ninth House: You have a mystical connection to foreign cultures and traditions. Try to travel to countries or cities near the sea. You tend to gravitate toward mystical or mysterious religions. This week, travel as much as you can, especially for business.

Pisces in the Tenth House: Your career might be hampered by your plethora of talents and possibilities. You might have two entirely different careers. You need to narrow your focus and ensure that your chosen career involves mysticism, movement, or something you feel deeply about. This week, you can advance your worldly pursuits dramatically.

Pisces in the Eleventh House: You might feel disappointed by your friends or groups. You thrive amongst friends who share your mystical outlook on life. This week, focus on friends, groups, and the organizations you belong to. You also might want to join a yoga class to meet new people.

Pisces in the Twelfth House: You are highly mystical and may exhibit a tendency toward drug abuse or self-destructive activities. You might have been killed in a past lifetime because of your mystical or religious affiliation. You might even have been burned or drowned. This week, focus on retreats, spiritual activities, and letting go of whatever you do not need.

The Age of Pisces: Let It Be!

As we step into the Age of Aquarius, we leave the tumultuous era of Pisces behind. The Age of Pisces centered on faith and religion. Countless traditions and creeds arose during this two-thousand-year span, including Kabbalah, Sufism, Islam, Gnosticism, Mahayana, Christianity, Afro-American faiths, and even the Church of Scientology, whose founder was a Pisces. The Age of Pisces also witnessed a zealous attachment to religion that seemed always to spin out of control. Many groups and individuals chose to abuse the name of God in service of their own political agendas. Jihads, crusades, witch hunts, religious genocide, and inquisitions sprouted all over the world like mushrooms after a rain. It was an age where everything suddenly became sacred by decree. Hebrew was a common language spoken for centuries, but when we entered the Age of Pisces, Hebrew transformed into the Holy Language. Latin, which the Romans used in daily life, suddenly became the holy language of the Holy See in holy Rome. The province dubbed Palestine by the Romans all of the sudden became known to the three monotheistic religions as the Holy Land. War, a mundane concept prior to the Age of Pisces, was relabeled a holy jihad or holy crusade.

Identify three people in your life who would benefit from your empathy and compassion. To step into their shoes and then extend compassion to them, reflect their energy back to them. Look too for places where you ought to set boundaries. This dance of compassion and detachment will allow you to learn about the upward soaring and downward diving fish within you.

Our job as conscious, loving, spiritual people is to let go of the fanatical, dogmatic tenets of organized religion and open our hearts to different spiritual traditions. It is time to realize that God loves us all, no matter what name we use for God. No one people, book, or doctrine holds a monopoly over God, and no religion retains copyright or exclusivity over the distribution of lots in heaven. There is nothing wrong with being religious, but there is something irreligious about hating people who believe in a different creed or lifestyle. After all, the word *religion* comes from the word for *tie back*. That very word mirrors the Pisces mission to realign everything together into One.

The Philosopher's Stone

The philosopher's stone is no magic rock. It is simply a symbol for imagination—the true treasure bestowed to all of us by the archetype called Pisces. "Imagination is more important than knowledge," said Einstein. Through the use of imagination and creative visualizations, we can move mountains, cure diseases, win Olympic gold medals (great athletes have for decades visualized their own perfect dive or gymnastic trick in their minds just prior to competing), and maybe, if Lennon was right, install world peace. One of my best friends, a Pisces and a choreographer, dancer, and acrobat, starred in the original cast of *Quidam* by Cirque de Soleil. She told me that before each performance, she would sit quietly and imagine each move of her dangerous and beautiful routine. That visualization served as a vital part of her warm-up, and, she felt, it saved her life many times over.

Pisces take the axiom "as above, so below" quite literally. While most of us aim to fix things in the below—if something is wrong with the car we take it to the mechanic, for example—Pisces sculpt things in the above. They say: "if 'as above so below' is true, then let's soar via our mystical imagination to the above and mend things up there. Let's unite with God and rectify the problem in the astral world, and it will then resolve itself on its own down here." It may sound far-fetched, but shamans, mystics, and healers have been operating this way for thousands of years. This is the real secret behind *The Secret*. Imagination is their tool. If you imagine improvement in your health—truly, truly visualize vigor day after day with unwavering conviction—your health will be enhanced. If, however, you remain lodged in self-pity and negativity, you will experience a more difficult time.

"The imagination is probably a person's least utilized health resource," says Martin L. Rossman, M.D., of the Academy for Guided Imagery. He asserts that imagination represents the language of the emotions and serves as the interface between mind and body. The Academy for Guided Imagery has documented numerous cases in which visualization helped to ameliorate suffering in patients with allergies, arthritis, asthma, and even cancer. For example, as documented in Burton Goldberg's book *Alternative Medicine*, Patricia Norris worked with a nine-year-old boy suffering from an inoperable brain tumor. She used the boy's favorite TV show, *Star Trek*, to lead him through a year of creative visualizations and guided imagery that aimed to have him envisage the destruction of his disease. At the end of the year, the tumor had disappeared.

This week, identify one thing you want to change in your life and imagine your perfect outcome every day when you wake up and before you go to sleep. Dedicate five minutes to conjuring vivid images of how your life and you will look and feel once you have fixed the problem. Imagine all the details with as much specificity as possible. And don't do it once. Picture your perfect Olympic dive, your perfect job, your perfect partner over and over and over. And remember the key phrase for Pisces—"I believe." You must believe. Before Jesus preformed a healing miracle, he always asked the patient, "Do you believe in me?" If the person did, the miracle transpired. The healing did not come from Christ. It emerged from the person's faith and imagination.

How to Get Along with Pisces

- Tell Pisces your dreams. Demonstrate that you are a dreamer too.

- Don't plan activities for too early in the morning. And don't talk to them before they've had their morning fix, whether it's coffee, their newspaper, or what ever helps them break from dream time.

- Whenever they get confused or overwhelmed with life, help them create a schedule or a plan that will provide them with a clear path. Offer them tools to connect to discipline and boundaries.

- Show vulnerability. Demonstrate that you have feelings and can sense others' pain.

- Pisces flow back and forth like water, sometimes cold and sometimes warm. If the Pisces withdraws now and then, don't take it personally. Like the tide, he or she will return.

- "All the rivers flow into the sea and yet the sea is never full," says Ecclesiastes. No matter how much emotion you pour into them, Pisces will feel the need for more feelings.

- Laughter, jokes, and silliness can help defuse the surfeit of the Pisces' emotional energy. Try these tactics. Or suggest a good nap together.

THE DARK SIDE OF THE FORCE: PISCES

Dependency and codependency present Pisces with grave problems. These afflictions will also loom as key issues in your house ruled by Pisces. Think about a dolphin that swims near the southern part of California and decides to cross down to Mexico. The dolphin will not wait in line at the border. It never registers for a passport. It does not recognize borders or the concepts of territorial waters. Pisces are like that. Because their emotional capacity is so rich, they can easily drown in their partner's energy or allow their partner to drown in them. This problem is not only limited to relationships but also applies to any type of addictions. Pisces live to escape. They frequently yearn to flee. Sometimes escape—through dreams or imagination—can truly benefit us, providing insight and action plans for how to deal with people or challenges here on earth. The trouble arises when we become addicted to the escape or the means we use to create it. Pisces' trials with boundaries often lead to addictions that sabotages their health and well-being.

Mystics in many cultures have used drugs for thousands of years. Shamans and healers ingested potent plants such as peyote or ayahuasca to induce an altered state of mind. In that higher state, they can reach beyond the confines of this material world and achieve heightened states of awareness. The problem lies not with the drug or hallucinogenic plant, but with the person who uses it. When taken by a practiced shaman or medicine man who has studied mysticism and herbs for years, and when ingested for a higher purpose, then the drug can serve as a tool as powerful as a Bible or Koran. But when used for recreation or abused repeatedly to escape the rigors of daily life, then the substance turns dangerous.

Pisces Michelangelo was bold enough to draw the image of God in the Sistine Chapel. Johnny Cash, who battled drug addiction and is famous for his concert at California's Folsom prison, was a Pisces.

For a related reason, Pisces also rule prisons. If it were up to the Pisces, they probably would choose to escape life all together. Therefore, to them, the body is like a jail and living in the material world of earth akin to doing time. Any addiction can resemble a prison, trapping us in its merciless grip. But prison—or at least the metaphor of confinement—can also serve as a boon to our spiritual growth. When we go on retreats or *vipassana* (one of India's oldest forms of meditation; the word *vipassana* translates as "seeing things as they really are"), we are required to refrain from many of our quotidian comforts. We do not speak. We fast. We sleep on the floor. We segregate men from women. To many, it sounds like a prison—a confined place with too many onerous rules. But the results of these deprivations are often extraordinary. Freed from the normal, from the everyday, we swim deeper into what truly matters, and the apparent confinement actually serves to shine clarity on the way things really are.

The innate Pisces empathy allows them to help others by absorbing pain and negativity. This method of healing is common in Afro-Cuban religions such as Santeria, where the high priestess takes on the malady of her patient. Her initiation into the mysteries of psychic medicine allows such a dangerous procedure. Her expertise provides a technique for accepting and then discharging the negativity without hurting anyone, especially herself. Most Pisces, however, don't possess such mastery. The motivation to help is admirable, but the negativity internalized by the Pisces can sometimes provide them with yet another reason to drink or take drugs or eat themselves into a stupor.

This week, identify one thing you want to change in your life and imagine your perfect outcome every day when you wake up and before you go to sleep. Imagine all the details with as much specificity as possible, then picture your perfect Olympic dive, your perfect job, your perfect partner over and over and over. And remember the key phrase for Pisces—"I believe." You must believe.

And often Pisces fall victim to spiritual vampires. You didn't think that Dracula was real? Well, energetic vampires abound. They don't suck blood from people's necks, but they do drain our energies and drench us in their negativity. Pisces in your chart highlights the area in your life where you will have to be wary of self-sacrifice and/or self-destruction. It shows the arena in which you might encounter people or situations that can drain you. So protect yourself. Do not wear black because this color absorbs energy. Take long baths with salt water. Scientific industries utilize special containers lined with salt to store radioactive materials, because the salt apparently absorbs the radiation. Salt can also absorb the negative radiation around you. Try to burn purifying sage in your house or office once a week. Wear an amethyst (in earrings or a necklace) because this crystal is reputed to dispel negative energies and radiate positive ones.

Pisces yearn to escape because they tend to suffer. And their primary challenge centers on realizing that while this world is, as Rabbi Nachman of Breslov says, "a narrow bridge to the afterlife," we still must make the best of our time here on earth. Though he acknowledged the illusory nature of reality, the Buddha advised us to "joyfully participate in the suffering of the world." Life is not that bad. This world has given us amazing natural treasures, cuddly animals, friends, conversation, laughter, and sex. And there is always the weekend to look forward to.

Combat the dark side of Pisces by creating your own special retreat, even for one day. Don't speak. Don't eat after midday. And try to meditate for at least two hours. See how high you soar via this spiritual practice. Watch for the clarity it brings to the challenges of your life.

THE HEBREW LETTER *Kuf*

Kabbalah assigned the Hebrew letter *Kuf* to Pisces. The curved part of the letter resembles the back of the head, or the human cortex, which is involved in imagination and dreaming, while the vertical line represents the spinal cord, which sends all these imaginative messages to the rest of the body. Research with PET (positron-emission tomography) scans shows that the optic cortex, which is located in the back of the head, lights up whenever a person visualizes and imagines.

Aquarius, the sign before Pisces, is called the water bearer. Pisces supplies the water, also known as the subconscious, or what C. G. Jung named the collective unconscious. Jung suggested that within the collective unconscious we find all the archetypes huddled together just as Pisces gathers all the rest of the astrological archetypes. The Hebrew letter of Aquarius is *Tzadik*, which means "the fishhook."

Where does the fisherman cast his fishhook? Into the ocean of Pisces. It is not surprising that the Age of Pisces, which ruled us for the last two thousand years, began with the emergence of Christianity, which employed the fish as one of its early symbols. Christ also walked on water and declared, "I will make you a fisher of men" (Matthew 4:18).

Meditate with the letter *Kuf* to bolster your psychic abilities and mystical insights. *Kuf* will also help you to interpret your dreams and access your subconscious.

The Parts of the Body

Pisces governs the feet and the lymphatic and immune systems. Medical professionals have discovered a link between the strength of our immune system and our thoughts and feelings. Pisces tend to take things too personally, and they absorb the negative energies of others. These stresses can lower the immune system and expose the body to hostile intrusions. So many Pisces fall prone to psychosomatic diseases or health problems that arise from the way they think or feel.

The healing art of reflexology postulates that the feet contain points that connect to all the organs in the body. By massaging and prodding specific areas of the feet, reflexologists strive to heal the corresponding organ. It makes sense. Pisces (feet) embodies all the other signs (organs). Because this sign rules the feet, Pisces tend to be graceful dancers. Many possess the ability to go into deep meditation or even trance while dancing or moving.

Combat the dark side of Pisces by creating your own special retreat, even for one day. Don't speak. Don't eat after midday. And try to meditate for at least two hours. See how high you soar via this spiritual practice. Watch for the clarity it brings to the challenges of your life.

This week, go dancing. You might be shocked at the transformation this joyous activity evokes. For example, a woman I know who has Pisces in her house of health and diet struggled for years with her weight. No matter what she tried—and she tried everything—she could not keep those pounds off. She was about to give up, but in the week of Pisces, she took a bellydancing class. At first she hated it because she was forced to expose her stomach. But a strange thing happened as she progressed in the class. She learned that in Arab world, a round, voluptuous woman is considered beautiful. She discovered that not every man on the planet desires an anorexic wife. These insights prompted her to change her diet. Instead of fretting about the amount of food she ate, she started paying attention to the quality of her meals. Now, after two years of belly dancing, she has lost twenty pounds. She is far from a size two, but she performs regularly in a trendy Middle Eastern restaurant, where she is paid to expose her belly.

THE COLOR OF PISCES: VIOLET-RED

The color of Pisces is violet-red. Alchemy associates this vibration with the serpent that bites its own tail and creates the endless circle, joining red, the lowest visible frequency, with violet, the highest visible frequency, creating a unified whole of high and low. This concept mirrors the formula "As Above so Below," the premise of all mystical doctrines. Pisces merges the end with the beginning to create the wheel of color, the wheel of fortune, the circle of life—Astrology.

WHAT SHOULD I FOCUS ON IN THE WEEK OF PISCES?

Mysticism, spirituality, and displaying empathy toward your fellow sentient beings is your mission this week. It is a perfect time to begin a new spiritual or mystical activity like yoga, chanting, or meditation. Go dancing or swimming. Try any activity that can throw you into a trance. Abandon your mind and your racing thoughts and anxieties for a week—or at least a little while. You might also want to take a class or read about different religions or spiritual traditions to prod you to recognize that all mystical doctrines are basically the same. They all point to a single place—God.

Meditate with the letter *Kuf* to bolster your psychic abilities and mystical insights. *Kuf* will also help you to interpret your dreams and access your subconscious.

The bank of symbols for Pisces include fish, dolphins, mermaids, the ocean, currents, compassion, empathy, circles, endings and beginnings, spirituality, religion, faith, mysticism, drugs, addictions, imagination, visualization, dreams, sleep, laziness, dancing, feet, immune system, lymph nodes, retreats, prisons, suffering, psychic healing, holiness, illusion, poetry, and enlightenment.

Your Pisces Week Checklist

- Meditate twice a day.
- Use creative visualization in your meditation to manifest what you need.
- Start a dream log.
- Speak the affirmation of Pisces: "I am at one with the flow of the universe, effortlessly attracting all that I need."
- Play the psychic game with your friends and family. Close your eyes and concentrate on a number from one to ten. Using your imagination, transmit that number to your companion. After a minute, ask him to guess the number. Take note of whether you are better at receiving psychic information or transmitting it. If you are a better receiver, then practice giving, and vice versa. This insight might serve as an indication of how you fare in life in general. Are you a person that gives too much and does not receive or a person that receives too much and needs to give more?
- Join a dance class or go out dancing.
- Rent some fantasy movies, musicals, biographies about religious figures or religious stories (such as The Last Temptation of Christ), or animated films.
- Practice seeing God in every person that you meet.
- Hang out near water. It could be an ocean, a river, lake, or fountain.
- Take long baths with salt water.
- Visit a house of worship or a park where you can contemplate the positive energies of religion.
- Make sure that you have a Bible or Koran or any other religious text at home. It's best to have them all. Read at least twelve pages of different religious texts to assimilate the feel and spirituality of different traditions.
- Work on creating boundaries. Try to identify and then check your addictions.

THE RITUAL OF PISCES: AUTOMATIC WRITING

Pisces' mystical bent can help us gain access to our higher self or God. Channeling is a medium by which we can tap higher wisdom. This spiritual practice requires that you relinquish your ego and allow something bigger to emerge through you. In essence, you become a pipe to higher wisdom. Pisces also rules all forms of divination such as the runes, I Ching, Tarot, and reading shells, tea leaves, or coffee grounds. *Divination* derives from the verb "to divine" — seeing the divine.

Late at night when you are tired and your mind is beat, sit in a comfortable place and light a white candle. Have a pencil and white piece of paper handy. Try to not blink as you stare at the flame for a few minutes. Think of a subject about which you need clarification. With your eyes half closed, start writing whatever comes into your head. Don't judge or criticize what

This week, go dancing. You might be shocked at the transformation this joyous activity evokes.

you write. Let it flow. Don't lift the pencil. Keep writing anything. After five minutes, stop and go to sleep.

When you wake up in the morning, flip the paper over and write whatever you remember from your dreams or any other feelings you might have right then. Do not read what you wrote the night before. Try to repeat this exercise every night for the next forty nights. On the fortieth night, read all that you have written. Circle all the sentences or paragraphs that you do not remember writing or feel might contain some higher wisdom. You will be surprised at how much information you will discover. Then compare what you wrote at night with the dreams you experienced. Whenever you need more clarification about any subject, try this exercise again.

FAMOUS PISCES

Sidney Poitier, Nina Simone, Frederic Chopin, Auguste Renoir, Victor Hugo, Elizabeth Taylor, Bugsy Siegel, Mikhail Gorbachev, Dr. Seuss (Theodor Seuss Geisel), Alexander Graham Bell, Antonio Vivaldi, Michelangelo, Gabriel Garcia Marquez, George Washington, Ralph Nader, Johnny Cash, Spike Lee, Albert Einstein, Rudolf Nureyev, Vaslav Nijinsky, and Edgar Cayce.

Conclusion

CONGRATULATIONS, YOU ARE A COSMIC NAVIGATOR!

You are now an official graduate of the Intergalactic School of Cosmic Navigation. You may stand up and throw your hat jubilantly into the sky.

Armed with this book's information on the planets, stars, and houses, you are ready now to interpret any chart with skill and wisdom. Test out your knowledge on your own chart, then tackle the charts of your friends and family. It is time for you to share your insight with others. The more you practice, the more adept an astrologer you will become.

For example, when a friend calls you up distressed over turmoil in her relationship, you now know what to do. Check the position of Venus, the planet of relationships, in her chart, and offer up the information that you discover. Then identify the sign that rules the seventh house, the house of relationships, and discuss with her the potential significance of that configuration. Read the appropriate information to her directly from the book. Then watch and listen to how she responds. You also might suggest that she begin to heal her problems by meditatively chanting *Yod Hey Vav Hey Tzevaot*, the name of God associated with the Kabbalistic sphere Eternity, the archetypal energy that guides Venus.

If another friend complains about an impasse with his mother, follow the astrological prescription: identify his moon (the symbol of mothers) sign; check for any planets in Cancer (the mothering sign); look into the fourth house, the house of the mother; and suggest that he chant *Shaddai El Hai*, the name of God associated with the Kabbalistic sphere of the moon, called Foundation.

Remember, you don't need to be as proficient and practiced as Tiger Woods, Yo-Yo Ma, or the Buddha are in their fields to walk onto the astrological stage, to begin interpreting charts, to begin helping yourself and others. My first astrologer, who was without question one of the most invaluable teachers I have ever encountered, read most of her insights out of a book. But she wasn't afraid, and the shrewd perceptions she conveyed literally awed me and changed the course of my life. You can do the same.

Advanced Studies in Cosmic Navigation

As a graduation gift, I invite you to matriculate into the cosmic navigator's Ph.D. program, which is nothing less than the rest of your life.

Look at the calendar. What sign are we in right now? Aries, Libra, Capricorn? Go back to the chapter that matches the sun sign of today. And become that sign all over again until the calendar switches over to the next. Then move with the sun and become that subsequent sign for an entire month. Try to channel all of the astrological archetypes for an entire year. Remember, Pisces, the last sign you read about in part III, is not an end, but a launching pad to another ride on the astrological merry-go-round.

So, for one whole year, assert yourself for the month of Aries (March 21 to April 19), attend to your relationships during Libra (September 23 to October 22), and focus like a laser on your career during the span of Capricorn (December 22 to January 19). Practicing Kabbalistic astrology for an entire year will allow you to assimilate the lessons of all the archetypes in a life-altering and fruitful way. It will present you with a continuous series of synchronicities that will open up possibilities that you never imagined. You will become a magus, an alchemist, and a wizard, shaping your genuine astrological destiny and actualizing all of your dreams.

The more you harmonize yourself with the energies of heavens, the easier you will flow with the ever-changing currents of life on earth. None of us can rectify our karma and fulfill all of our aspirations in just twelve weeks. What would we do for the rest of our eighty or ninety years? The cosmic navigator graduate program lasts a lifetime.

You can now apply the insights and techniques that you learned every day in every area of your life. The more you do that for yourself, the more charts you read, the more you teach other people the lessons of the stars, the more control you will wield over your destiny, and the closer you will move toward a continual state of serenity and joy.

Beyond the Stars: What's Next For Humanity

We live in a world in which books and movies on the Rapture, the apocalypse, and other doomsday scenarios have gained greater and increasing traction. The addition of the very real fears of terrorism, religious fundamentalism, global warming, pandemic, and other fatalistic prophecies offers even less hope to all humans traveling on the blue spacecraft called earth. As a cosmic navigator, you have assumed the responsibility and privilege of living a positive alternative. Having traveled to the farthest reaches of your consciousness and the stars, you have acquired the tools that can help others to overcome their fears of the future and redesign their lives exactly as they want them.

You are the cosmic navigator. You hold enormous power. And with great power comes great responsibility. You undoubtedly will notice that more and more people will seek you out for information, assistance, understanding, and wisdom about themselves and their challenges. Spread what you have learned. Show them by the example of your life. Sagittarius, the traveler and the teacher of the zodiac, guides you, the cosmic navigator. Sagittarius teaches optimism and hope. Broadcast your own optimism and hope. The more brightness you emanate into the world, the brighter the world will become.

Kabbalah asserts that by working on your own *Tikkun,* by repairing your personal fears and negativity, you actually help to fix the entire cosmos. For example, when you spruce up the landscaping in your front yard, you inspire you neighbors to match your efforts, and you raise property values along the entire block. Similarly, when you extend compassion to someone in need, you amplify the cosmic energy of compassion in some invisible but profound way. When you laugh out loud, it becomes contagious, triggering others to smile and laugh too. And when you tune yourself to the optimistic emanations of the stars, you multiply that harmony within your small circle—and in the globally connected Age of Aquarius—across the globe as well.

THE TIPPING POINT

According to many different spiritual traditions, we have entered a crucial phase in human evolution—a period in which we must take full responsibility for our past and present behavior. These doctrines purport that in this age the reactions to our actions occur almost immediately. The Mayans, for instance, predict the end of time in 2012. This prophecy sounds rather grim and apocalyptic, but many mystics interpret it in a happier way. They claim that it simply suggests that the time lapse between action and reaction will vanish. The world will continue, but instead of having to wait for the karma of our action in one life to appear in our next incarnation, we will witness the consequence of our behavior right away. We see this time-less theory in effect as the pollution and carbon we pump into our air and water obliterates the ozone and dramatically alters environmental conditions worldwide in just a few years. You probably have noticed this same squishing of time in your personal life as well. We don't have lifetimes anymore to fix ourselves and the universe too. We have this moment and the actions we take today.

So what do we want? Do we crave fear, war, ignorance, intolerance, and apocalypse? If we think and act like we do, if we concentrate on those misfortunes, the result will be swiftly unfortunate. Or do we want fulfillment, abundance, and peace both for ourselves and all humankind? The compression of time awards us complete control. We can decide to make this place a heaven right now, or we can surrender to our fears and turn our earth into a living hell. Enough people have decided for now to propagate the bleaker narratives. You and the fellow warriors of Light that you inevitably will attract can swing the balance toward a more optimistic scenario.

In my extensive travels to various cultures and nations, I have met with mystics from a variety of traditions. When I ask about the future of humankind, they all unanimously reply that our future has not yet been determined. They contend we are nearing a tipping point. The future can go either way. As a cosmic navigator, you can mold your own astrological destiny. You gravitated to that realization because you can craft the destiny of all of us too. We have arrived at this critical junction together. And our future is not written in the stars, but in our hearts.

Have a great life. And if I don't see you in this lifetime, don't be a stranger in the next.

Love,
Gahl
New moon in Scorpio

The Beginning . . .

Selected Bibliography

Aivanhov, Omraam Mikhael. *The Zodiac, Key to Man and to the Universe*. Frejus Cedex, France: Prosveta, 1999.

Arroyo, Stephen. *Astrology, Psychology and the Four Elements*. Sebastopol, CA: CRCS Publication, 1975.

Campbell, Joseph. *The Inner Reaches of Outer Space*. Novato, CA: New World Library, 2002.

Campbell, Joseph, and Bill Moyers. *The Power of Myth*. New York: Broadway Books, 1988.

The revered scholar of myth managed to bestow scientific and anthropological credibility to the stories of spirituality. His work helped open the door to the importance and vitality of the world's ancient myths and religious rites.

Capra, Fritjof. *The Tao of Physics*. Boston: Shambhala, 1975.

Appealing to spiritualists and academics both, this book illustrates that the intangible axioms of metaphysics jibe rather perfectly with the quantifiable laws of science.

Ehrenreich, Barbara. *Blood Rites*. New York: Metropolitan Books, 1997.

A social anthropological study of the ceremonies and rituals of various cultures throughout history.

Gauquelin, Michel. *Cosmic Influences on Human Behavior*. Santa Fe, NM: Aurora Press, 1994.

The most serious attempt to find a scientific support to astrology.

Goldberg, Burton. *Alternative Medicine: The Definitive Guide*. Tiburon, CA: Future Medicine Publishing, 1994.

A great encyclopedia that covers almost all holistic medicine modalities.

Green, Liz. *Astrology for Lovers*. York Beach, ME: Samuel Weiser, 1980.

By far, one of the best and most entertaining astrology books that combines in-depth material as well as funny stories.

Halevi, Z'ev ben Shimon. *Adam and the Kabbalistic Tree*. York Beach, ME: Samuel Weiser, 1974.

Hauck, W. Dennis. *The Emerald Tablet*. Harmondsworth, New York: Arkana, 1999.
A thorough and scholarly digest of the history of alchemy and its applications.
His Holiness the Fourteenth Dalai Lama, and Howard C. Cutler. *The Art of Happiness:*
  A Handbook for Living. New York: Riverhead Books. 1998.
An authentic work of compassion that poses Western-thinking dilemmas of the
  contemporary world to the Dalai Lama. It demonstrates how the ancient wisdom
  of Tibetan Buddhism can enrich anyone's life today.
Kaplan, Aryeh. Sefer Yetzirah: *The Book of Creation*. York Beach, ME: Samuel
  Weiser, 1997.
Probably the finest and most complex book on the Kabbalah available in English, it
  translates and interprets the oldest and most essential Kabbalistic text known to man.
Kirsch, Jonathan. *Moses: a Life*. New York: Ballantine Publishing Group, 1998.
Any of Kirsch's books invigorate the old Bible stories by bringing a fascinating human
  shape to these sacred characters.
Lineman, Rose, and Jan Popelka. *Compendium of Astrology*. Westchester, PA: Schiffer
  Publishing, 1984.
A great book for learning how to cast charts by hand.
Miller, R. Anistatia, and M. Jared Brown. *The Complete Astrological Handbook for the
  Twenty First Century*. New York: Schocken Books, 1999.
Munk, L. Michael. *The Wisdom of the Hebrew Alphabet*. Brooklyn, NY: Menorah,
  1983.
Nietzsche, Friedrich. *Thus Spake Zarathustra*. Los Angeles: Pomona Press, 2006.
Sasson, Gahl, and Steve Weinstein. *A Wish Can Change Your Life*, New York: Fireside,
  2003.
Scholem, Gershom. *On the Mystical Shape of the Godhead*. New York: Schocken
  Books, 1976.
Scholem applied the modern academic field of rigorous research to the Kabbalah.
Sogyal Rinpoche. *The Tibetan Book of Living and Dying*. San Francisco:
  HarperSanFrancisco, 1994.

About the Author

Gahl Eden Sasson is a spiritual teacher who has earned a wide and enthusiastic following across the United States, Europe, and the Middle East. He is the author of *A Wish Can Change Your Life* and a regular contributor to *Olam*, the world's largest-circulation magazine on Kabbalah, alongside such notables as Deepak Chopra, Arianna Huffington, Larry King, and Shimon Peres. His unique interpretations of Kabbalist lore appear in more than three million copies of the magazine worldwide.

Sasson served on the faculty of Deepak Chopra's multi-media project, MyPotential, teaching both Astrology and Kabbalah. He has been profiled in dozens of U. S. publications and has appeared on both radio and television, including CNN and ABC News. He teaches ongoing workshops on Kabbalah, Mythology, and Astrology throughout England, Israel, Turkey, Mexico, and the United States.

Born in Israel, Sasson has traveled extensively in India, Nepal, Thailand, the Philippines, Australia, Sri Lanka, and Central America. He holds a degree in Psychology from the University of Haifa and studied Astrology and Kabbalah at the Golden Circe Esoteric School in Guadalajara, Mexico, where he is now a keynote speaker. He currently resides in Los Angeles. Visit Gahl Eden Sasson at *www.CosmicNavigator.com.*